S104 Exploring science
Science: Level 1

The Open University

Exploring Earth's History

Prepared by Steve Drury

This publication forms part of an Open University course S104 *Exploring science*. The complete list of texts which make up this course can be found on the back cover. Details of this and other Open University courses can be obtained from the Student Registration and Enquiry Service, The Open University, PO Box 197, Milton Keynes MK7 6BJ, United Kingdom: tel. +44 (0)845 300 60 90, email general-enquiries@open.ac.uk

Alternatively, you may visit the Open University website at http://www.open.ac.uk where you can learn more about the wide range of courses and packs offered at all levels by The Open University.

To purchase a selection of Open University course materials visit http://www.ouw.co.uk, or contact Open University Worldwide, Michael Young Building, Walton Hall, Milton Keynes MK7 6AA, United Kingdom for a brochure. tel. +44 (0)1908 858793; fax +44 (0)1908 858787; email ouw-customer-services@open.ac.uk

The Open University
Walton Hall, Milton Keynes
MK7 6AA

First published 2008

Edited and designed by The Open University.

Typeset by SR Nova Pvt. Ltd, Bangalore, India.

Printed in the United Kingdom by Halstan & Co. Ltd., Amersham, Bucks.

ISBN 978 1 8487 3167 7

2.1

Contents

Chapter 1 Introduction

Every part of the Earth system moves and changes continually, although sometimes very slowly. Each component of the system, however small, has some effect on all the other components (Book 2). Our home world is a far more dynamic place than the other planetary bodies in the Solar System. The course of Earth's history since it formed 4.6 billion years ago has emerged from understanding the many processes that have left their mark in rocks, and from judging the times over which they took place. However, the timescales involved are huge; far beyond human experience. They span thousands (ka), millions (Ma) and even billions (Ga) of years. (You met the notation Ma and Ga in Book 1, Box 3.3. In this book the abbreviation ka is also used.)

Given such timescales, all kinds of event might have happened on Earth. Some events would have been familiar, such as volcanic eruptions or the build-up of sediment, but the influence of others that might seem extremely strange or rare today cannot be ruled out. The emergence of an organism that can contemplate itself and its surroundings, and consciously manipulate them to survive and develop, is one such rarity; a one-off event, late in the Earth's history. How **hominins**[1] emerged 4.6 Ga after the Earth formed is bound up intimately with *all* of the Earth's previous history, and that alone makes studying geological evolution compelling. We are part of the Earth system, as were our distant ancestors; a point powerfully made by Figure 1.1.

Figure 1.1 Footprints of two *Australopithecus afarensis* individuals preserved in a 3.6 Ma volcanic ash deposit at Laetoli, Tanzania. They may have been an adult male and a female, or an adult and a juvenile. The tracks prove that *A. afarensis* (perhaps an early human ancestor) walked on two feet. Accompanying the hominin tracks are those of a small feline predator and an extinct horse.

Despite a limited personal experience of time, our imagination is sufficiently flexible to visualise what we learn from stories of the past, either written or passed down in oral tradition. Writing first appeared in what is now Iraq 300 to 400 generations (about 6 ka) ago. Much of written history since then is fragmentary, and is often more about the deeds of prominent individuals and major events, rather than the changing circumstances of ordinary human life. Reconstructing mundane events involves collecting many kinds of evidence.

This book aims to introduce you to judging the passage of time from features preserved in rocks and 'reading' the evidence in them for geological events upon and within the Earth. Books 1 and 2 revealed the complexity of the Earth system in which all processes are interwoven. The way the Earth 'worked' since it formed almost certainly involved such global connectivity. Expressed in products of geological and biological processes – rocks and fossils – it involved chemical and physical processes too, making the study of the Earth system truly interdisciplinary. However, it is quite likely that many processes outside direct human experience also occurred. None the less, the key to understanding events in the past lies in what is known about the modern world.

[1] Humans are members of the family Hominidae, which also includes orangutans, gorillas and chimpanzees. To set us and species that were probably our ancestors apart, we are said to belong to the sub-tribe Hominini of the tribe Homininae (includes chimps). So the general name for us and our closest ancestors is hominin.

History depends, of course, on putting known events into a time sequence. Chapter 2 shows how to construct such a framework for the events that rocks record. A history of the Earth's surface environment depends on signs preserved in sedimentary rocks. However, because a host of different conditions characterise different places, the sediments being deposited around the world at any one time will differ from place to place too. Those in one locality may be beautifully preserved and full of fascinating information, but how do we relate observation and interpretations there to other sedimentary rocks elsewhere in the world? Without such a global correlation, the geological history recorded at isolated places would be much like human history that referred to records at individual cities; i.e. it would lack any wider context. Because of biological evolution, fossil species provide a 'signature' (but not a measure) for their age *relative* to other species, and enable fossil-bearing sediments from every continent to be matched or correlated in time.

The Earth's vigorous behaviour at any particular location forms and preserves different rock types – igneous and metamorphic, as well as sedimentary – in a 'stop–start' manner; different processes shifting from place to place. Every local geological record is full of gaps. Observing and interpreting the geometric relationships between different rocks and the structures they contain helps to place those features, and the events that formed them, in *relative* time order. But relative time sequences fall well short of revealing how the planet evolved. Geologists are able to order events in an absolute, global timescale by exploiting the radioactive decay of naturally unstable isotopes as a means of dating suitable rocks. You will see in Chapter 2 that this has allowed geologists to reconstruct a geological timescale that extends back to around half a billion years after the Earth formed.

The sequence of fossils and other biological evidence that occurs in sedimentary rocks documents the course of biological evolution. Chapter 3 examines that evidence in order to highlight evolutionary milestones in the context of the Earth system; how global changes affected evolution, and how major steps taken by life changed parts of the inorganic world.

Non-biological components of the Earth system evolved too. Their importance lies partly in repeatedly creating and changing the conditions for biological evolution. Discovering and understanding such inorganic changes relies on being able to reconstruct past surface environments, together with deeper magmatic and tectonic upheavals, from features exposed in sedimentary, igneous and metamorphic rocks. Chapters 4 to 6 develop the observational tools that make it possible to tease information of all kinds from rocks now exposed at the surface. Deductions at different places, using the skills you will learn as you work through the book, have made it possible to visualise geographical as well as geological evolution on a global scale.

The Earth's history is preserved in three dimensions (3D) – rocks do not merely appear at the surface but may extend into the crust beneath. Erosion has removed rocks that once lay above the present surface. Geological maps show this 3D record in time, and also provide many clues to detecting past events on a grand scale. Chapter 7 introduces you to maps of this kind, using the long geological history of the British Isles as an example. Another form of map represents a 'snapshot' in time, deduced from geological observations, that shows the ancient geography of an area – how its landscape might have looked and where it was in relation to other areas at the time. The British Isles provide good examples that fit into global reconstructions of how the world has changed over the last billion years of its evolution.

Allegedly, only humans ask the question 'Where did we come from?' and wonder about the future. Chapter 8 examines some aspects of our past, present and future as part of the Earth system but cannot fully satisfy our curiosity. In many respects human evolution was a case of being carried along passively by broad environmental processes, subject, like all other organisms, to selective pressures (Book 5, Chapter 9). However, there is one difference: since 2.5 Ma our upright or bipedal hominin ancestors used tools (Figure 1.2). More important, they also deliberately made them from suitable materials, developed them and passed on the necessary skills for hundreds of thousands of years, as shown in the sequence (a)–(c) in Figure 1.2. Humans can now live on or roam across even the most inhospitable areas on Earth, and continually change the world, both by design and by accident, on a growing scale. Humans are the only organisms that are active in this sense. We seem thus to have risen somewhat above evolution in the purely Darwinian sense, by surrounding ourselves increasingly with what *we* have created, rather than purely natural materials.

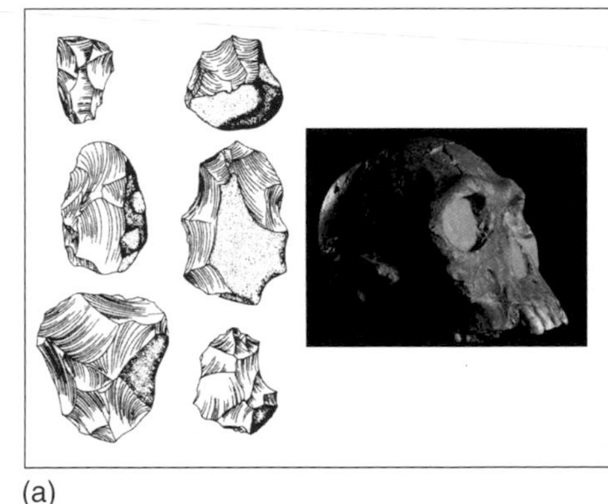

(a)

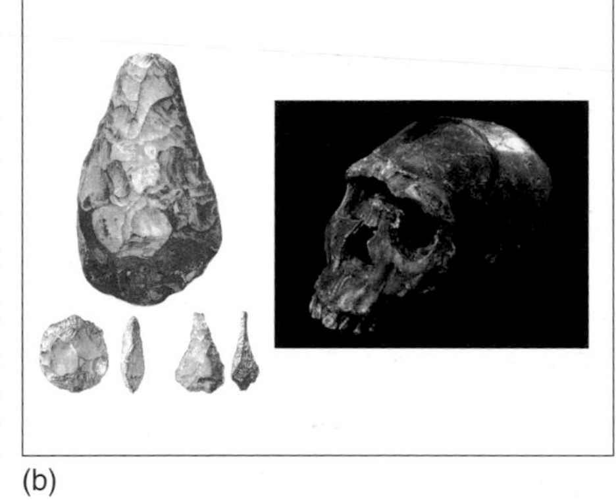

(b)

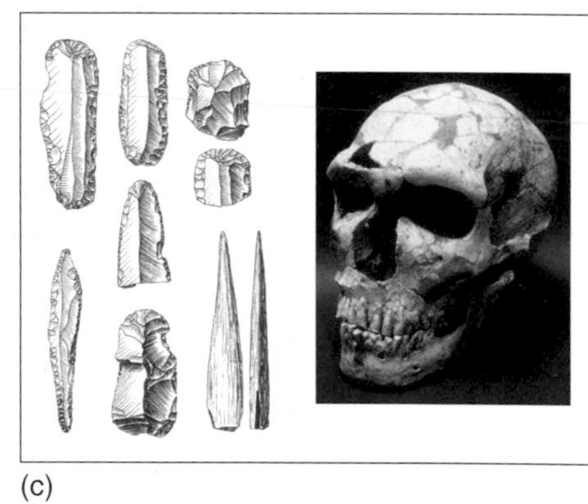

(c)

Figure 1.2 Stone tools and their likely makers. (a) The oldest stone tools (2.5 Ma) from Gona in northeastern Ethiopia, possibly made by *Homo habilis* or an earlier unknown hominin about 2.5 Ma ago. These are often called Oldowan, from the place where they were first discovered, Olduvai Gorge in Tanzania. (b) Bifacial tools, including a 1.5-Ma-old hand axe, made by *Homo ergaster*. These are generally referred to as Acheulean, from a site at St Acheul in France. (c) Blade tools from Le Moustier in Central France, made by *Homo neanderthalensis* at around 35 ka, thus defining the Mousterian 'culture'. (The tools in parts (a) and (c) from Nature Publishing Group. Reprinted by permission from Macmillan Publishers Ltd, http://www.nature.com/index.html)

1.1 Planning your study of Book 6

The topics in this book fall naturally into three parts: Chapters 2 and 3, on geological time and biological evolution; Chapters 4, 5 and 6, showing how observations of rocks give clues to the processes operating in the past; Chapters 7 and 8, applying what you have achieved in earlier chapters. Most of the activities involve the specimens in the Practical Kit, or computer-based resources, and you will probably need to study at a table to do them. Table 1.1 shows where these activities occur in the book.

Table 1.1 Activities needing other resources.

Chapter	Section	Activity	Time/min	Resource
2	2.2.1	2.2 Different animal groups	90	Practical Kit specimens
4	4.1	4.1 Igneous minerals	60	Computer-based resource
	4.2	4.2 Basalt and granite (1)	15	Practical Kit specimens
	4.2.2	4.3 Basalt and granite (2)	15	Practical Kit specimens
5	5.1	5.1 Examining sedimentary materials in soil	60 (over 24 h)	Practical
	5.2.2	5.2 Sedimentary grains, transport and sorting	60	Computer-based resource Practical Kit specimens
6	6.1.1	6.1 Comparing metamorphic rocks	30	Practical Kit specimens
7	7.1.3	7.2 A geological field trip	60	Computer-based resource
	7.3.1	7.3 How Pangaea was made	30	Computer-based resource
	7.3.2	7.4 The break-up of Pangaea	30	Computer-based resource

Use the course calendar on the course website as a guide to help plan your study.

Chapter 2
Tracking environmental change

A core extracted from the mud beneath a lake bed, such as the one you saw in Book 1, Section 3.4.1, records the build-up over time of sediment and whatever fell into the lake. Unless the lake occasionally dried out or froze completely, deposition of sediment would have been continuous. Hence the deeper the layer, the older it is. This ordering is known as the **principle of superposition** and it provides a means of **relative dating**. It may seem an obvious indicator for a geological time sequence, yet the principle was first recognised only in the mid-17th century, by the Danish geologist Nicolaus Steno (1638–1686), from his study of sedimentary rocks in Italy. Steno observed not only that the rocks had been laid down as a sequence of near-horizontal layers but also that those layers might be folded, or even turned upside-down, by later events.

The variation of tree pollens in a core taken from a lake bed (Book 1, Figure 3.14) records changes in the density of woodlands near the lake, and also in the types of tree that once grew nearby. Studies of modern woodlands in different climates provide the key to understanding how past changes in the proportions of pollen from different trees reflect shifts in climate around the lake. Pollen is therefore an indirect pointer to or **proxy** for past climates.

■ Book 1 gave the impression that pollen records can be converted to a history of changing mean surface temperature but what other aspects of climate and locality might affect vegetation?

□ Precipitation, windiness, length of seasons and ranges of daylight hours would also be important.

You may also have realised that different kinds of tree favour different soil types and drainage conditions. Useful though a pollen record may be for visualising past environments, it is a proxy for many things other than temperature. Figure 3.16 in Book 1 is useful only in general terms: for the range of mean temperatures tolerated by a 'blend' of trees; and for indicating 'warm' or 'cold' conditions at only a single geographic point. If there were proxies for individual attributes of climate, a more rigorous approach would be possible, especially if the proxies expressed regional or even global changes. In Section 2.1 you will meet such proxies that have revolutionised understanding of 2.5 Ma of global climatic change during the last ice age – the crucial period of human evolution.

For any local record (such as pollen records) to contribute to regional and global history, events recorded by it must somehow be related to time, rather than just their depth in the record. Only then can many isolated records be meaningfully compared. If records from different areas contain distinct evidence for the same short-lived regional or global event, matching or **correlation** between many records can be achieved.

■ Based on your knowledge of Book 2, suggest some widespread events that might leave signs in the rock record and provide useful relative time markers of this kind.

□ Explosive volcanic eruptions may deposit thin layers of ash over huge areas. A reversal of the Earth's magnetic polarity is an example of a truly global event. Its effect on the magnetisation of sediments can be detected, as well as that in lavas (Book 2, Section 7.3.1).

As you will see in Section 2.2, another means of correlation exploits speciation and extinction of organisms (Book 5, Chapters 14 and 15) by using fossils. This is the main method that led to a generally accepted geological timescale, in the relative sense, which you will meet in Section 2.3.

Correlation still leaves out the issue of absolute time, and therefore any ability to judge the *rates* of changes. Assessing these rates demands a framework expressed in years – ka, Ma, etc. – that has been established by **absolute dating** of the rocks involved. Also, many sequences of sedimentary rocks contain evidence for breaks in deposition (Section 2.4) that stem mainly from changes in tectonic motions or from rises and falls in global sea level. Absolute dating of rocks above and below such a break shows how long sedimentation was absent and helps to connect the break to regional or global processes that may have been responsible for it. Many geological events are episodic – they start and stop – shifting from place to place around the globe. Although particular features observed in exposures of rock can place such events in local, relative sequences (Section 2.4), only absolute dating can link them to a global, tectonic context. The most important means of absolute dating exploits the radioactive decay of several unstable isotopes (Section 2.5) but, for technical and financial reasons, not every exposed rock can be dated in this way. So an important approach is to use a few absolute dates to *calibrate* the geological record established by relative dating.

In Book 4 you met isotopes written as, e.g. carbon-14; the element name followed by the isotope's relative atomic mass. The form ^{14}C is more usual, and is used here and in Book 7.

Dating based on the radioactive decay of ^{14}C (radiocarbon dating) in charcoal grains from forest fires that occur in lake-bed sediments has helped to correlate pollen records across Europe. Comparing many local records that are calibrated to time shows how European woodland re-established itself after the last advance of glacial ice (Figure 2.1).

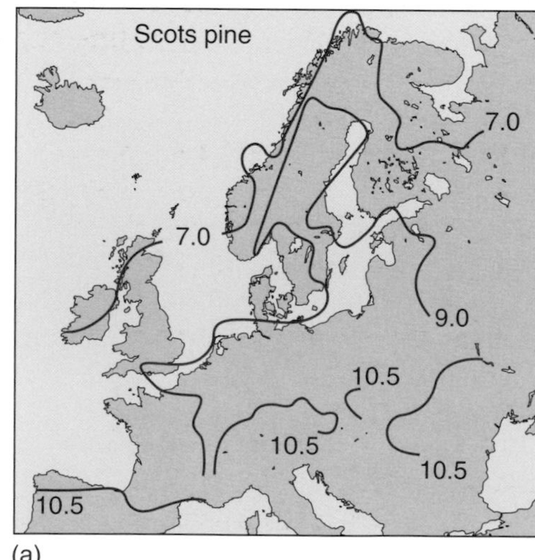

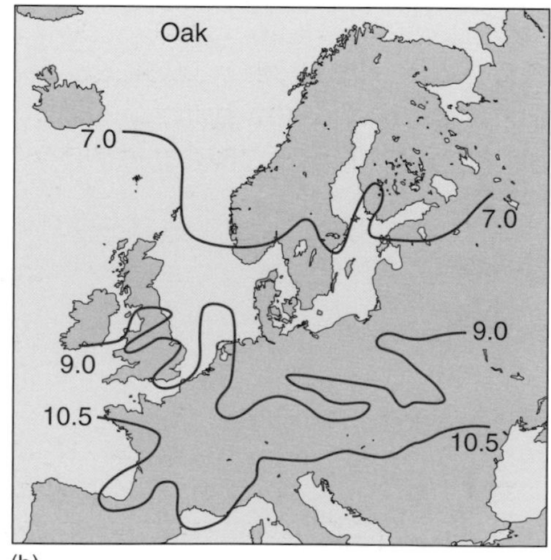

Figure 2.1 Analysis of European tree-pollen records, calibrated using radiocarbon dating, showing the advance of (a) Scots pine (*Pinus sylvestris*) and (b) oak (*Quercus* sp.) as the global climate warmed since 10.5 ka. The lines show the northernmost limits of each species at different times, in ka.

■ From the information in Figure 2.1, which species of tree appeared first in the British Isles?

□ Oak was established over most of southwestern England by 9 ka, whereas Scots pine began to grow there later, becoming established by 7 ka.

Dramatic discoveries about changing climate have emerged from unbroken sequences extracted as cores through the Greenland and Antarctic ice caps, and through sediments on the deep ocean floor. The last part of that climate record spans the period since 140 ka when modern humans from Africa began to populate the rest of the habitable world.

2.1 Records of continuous climate change

On the highest parts of the Antarctic and Greenland ice caps, annual snowfall exceeds the amount of summer melting. Snow therefore builds up each winter. Compaction transforms snow into solid ice that preserves signs of each summer's melted surface. The ice is thus layered year on year (Figure 2.2a), creating a perfect opportunity for both relative and absolute dating.

It is possible to count annual layers in cores through the Greenland ice cap back to 85 ka, corresponding to a depth of about 2800 m. Below that depth the ice has lost its layering. For these earlier times, mathematical models of how ice flows and becomes compacted, derived from the younger layered record, are used to convert from depth to age.

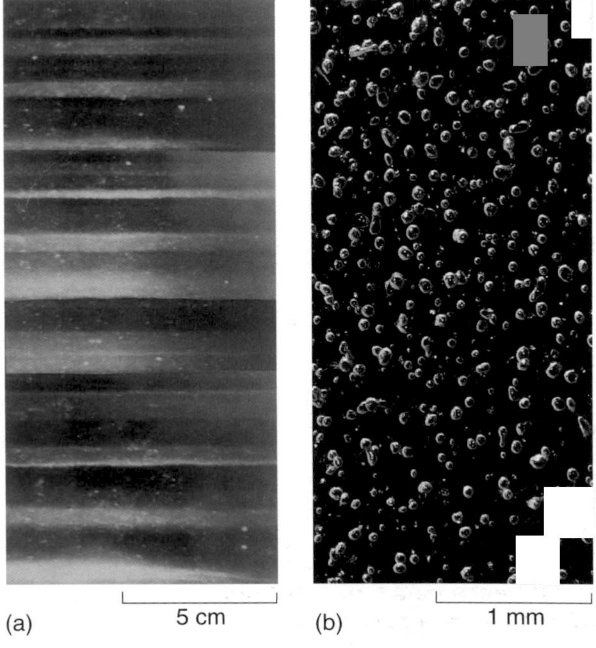

Figure 2.2 (a) Annual ice layers in a core drilled from deep in the Greenland ice cap. (b) Bubbles of air in glacial ice that were trapped at the time snow fell, in this case several tens of thousand years ago.

Glacial ice contains more than frozen water. Each year, snowflakes trap samples of the atmosphere, which eventually become bubbles in the ice (Figure 2.2b). These bubbles record the atmospheric greenhouse gases carbon dioxide and methane when each layer formed. Each layer also contains wind-blown dust scoured by wind from the land surface (Section 2.1.1); particles of salt precipitated from sea spray; smoke from forest fires; ash from volcanic eruptions, and, in the uppermost layers, various emissions from industry – for example, concentrations of lead and copper in the Greenland ice have increased since pre-Roman times. Atmospheric circulation efficiently mixes gases and fine dust particles entering the air from all parts of the Earth. As a result of this mixing, gas and dust measurements through ice cores chart changes that affected entire hemispheres and even the whole planet. So ice cores can be considered to be more than a 'local record' of environmental conditions.

Beyond the edges of the continental crust lies the quietest place on Earth: the deep ocean floor. A kind of 'snow' continuously falls there too (Book 1, Section 7.3.4). It consists mainly of the remains of dead organisms – both hard parts and undecayed organic matter – together with fine clays, volcanic dust and even minute particles of extraterrestrial materials. As you will see in Section 2.1.3, although the continuous records preserved in sea-floor sediments do not have the convenience of annual layers, they generally accumulate at a steady rate for long periods. Absolute dates at a few levels therefore enable depth to be calibrated against time. Individual samples extracted from cores driven through the sediments can represent an average over 100 to 1000 years, depending on the rate of sedimentation and the spacing between samples from the core. So marine sediment cores rarely yield the detail of ice cores.

Ocean-floor sediments contain the shells of tiny marine organisms called foraminifera (Book 1, Figure 7.5b). **Planktonic** species of foraminifera live in the top few hundred metres of ocean water. These foraminifera subsist on photosynthetic phytoplankton (Book 2, Section 2.1.1) that thrives in the sunlit zone. **Benthic** species live in deep water and on the ocean floor where they scavenge dead organic matter that sinks from higher levels. Small as they are, foraminifera shells in ocean-floor sediments are sufficiently varied in shape that specialists can link most species to specific habitats.

Different species of planktonic foraminifera live in various surface-water conditions. For example, some live only under floating sea ice whereas others live in cold water free of ice. There are also temperate and tropical species. Variations in planktonic species in a sediment core give a broad idea of changing sea-surface temperature at the site. Because present-day foraminifera species are found as fossils in the sediment cores, as far back as 1 Ma ago and in some cases beyond that, they are important indicators of past oceanic conditions. Such species can be used as environmental proxies in an analogous way to tree pollens in lake sediments. In contrast, the deep-water habitat of benthic foraminifera has a very stable, low temperature. As a result, benthic species in a sediment core do not change much with time, although they also have an important role in analysing climatic change (Section 2.1.3).

2.1.1 The dust of time

Raindrops that have dried on a car sometimes leave traces of very fine, yet annoyingly abrasive dust. Occasionally, it forms a very obvious yellow-orange coating, generally after major dust storms in the Sahara desert. The finest particles lifted by the storm remain suspended in the atmosphere long enough for lower-atmosphere circulation to carry them to higher latitudes. The annual layers in the Greenland ice cap preserve such dust, but only rarely with a concentration visible to the unaided eye.

■ What large-scale climatic processes might result in variations in the dust content of annual ice layers?

□ The most obvious factor is windiness but variations in global humidity are more important. Fine particles in sediment or soil exposed on bare, dry surfaces are easily blown away. The higher the humidity, the more vegetation and soil moisture there is at the land surface. Both tend to hold sediment grains in place. Greater rainfall in humid times would also remove dust from the atmosphere at lower latitudes before reaching the ice sheets.

As mentioned earlier, because of atmospheric circulation the dust in Greenland ice cores represents conditions thousands of miles away, even the entire Northern Hemisphere. The more arid the global conditions, the larger the area of bare, dry surfaces and the more dust that can be blown into the atmosphere. The dust record in ice cores is therefore an important climate proxy.

Dust particles are too tiny to count in thousands of ice layers, so an automated method has been devised. The continual accumulation of volcanic sulfur dioxide gas in snow makes glacial ice slightly acid so that it conducts electricity. Wind-blown dust, on the other hand, contains a proportion of carbonates that neutralise the acid, thereby tending to reduce the electrical conductivity of ice. (Electrical conductivity is a measure of the ease with which an electric current will flow through a material; i.e. Book 3 Section 7.2.) So measurements of electrical conductivity to deduce variations in acidity through an ice core give a proxy for atmospheric dustiness; high acidity signifies low dust content, whereas low acidity values reflect more dusty conditions.

Figure 2.3 plots acidity derived from electrical conductivity measurements (horizontally) against age (increasing downwards) in a Greenland ice core. As you saw in Book 1, this style of plot is sometimes useful for visualising time sequences in layered sequences, such as glacial ice and sedimentary strata, in which age increases with depth in a core, or in a cliff exposing sedimentary rocks.

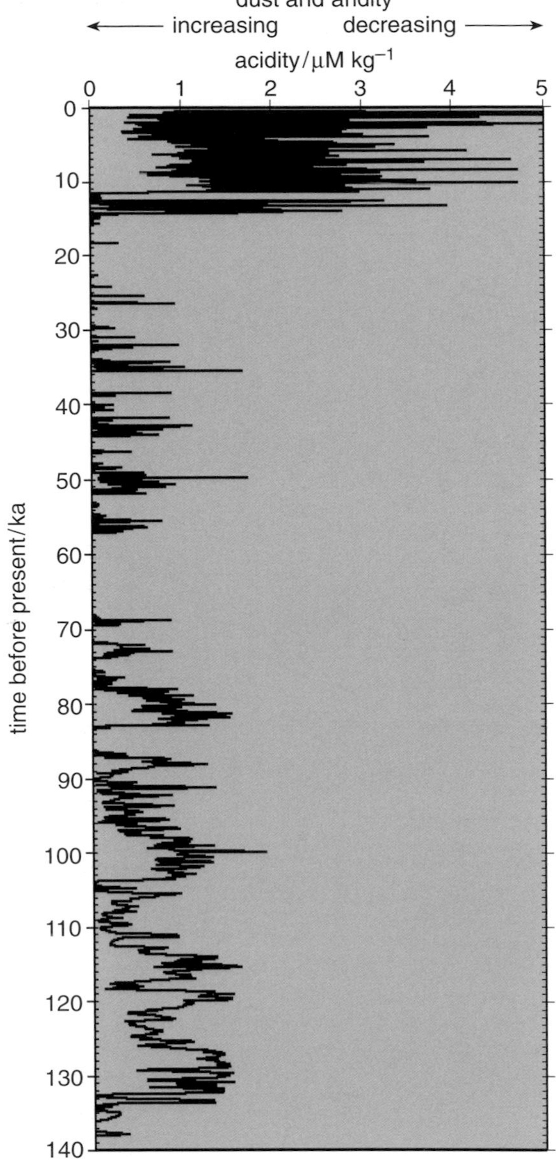

Figure 2.3 Changes since 140 ka in the acidity of ice beneath the summit of the Greenland ice cap. This is about the same time range as in the pollen diagram from France in Book 1 Figure 3.15. (*Note*: acidity is expressed in micromoles of hydrogen ions in a kilogram of ice (μM kg^{-1}) but you don't need to worry about the units.)

Figure 2.3 records an immense amount of information: acidity measurements are for every 3–10 years for the last 10 ka, and then increasing in steps to about every 300 years at 140 ka. The data are extremely variable, but the sharp variations are not instrumental 'noise' and represent the natural variability of atmospheric dustiness through time. With such highly variable data, *interpretation relies on looking for patterns rather than at each tiny peak or dip*. To help you to start interpreting the figure, consider first the lower section of the graph. At 140 ka the Northern Hemisphere was dry, windy and very dusty and continued to be so until about 134 ka, when dust decreased suddenly to signify an increase in Northern Hemisphere humidity. From 134 to 110 ka there were two periods (127–121 and 119–117 ka) of increased dust levels and therefore climatic dryness (aridity), although neither reached the extreme aridity of 140 ka. From about 113 ka dust levels began to rise again.

Question 2.1

What are the *overall* trends in dustiness and aridity in Figure 2.3 over the last 110 ka? (Remember that the acidity proxy decreases as dust content in ice increases and that increasing dust implies decreasing humidity.)

The fully modern human species (*Homo sapiens*) emerged in Africa between about 150–200 ka. Humans began to migrate out of their home continent to populate the rest of the habitable world at about 85 ka. Interestingly, Figure 2.3 shows that this exodus took place during a period of major changes in aridity. The next two sections explore other aspects of climate change to seek possible explanations for major events in human prehistory.

2.1.2 Oxygen isotopes in ice: keys to Greenland's climate

The evidence for complicated changes in aridity from the dust record in the Greenland ice cap is, by itself, divorced from a more familiar expression of climate: temperature. Oxygen atoms, the dominant components (by mass) of ice, hold the key to constructing a record of air temperatures over Greenland. More precisely, the key to measuring those ancient temperatures lies with different isotopes of oxygen (Book 4, Section 3.2), and how simple processes in the water cycle affect their proportions in ice.

Despite their different relative atomic masses (RAMs), all the isotopes of an element have the same chemical properties, which stem from their fixed number of electrons. Yet their different RAMs give each isotope slightly different *physical* properties. So they are affected in subtly different ways by physical processes, such as melting and vaporisation, and freezing and condensation.

Oxygen comprises three isotopes with RAMs of 16, 17 and 18 (denoted ^{16}O, ^{17}O and ^{18}O, respectively). Each is a **stable isotope** that does not undergo radioactive decay. Of the three, ^{16}O accounts for more than 99% of oxygen on Earth, and ^{18}O makes up most of the balance; ^{17}O is present in very tiny amounts. Very precise measurements of the relative amounts of each isotope in small ice samples are made using a mass spectrometer that separates atoms according to their RAM and their atomic number. In the Greenland ice core the relative proportions of ^{18}O to ^{16}O in the ice varies considerably with depth and thus with the age of the samples.

The relative proportion of two isotopes in a sample is expressed by the ratio of their abundance, for example, the amount of ^{18}O divided by the amount of ^{16}O (i.e. $^{18}O/^{16}O$). To compare the value of this ratio in different samples, each measured value must be expressed in a standardised way as a fractional difference between it and the $^{18}O/^{16}O$ ratio measured in a standard material. In this case the standard is present-day seawater. The fractional difference is:

$$\frac{(^{18}O/^{16}O)_{\text{sample}} - (^{18}O/^{16}O)_{\text{standard}}}{(^{18}O/^{16}O)_{\text{standard}}} \tag{2.1}$$

Ratios are often expressed as a percentage, for example 0.5 as 50%. But Equation 2.1 produces very small numbers. Rather than expressing it as a percentage (%), it is conventionally expressed as per mil (per thousand, denoted ‰). As a fraction is converted to per cent by multiplying it by 100, so converting the fraction given by Equation 2.1 to per mil involves multiplication by 1000. This fractional difference is known as the **delta value**, in this case denoted $\delta^{18}O$ (said as 'delta eighteen oxygen').

You will not need to apply the equation in this course, but you should be able to see the following:

A sample whose oxygen isotopes are identical to those in the standard has a $\delta^{18}O$ value of 0‰, i.e. there is no difference. Negative values of $\delta^{18}O$ show that somehow ^{18}O has been depleted relative to ^{16}O in the sample, and positive values of $\delta^{18}O$ occur in samples that are enriched in ^{18}O.

Moving away from the equation that defines what the delta value $\delta^{18}O$ is, it is important to know what causes the $\delta^{18}O$ value of ice to vary.

Scientists have measured the $\delta^{18}O$ in snow that falls today on parts of the Greenland ice cap that have different mean annual air temperatures. The results show that the $\delta^{18}O$ of the snow depends on air temperature (Figure 2.4). Snow formed at very low

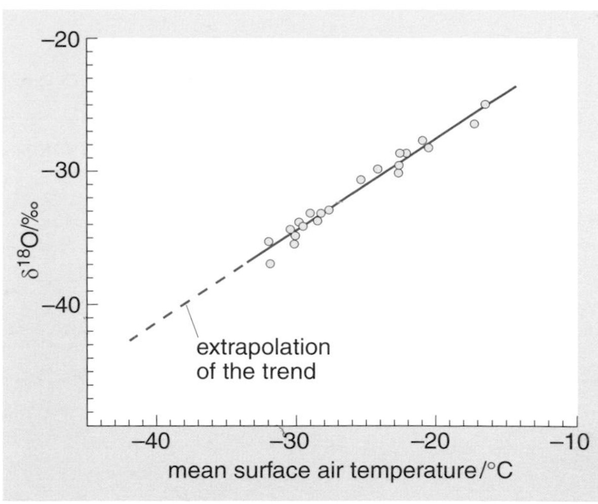

Figure 2.4 The $\delta^{18}O$ values in modern snow falling at different places in Greenland versus the mean surface air temperature. The dashed line shows the linear trend extended to lower temperatures. *Note*: the more negative the $\delta^{18}O$ value, the less ^{18}O is present in the ice.)

temperatures has a lower $\delta^{18}O$ and therefore contains less ^{18}O than that formed at higher temperatures; i.e. the heavier isotope (^{18}O) more easily enters the ice structure in snow when snowflakes crystallise at higher temperatures. The $\delta^{18}O$ values in Figure 2.4 can therefore be used to work out past variations in the mean air temperature over the site from the $\delta^{18}O$ in ice core samples.

Figure 2.5a shows how $\delta^{18}O$ varied in a Greenland ice core between 140 ka ago and the present day. The variations in $\delta^{18}O$ represent shifts in mean surface air temperature over central

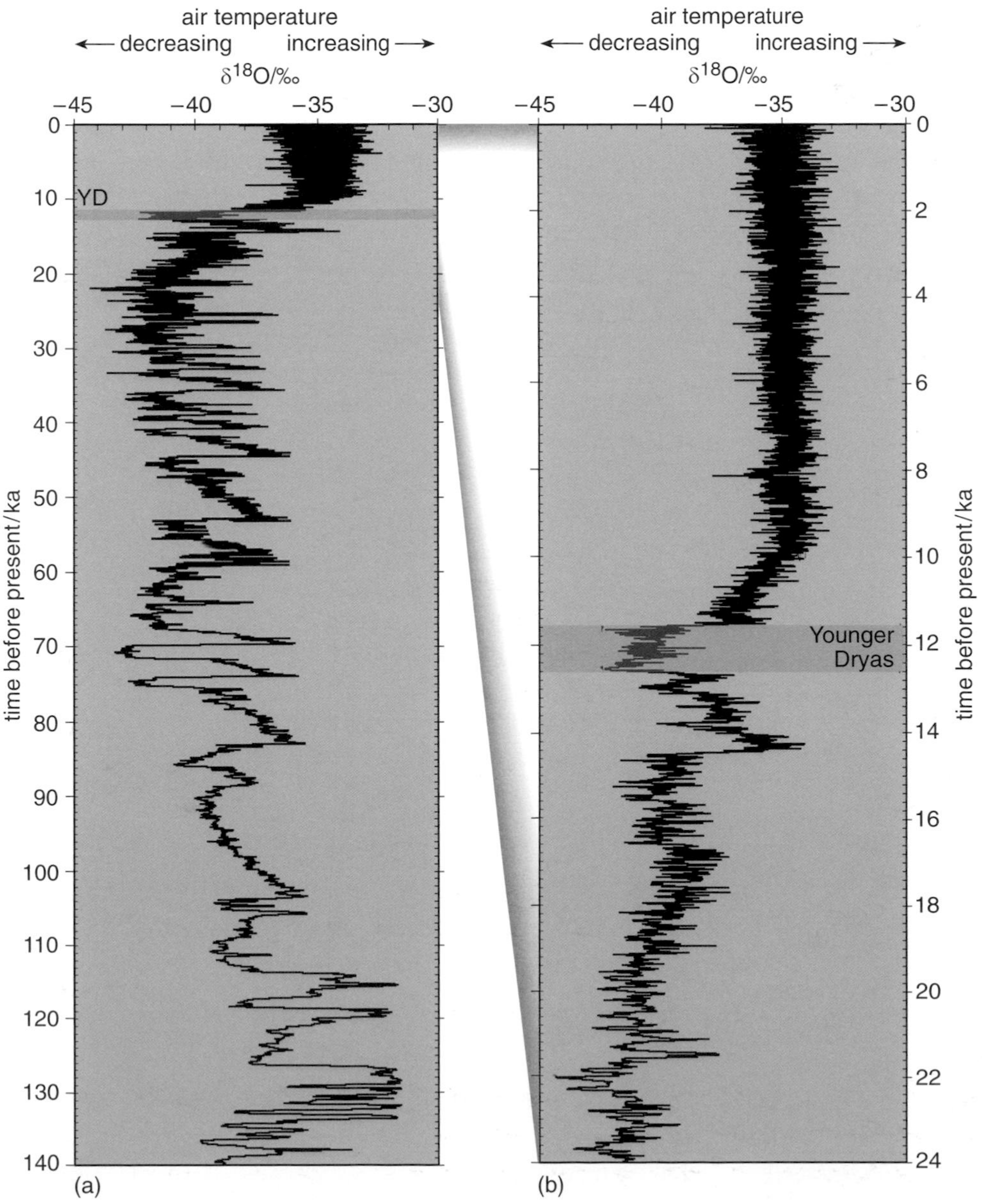

Figure 2.5 Variations in $\delta^{18}O$ in ice (a proxy for mean surface air temperature) from a core through the Greenland ice sheet: (a) for the last 140 ka (YD is the Younger Dryas); (b) for the last 24 ka. As in Figure 2.3, the measurements accurately express real variations rather than sudden, random fluctuations caused by instrumental noise.

Greenland, which you can judge by referring to Figure 2.4. Despite numerous short-term fluctuations, the $\delta^{18}O$ values over the last 10 ka are around –35‰ and so indicate long-term climate stability over that period (Figure 2.5).

Question 2.2

Using Figure 2.4 to convert $\delta^{18}O$ values in Figure 2.5a to mean surface air temperatures, roughly:

(a) What was the mean surface air temperature over the last 10 ka?

(b) What was the lowest surface air temperature recorded in the core?

(c) When was that lowest surface air temperature reached?

(d) When was the last time that surface air temperatures over Greenland were as high as the mean for the last 10 ka?

The coldest time over the Greenland ice cap was about 22 ka ago, the whole period from about 30 to 20 ka being almost as cold. So, how fast did central Greenland warm up since 20 ka? Spend a few minutes looking at the detailed plot in Figure 2.5b.

From about 20 to 15 ka temperatures rose sluggishly. Temperatures rose rapidly from 15 ka to reach almost present levels by 14.5 ka, but the warmth did not last. At 12.6 ka temperatures plummeted to almost the levels of 10 ka earlier, perhaps in as little as a decade. The climate warmed up almost as rapidly about a thousand years later. This almost-glacial millennium is called the Younger Dryas, after *Dryas octopetala* (the mountain avens), an alpine member of the rose family whose pollen dominates lake sediment cores of the period. In Britain, remnants of mountain glaciers grew and sculpted much of the present upland scenery. The close of the Younger Dryas was followed by steady warming to the current period of warmth that has lasted since 10 ka ago.

Looking back beyond the 30–20 ka period of minimum temperatures, Figure 2.5a shows several cycles of warming and then cooling that are irregularly spaced. Between 65 and 90 ka there are four cycles that are sufficiently clear for you to explore the relationship between temperature variations and the acidity proxy in ice for aridity in Figure 2.3.

Activity 2.1 Comparing climate proxies from the Greenland ice cap

We expect this activity will take you approximately 10 minutes.

With the help of a ruler, read off the dates (to the nearest 1 ka is fine) of the highest temperatures in each of the four cycles between 65 and 90 ka shown in Figure 2.5a.

Mark these dates on the time axis of Figure 2.3.

In a few sentences, describe the relationship between temperature over the Greenland ice cap and the dust proxy for aridity.

Now look at the comments on this activity at the end of this book.

The two proxies from the Greenland ice match quite well, and show that every fall in temperature over Greenland was accompanied by an increase in aridity that probably affected the whole Northern Hemisphere. (Likewise, as Greenland warmed, conditions elsewhere became more humid.) Over about 90 ka, from 110 to 20 ka, the world became increasing cold and dry, albeit relieved from time to time by short periods of relative warmth and humidity. This was the time of the last glacial period, yet conclusive evidence for the growth and shrinkage of glacial ice on land comes from a surprising source.

2.1.3 A message from the abyss

The outwardly featureless muds in ocean-floor cores (Figure 2.6a) are enlivened when seen through a microscope (Figure 2.6b). They fossil teem with tiny shells of foraminifera of many kinds, both planktonic and benthic. These fossil remains are the source of intensively studied proxy records, but they are sometimes accompanied by wind-blown dust and pollen, and fragments of rock dropped by melting icebergs.

Figure 2.6 Materials in ocean-floor sediment cores. (a) Part of a core which suggests that the muddy sediments do not vary much. (b) Microscopic view of ocean-floor sediment: much of the material comprises minute skeletal remains of organisms that once lived at different depths in ocean water. The image is about 2 mm across.

Having been deposited continuously, deep-ocean sediments complement ice-core records. The information that they provide extends the climate record globally, because sediment cores can be obtained from a range of latitudes in all the ocean basins. A disadvantage stems from creatures that live in the top few centimetres of the ocean bed; they stir up the sediment after it has settled. As a result, the time record becomes blurred, so that there is little point in sampling closer than every 5 to 10 cm through the cores. That limits the time resolution of ocean-floor proxy records to around 100 years compared with the potential yearly resolution in ice-core data.

Foraminifera shells are made of calcium carbonate ($CaCO_3$). The living organism extracts Ca^{2+} and CO_3^{2-} ions from seawater to secrete its shell, so the shells contain samples of the elements Ca, C and O contained in the seawater where they lived. As with ice, temperature has an effect on the relative proportions of ^{16}O and ^{18}O that the foraminifera take up. In the top few hundred metres of the oceans where planktonic species live, seawater temperature will vary with overall climate, but will also change over very short timescales because of shifts in warm and cold surface currents. Oxygen isotopes from fossil planktonic species thus give only a guide to varying sea-surface temperatures in the past. The benthic forms provide a very different proxy. They live at the ocean bottom, where water temperature remains constant for hundreds of thousand years, barely above 0 °C. Free of variations caused by temperature, changing oxygen-isotope proportions in benthic foraminifera provide clues to other processes, which are part of the water cycle.

When water evaporates from the ocean surface, water molecules containing ^{16}O – the lightest isotope of oxygen – evaporate slightly more readily than those containing the heavier ^{18}O.

■ What happens to the proportion of ^{18}O in the remaining liquid water?

□ The water becomes slightly enriched in ^{18}O, while the proportion of ^{16}O in atmospheric water vapour increases.

If some of the evaporated water falls on land as winter snow, but a proportion of that snow fails to melt in succeeding summers, it becomes ice and eventually may contribute to glaciers. Such long-lived land ice stores the excess ^{16}O produced by evaporation. A build-up of glacial ice on land gradually enriches seawater in ^{18}O. As a result, the $\delta^{18}O$ value in seawater *increases* (Figure 2.7).

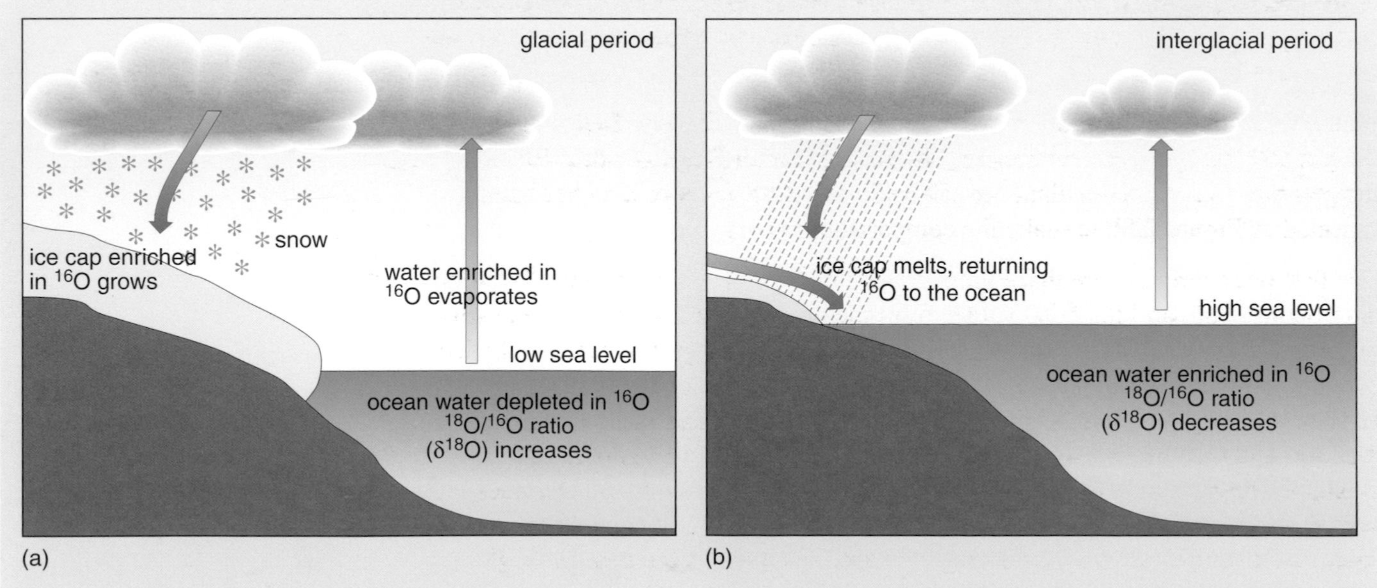

Figure 2.7 How sea-surface evaporation causes ^{16}O preferentially to enter atmospheric water vapour and then ice caps, the effects on the proportion of ^{18}O in seawater, and how this relates to changing sea level: (a) during an ice age; (b) during a warmer interglacial period.

Conversely, as glacial ice melts it releases floods of isotopically 'light' water to the ocean, and $\delta^{18}O$ *decreases*. These isotopic changes are passed on to the oxygen taken up by foraminifera to make their shells. Benthic foraminifera live in deep water where the temperature stays constant, so their shells inherit *only* the changes in $\delta^{18}O$ that are due to the waxing and waning of ice sheets on the land surface. Accumulating through time in ocean-floor sediments, the shells of dead benthic foraminifera steadily build up a proxy record of large-scale glaciation, in the form of changing $\delta^{18}O$.

■ What else happens to the ocean as ice caps grow and then melt?

□ Its volume changes, so global sea level falls and rises respectively.

The $\delta^{18}O$ record from benthic foraminifera in ocean-floor sediment cores is therefore a proxy for global sea level, as well as for the waxing and waning of ice caps. Yet the volume of seawater is so immense (about 1.4×10^9 km^3) that only huge changes in the volume of ice caps would have an effect on this record. So, how big *were* ice caps in the past compared with their present sizes?

■ What evidence might indicate the former extent of glacial ice?

□ The distinctive sediments, or tills, which moving glaciers pick up, transport and dump where they melt.

The extent and present latitude of ancient tills allowed Alfred Wegener to propose that the southern continents had once been united in Pangaea (Book 2, Section 7.1). Much more recent tills (from the last few hundred thousand years) extend to as far south as 40° N in North America and around 50° N in Europe, almost reaching London and laying beneath Berlin. Tens of million square kilometres of now-vegetated land must have once lain beneath several kilometres of ice. Such ice caps were big enough to affect sea level significantly. So ocean-floor oxygen isotopes can resolve the timing of changes in the amount of land ice and the sea level.

Figure 2.8a shows the variation of $\delta^{18}O$ in benthic foraminifera shells over the last 140 ka. Spend a few minutes comparing it with the proxy data for air temperature over the Greenland ice cap in Figure 2.5a. (Figure 2.5a has been repeated as Figure 2.8b to make the comparison easier.)

The first points to note are that Figure 2.8a shows much less short-term variation than Figure 2.8b, and the $\delta^{18}O$ values from the ocean-floor sediments are positive instead of negative. The greater variation in Figure 2.8b is partly because the ice-core data involve far more samples than do those from the ocean floor. Another reason for the relative smoothness of Figure 2.8a is that huge masses of glacial ice form and melt slowly over hundreds of years, whereas air temperature can change from year to year. Overall, however, the trends shown by $\delta^{18}O$ values in both plots are similar: shifts to the left from around 125 ka to about 20 ka in both cases, indicating cooling and growing ice caps. What about the detail though?

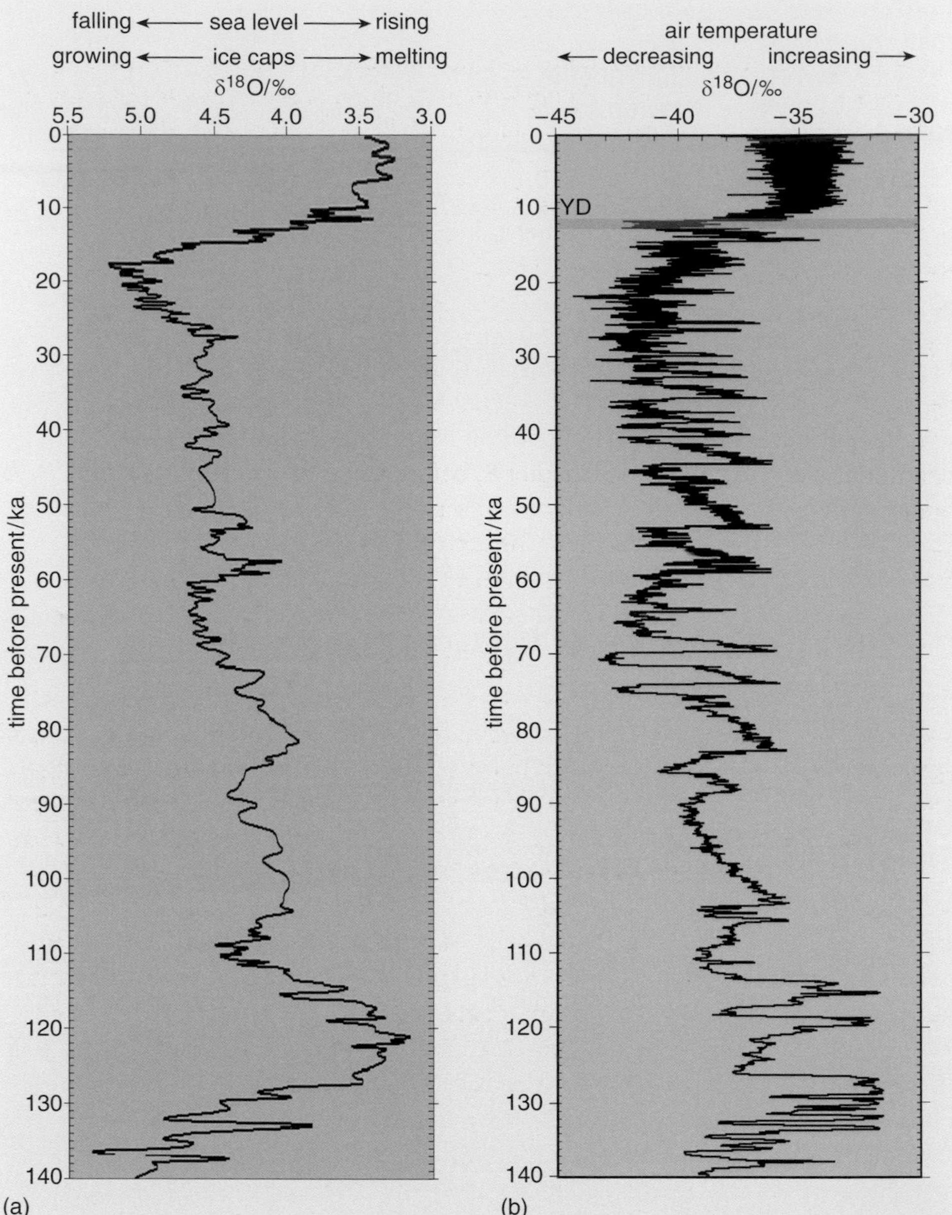

Figure 2.8 (a) Variation over the last 140 ka of $\delta^{18}O$ in benthic foraminifera from ocean-floor sediments. This is a composite of data from several ocean-floor cores. (b) Variation over the last 140 ka of $\delta^{18}O$ in a Greenland ice sheet. (This is a repeat of Figure 2.5a.)

■ Figure 2.8b shows prominent patterns of changing temperatures over the Greenland ice cap at around 113–105, 86–75, 60–57, and 57–50 ka. Do these also occur in the record of land ice shown in Figure 2.8a?

□ All four patterns occur in Figure 2.8a, but they are not exactly the same as in Figure 2.8b; they are smoother and often less pronounced.

There are several differences between the Greenland ice record and that of ocean-floor sediments. Most notably, whereas the lowest temperatures occurred over the Greenland ice cap at 22 ka, land ice reached its greatest volume 4 ka later (as recorded in the ocean-floor sediments). The period around 18 ka is known as the **last glacial maximum**.

2.1.4 The human connection

A human perspective on the record of temperature and Northern Hemisphere aridity is interesting. The earliest signs of agriculture and permanent settlements appear in the archaeological record at about 10 ka in the region of the present Middle East and Black Sea, i.e. after the climate had become stable. Britain's earliest agriculture began at about 6.5 ka, but there is evidence that forager-hunters had lived there during the warming after 20 ka, and through the frigid millennium of the Younger Dryas. The dramatic shifts in climate before 10 ka made a nomadic forager-hunter lifestyle obligatory everywhere. At high latitudes intense cold and advancing ice made life almost impossible. In the tropics, increased aridity would have reduced vegetation so that game declined or migrated. Our ancestors had to be free to move quickly, to survive when the climate worsened and to exploit new opportunities of warming conditions. As you will see in Chapter 8, before about 85 ka, fully modern humans (*Homo sapiens*) lived only in Africa and occasionally in the Middle East. About that time they began to migrate into Eurasia, eventually reaching Europe at around 50 ka. There they came into contact with the Neandertals (*Homo neanderthalensis*), forager-hunters who had occupied Europe since at least 230 ka and had survived previous glacial episodes.

Fully modern humans emerged in Africa between 150 and 200 ka, migrated to Asia, and eventually spread everywhere except to Antarctica. Yet, until the rise of agriculture around 10 ka, the global human population was probably never more than a few million, and during periods of quickly worsening global climate there is evidence that it fell much lower than that. As well as repeated climate changes that sometimes threatened and sometimes benefited humanity, these times also witnessed major changes in sea level. Some climate changes, such as the onset of the Younger Dryas, could have happened within a human lifespan. These events reshaped the face of the world as it would appear from space, not only blanketing vast areas with ice, and changing coastlines, but also shifting vegetation zones by up to several thousand kilometres. Chapter 8 returns to the broad climatic and environmental context of human evolution and migrations.

2.2 Marking time in sedimentary rocks

Having studied an example of a continuous record in ocean-floor sediments, you may be thinking that they and other sedimentary rocks can be used to extend detailed climate history back millions or even billions of years. However, modern ocean floors started forming about 180 Ma ago (Book 2, Section 9.4), when Pangaea began to break apart (Book 2, Section 7.1). Ocean floor which once surrounded that supercontinent has long since disappeared down subduction zones. So, information like that in Figure 2.8 is available only since 180 Ma ago.

The land and shallow seas that are underlain by continental lithosphere cannot be subducted into the mantle because of the low density of the continents. Consequently, they are able to preserve records of sedimentation since the times when each segment of continental crust first formed. The age of the continental crust extends far beyond 180 Ma, in a few places to almost 4 Ga. However, none of the continents have a complete sedimentary record; it has to be pieced together from evidence collected at many different places.

- ■ Suggest two important reasons for this incomplete record of sedimentary rocks.
- □ Continental crust forms at convergent plate boundaries, and continental drift may result in continent–continent collision. Both processes force up the Earth's surface, either as volcanoes or as deformed and metamorphosed mountain belts (Book 2, Chapters 8 and 9). Uplifted surfaces are exposed to weathering and erosion. So older rocks, including sediments, are stripped away while debris from the erosion eventually forms new sediments (Book 2, Chapter 5).

Where they *are* preserved, sedimentary rocks generally take on the distinctive form of a 'layer cake' of beds or strata. In sedimentary sequences younger strata sit on top of older ones – unless huge tectonic forces have turned them upside down. (These tectonic forces are considered further in Chapter 6.) The study of **stratigraphy** (from the Latin, 'description of strewn things') stems from the simple principle of superposition. Figure 2.9 shows sedimentary rocks that are part of a sequence deposited on a surface underlain by continental crust. Unlike ocean-floor sediments, the sequence contains several different-looking kinds of sedimentary strata, whose relative age decreases upwards. The changing appearance of the strata suggests that the materials, and perhaps conditions of sedimentation changed with time. There are sharp breaks between the different sedimentary rock types, so those changes seem to have happened suddenly.

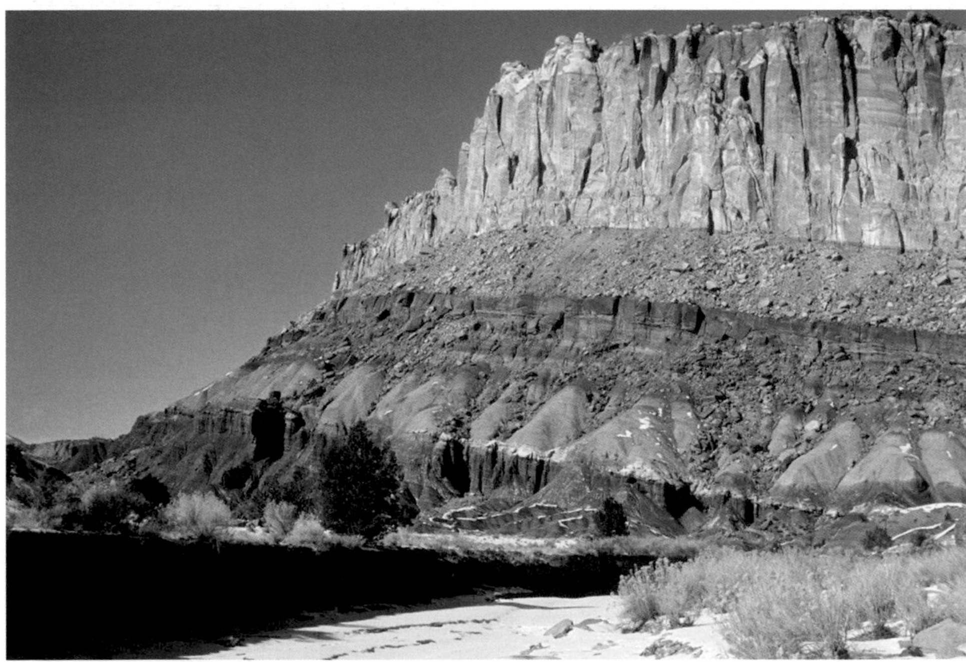

Figure 2.9 Varied sedimentary rocks exposed in Utah, USA. According to the principle of superposition, the oldest strata are at the bottom. The clear differences in colour and other attributes from layer to layer are the result of changing conditions of sedimentation.

Book 2, Section 5.2.2 briefly describes the processes of weathering, erosion, transportation, and deposition involved in the formation of sedimentary rocks. Many sedimentary rocks are made of mineral and rock fragments. Others comprise skeletal debris made from calcium carbonate, formed when organisms extract that compound's chemical components from water to form their hard parts. More rare are sedimentary rocks made of compounds, such as sodium chloride or calcium sulfate, that come out of solution as a result of the evaporation of water (Book 4, Section 4.1). There are also carbon-rich sediments formed by the accumulation of dead organisms; for example, coal and hydrocarbon-rich muds. All kinds of features within such sediments help re-create a story of their formative environments (Chapter 5). The question here is, do simple sedimentary sequences deposited on land and on the shallow sea floor, as exemplified by Figure 2.9, contain a *continuous* record of events? The answer is, only if conditions continuously favoured deposition. Interruptions to the deposition by erosion would result in discontinuous records.

■ How do you think the variability of conditions on the land surface and beneath shallow seas differs from that on the deep-ocean floor?

□ They vary in both time and space, whereas conditions in deep water generally stay about the same.

Question 2.3

What variations in conditions (i) beneath shallow seas and (ii) on land, would you expect to have an effect on the sediments that build up?

Kinetic energy (Book 3, Chapter 3) drives many sedimentary processes on land and in shallow seas. Energy levels can be far higher than in the deep oceans, but that does not imply that quiet conditions never occur. Flat areas of land, sheltered coasts and the deeper water of continental shelves have low energy. Yet, as your answer to Question 2.3 may suggest, the available kinetic energy can change dramatically everywhere except on the deep-ocean floor. Places where sediments once accumulated steadily may eventually be stripped of them, if the local conditions become more energetic. That would leave a gap in the local geological record. Yet those shifted sediments will be transported elsewhere to build up again.

Geographic variation in the type of sedimentary deposition and breaks in deposition greatly hinder the place-to-place correlation of sedimentary sequences using the rocks alone. Reconstructing the Earth's history depends on discovering what was happening in different parts of the world at any particular time. Which areas were above sea level then, and which were shallow seas? Where were mountain ranges forming by continental collision, or through volcanic activity? Where did different climates prevail? And so on. None of these questions could yield a useful answer without an indicator of the passage of time that is common to all parts of the world, or at least over large regions.

2.2.1 Fossils and time division

The surveyor and geologist William Smith (1769–1839) surveyed canal schemes all over England, and had to examine rocks professionally. He noticed that different fossils occur in rocks that, from the principle of superposition, formed at different times. Although he did not ascribe these differences to evolution, Smith used fossils as a means of recognising particular beds. For instance, he could correlate certain beds of chalk in the North Downs of southern England with others in the South Downs, because each contained particular types of fossil which differed from those in the identical-looking chalk beds above and below.

Smith's second breakthrough was to correlate apparently *dissimilar* sedimentary strata because they contained *similar* fossils. For instance, widely separated limestone and sandstone beds, although quite different rocks, sometimes contained the same fossils. This suggested to him that both kinds of sediment were deposited in *different* environments at the *same* time. Smith's third and crucial observation was that the same changes in fossil assemblages from older to younger beds were repeated in rock sequences of different parts of the British Isles. His **principle of faunal succession** proposed that each sequence of rocks that contained the same fossil assemblage represented a particular span of time. Smith was then able to correlate widely separated occurrences of rock and in 1815 he published the first geological map of England, Wales and part of Scotland.

As fossil collections grew, it became clear that most fossils had anatomical features similar to those found in living organisms; the basis for theories of evolution extending far into the past (more of this in Chapter 3). Those features also gave some clues to the possible habitats of extinct organisms. So, as well as recognisably subdividing the passage of time, fossils can help to define the environments in which sedimentary rocks formed.

Throughout this book, you need not worry about the detailed names of fossil organisms.

The smallest division using fossil evidence – a **zone** – is the time from the first appearance of a species to its disappearance. A sequence in time of several zones might be known exactly, but the *duration* of each zone is not. Individual species are now known (thanks to radiometric dating; see Section 2.5.1) to survive typically for a few hundred thousand years to a few million years. A few last much longer, for example the brachiopod *Lingulella* (Book 5, Chapter 1), and would be of little use in stratigraphy. A species with a small geographic range would also be of little use. Most fossil organisms capable of providing time 'zonation' are animals. To be useful in identifying such zones over wide areas an animal species needs:

- unique anatomical features that are easily recognised
- a rapid pace of evolution and extinction
- a wide geographic range – the most useful are free-swimming or floating marine animals, including those whose larvae float and drift in currents, such as corals
- parts that are efficiently preserved, so that fossils occur in sediments deposited in different environments
- to be abundant and therefore easy to find.

The first is the most important, for obvious practical reasons, but accurately identifying fossils to species level is a skill beyond the scope of this book. However, it is not difficult to place a fossil into one of the more fundamental anatomical groupings, using some simple observations of its **body plan** (i.e. the layout of its body parts). The most basic of these is whether it shows *symmetry*. For example, a human skeleton is largely the same either side of a plane that runs through the nose to the join of the legs. This is called **bilateral symmetry**. The embryonic forms of many living animals show such a bilateral symmetry, even those that are not obviously symmetrical when fully developed. They are members of a broad group encompassing many phyla called **bilaterians**. There are other organisms that are not bilaterians, and there is a brief discussion of the division in Chapter 3.

As fellow bilaterian animals, we are related to slugs and lobsters, although very distantly. The fact that both sides of the human skeleton stems from a backbone sets us apart from the other bilaterians, as members of the phylum Chordata, sub-phylum Vertebrata. Lesser anatomical differences separate our vertebrate class, order, family, genus and species: mammals; primates; hominins; *Homo*; *H. sapiens*. Today relationships or clades can be expressed for living organisms in terms of degrees of similarity in their DNA (Book 5, Section 3.3). For fossils, only anatomical comparisons can form a basis for inferring genetic relationships, in terms of degrees of similarity (and difference) in form.

Activity 2.2 Different animal groups

We expect this activity will take you approximately 90 minutes.

For this activity you will need the six fossil replicas and the hand lens from the Practical Kit.

The aim is to observe a few features shown by the fossils that highlight their anatomical differences, and in two cases some similarity. Most of the features are easily visible, but the hand lens may help resolve some details.

Examine each fossil, only using the hand lens if necessary, and enter your observations for each column in Table 2.1.

The row for fossil D is completed for you, so start by checking the comments against your own observations. (*Note*: only half of fossil D is visible, the hidden half being a near-mirror image of what you can see – so it shows bilateral symmetry across a plane roughly represented by the flat surface on which it rests.)

You should not expect to become a fossil expert in 90 minutes, but you should be able to observe and record some body features in a systematic fashion.

Table 2.1 Simple observations of some features of common animal fossils.

Fossil	Symmetry	Segmented?	Coiled?	Made of plates?	Other features
A	Bilateral	Yes	No		Ridged pattern along length
B	No (each piece yes)	Yes in whole (each piece no)	No	Possibly	lots of joined circular pieces
C	No	Yes	No	Possibly	Branched from main stem
D	Bilateral	No	Yes	No	Frilled pattern on shell
E	Bilateral	No ?	No	No	2 joined shells plates.
F	Bilateral (multi lateral)	No	No	Yes	Star shaped patterns

Question 2.4

Which of the fossils are bilaterian and which are non-bilaterian animals?

B: A, D, E
Non B, F, C

You will learn more about the six animal fossils from the extended comments on this activity at the end of this book, where you can check your entries in Table 2.1. Read those comments before continuing.

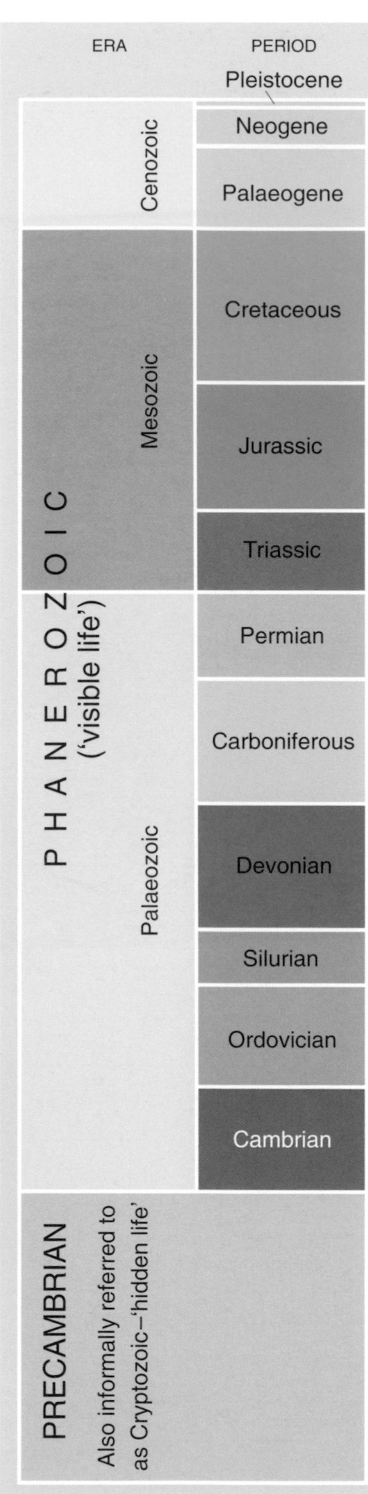

Figure 2.10 The stratigraphic column, divided into geological Eras and Periods, the oldest being at the bottom.

All the fossils in the Practical Kit are from groups that are exclusively marine. Finding them or fossils of closely related organisms in a sedimentary rock points clearly to sedimentation having occurred on the seabed. Almost all the fossils used in subdividing time and global correlation are of marine organisms, since they are most likely to satisfy the five essential criteria listed earlier.

All land-dwelling life forms evolved from saltwater ancestors (Chapter 3), so it is signs of their *adaptations* to living on land or in freshwater that signify the environment of sedimentary rocks that contain their fossils.

Most of the animals whose shells you might find on a beach are members of the phylum Mollusca, either single-shelled gastropods (limpets, whelks, periwinkles, etc.) or bivalves (mussels, cockles, clams, etc.). The other main molluscan class – the cephalopods – are exclusively marine. However, there are bivalve and gastropod families that are exclusive to freshwater, and some, such as snails and slugs, live happily on dry land. So neither bivalve nor gastropod fossils on their own can clearly signify marine deposition of the sediments that preserve them. If a bed that contains fossil bivalves or gastropods also yields coral, echinoid or cephalopod fossils, the accompanying mollusc species would also be demonstrably marine, and therefore suitable as environmental indicators in their own right. Likewise, fossil bivalve and gastropod species found in sedimentary beds that contain abundant remains of woody plants become indicators of non-marine conditions.

The very simplest environmental division separates saltwater marine conditions from those that were either on dry land or in fresh water – **terrestrial conditions**. Fossils are good indicators of which conditions prevailed at times in the past, but more details of the environment emerge from features preserved in sedimentary rocks themselves (Chapter 5).

2.3 The stratigraphic column

William Smith's discovery of faunal succession, as well as laying the basis for piecing together biological evolution, allowed stratigraphy to triumph. Changes in the kinds of organisms preserved in sedimentary rocks provided a means of subdividing the Earth's history. This division became known as the **stratigraphic column** (Figure 2.10).

The different levels of division depended on how dramatic the changes in fossils were. The greatest division is between the **Phanerozoic** Eon of 'visible' life (from the Greek *phaneros*, meaning visible, and *zoion*, meaning an animal) and earlier times when rocks show few, if any, tangible signs of fossil organisms. In the 19th century the oldest rocks known to contain fossils were first described from North Wales, and were dubbed the Cambrian. Unsurprisingly, the fossil-free, older rocks became widely known as the **Precambrian** (a more apt term is Cryptozoic – meaning 'hidden life' – but this is rarely used). Abundant fossils allow an intricate subdivision of the Phanerozoic. The most profound faunal differences helped to define three Eras: the **Palaeozoic** ('ancient' life), **Mesozoic** ('middle' life) and **Cenozoic** ('new' life).

Eras are divided into Periods, which are named arbitrarily according to where they were first described (Figure 2.10). Some use the Latin names of Welsh tribes, as in Ordovician. Others are named after the regions where they were first described, such as Permian from Perm in Russia. There are even Periods named after the most common sedimentary rock formed during that time: the Cretaceous is from the Latin for chalk (*creta*).

Geologists often refer to a stratigraphic division by its adjective (e.g. Phanerozoic, Cenozoic, Cambrian), without the associated noun Eon, Era or Period.

Faunal divisions at smaller time intervals, down to that of the zone, proliferate within Periods, but they are not necessary in this book. You will sometimes find references to the Upper and Lower parts of geological Periods: the formal terms for their later and earlier parts. A more important issue is that, until the mid-20th century, geologists had intricately divided a sequence among sedimentary rocks in *relative* time, but had no consistent idea of the timing of events or the duration of stratigraphic divisions in an *absolute* sense. This posed a whole series of challenges concerning other kinds of geological observation. There were stratigraphic gaps in some areas that were filled in others. Among sedimentary rocks there were also clearly volcanic layers. How long did they take to accumulate? There were abundant exposures of coarse igneous rocks that had crystallised deep in the Earth, which had neither layering nor fossils. When had they formed? There were even larger areas underlain by crystalline, sometimes layered metamorphic rocks, so transformed that any fossil content had disappeared. Fossiliferous sedimentary rocks (i.e. rocks containing numerous fossils) in many areas were contorted or fractured into complex forms that 'scrambled' the stratigraphic record. When did this deformation happen and how long did it take? In Section 2.4 several geological 'tools' are introduced that help unravel the *relative* time relationships of igneous, metamorphic and deformational events. However, neither they nor the stratigraphic column make proper sense unless they can be judged in real, *absolute* time. The most successful tool for doing this is radiometric dating, which is introduced in Section 2.5.

2.4 Filling the gaps in relative time

The clearest cause of a gap in a sedimentary sequence results when the Earth's surface is above sea level and has sufficient topographic relief for erosion to dominate over deposition. That can happen if sea level falls but is more likely if the surface of the continental crust is uplifted by tectonic forces.

■ In which tectonic setting is such uplift likely to occur?

□ At convergent plate margins, especially where the continental parts of two plates collide (Book 2, Figure 8.16).

Continent–continent collision usually forms mountain belts. These uplifted areas are the focus for intense erosion, which can take tens to hundreds of million years to wear down the surface to a level when sediments can be deposited once again. Another feature of mountain belts is more dramatic (Book 2, Section 8.6); the collisional tectonic forces buckle older crust, including sedimentary rocks, which thickens the crust. Parts of the crust are driven deep below the surface so that their temperature increases and they are subject to enormous pressure. As a result, they become metamorphosed; they may even begin to melt. Through erosion and uplift, such transformed rocks eventually form the surface on which sedimentary deposition can begin once more. A simple example of the outcome is shown in Figure 2.11.

Figure 2.11 An unconformity separating folded rocks from unfolded sedimentary rocks in Utah, USA.

Figure 2.11 shows a series of flat sedimentary strata directly above more complicated older structures, the boundary that separates the two showing as a horizontal line. If the younger sedimentary rocks were stripped away, the boundary would be revealed in 3D as a flat surface. Since the simple, younger structures above the boundary do not conform to the more complex, older structures below, the boundary is known as an **unconformity**. The folded structure beneath it signifies that tectonic forces buckled a series of older layered rocks. The unconformity also shows that the buckled rocks were exposed to weathering and erosion. So the almost flat surface of the unconformity represents the final landscape after erosion had reached its limit: a plain or a surface of marine erosion. That surface then became the base for deposition of the younger sediments that lie above it. Not only does this unconformity represent a gap in time, it also gives clues to what caused that break in sedimentation.

2.4.1 Signs of igneous, tectonic and metamorphic events

The layered rocks beneath the unconformity in Figure 2.11 obviously buckled after those rocks had formed. They are sedimentary rocks and, if the age of the uppermost deformed layer is known, that gives a *maximum* or oldest date for the tectonic event. Likewise, knowing the age of the undeformed sediments above the unconformity gives the *minimum* or youngest age for the tectonic event.

Figure 2.12a shows a different kind of geological relationship separating very different kinds of rock. The textures and structures in the rocks either side of the two sharp boundaries give a clue to what the relationship signifies.

(a)

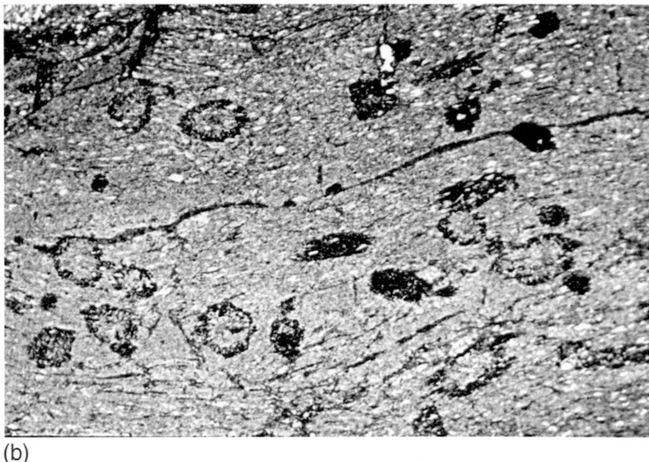

(b)

Figure 2.12 (a) A cross-cutting rock relationship. (b) Minerals which grew in a sedimentary rock when it was metamorphosed (the field of view is about 10 cm across).

■ Describe the rock in the pale band and those on either side of it (in Figure 2.12a), and suggest what kinds they are (there are two).

□ The rock between the two boundaries shows no layering. It contains some large crystals with quite regular shapes; it is probably a slowly cooled *igneous* rock, similar to Kit Specimen 6, the granite. The other rock shows crude layering perpendicular to the boundaries of the igneous rock, but the particles it is composed of are not visible. It could be either a *sedimentary* or a *metamorphic* rock; in fact, it is sedimentary.

The two boundaries cut across the layering and are therefore younger. As the boundaries enclose an igneous rock, this **cross-cutting relationship** is good evidence for the intrusion of igneous magma into an older series of rocks. In this case, the magma cooled slowly to crystallise as granite. Magmas may also be extruded at the surface, to form lavas and pyroclastic rocks (Book 2, Section 4.1). By spreading across the surface they may form layers and look superficially like sedimentary strata, but their very different internal textures soon give them away. Such extrusive igneous layers within sequences of sedimentary rocks are crucial for calibrating the stratigraphic column to an absolute timescale (Section 2.5). Absolute dating of an igneous intrusion only conveys a *minimum* age for the rocks and structures that it cuts.

■ What else would you expect to have happened to the sedimentary rock in Figure 2.12a, close to the magma that was cutting through it?

□ It would have been heated strongly and may shows signs of metamorphism, i.e. the growth of new minerals.

Figure 2.12b shows another sedimentary rock close to an intrusive igneous contact. The thin (~1 mm) sedimentary layering is still discernible, but growing across it are large (~1 cm) crystals of a new metamorphic mineral called andalusite (Al_2SiO_5), which forms when muddy sediments are strongly heated at shallow depths in the crust.

Unconformable, cross-cutting and mineral-growth relationships give clues to the relative ages of different rocks and structures produced by different geological processes. 'Common-sense' interpretation of relationships can be applied to virtually every geological feature that expresses the relative ages of different kinds of event.

Question 2.5

Figure 2.13 is a sketch of a cross-section summarising several relationships observed in an area of well-exposed rocks. The main features are labelled A to G. From the relationships shown write a short account (up to 175 words) of the geological history of the area as a sequence of events in relative time. Write your account starting with the oldest event, and work progressively through younger ones. (*Hint*: before you start writing, find the youngest and simplest feature and work backwards to discover progressively earlier ones.)

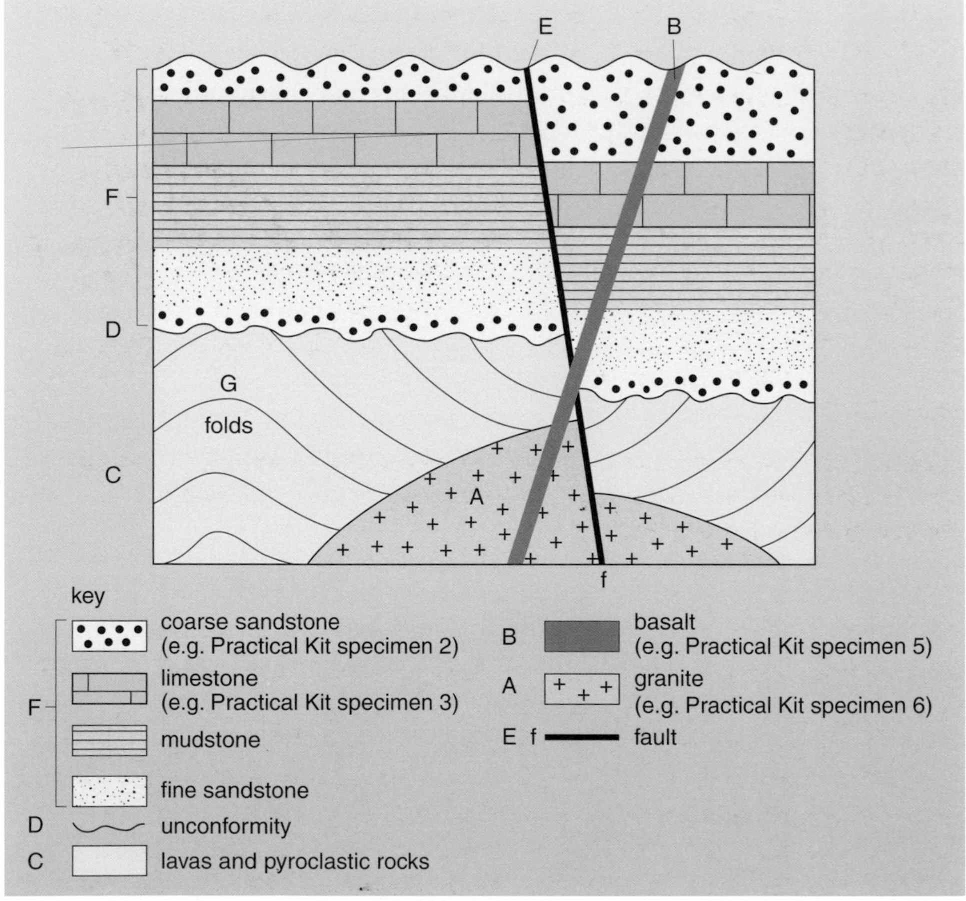

Figure 2.13 Geological cross-section for use with Question 2.5.

2.5 Measuring geological time

As discussed in the previous section, methods of placing events in a time sequence relative to one another were being used from the late 18th century onwards, and the use of fossils as time markers began shortly afterwards.

The first attempt to find out when the Earth formed used an estimate of how long it would take for the saltiness of seawater to build up from the very dilute concentrations of sodium and chloride ions in river water. The estimate had to make several assumptions: the rates of transport of ions to the oceans have always been the same; seawater started as freshwater; sodium and chlorine never leave aqueous solution and always stay in the sea. This approach suggested that the oceans formed 90 Ma ago – such a great age that it disturbed many people in the 19th century. However, the assumptions were flawed, one in particular failing to acknowledge that seawater can evaporate to precipitate sodium chloride, and that such salt deposits can be buried (Chapter 5), thereby removing both ions from seawater.

Another attempt divided an estimate of the total volume of all sedimentary rocks by an estimate of the present rate of sediment deposition. That is also flawed, for two reasons: sedimentary rocks can be eroded and their contents recycled; modern rates of sedimentation vary enormously and would have done so in the past.

The physicist Lord Kelvin (William Thomson; 1824–1907) observed in the late 19th century that the temperature in mines increases with depth. This shows that the Earth is losing heat from its interior. Assuming that the whole Earth was originally molten, Lord Kelvin calculated how long it would take to cool to its present state by conduction, and came up with 20–40 Ma. Shortly after his widely publicised efforts it became clear that there are naturally radioactive isotopes within the Earth that continually supply heat, so he was wrong as well. As suggested in Book 1, Chapter 4, it is now clear that the Earth loses heat mostly by convection and that drives plate tectonics. Heat conduction takes place only through the lithosphere.

The discovery of radioactive decay was to provide the means not only to estimate when the Earth came into being but also to give meaningful dates to many of the rocks that have formed since then.

2.5.1 Absolute ages from radioactive decay

Many elements consist of several stable isotopes (Section 2.1.2). A few elements have isotopes that naturally contain excessive numbers of neutrons relative to protons in their nuclei, making them inherently unstable. The more unstable the neutron–proton balance, the greater the chance that the atom will break down at any instant by radioactive decay, to form a stable isotope of another element. Book 7 discusses radioactive decay in more detail. For now, you just need to know that the end product is a stable isotope called a **daughter isotope**, which has formed by the decay of the original, radioactive **parent isotope**.

By decaying, the abundance of a radioactive parent isotope decreases with time, while its daughter isotope becomes more abundant. Since every nucleus of a particular radioactive isotope has a particular chance of decaying or staying intact, this decay averages out among billions of atoms to a constant, measurable rate. The proper expression for this rate is the number of nuclei in 1 kg of the isotope that are likely to decay in one second. A more useful expression, however, is the time taken for half the radioactive nuclei in an isotope sample to decay – the isotope's **half-life**. Half-lives range from fractions of a second for some rare, artificially produced isotopes, to over a hundred billion years for a few naturally occurring isotopes. Every isotope has a particular half-life that enables the age of a sample to be deduced. Activity 2.3 takes you through a simplified case to illustrate how an isotope's half-life bears on absolute or **radiometric dating**.

Activity 2.3 Radioactive decay: the key to absolute time

We expect this activity will take you approximately 30 minutes.

Task 1

Suppose a mineral sample contains, in addition to the elements that make up its bulk, 1024 atoms of a radioactive isotope whose half-life is 3 days.

(a) Starting with 1024, calculate the number of atoms of the parent isotope that remain after 3, 6, 9, 12 days and so on; for example, after 3 days 512 atoms remain. Record the number of half-lives that have elapsed and the remaining number of atoms (P) of the parent isotope in Table 2.2, in the appropriate rows.

(b) Now calculate the number of atoms (D) of the daughter isotope after each half-life, and record them in Table 2.2.

Table 2.2 For Tasks 1 and 2 of Activity 2.3.

Time/days	0	3	6	9	12	15	18	21	24	27	30
Half-lives/n	0	1	2	3	4	5	6	7	8	9	10
Atoms of parent isotope/P	1024	512	256	128	64	32	16	8	4	2	1
Atoms of daughter isotope/D	0	512	768	896	960	992	1008	1016	1020	1022	1023
D/P ratio by division	0	1	3	7	15	31	63	127	255	511	1023
D/P ratio by Eqn 2.7		1	3	7	15	31	63	127	255	511	1023

(c) Plot on Figure 2.14 the numbers of parent (P) and daughter (D) isotope atoms (vertical axis) against time (horizontal axis), expressed as the elapsed number of half-lives (n). Draw a smooth curve through each set of data points, using different colours or line styles for each, and briefly describe the shape of the two graphs.

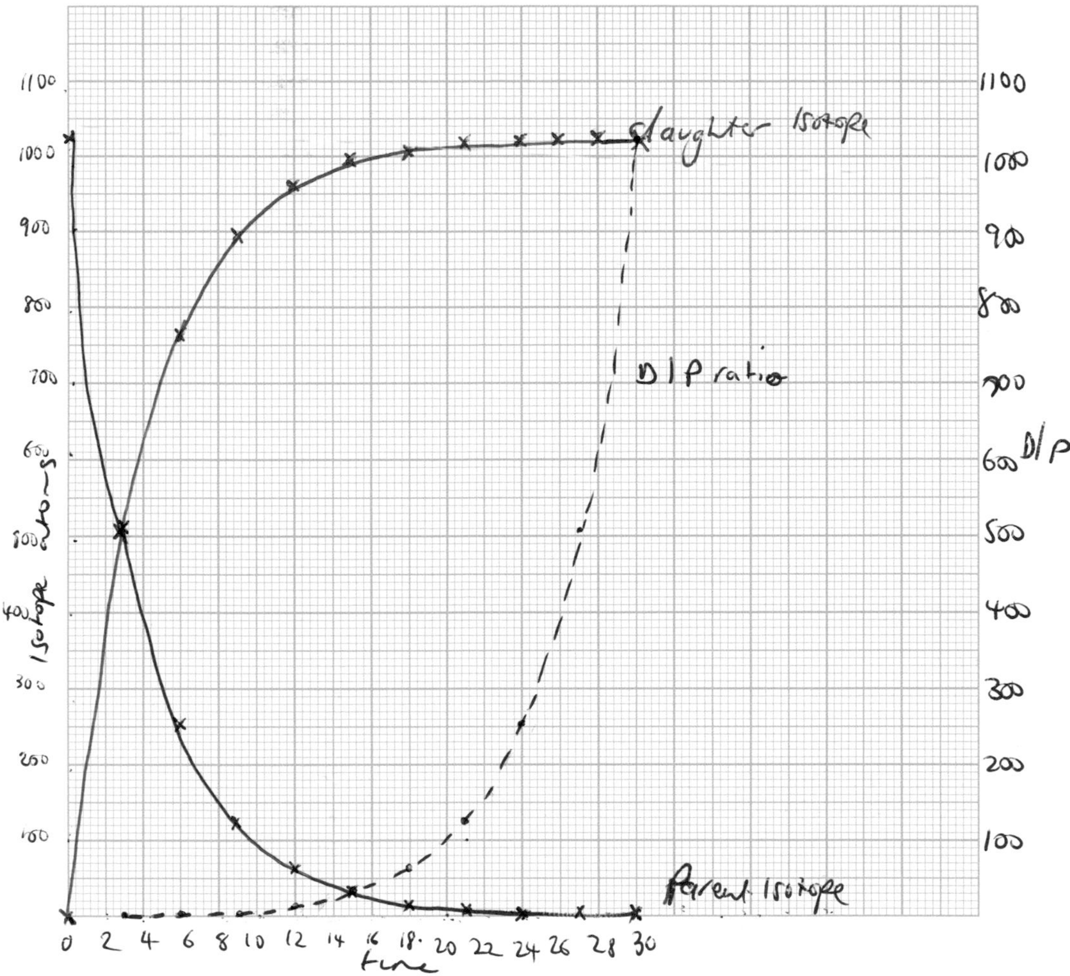

Figure 2.14 Graph paper for use in Activity 2.3.

Two algebraic expressions can be derived from your results in Task 1:

- At any time the sum of the atoms of parent and daughter isotopes ($P + D$) is equal to the original number of atoms of the radioactive parent (P_0), expressed mathematically as:

$$P + D = P_0 \tag{2.2}$$

- The number of atoms of the parent isotope (P) after n half-lives is the original number (P_0) divided n times by 2 (i.e. divided by 2^n), or:

$$P = \frac{P_0}{2^n} \tag{2.3}$$

So, how do these relationships help in calculating an age from radioactive decay? Both P and D can be measured in a sample of a mineral known to contain an element that includes a radioactive isotope as well as stable isotopes. For instance, natural rubidium includes some ^{87}Rb, which is radioactive and very slowly decays to a stable isotope of strontium, ^{87}Sr. So a mineral that contains rubidium will also contain some of this daughter isotope that has accumulated since the time the mineral formed. If that mineral occurs in an igneous rock, it will have accumulated ^{87}Sr produced by ^{87}Rb decay from the time the mineral had crystallised from magma and cooled down.

A mass spectrometer can measure amounts of both parent and daughter isotopes at extremely low abundances (parts per billion by mass) to determine the relative amounts of one to the other, i.e. as D/P. So, what does that proportion convey?

Rearranging Equation 2.2 gives:

$$D = P_0 - P \tag{2.4}$$

which is how you worked out D in Task 1 for each half-life.

Rearranging Equation 2.3 gives:

$$P_0 = 2^n P \tag{2.5}$$

So the proportion of daughter to parent isotopes is given by combining Equation 2.5 with Equation 2.4 (see Book 3, Section 5.6):

$$D = 2^n P - P = P(2^n - 1) \tag{2.6}$$

and so:

$$D/P = 2^n - 1 \tag{2.7}$$

The value of this **daughter to parent ratio** (D/P) depends on how many half-lives (n) that have elapsed since the parent isotope entered the mineral being dated. It is this relationship that allows a mineral to be dated. The elegance lies in not having to know how much of the parent isotope (P_0) was originally present when the mineral formed.

Task 2

From the values for P and D in Table 2.2 that you calculated at half-lives 1 to 10, calculate D/P by dividing D by P, and then by using Equation 2.7. Record these values of the daughter to parent ratio (D/P) on Table 2.2, and plot them on Figure 2.14 in a different colour or line style. You will need to make another axis on the right-hand edge of Figure 2.14, using 1 cm for $D/P = 100$, etc.

Read the comments on this activity at the end of this book before continuing.

Activity 2.3 demonstrates two ways in which the daughter to parent ratio (D/P) produced by the decay of a radioactive isotope in a sample gives a time since the sample formed. One is mathematical, the other graphical, and both show an age in multiples of the isotope's half-life. That seems simple enough but, in practice, there are two important conditions.

- Atoms of both parent and daughter isotopes must remain locked in the sample; if either is added from outside or lost, the calculated age is not the true age.
- This simple approach only works if there were no daughter atoms in the sample when it formed.

For many isotope systems corrections have to be made to overcome both these challenges, which are beyond the scope of this book. However, one widely used and extremely precise method of radiometric dating avoids them.

The mineral zircon (zirconium silicate, $ZrSiO_4$) is sometimes used as a cheap substitute for diamond in jewellery. It forms in small amounts (less than 1%) when magmas crystallise. Zircon concentrates uranium to much higher levels than those in the magma from which it crystallises, which is why it is commonly used in radiometric dating. Crystals of zircon can be dated using two schemes for the decay of the two naturally radioactive uranium (U) isotopes to stable isotopes of lead (Pb): ^{235}U to ^{207}Pb and ^{238}U to ^{206}Pb. Both these U–Pb decay schemes involve a sequence of intermediary radioactive isotopes, but end in a stable, but different daughter isotope of lead. Zircon is very handy because, although its structure can incorporate uranium atoms, it contains very little lead other than that produced by uranium decay. It is also extremely stable with a 'tight' molecular structure, into and from which atoms rarely move. Zircon avoids both of the practical constraints described above and hosts both uranium decay schemes. This means that $^{207}Pb/^{235}U$ and $^{206}Pb/^{238}U$ are two *independent* D/P ratios; they involve half-lives of 704 Ma and 4470 Ma, respectively.

Question 2.6

The value of $^{207}Pb/^{235}U$ (the D/P value) in a zircon sample from a granite intrusion is 3.0. What is the age of the zircon and hence the granite to two significant figures? (*Hint*: you will need to use your completed Table 2.2.)

Not every rock or mineral is suitable for radiometric dating. Some sedimentary rocks contain minerals that grew while sediment was being deposited. Of these minerals a few contain traces of radioactive ^{87}Rb and can be dated, but they are rare. Many sediments contain organic carbon compounds. Since ^{14}C is a naturally produced radioactive isotope, it might seem that radiocarbon dating can give an absolute age to most sediments, back to the very earliest ones. Sadly, that is not possible. The half-life of ^{14}C is only 5.73 ka. The oldest achievable radiocarbon ages, using present techniques, are no more than about 50 ka. Had all ^{14}C formed, like most other natural isotopes, long ago in exploding stars (more of which in Book 7), it would now be undetectable. The reason why ^{14}C is available for dating very young geological events is because of its continual formation from nitrogen (^{14}N) in the upper atmosphere by the effects of cosmic rays.

The most commonly dated rocks are igneous in origin. Their importance is shown by the relationships that you considered in Question 2.5 and Figure 2.13. A radiometric date for the igneous intrusion A gives a *minimum* age for the tectonic event that produced the folds G, and a *maximum* age for the fault E. Similarly, the narrow igneous intrusion B represents the youngest event, apart from erosion that produced the modern land surface, and gives a minimum age for the youngest (uppermost) of sediments F.

The stratigraphic column of the Phanerozoic, so finely divided by fossils before radiometric dating was invented, now has a global, real-time framework. Using Smith's principles, palaeontologists in the 19th and 20th centuries were able to match stratigraphic sequences on every continent. Where the stratigraphic column in one place was missing some sedimentary strata, another location filled in the gap. Except for the Precambrian rocks, devoid of tangible fossils, geologists knew where they were in the sequence, but didn't know their true age.

Because plate tectonics never stops, volcanoes have been active somewhere at the Earth's surface at all times in the past. While volcanism continued in an area, sedimentary strata were interlayered with lavas and pyroclastic rocks. So, on a global scale, the Phanerozoic stratigraphic column can be calibrated by radiometrically dating the volcanic layers. Instead of a well-known sequence of events, the Phanerozoic became a quantitative history.

Without fossils as time markers in sedimentary sequences, the Precambrian was far more difficult to date. Moreover, its rocks had undergone many more igneous, metamorphic and deformation events than had those of the Phanerozoic, making Precambrian geology on every continent more complex than that of the Phanerozoic. Again, the igneous rocks provided the key to ordering events from region to region in a time frame, but details of the global sequence are still not fully agreed. Consequently, the division of the Precambrian is 'coarser' than that of 'the times of visible life'.

2.5.2 The Geological Time Scale

You are not expected to remember all the names in Figure 2.15, or their sequence, but they are used in the rest of this book.

Figure 2.15 is a simplified version of the International Geological Time Scale agreed by the International Commission on Stratigraphy (last revised in 2004). The vertical scale of both columns is linear; the time since the emergence of the first common fossils at 542 Ma is enlarged for clarity. Figure 2.15 has been repeated in the Appendix at the back of this book, for ease of reference.

A striking feature of the timescale is how little of geological time has been divided using fossils: about one-ninth. Four billion years passed before the appearance of organisms capable of being preserved and easily distinguished anatomically. The Earth and the other planets formed around 4560 Ma, a time deduced from radiometric dating of meteorites. However, no rocks with that age are known on Earth, possibly because vigorous plate tectonics on the early Earth could recycle oceanic lithosphere so quickly that little continental crust was able to stabilise. The oldest known rocks occur on the east shore of Hudson Bay, Canada, and are metamorphosed sedimentary rocks. They have been dated radiometrically at 4280 Ma. However, there are traces of the missing, earlier 280 Ma Geoscientists dated grains of zircon that had been transported into and preserved by a 3000 Ma Australian sedimentary rock to find out the age of the igneous rocks from which those grains had come after weathering and erosion. Out of many that gave slightly older ages than the sediments, to their surprise, they found 17 tiny zircon grains ranging in age from 4000 to 4400 Ma. The oldest of those grains represent igneous processes from shortly after the Earth formed, but their parent igneous rocks have not been found. Being so robust, the zircons may have been through the rock cycle several times before coming to rest in the Australian sedimentary rock.

The 19th century stratigraphic division stemmed from features in the fossil record, and still lies at the heart of the geological timescale. The greatest division is that separating the Phanerozoic Eon from the Precambrian, now placed at 542 Ma. Fossil evidence divides the Phanerozoic into the Palaeozoic, Mesozoic and Cenozoic Eras and further still into Periods.

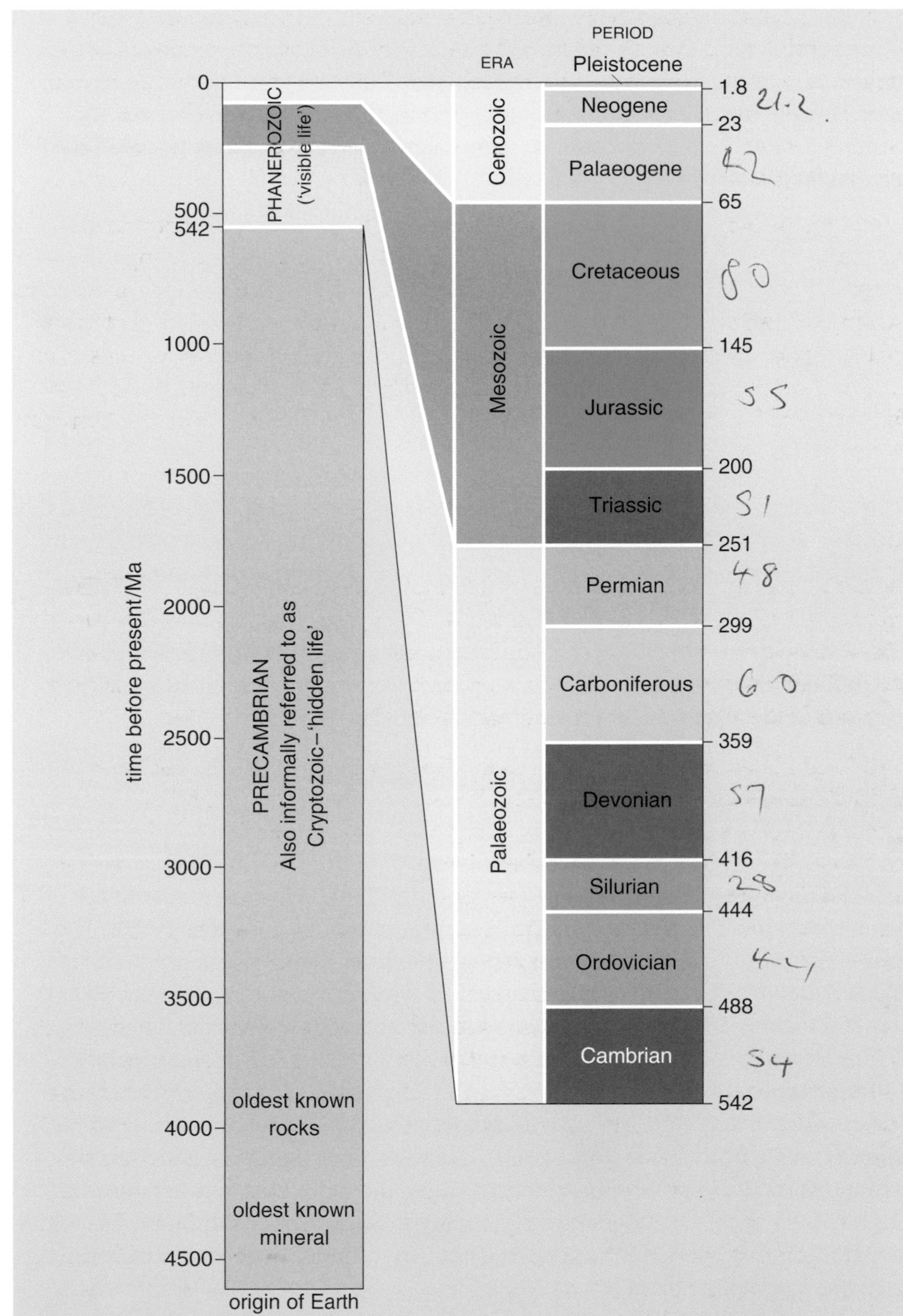

Figure 2.15 The main divisions of the International Geological Time Scale. The times of the major boundaries are almost all based on high-quality radiometric dating. Divisions in the Precambrian are omitted. (This figure has been repeated in the Appendix for ease of reference as you study this book.)

■ Work out the duration of each Period in the Phanerozoic timescale. Is there a regular timespan for the individual Periods?

□ Not at all: every Period lasts more than 20 Ma, but their duration ranges up to 80 Ma in the case of the Cretaceous.

Despite the different durations, the basic division of the Phanerozoic using fossils was not arbitrary. Many of the Period boundaries mark striking changes in many, and sometimes all, groups of fossil organisms. The course taken by life has not been entirely one of steady evolution, as envisaged by Charles Darwin (Book 5, Chapter 14). In fact, there could be no greater understatement; as you will see in Chapter 3, during the last half-billion years, life as a whole has experienced several huge upheavals that have little to do with biological evolution, except that they interrupted it and changed its course.

2.6 Summary of Chapter 2

Time, in a geological sense, can be judged from relationships that show relative ages, or by absolute dating. Annual layering in continuously accumulated glacier ice can give an absolute age to ice-core samples, but the absolute ages of rocks are generally estimated using the decay of radioactive isotopes incorporated into them when they formed. Radioactive decay is regular, and is expressed as a half-life. As the radioactive parent isotope decays, so the daughter isotope grows in abundance at the same rate, and the measurement of the parent-to-daughter ratio in a rock or mineral sample is related to the sample's age.

Fossils that satisfy several criteria provide a means of establishing the relative, stratigraphic age of sedimentary rocks. Used on a regional to global scale, they provide a means of correlating widely separated rock sequences, and the geological processes that formed them. Fossils provided the first detailed subdivision of the stratigraphic column, but one lacking any sense of real or absolute time. Radiometric dating has provided the absolute ages to calibrate the Geological Time Scale.

Establishing a geological history requires far more information than a series of dates and global correlation of rocks. Many processes in the Earth system leave their mark on the properties of geological materials – their chemistry, minerals and internal structures – features that can be used as proxies for the processes and factors that affect them. The proportion of the ^{18}O isotope relative to ^{16}O, expressed as the δ^{18}O value, is a proxy for two variables: the air temperature at which snow forms and the amount of ice that has built up on land. Changes in δ^{18}O in ice cores establish a detailed record of changing air temperature over an ice cap. Changes in δ^{18}O in the shells of deep-water foraminifera in ocean-floor sediments are a proxy for the volume of ice stored on land, and thereby for global sea level. Variations in the electrical conductivity with depth through ice cores is a proxy for the amount of dust in the atmosphere and, from that, a measure of varying regional to global aridity.

Proxy records from ice and deep-sea sediment cores show similar features for the last 140 ka. From a 10 ka period of global warmth about 130 ka ago, in Greenland the air temperature fell and both the total volume of land ice and aridity increased over 100 ka, to reach the last glacial maximum at around 20 ka. The climate changed in a markedly irregular manner.

Your study of this chapter involved: comparing information given in diagrams and graphs; describing and interpreting that information; applying it more widely, and summarising your findings. You have also developed and practised some key mathematical skills, and made observations on specimens and recorded your results.

Chapter 3
The record of life on Earth

The oldest rocks in the geological record are metamorphic rocks formed 4000 Ma ago, although a few igneous zircon crystals are known to have formed as far back as 4400 Ma. But when did life stamp an irrefutable mark in the geological record? What constitutes strong evidence for biological processes, before the appearance of organisms with hard parts, is a matter of some debate. Such evidence would occur only in sedimentary rocks that have not been strongly metamorphosed. The further back in time, the more likely it is that mountain-building events thoroughly transformed pre-existing rocks. So rocks in which to look for the oldest signs of life are rare. Set in a vast area of metamorphosed igneous rocks, one small part of West Greenland contains 3800-Ma-old, fine-grained metamorphosed rock layers between basaltic pillow lavas (Figure 3.1). The fine-grained materials probably formed as muddy sediments around hot springs on the ocean floor (Book 2, Section 7.3) and are a target for scientists interested in life's origin. However, examination with high-powered microscopes has yet to reveal even the most humble single-celled organism.

Figure 3.1 Pillow lavas in Isua, West Greenland, which are 3800 Ma old.

3.1 The oldest organic signs

The earliest sedimentary rocks that have undergone little metamorphism formed about 3500 Ma ago and are found in South Africa and West Australia. Among them are limestones formed from calcium carbonate, which contain curious structures. Thin concentric layers make up irregular mounds ranging in size from centimetres to metres (Figure 3.2a). Similar structures form today in salty lagoons (Figure 3.2b). They are **stromatolites**, constructed from films of calcium carbonate secreted by cyanobacteria cells as they excrete excess calcium ions. Cyanobacteria are prokaryotes (Book 5, Chapter 3) which photosynthesise and release oxygen as a by-product. The stromatolites themselves do not preserve cyanobacteria cells. However, fine-grained sediments interlayered with them do contain microscopic structures bearing some resemblance to cells; some researchers believe they are organic, while others insist they are inorganic. So, direct observations cannot *prove* that life was established 3500 Ma ago. Discussion of the earliest life and its origin is a central theme of Book 8.

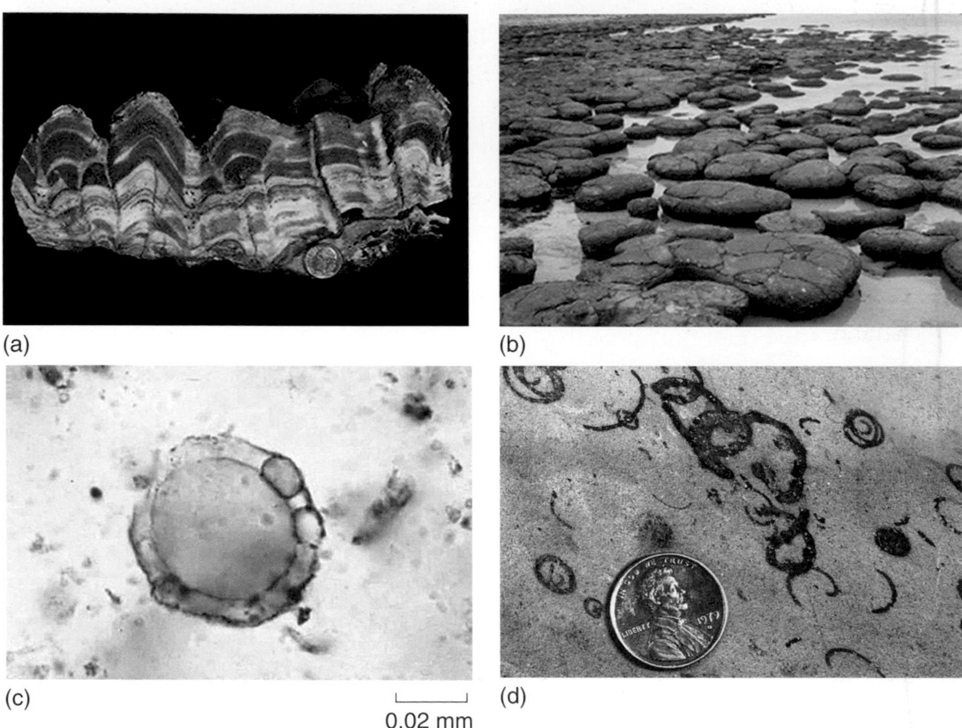

Figure 3.2 (a) A candidate for the world's oldest tangible evidence of living processes: a 3500-Ma-old stromatolite from Western Australia in cross-section. The specimen is 20 cm across. (b) Living stromatolites in Shark Bay, Western Australia. They are about 0.5–1.5 m across. (c) Fossil cyanobacteria cell from the Gunflint Chert, Ontario, Canada. (d) *Grypania*, the first eukaryote from Michigan, USA; the coin is ~1 cm across.

The oldest known fossils of single-celled organisms occur in the Gunflint Chert of Ontario, Canada, a rock once used in the firing mechanism of muskets. The example shown in Figure 3.2c is very like a modern cyanobacteria cell but, at around 2100 Ma old, it is a youngster relative to the oldest stromatolites. Sedimentary rocks of a similar age in Michigan, USA, contain a larger and more advanced fossil made from a carbon film (Figure 3.2d).

■ From its size, what fundamental kind of organism do you suspect the fossil in Figure 3.2d to be?

□ Its size suggests that it is multicellular, probably a fossil eukaryote (Book 5, Chapter 3) and perhaps a primitive alga.

An age of 'only' 2100 Ma for the first convincing prokaryote and eukaryote fossils is interesting in several ways. Since eukaryotes evolved from prokaryotes (Book 5, Section 4.3), that giant evolutionary step must have occurred before 2100 Ma.

Eukaryotes are organisms that need oxygen to survive, so their first appearance signifies that the Earth's atmosphere and oceans must have contained free oxygen. Conversely, many living prokaryotes thrive in anaerobic conditions and, indeed, free oxygen is highly toxic to them. Prokaryote life probably originated when seawater and air contained little, if any, free oxygen. The appearance of abundant free oxygen was perhaps the second most important step in the evolution of life on Earth, after the origin of life itself.

In today's atmosphere, metallic iron oxidises to rust, a form of iron oxide, $Fe_2O_3.nH_2O$ (Book 4, Section 8.5).

■ What charge is associated with iron in this rust, in order for the formula to balance?

□ It is 3+, being three electrons short of a stable outer shell (i.e. three O^{2-} ions are balanced by two Fe^{3+} ions).

This Fe^{3+} ion is one of two formed by iron, and it happens to be highly insoluble; that is why you cannot wash rust off an old car. The other ionic form of iron is Fe^{2+}.

■ What is the difference between the two ions?

□ Fe^{2+} has one more electron in its outer shell than Fe^{3+}, and by comparison is *reduced* (Book 4, Section 8.3).

The reduced Fe^{2+} ion is highly soluble but it only occurs in natural aqueous solutions today where conditions are reducing, i.e. where electrons are easily gained. In the oxidising conditions (where electrons are easily lost) that now pervade most of the Earth's surface, insoluble Fe^{3+} dominates, in the form of brightly coloured hydrated oxide minerals which are essentially the same as rust.

Geologists have looked for evidence of when free oxygen began to dominate surface processes in rare rocks that formed as ancient soils. Before about 2400 Ma, none of these old soils are red, but those of younger ages are. Oxygen must have begun to pervade the atmosphere and many other environments only after 2400 Ma.

■ Where did the oxygen come from?

□ Oxygen is a by-product of photosynthesis, probably by the cyanobacteria which secreted stromatolites.

Eukaryotes may have evolved where cyanobacteria provided oxygen locally. Elsewhere, the oxidation of dissolved Fe^{2+} ions and of dead organic matter would have consumed oxygen so efficiently that none would have entered the atmosphere or the bulk of the oceans. Only when oxygen production exceeded consumption about 2400 Ma ago was it able to accumulate as a free element.

3.1.1 Signals from life's chemistry

Although the oldest sedimentary rocks do not contain fossils, they do provide two kinds of proxy evidence that may signify life's chemical influence. The first results from biological production of complex organic molecules through a stepwise process of reduction that begins with autotrophism (Book 5, Section 2.3). In the oxygen-poor early world, these compounds had a greater chance of preservation than in the Phanerozoic (except where they accumulated to form crude oil – as you saw in Book 4, Chapter 12). If found, such 'biomarkers' would be excellent evidence that there was life at the time. Indeed, biomarkers accompany the first stromatolites at about 3500 Ma.

The second proxy for biological processes results from their effect on the proportions of stable isotopes of carbon, which is analogous to the changes in oxygen-isotope proportions caused by inorganic processes (Section 2.1.2). The reduction of CO_2 and H_2O to produce carbohydrates by autotrophic organisms selectively takes up the *lighter* of the two stable isotopes of carbon: ^{12}C rather than ^{13}C. As a result, carbon that has been taken into autotrophic cells (and those of the heterotrophs which consume them) has a lower ratio of ^{13}C to ^{12}C than common carbon. Usefully, different autotrophic metabolisms have different effects on that ratio, to the extent that broadly different groups of organisms have their own carbon-isotope 'signature'. The stromatolite-bearing 3500-Ma-old sediments of Western Australia and South Africa have a diversity in carbon isotopes which suggests several prokaryote metabolic pathways and, arguably, traces of the earliest eukaryotes.

Despite the discovery of 2100-Ma-old eukaryote fossils, sedimentary rocks which formed in the next 1500 Ma contain only a few single-celled fossils. Yet during those late Precambrian times the carbon-isotope proxy for living processes went through some of its greatest changes in geological history (Figure 3.3); there seems to have been a lot happening at the level of microscopic life forms. What was happening in evolutionary terms can only be guessed at, but something

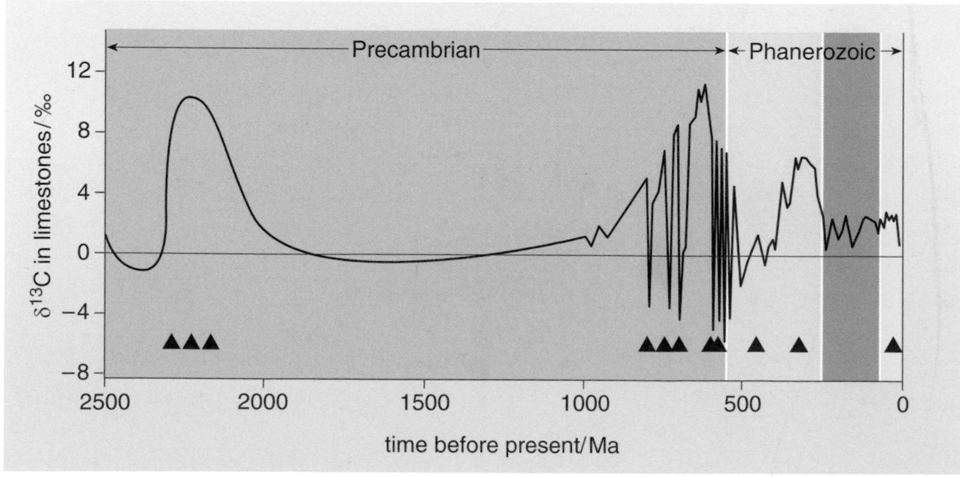

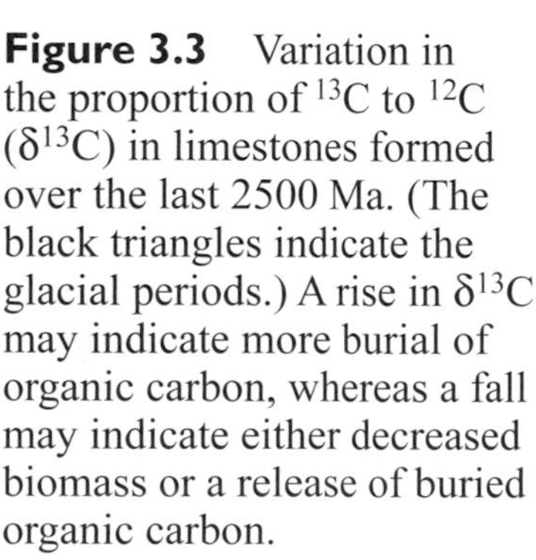
Figure 3.3 Variation in the proportion of ^{13}C to ^{12}C ($\delta^{13}C$) in limestones formed over the last 2500 Ma. (The black triangles indicate the glacial periods.) A rise in $\delta^{13}C$ may indicate more burial of organic carbon, whereas a fall may indicate either decreased biomass or a release of buried organic carbon.

odd seems to have recurred. Figure 3.3 shows how the proportion of ^{13}C relative to that of ^{12}C (represented by $\delta^{13}C$) in marine limestones has changed over the last 2500 Ma. (This delta value is derived in much the same way as that for oxygen isotopes (Section 2.1.2) but the standard material used is carbon in the calcium carbonate shell of a large fossil found in South Carolina, USA.) What the changes in $\delta^{13}C$ might signify requires some explanation.

Marine autotrophic organisms preferentially extract more ^{12}C than ^{13}C from the CO_2 dissolved in seawater. If their dead remains, containing an excess of ^{12}C, are buried (as organic carbon) in sediments, the $\delta^{13}C$ value of carbon dissolved in seawater therefore *increases*. (*Note*: this process is analogous to the way $\delta^{18}O$ increases in seawater when ice builds up on land (Section 2.1.3).) When marine limestones form, their calcium carbonate incorporates carbon from seawater. The value of $\delta^{13}C$ in seawater at a particular time is therefore transferred to the limestone beds which formed at that time.

The $\delta^{13}C$ value of seawater and of limestones *decreases* during a decrease in the total mass of living organisms, when living processes take up less ^{12}C, or if older sediments rapidly release buried organic carbon that is enriched in ^{12}C. Figure 3.3 may chart life's ups and downs during a critical period in its history.

After 2300 Ma, $\delta^{13}C$ in seawater rose rapidly and for more than 200 Ma remained far above previous levels and those that followed. This period included the first irrefutable fossils (Figure 3.2c, 2100 Ma). The rise in $\delta^{13}C$ can be explained by a dramatic increase in the total mass of living organisms, together with increased burial of organic carbon. In the following billion years $\delta^{13}C$ decreased to steady levels of around 0‰, possibly reflecting a decreased biosphere whose overall mass changed little. The last billion years show extremely complex patterns.

■ How does $\delta^{13}C$ in limestones change in Figure 3.3 between 1500 and 500 Ma?

□ Broadly, it rises fairly smoothly until about 800 Ma, and then becomes very erratic, with a succession of extreme highs and lows. In more detail, between 800 and 500 Ma there were seven major changes from high to low values, greater in magnitude and pace of change than at any time since 500 Ma.

During the $\delta^{13}C$ peaks in the late Precambrian, vast amounts of dead organic matter, enriched in ^{12}C, were buried in marine sediments. Interestingly, the highest value of $\delta^{13}C$, around 600 Ma, was about twice as high as the maximum reached in the Phanerozoic. This may have been because the biosphere had a much greater mass than during the Phanerozoic so that more organic carbon was available for burial. The rapid decreases in $\delta^{13}C$ may represent short periods when either overall living biomass collapsed (so that ^{12}C built up in seawater), or older buried organic carbon, containing low levels of $\delta^{13}C$, was released in vast amounts from sea-floor sediments, perhaps as methane, a product of anaerobic decay in such sediments.

An interesting feature of Figure 3.3 is that periods of massive change in the carbon-isotope content of Precambrian seawater coincide with evidence for widespread glaciation. Tills of those ages are abundant, and oddly, the evidence for late Precambrian glacial episodes includes many examples from what were then tropical latitudes. For some reason, ice sheets spread over the whole planet for long periods. These have been called 'Snowball Earth' episodes. The last such global glaciation occurred at around 600 Ma. Then, another sudden change enters the geological record: sediments deposited above 600-Ma-old tills on several continents are full of evidence for large, multicelled organisms.

3.2 The earliest common fossils

Sediments deposited between 590 and 565 Ma in China preserve exceptional details of algae, sponges, possible corals and even embryos of unknown but probably bilaterian animals (Figure 3.4). Some of the fossils shown in Figure 3.4 are imprints in sediment of large soft-bodied organisms that show signs of segmentation, radial division and a variety of other body plans. From about 575 Ma large numbers of such fossils occur globally. They are known collectively as the Ediacaran fauna, from the Ediacara Hills of South Australia, where palaeontologists first described them. Some superficially resemble modern animals, such as jellyfishes and sea pens (phylum Cnidaria), but others seem to have left no living descendants. All Ediacaran animals completely lack hard parts; they are **trace fossils**. That such delicate animals left abundant clear traces in sediments that buried them implies that none of them could bite or burrow to eat the buried, rotting corpses of their companions. Recent research suggests that some of them lived by absorbing dissolved organic compounds through their skin. The abrupt appearance of large Ediacaran animals coincides with chemical evidence for increased amounts of dissolved oxygen in seawater; probably caused by increased photosynthesis and burial of organic carbon.

The youngest Precambrian sediments foretell another major change, sometimes containing small (1–2 mm) shelly fossils (Figure 3.5a). Then, at the base of the Cambrian, the first signs of burrowing animals appear (Figure 3.5b). Above that level, every modern phylum and many modern classes of animals appear as fossils made from the first hard body parts. This sudden appearance at 542 Ma of common **body fossils** has been called the **Cambrian Explosion**. However, comparison of the genetics of living animals of all kinds and the use of 'molecular clocks' (Section 3.2.1) shows that animals began to evolve long before the start of the Cambrian. So how did hard parts ever appear? They were possibly adapted from solid materials formed as calcium, hydrogen-carbonate and phosphate ions were excreted from cells. Toughening of soft parts by such mineral deposition would have conferred a potential selective advantage, in either predation or defence. Yet no evidence has emerged of an environmental trigger for the Cambrian Explosion. Whatever their cause, once hard parts appeared a wide range of new ecological opportunities became available for exploitation, promoting the rapid evolution of the animals.

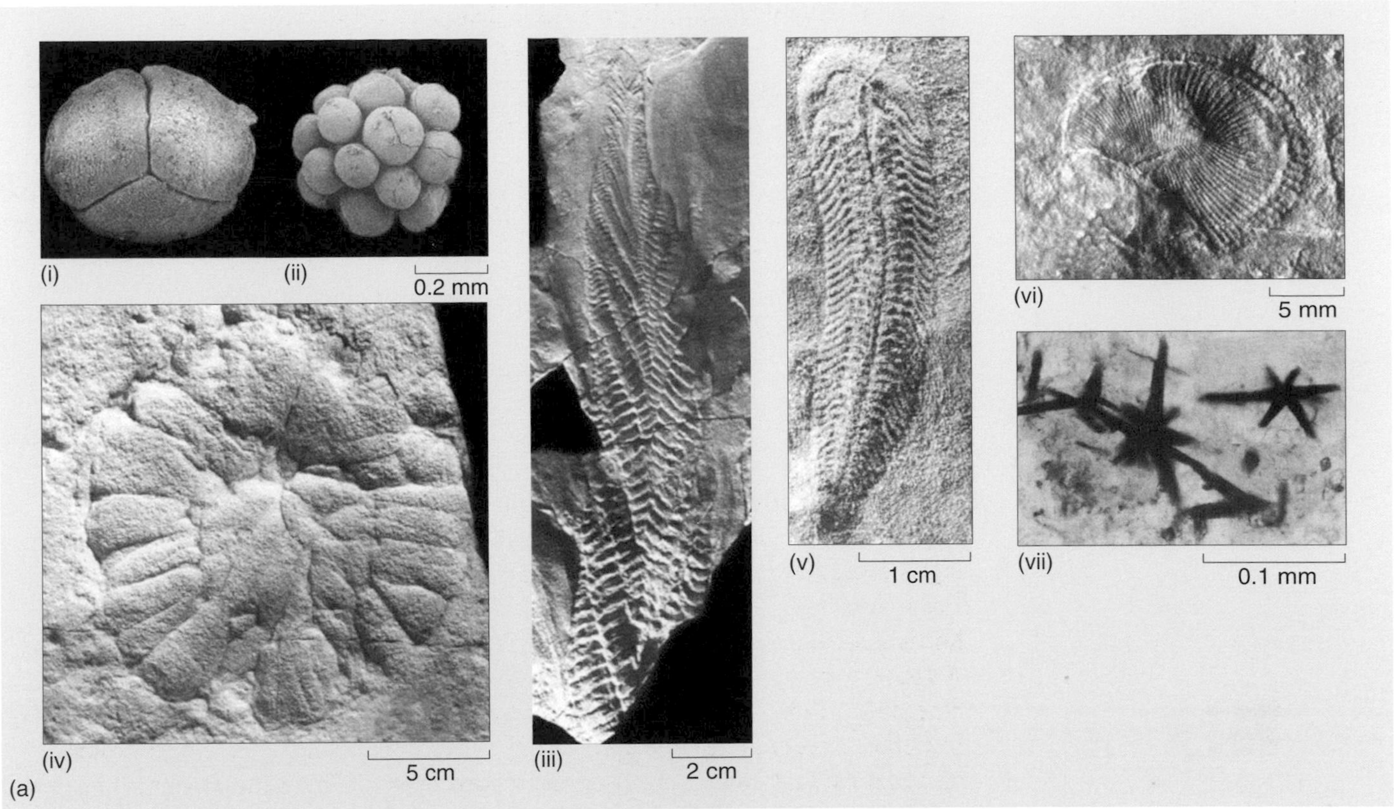

(i) (ii) 0.2 mm

(vi) 5 mm

(v) 1 cm

(vii) 0.1 mm

(iv) 5 cm

(iii) 2 cm

(a)

(b)

Figure 3.4 The earliest animals. (a) Some fossils from the late Precambrian ((iii) to (vi) are impressions of bodies in sediment): (i), (ii) bilaterian embryos; (iii) unknown organism, once assigned to sea pens; (iv) cnidarian polyp; (v) worm-like animal of unknown affinities; (vi) jellyfish-like animal of unknown affinities; (vii) sponge spicules. (b) Reconstruction of animals of the Ediacaran fauna living on the late Precambrian seabed. The largest organisms are about 15 cm long.

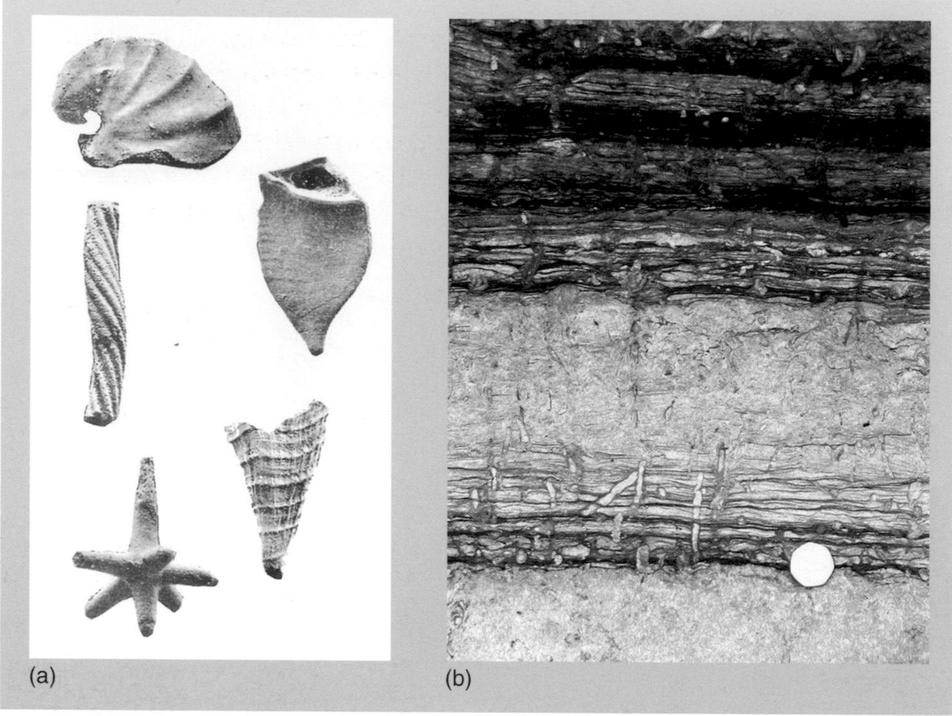

Figure 3.5 Signs of a pending evolutionary change. (a) Small shelly fossils, no more than a few mm in size, found in sedimentary rocks just below the Cambrian. (b) Burrows in the lowest Cambrian sedimentary rocks.

■ In what ways might the novelty of hard parts drive a general evolutionary burst?

□ At the simplest level, protection or support by hard parts would strengthen the animal's body so that life exposed to more energetic conditions, including more rapid movement, would be possible. Support provided by skeletons would also have given animals the potential to become larger. Hard parts would offer protection against predation, so that predators increasingly would need hard, sharp means of penetrating those defences.

Although there are other factors in adaptive radiation (the branching in a phylogeny; e.g. Book 5, Figures 3.6 and 14.7), natural selection based on 'armour versus arms' would have promoted diversification. Many Cambrian animals adapted for predation could pursue food much more actively than the Ediacaran fauna by scuttling over the sea floor, swimming actively and burrowing. Most animal phyla show organisation of the body into specialised areas, especially a head end with food trapping and sensory organs, a tubular gut and limbs.

■ Many living burrowers are soft-bodied, yet the first signs that burrowing had disturbed sediments appears only at the base of the Cambrian. Why might that have occurred?

□ Before predation using hard parts, soft-bodied animals feeding above the sediment surface would have been in no danger. So there would have been no selective advantage in burrowing or developing new means of collecting oxygen. After the Cambrian Explosion, soft animals which evolved a burrowing lifestyle would not only escape predation but also find a previously unexploited source of buried food – a positive pressure for adaptation.

Fossils in Cambrian rocks are quite diverse but occasionally geologists find sedimentary rocks that accumulated in conditions that were unusually suited to preserving more organisms. The famous Middle Cambrian Burgess Shale from British Columbia, Canada, is a mud deposited by a submarine landslip that transported sediment and organisms into deep water that lacked oxygen. The animals died, but their bodies were not scavenged, so even rare beasts of the time, both soft and with hard parts, occur as wonderfully preserved fossils (Figure 3.6).

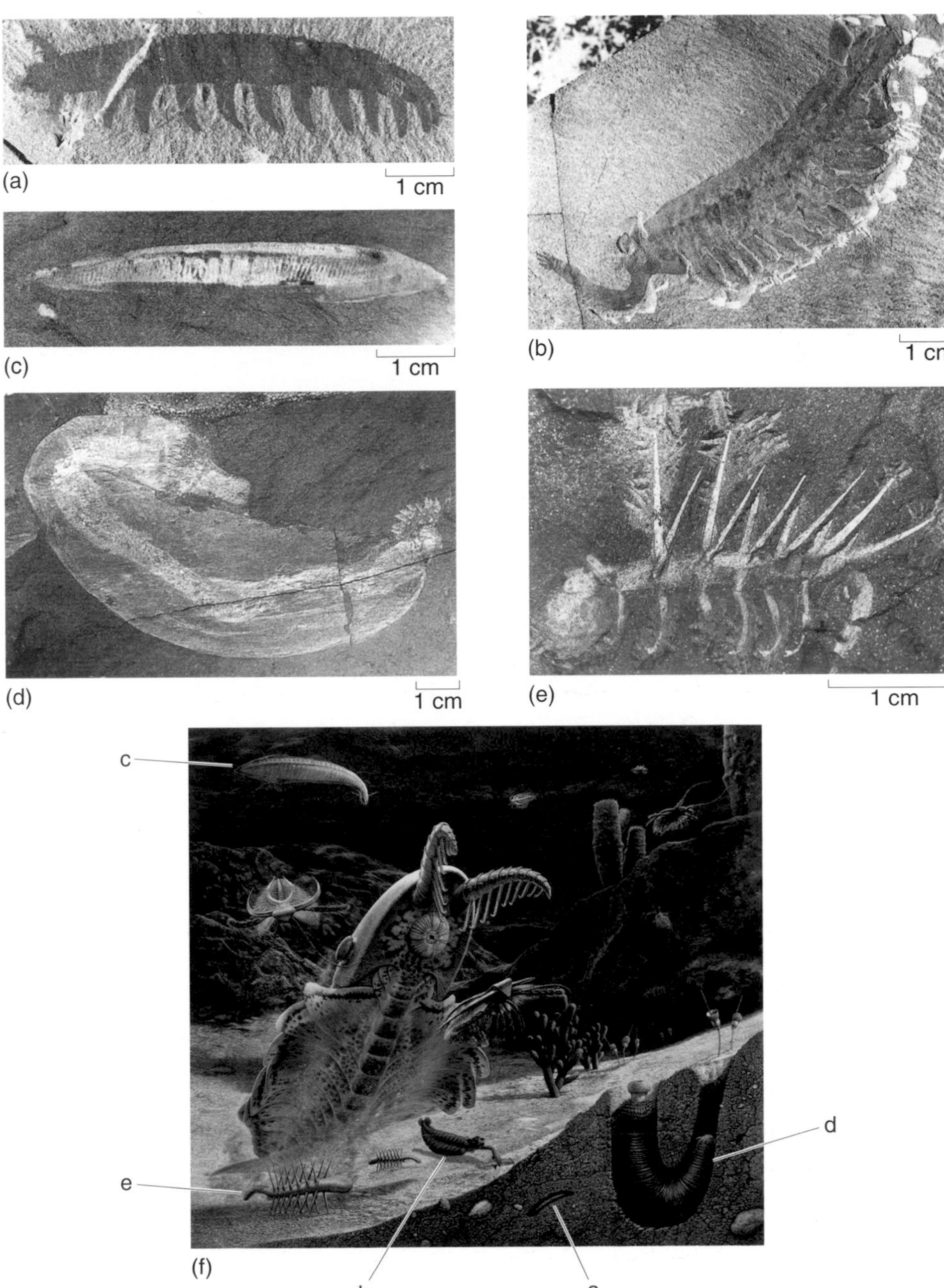

Figure 3.6 Animals of the Burgess Shale. (a) *Ayshia*, a velvet worm; (b) *Opabina*, which had five eyes but is from an unknown phylum; (c) *Pikaia*, an early chordate; (d) *Ottaiai*, a priapulid or penis worm; (e) *Hallucigenia*, from an unknown phylum. (f) A reconstruction from the Burgess Shale fauna of sea-floor life in the Middle Cambrian based on fossilised body parts: *Anomalocaris*, the largest known Cambrian predator, threatens five-eyed *Opabina* and its prey, and *Hallucigenia*.

Only about 15% of the Burgess Shale fossils are of shelly organisms that dominate Cambrian fossil assemblages elsewhere.

■ Why is it important to bear this in mind when trying to interpret other, less complete fossil assemblages?

□ They too may also have been dominated by soft-bodied animals, even if the only fossils they now contain are of hard-bodied ones.

Most fossil assemblages under-represent animal diversity, the most common organisms with the strongest bodies usually being dominant.

About twelve of the Burgess Shale phyla persist to the present day, including *Pikaia* (Figure 3.6c and 3.6f), an early chordate (the group to which vertebrates belong). *Anomalocaris* (Figure 3.6f) is an early arthropod; the largest known Cambrian animal, which may have grown to two metres long. The priapulid worms of the present day (Figure 3.6d and 3.6f) are a phylum on their own. About a dozen other types of Burgess Shale fossils are so unlike anything living today and so different from each other that they were thought initially to belong to long-extinct phyla (for example, the bizarre *Opabina* and *Hallucigenia* in Figures 3.6b, 3.6e and 3.6f). In fact, their oddity may have stemmed from blurred boundaries between major categories of animal life that had only recently evolved from soft ancestors. Cambrian diversity was perhaps an unpruned 'bush of diversity', not fully tested for fitness by competition. Extinctions in the Upper Cambrian terminated some of the branches, leaving more distinct phyla that have remained to this day.

So when *did* animals first appear and when did they diversify into fundamentally different body plans? As so often, the present is a key to the past: in this case the phylogeny (evolutionary history) of living organisms based on differences between their DNA.

3.2.1 Molecular clocks and the diversification of animals

The classification of species according to their anatomy has been revolutionised by comparing them according to molecular differences in their DNA (Book 5, Section 14.4.3). A good example is the phylogenetic tree of Galápagos finches (Book 5, Figure 14.7). Having evidence for the pace of DNA mutations that led to differences between the finch species, and assuming that the pace has remained constant, helps to date each evolutionary branching; a **molecular clock**. The timing of separation between the most basic animal groups is beginning to emerge from the same approach.

The embryos of most living animals have anatomical similarities. Embryonic bilateral symmetry informally groups many phyla as bilaterians (Section 2.2.1). Three such phyla anatomically belong to the super-phylum Deuterostomia: Chordata (such as vertebrates like ourselves), Echinodermata (such as sea urchins) and Hemichordata. Figure 3.7a shows the molecular relationships of 15 different deuterostomes. (You saw a similar diagram in Figure 3.6 of Book 5.) The distance leftwards to where two branches meet expresses the degree of difference between the DNA of the two linked organisms. By assuming a constant rate of accumulation of mutations that are neither favoured nor disadvantageous, the magnitude of that molecular difference can be expressed roughly as a time in the past when the common ancestor of modern animals on both branches lived.

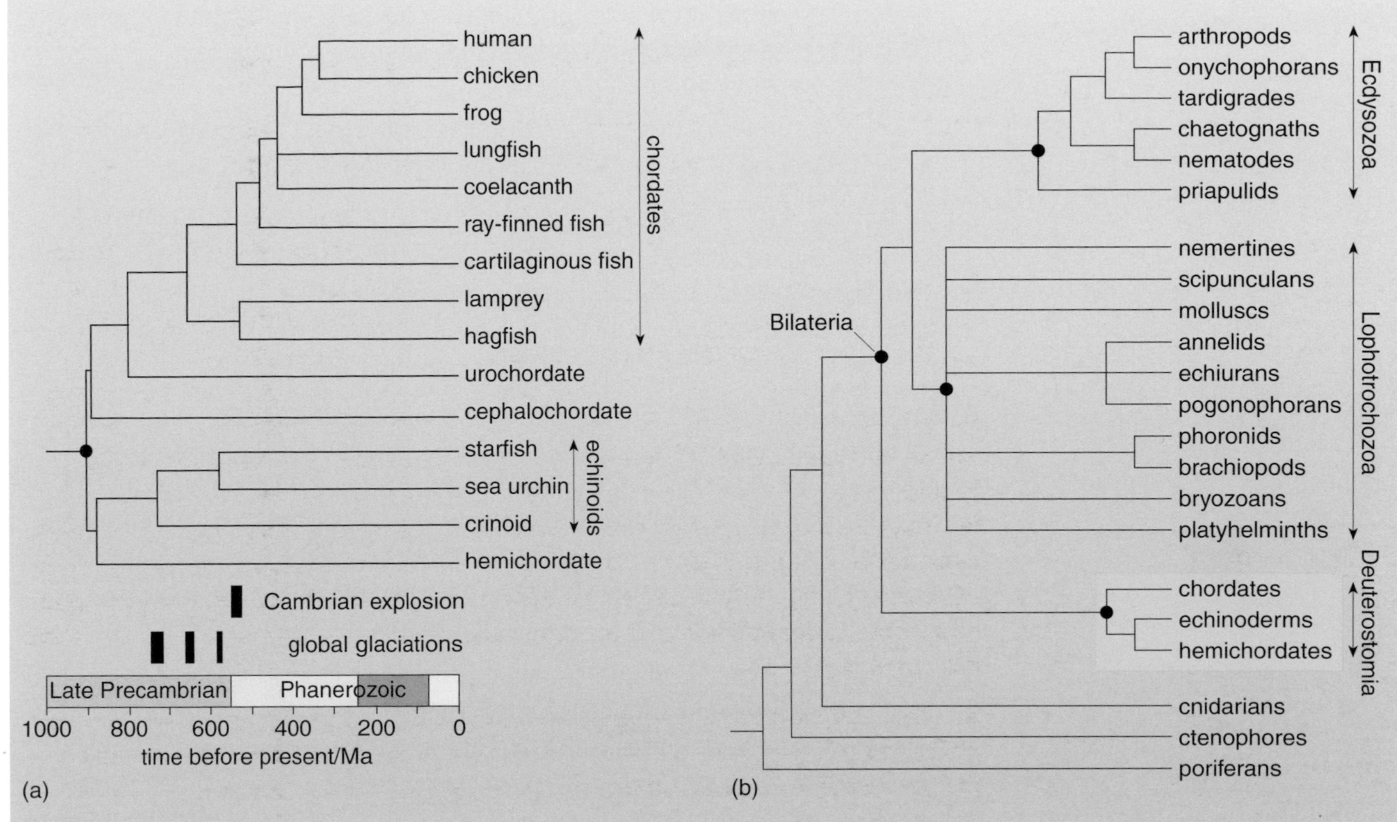

Figure 3.7 Phylogenetic trees of animals. (a) Various groups of deuterostomes, with approximate dates of branching determined using molecular clock methods (age key below). (b) Branching among animal phyla. This phylogeny is not scaled to time, but the part covered by (a) is highlighted so that you can judge the relative timing of other, more fundamental branching. The large dots in both trees emphasise important branchings.

■ When did the last common ancestor of humans and domestic chickens probably live?

□ From Figure 3.7a, this was about 330 Ma ago (in the Lower Carboniferous).

You may have read elsewhere that birds evolved from dinosaurs, and that dinosaurs were reptiles. The ancestors of mammals were reptiles too. So the last ancestor that we shared with a chicken was probably a reptile. According to the molecular clock for deuterostomes, the last common ancestor of chordates and echinoids lived about 900 Ma ago, long before the Cambrian Explosion.

Figure 3.7b shows a molecular phylogeny for the entire Animal Kingdom. The split of the bilaterians that led to deuterostomes was earlier than the evolutionary separation of all the other bilaterians.

Except for unsuspected genetic links between a few groups of living animals, molecular phylogeny has proved how reliable the anatomical scheme of classification launched by Linnaeus has been (Book 5, Section 3.5). The big surprise is the great age of the basic diversity among living animals, which apparently was established long before the appearance of body fossils. The Cambrian Explosion seems not to have been especially significant in a genetic context. Yet, new selection pressures affected animal evolution once hard parts conferred protection and/or armament.

3.3 Life's ups and downs in the Phanerozoic

Since William Smith's discovery of practical uses for fossils (Section 2.2.1), large, time-ordered collections have accumulated for all continents. There are now sufficient fossils of different species, genera, families, etc. to look for changes in overall biological diversity since 542 Ma, as well as to assemble the evolutionary relationships within and between individual groups.

Today, life scientists can study an embarrassment of riches in the living world. So much so that many species, genera and families have probably yet to be discovered and related to those that are known. You may be surprised to learn that as recently as 1995 Danish marine biologists announced to the world a creature (*Symbion pandora*) which lives on bristles surrounding the lips of lobsters. Being unable to match its body plan with that of any existing phylum, they had to create a new one – the Cycliophora.

Properly documenting ancient life is not easy because fossils are hidden inside rocks. Yet there is a more intractable challenge. There is only a tiny chance that any particular individual that died in the past did so under conditions that would preserve recognisable traces. Even the corpse of a whale falling to the ocean floor, where you might expect it to be preserved, can vanish in a few years (Figure 3.8). Every kind of organism benefits from the death of others, by either scavenging proteins or thriving because of nutrients released by decay. On land, weather and moving water, combined with highly oxidising conditions, return biological materials to the inorganic world far more rapidly than any process on the ocean floor.

Although more protected from complete break-up and oxidation than land-living organisms, dead marine organisms also become degraded. Shelly material and bone have more chance of preservation than soft tissue, despite the fate of the grey whale in Figure 3.8. Invertebrate animals, whose hard parts contain little nutriment, are the most likely to become fossils. So what chance is there for softer and more humble life forms? To become fossils, soft parts must quickly be buried to escape total oxidation, as in the case of the Burgess Shale fauna. Few environments where sediments are deposited ensure that vital requirement. The slim chance of preservation is also improved if the individual organism is one of a great many of the same species.

The fossil record is seriously incomplete because of the vagaries of preservation. By no means has every species that ever lived been preserved, let alone found. Geologists get only an infrequent glimpse of the full species diversity from rocks such as the Burgess Shale (Figure 3.6).

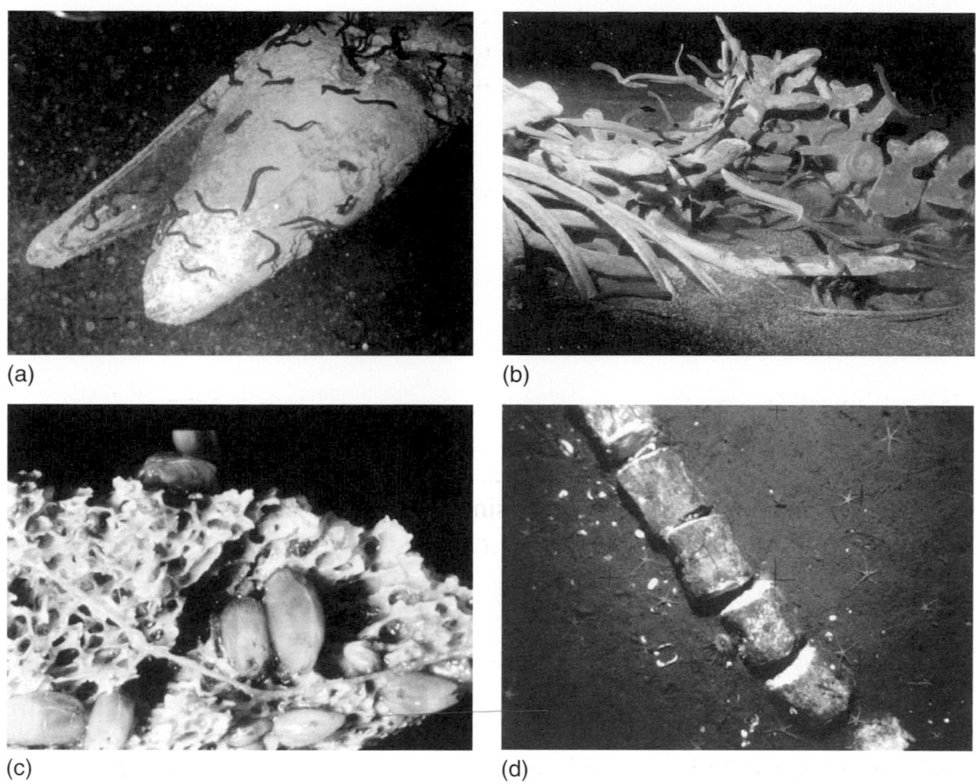

Figure 3.8 What happens to dead whales. (a) The corpse of a 21 m long, 35 tonne grey whale on the deep ocean floor, six weeks after dying. Large lumps have been torn from the carcass by deep-water sharks, but most of the feeding is by toothless hagfish which suck the decaying flesh from the bones. (b) After 18 months, only the bones are left. (c) These are colonised by several kinds of bacteria which cause slow decay, so that small molluscs can enter bones to consume the fat-rich tissue. (d) After a decade, only the largest bones remain but they too are broken down because they contain protein in pore spaces. The final sign that a whale once lay here is the increased colonisation by bacteria and other organisms of the now nutrient-rich sediment beneath it.

■ Although classified at the species level, fossils are catalogued in families (Book 5, Section 3.2). Why would the taxonomic level of family be likely to represent diversity more usefully and accurately than that of the species or the genus?

□ Fossil records of species or genera will be biased towards common, sturdy ones and those living where sedimentation was rapid. Families group together several genera and species which have features in common. So, the discovery of just a single member species indicates that the family to which it belonged was indeed around at the time. Whereas it would be impossible to discover all genera and species that had ever lived, it is far more likely that most of the families that ever lived show up in the fossil record.

There are about 2400 animal families living at present. How does this compare with the fossil record of animal families? Figure 3.9a shows the variation in number of families of all organisms found as fossils during the Phanerozoic.

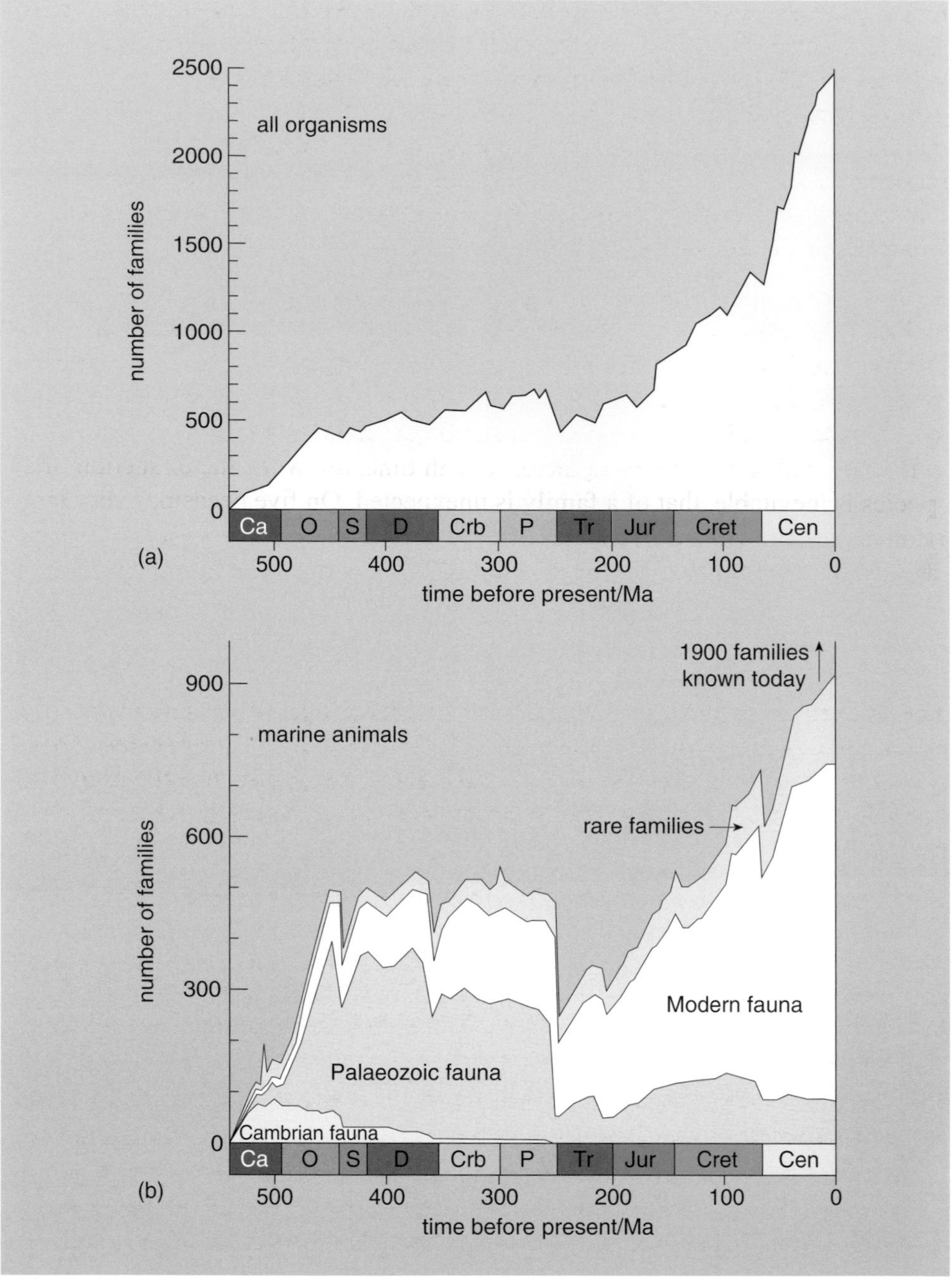

Figure 3.9 Varying numbers of families of: (a) all fossil organisms; (b) marine animals, since 542 Ma, divided into the dominant faunas present just after the Cambrian Explosion, throughout the Palaeozoic, and during the Mesozoic and Cenozoic ('Modern' fauna). (*Note*: the origins of all three faunas can be traced back to the start of the Phanerozoic.)

Question 3.1

Describe briefly (in about 150 words) how the number of recorded families in Figure 3.9a, and therefore global biological diversity, has changed during the Phanerozoic Eon, referring to the time before present and the geological Eras and Periods.

Overall, life on Earth increased in diversity during the Phanerozoic. For some reason an early increase slackened off after about 440 Ma until the Jurassic Period, and the greatest surge in diversity occurred during the last 200 Ma. Considering only marine fossil faunas adds detail to the broad picture. Figure 3.9b divides marine animal families into three groups: Cambrian fauna which dominated the Cambrian Explosion; Palaeozoic fauna dominating the rest of the Palaeozoic Era and Modern fauna that were most abundant through the Mesozoic and Cenozoic. There is also a category of fossil families that are very rare and known only from rocks such as the Burgess Shale, which preserve organic remains better than more common sedimentary rocks. By 'stacking' the faunas the diagram shows how the total number of families at any time is made up of different proportions of the three faunas. Overall, marine diversity dramatically fell five times: at the end of the Ordovician, Devonian, Permian, Triassic and Cretaceous Periods.

At any time in geological history some species inevitably would have become extinct, while others would have been emerging through natural selection. Detailed work on fossil species in several families at different times shows that, on average, the rates of extinction and speciation have been roughly balanced for long timespans. Diversification has ensured that, if anything, the normal trend is for the number of families to increase with time. So, while the extinction of a species is inevitable, that of a family is unexpected. On five occasions very large numbers of families were wiped out, never to return. These geologically sudden 'die-offs' are among the most awesome and yet enigmatic events known.

3.3.1 Mass extinctions

The five largest downturns in diversity represent episodes of such accelerated extinction of species that every member of a host of families disappeared. That is why these episodes are called **mass extinctions**, as opposed to extinctions normally expected in steady species turnover. The main losses in the 'Big Five' mass extinctions were as follows:

1. Upper Ordovician (~440 Ma). Many types of trilobites, brachiopods, echinoderms and corals.
2. Upper Devonian (~360 Ma). Many marine families, especially those of tropical reef-dwelling organisms such as corals, brachiopods, bivalves and sponges.
3. Upper Permian (~250 Ma). Nearly 60% of marine families (as much as 95% of marine animal species may have disappeared). Trilobites and water scorpions disappeared completely. Virtually all corals became extinct, and reefs were eliminated. Crinoids, brachiopods, bivalves and gastropods had huge losses. Many groups of terrestrial amphibians and reptiles perished.
4. Upper Triassic (~200 Ma). Major losses of cephalopods, gastropods, brachiopods, bivalves, sponges and marine reptiles. On land, many insect families became extinct, as did yet more reptiles and large amphibians.
5. Upper Cretaceous (~65 Ma). Ammonites, large marine reptiles such as plesiosaurs and, on land, dinosaurs and pterosaurs were extinguished completely. Groups that had major losses included foraminifera, brachiopods, bivalves and sea urchins. Vertebrate groups which were affected only slightly include fishes, amphibians, crocodiles, snakes, turtles and mammals. Flowering plants, including hardwood trees, were also affected. *Note*: extinction at the Cretaceous–Tertiary boundary is known as the **K–T event** (K is the abbreviation for Cretaceous; Tertiary is the old name for the start of the Cenozoic. Although not used now, it is still used when referring to the K–T boundary.)

Figure 3.10 shows in more detail the percentage of marine animals at the level of genus that became extinct during the Phanerozoic. You can see that, as well as the Big Five, there are several lesser events. The prominent extinction peaks during the Cambrian are a result of that Period having far fewer genera in total than in younger Periods, so that any losses would constitute a high percentage and the peaks are thus exaggerated.

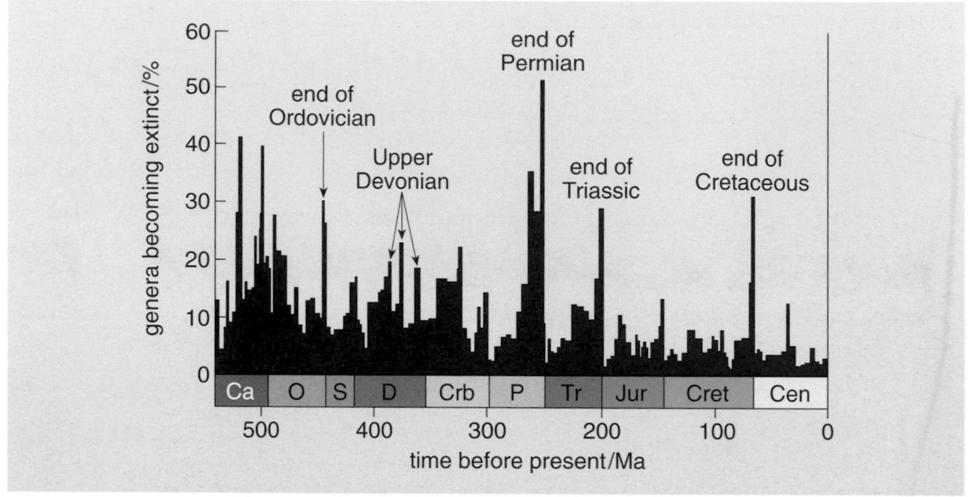

Figure 3.10 Plot showing estimated percentages of known marine animal genera becoming extinct during the Phanerozoic. The widths of the bars are uneven and cover the duration of lesser stratigraphic divisions of geological Periods.

Although the terrestrial fossil record is less complete than that from marine sediments, for the time when animals first colonised the land about 400 Ma ago (Section 3.4), it shows the similar features as Figure 3.9b.

■ What can you deduce about mass extinctions from the similarity between marine and terrestrial fossil records?

□ Whatever caused the mass extinctions was global in scope, and affected land and marine environments.

Each of the Big Five mass extinctions affected families in all phyla, classes and orders. Whatever the causes, they were generalised in their effects. So, what might those causes have been?

3.3.2 'Smoking guns'

The mass extinction at the end of the Cretaceous Period is celebrated for wiping out the dinosaurs but they were by no means its only victims. A wide range of animals and plants was affected, and many species of microscopic organisms. The first evidence for its cause emerged from unrelated research. In the 1970s, father and son Luis and Walter Alvarez, with colleagues from the University of California at Berkeley, were trying to estimate deposition rates of ocean-floor sediment layers using changes in their concentration of the metal iridium.

Iridium is extremely rare in the Earth's crust but much more abundant in meteorites. Assuming that meteoritic dust falls at a regular rate, variations in the pace at which sediments accumulate would give higher iridium concentrations in a given thickness of slowly accumulating sediment than in the same thickness of rapidly accumulated sediment. In deep marine sediments from Gubbio in central Italy, which ranged across the K–T boundary, 10 mm of clay marking the boundary (Figure 3.11a) contained up to 30 times the level of iridium than in other layers. That could have been due to sediment accumulating 30 times more slowly than normal. However, the team claimed boldly that the mass extinction was due to a huge meteorite impact which supplied the iridium. Iridium analyses at K–T sections elsewhere gave the same result and ruled out the slow sediment accumulation model.

(a)

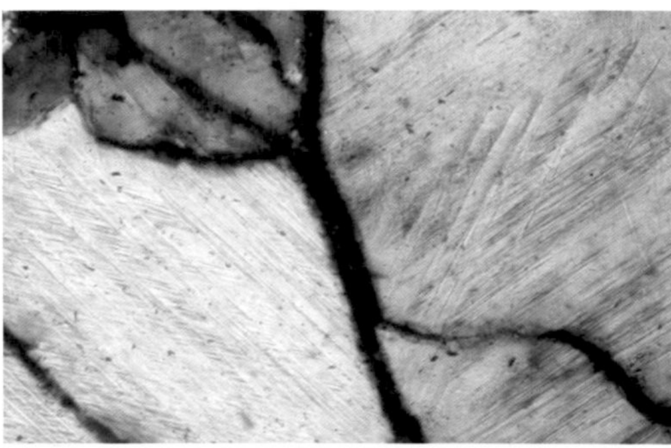

(b)

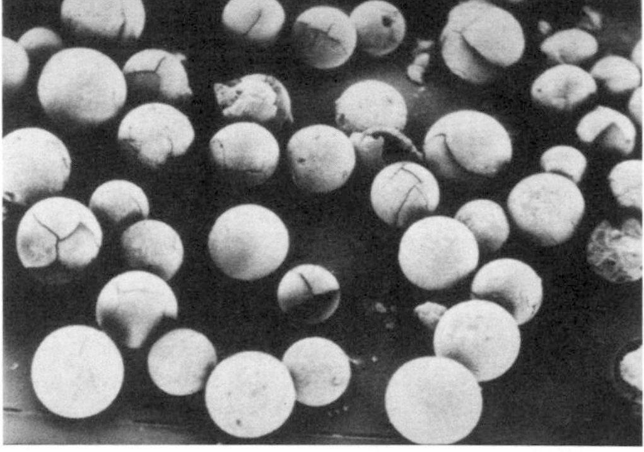

(c)

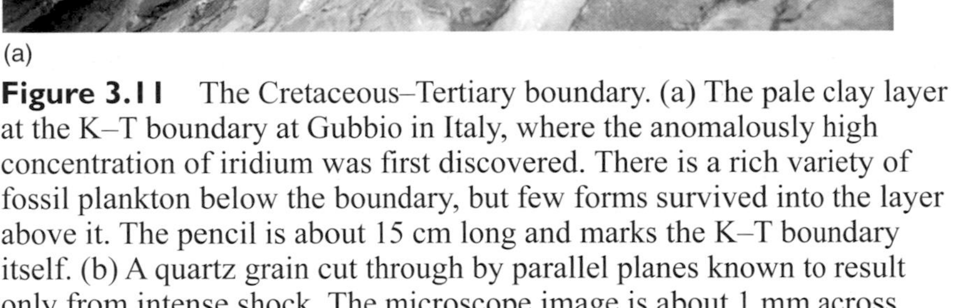

Figure 3.11 The Cretaceous–Tertiary boundary. (a) The pale clay layer at the K–T boundary at Gubbio in Italy, where the anomalously high concentration of iridium was first discovered. There is a rich variety of fossil plankton below the boundary, but few forms survived into the layer above it. The pencil is about 15 cm long and marks the K–T boundary itself. (b) A quartz grain cut through by parallel planes known to result only from intense shock. The microscope image is about 1 mm across. (c) Millimetre-sized glass spheres formed by rapid cooling of droplets of molten rock.

Publication by the Alvarez's team in 1980 opened the greatest debate in the geosciences since the discovery of sea-floor spreading. Researchers flocked to the now-famous sites to sample the boundary layer, to see what else they might find. Figure 3.11 shows examples of other evidence confirming that there had indeed been an impact. It must have been huge as many sites around the world contain these anomalies (Figure 3.12a). As well as common grains of quartz showing structures uniquely formed by intense shock (Figure 3.11b), there are occasional minute diamonds formed under extremely high pressures. Tiny glass spheres formed as chilled droplets of molten rock were flung into the atmosphere by the impact (Figure 3.11c).

The only missing information was an impact crater blasted out by the hypothesised meteorite. Eventually, geophysicists examining variations in the gravitational and magnetic fields in the southern Gulf of Mexico noticed a series of circular features about 300 km across at the coast in the Mexican province of Chicxulub (pronounced 'chick-shulub'). They indicated a large buried structure (Figure 3.12b). Drilling proved not only that the circular feature was an impact crater but also that it had formed 65 Ma ago, at the K–T boundary: a 'smoking gun' by any standards.

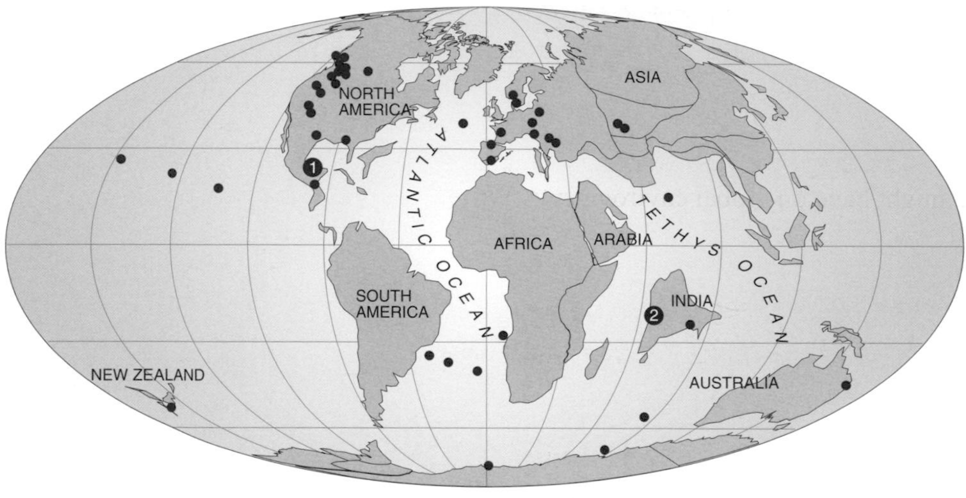

(a)

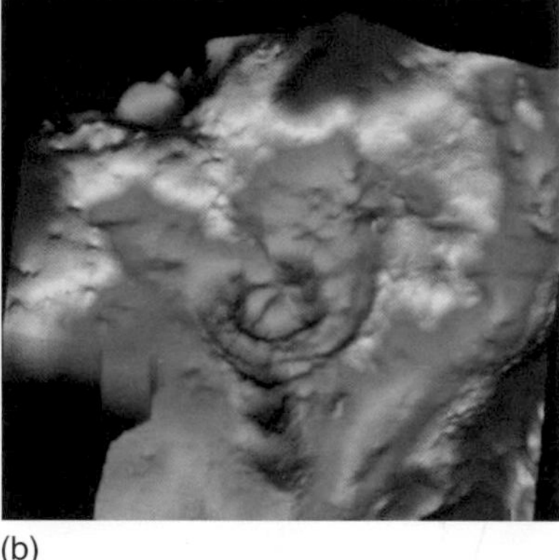

(b)

(c)

Figure 3.12 Possible causes of the K–T mass extinction. (a) Global distribution of iridium anomalies at the K–T boundary, the Chicxulub Crater (purple dot 1) and the site of huge volcanic eruptions in northwestern India (purple dot 2). The map shows the positions of continental masses at 65 Ma, but with their present-day coastlines for clarity. (b) Image of the gravity field over the buried Chicxulub Crater viewed as if it were 'illuminated' topography – the rainbow colours are from blue, low gravity, to red, high gravity. (c) Repeated lava flows in the Indian flood basalts – the cliffs are up to 1 km high.

However, the plot thickened with the discovery of another potential culprit. Roughly on the other side of the world from Chicxulub, in northwestern India, there are great thicknesses of basaltic lava flows that cover a huge area (Figure 3.12c). Before erosion, there may have been up to 1.5×10^6 km^3 of these **flood basalts** in northwestern India. They formed at the end of the Cretaceous, when India drifted over a hot spot beneath what is now the Indian Ocean. Detailed radiometric dating revealed a surprise; the immense magma volumes emerged in only 1–2 Ma, bracketing the K–T boundary. No one has witnessed a flood basalt event, but what one might have done to the environment can be estimated by considering what modern volcanism emits (Book 2, Chapter 4).

Question 3.2

Try to imagine from your study of Books 1 to 3 what effects (a) the impact of a large (~10 km diameter) meteorite travelling at a speed of 15 km s^{-1} and (b) a massive outpouring of magma, might have on global environments. Write a paragraph (about 50–100 words) for each scenario.

Although both events would make the adjective 'awesome' completely inadequate, if we did witness them, their most devastating influence would have been stealthy.

■ What would have been the effects on climate of (a) CO_2 and (b) dust?

□ (a) CO_2 is a greenhouse gas, so the global mean surface temperature would rise; (b) dust in the upper atmosphere increases the Earth's albedo, i.e. scattering some of the incoming solar radiation back to space (Book 1, Section 4.4) and so would result in cooling.

In the stratosphere, SO_2 forms tiny sulfuric acid droplets which also increase albedo. This would also result in global cooling.

■ What other effect might the gases have had?

□ Both CO_2 and SO_2 dissolve in rainwater to make it acid, which would decrease the pH of ocean surface water.

The important point to note is that these three products (CO_2, SO_2 and dust) of either meteorite impact or volcanism affect the atmosphere and so spread around the world quickly – the prerequisite for mass extinction. A notable feature of the K–T extinction was the collapse of the population of foraminifera – marine zooplankton with calcium carbonate shells. That may have resulted from a decrease in pH (increased acidity) of near-surface seawater but, equally likely, less sunlight would reduce photosynthesis. Phytoplankton are at the base of the food web for the rest of marine life. A similar scenario can be surmised for life on land, i.e. the reduced growth of land plants. Drastically reduced food, even for a few months, could trigger massive animal extinction by starvation. Neither dust nor SO_2 stay in the atmosphere for more than a few years; they are rained out. However, the collapse of photosynthesising organisms would have reduced the potential for the biosphere to remove CO_2 from the atmosphere. So, global warming would continue until the recovery of photosynthesising organisms, which provide the dead organic matter for the burial of carbon in sea-floor sediments. Perhaps for several hundred thousand years, global ecosystems would have changed drastically. To the acute extinction by starvation would be added chronic adverse pressures as habitats were drastically transformed.

There is no doubt that the meteorite impact or volcanism, or perhaps a combination of both, caused the K–T mass extinction; but there are unexplained aspects. Slower, yet important changes in the Earth system had built up throughout the Upper Cretaceous; sea level had begun to fall and global climate to cool. Some animal groups had begun to decline well before the K–T event. Ammonites were entirely exterminated at 65 Ma, yet families of other cephalopods, such as squid and the similar *Nautilus*, survived. While dinosaurs perished, some reptilian groups, early mammals and birds remained.

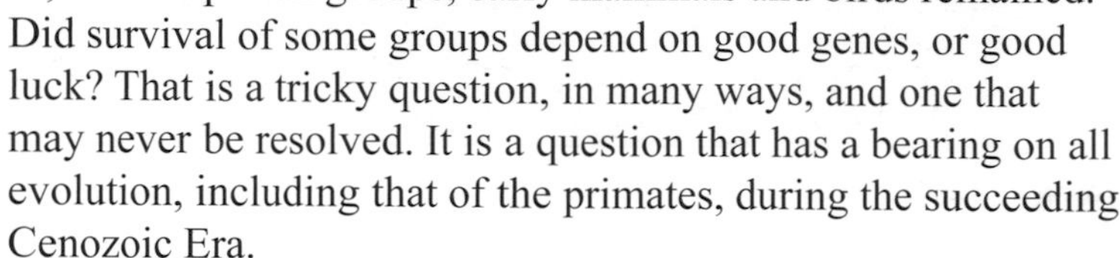

Did survival of some groups depend on good genes, or good luck? That is a tricky question, in many ways, and one that may never be resolved. It is a question that has a bearing on all evolution, including that of the primates, during the succeeding Cenozoic Era.

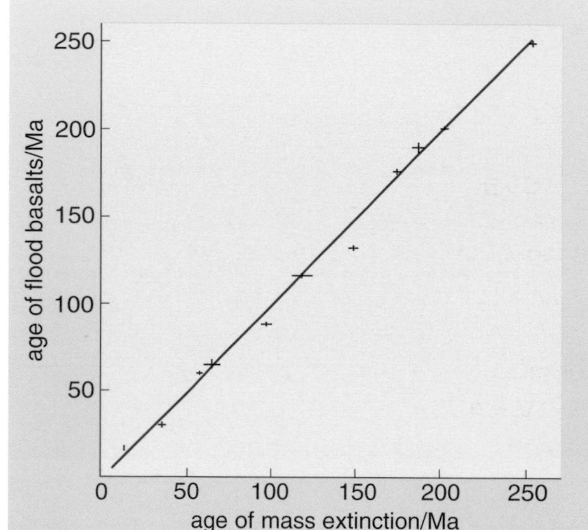

Figure 3.13 Ages of flood basalts, against ages of mass extinction. Allowing for uncertainties, most of the data fall on or close to a straight line joining points with the same age on each axis.

At the time of writing (2007), research focused on other mass extinctions has produced no more than a few inconclusive hints at the influence of extraterrestrial bombardment. The biggest mass extinction at the end of the Permian – around 95% of all species living at the time are estimated to have been wiped out – coincided with the largest flood-basalt event known in geological history. As much as 10×10^6 km^3 of Upper Permian lava may have emerged in a little over 2 Ma and much still covers part of Siberia.

Unlike fossils, flood basalts are neither easily overlooked nor eroded away. During the last 250 Ma since the near-end of life on Earth at the close of the Palaeozoic Era (end of the Permian), geologists have found evidence for and dated 10 flood-basalt events. Figure 3.13 shows a plot of the ages of flood basalts against the accepted ages of significant mass extinction events, including the major ones at the ends of the Permian, Triassic and Cretaceous.

- ■ What might you conclude from the plot in Figure 3.13?

- □ At first sight, the close fit of ages for both mass extinctions and flood basalts to a straight line seems to be convincing evidence for major volcanism repeatedly having *caused* mass extinctions.

Now examine Figure 3.14, which expresses the same data differently.

- ■ Do the data for extinction and flood basalt in this form support the hypothesis that flood basalts cause mass extinctions?

- □ Although the durations of the Siberian (Upper Permian), Central Atlantic (Upper Triassic), northeastern Indian (Lower Cretaceous) and western Indian flood basalt volcanism bracket the extinctions, some have no associated extinction, and others follow extinctions.

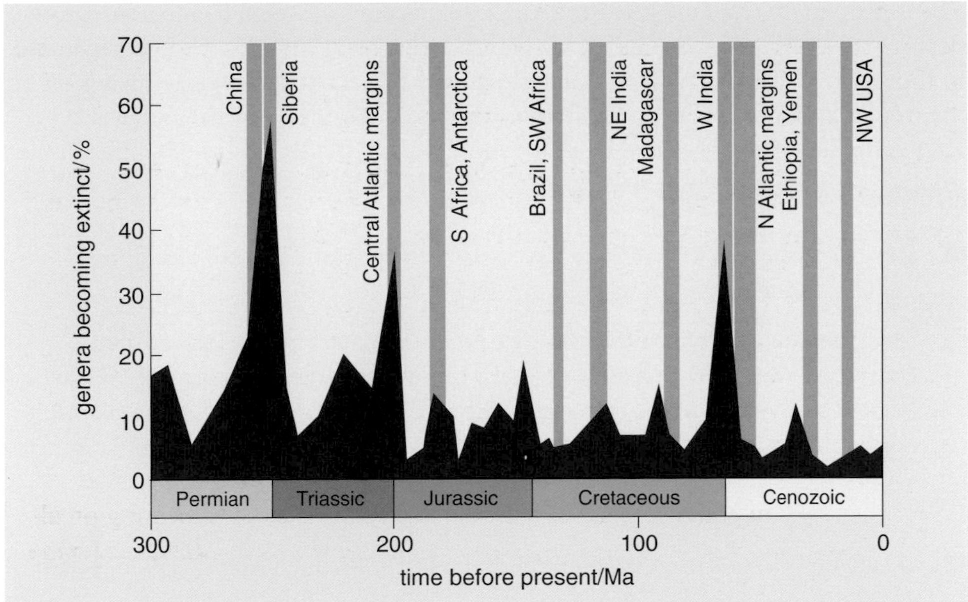

Figure 3.14 Plot of the percentage of genera becoming extinct since 300 Ma. Note this is based on Figure 3.10, but the extinctions are from longer divisions of each geological period. The duration of flood-basalt events is superimposed as vertical orange bars so that the two phenomena can be compared.

Clearly, not every flood-basalt event directly triggers mass extinction, despite their apparent closeness in time. Four of the mass extinctions in the last 250 Ma seem to be associated with flood-basalt events; but the 'fuzziness' of the data makes it hard to justify the certainty of direct, causal links.

The interactions involved in plate tectonics, in the Earth's ocean–atmosphere system and in its ecosystems are extremely complex. Between them they may result in fundamental changes, *without* needing to invoke catastrophic impacts or volcanism, for example: climatic cooling and aridity; global warming; rise or fall in sea level; changes in oceanic circulation that reduce dissolved oxygen in shallow waters; changes in atmospheric chemistry. The Upper Ordovician event coincided with evidence for a massive glaciation in what is now Africa, and resulting global falls in sea level. Events at the end of the Devonian and the Triassic correlate with evidence for sudden falls in atmospheric oxygen levels. Establishing cause and effect during extinctions, and precisely which biological attributes – or lack of them – led to the demise of a particular species, is difficult, even for individual species extinctions that biologists have witnessed.

3.3.3 Recovery and evolutionary radiations

Variation in the number of marine animal families during the Phanerozoic shows another remarkable feature (Figure 3.9b). After the two massive extinctions at the end of the Palaeozoic and Mesozoic Eras, diversity fell, took time to recover and then, in each case, rose to higher levels than before the extinction event. After the extinction at the end of the Permian, recovery took 100 Ma, until the end of the Jurassic. Figure 3.9b reveals further interesting features. There were a few representatives of each fauna as far back as the Cambrian Explosion, but the destiny of each fauna was different. To make this clear they are plotted separately in Figure 3.15. The features to note are: what happens to each fauna during the mass extinction at the ends of the Ordovician and the Permian and at the K–T boundary; increases and decreases in diversity of the faunas; changes in the relative proportions of the faunas.

■ Describe briefly the changing diversity through the Phanerozoic in the Cambrian fauna shown in Figure 3.15.

□ This fauna was the first to diversify, reaching a peak at the end of the Cambrian. Thereafter, it slowly lost families, including a major fall at the end of the Ordovician, and is so poorly represented today that it is imperceptible on the graph. *Lingulella*, a brachiopod, is a Cambrian survivor (Book 5, Figure 1.2).

■ Describe briefly the changes in the Palaeozoic fauna during the Phanerozoic.

□ The Palaeozoic fauna rose rapidly to a peak of about 350 families in the Ordovician. Although greatly reduced by the mass extinction at the end of the Ordovician, it recovered and then declined gradually during the rest of the Palaeozoic. The mass extinction at the end of the Permian had by far the greatest effect on this fauna, and the number of families fell from about 240 to 60. (A few families in each group – except for the Graptolithina – survived.) Despite some recovery in the Mesozoic, the number of families never again rose above about 125, and their contribution to overall faunal diversity declined as the Modern fauna expanded (Figure 3.9b).

■ What happened to the Modern fauna during the Phanerozoic?

□ The number of Modern families grew during the Palaeozoic Era, but was outpaced by the other two. Some families disappeared in the mass extinction at the end of the Permian, but far fewer than in the Palaeozoic fauna. Thereafter, Modern fauna began to dominate, and account for all the growth in diversity during the last 250 Ma, despite significant losses at the K–T boundary.

Apart from the first 100 Ma, overall diversity in the Palaeozoic seas did not change much. The causes for the post-Permian change from this prolonged era of static diversity to rapid growth are the subject of speculation. Were animals of the Modern fauna favoured by especially good luck or by 'good' genes? Whichever, the wipe-out of the Palaeozoic fauna at the end of the Permian created opportunities for survivors among the Modern fauna. There would have been many vacated niches to expand into, but such an enormous growth in diversity (more than quadrupling) must have involved an increase in niches too. How could that be? Ironically, one reason was the survival of a few families of

Figure 3.15 Changes during the Phanerozoic in the number of families in the three marine faunas (Figure 3.9b), including representatives of the main animal groups (classes and orders) in each.

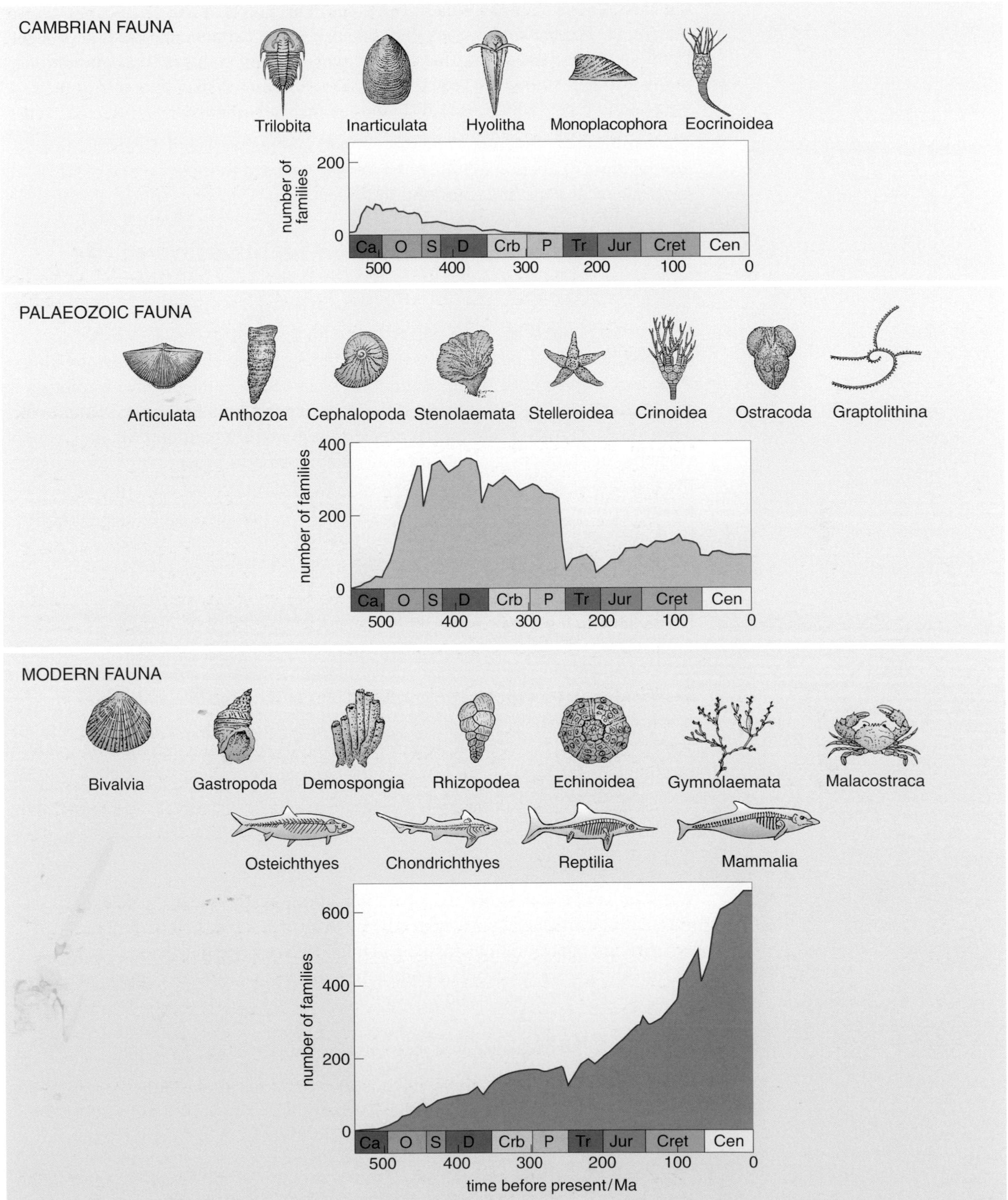
CAMBRIAN FAUNA
Trilobita
Inarticulata
Hyolitha
Monoplacophora
Eocrinoidea
number of families
200
0
Ca O S D Crb P Tr Jur Cret Cen
500 400 300 200 100 0
PALAEOZOIC FAUNA
Articulata
Anthozoa
Cephalopoda
Stenolaemata
Stelleroidea
Crinoidea
Ostracoda
Graptolithina
number of families
400
200
0
Ca O S D Crb P Tr Jur Cret Cen
500 400 300 200 100 0
MODERN FAUNA
Bivalvia
Gastropoda
Demospongia
Rhizopodea
Echinoidea
Gymnolaemata
Malacostraca
Osteichthyes
Chondrichthyes
Reptilia
Mammalia
number of families
600
400
200
0
Ca O S D Crb P Tr Jur Cret Cen
500 400 300 200 100 0
time before present/Ma

the class Anthozoa in the Palaeozoic fauna. This group of cnidarians includes the corals. The few anthozoans that did survive the extinction at the end of the Permian themselves diversified into the reef-building corals that are so familiar today. Modern reefs offer vastly more ecological niches than the reefs in Palaeozoic times, which were little more than shelly mounds.

The evolutionary outcomes of mass extinction – recovery and diversification – are the topic of Section 3.5. First, however, you need to focus on one of life's great physical steps: the colonisation of the land.

3.4 Crossing the great frontier: invasion of the continents

Life, to be blunt, consists of bags filled with dirty water (cells), whose component compounds and ions engage in something chemically astonishing. That fact alone points to life originating somewhere in the oceans. Evolution in the oceans produced enormous diversity, among both prokaryotes and eukaryotes. However, the land remained barren until about 400 Ma ago, except perhaps for sturdy cyanobacteria that today form thin veneers on rock, even in the driest deserts. For even the most advanced Cambrian animal, the land was an alien place: prone to drying out; highly oxidising since 2400 Ma; scoured by winds and powerful rivers; and subject to temperature extremes of –60 °C to +50 °C. To exploit the land's potential as a permanent resident, an exploring eukaryote would first need to carry its own water supply. Without an abundant, reliable food source, nothing would induce a Palaeozoic animal to venture across the water's edge.

Of course, the land surface does get wet. Water seeps into porous rocks as well as flowing in rivers and ponding in lakes. Far back in the Precambrian there would have been coastal swamps and mudflats but they would have been lifeless above water level. Terrestrial sediments of Ordovician age yield the first traces of rudimentary land plants, but it was in the Silurian Period that land plants became widespread, to lay the base of a food chain.

3.4.1 Land plants

Water on land contains few dissolved ions. Fresh water bursts the cells of multicellular marine algae (seaweeds) by diffusing across cell membranes to equalise ion concentrations inside and outside. Yet, once they had evolved, marine algae were probably as common in the past along the seashore as they are now.

■ Suggest three reasons why seaweeds favour near-shore habitats.

□ (i) In shallow water there is abundant sunlight for photosynthesis. (ii) Drying during the tidal cycle allows the distribution of spores by wind. (iii) Shallow water gives a firm footing for attachment to rocks or sediment.

The first two reasons apply even more on dry land, thereby creating selection pressures towards its colonisation. The first requirement is a coating to maintain cell water in the right amount and with the appropriate concentrations of ions. However, marine plants photosynthesise efficiently because the buoyancy of their fronds spreads out the surface exposed to sunlight. Without water they flop down, so adaptation is also needed to develop more rigid plant tissue to overcome gravity. This carries a bonus: the higher the fruiting parts of a plant, the more likely that spores are distributed by wind. Figure 3.16 shows two of the earliest land plants.

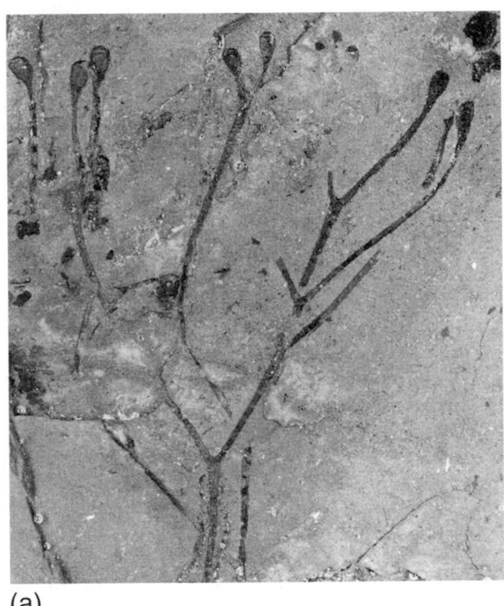

(a)

(b)

Figure 3.16 Early land plants. (a) A well-preserved fossil plant from the Silurian of Wales. The photograph is about 5 cm from top to bottom. (b) An artist's impression of Lower Devonian plants, fringing a lake. They are about 45 cm tall.

Sedimentary rocks deposited in lowland river flood plains at the end of the Devonian (360 Ma) contain plants tall enough to be called trees, with cells organised as wood, roots and complex branching systems. Most were ferns, still propagating like their marine ancestors through spores. A few had evolved seeds that protected fertilised ovules and gave them a nutrient store. These early plants were sufficiently well-endowed to take advantage of life on land to spread far across the surface. Flowering plants with proper fruits to enclose seeds did not emerge until more than 200 Ma later in the Lower Cretaceous.

The Carboniferous period is aptly named after the massive coal deposits laid down in the tropics of the time. Carboniferous coal reserves are close to 10^4 Gt (10^{16} kg), about one-tenth of which is currently profitable to extract. Coal formed from plants, some of tree size, which died in vast tropical swamps on the supercontinent of Pangaea (Book 2, Figure 7.3). Many early plants thrived in waterlogged conditions (Figure 3.17), so aerobic bacteria did not completely oxidise fallen debris, which accumulated as peat. Burial and then compression of carbon-rich peat slowly transformed it into coal. This product of Carboniferous photosynthesis was the main fuel for the Industrial Revolution in the 19th century. It is still the largest energy source for electricity generation, and contributes heavily to the increase in atmospheric CO_2 and to global warming (Book 1).

Figure 3.17 Reconstruction of an Upper Carboniferous low-latitude coal swamp.

■ Suggest two chemical outcomes of the formation of Carboniferous coal.

□ With vast amounts of carbon being buried, the photosynthesis that 'fixed' it in plant tissue would have significantly reduced the CO_2 content of the Carboniferous atmosphere. The main waste product of photosynthesis is oxygen, so atmospheric oxygen levels would have risen commensurately.

Reduced atmospheric CO_2 helps explain why a massive continental ice sheet blanketed the southern part of Pangaea from 60° S to the South Pole (Book 2, Figure 7.3). The Carboniferous to Lower Permian was probably the longest period of global cooling in the Earth's history. The inevitable rise of atmospheric oxygen, once plants began to colonise the land, would have provided a significant boost for animals to follow plants across the frontier.

3.4.2 Animals emerge onto the land

All animals need oxygen, and several different ways to absorb this vital gas have evolved. Marine arthropods had already evolved a simple way of doing so, which needed little modification to work with gaseous oxygen. Rotting early land plants would have been a tempting food source for shallow-water, vegetarian arthropods. Selective pressures on predatory arthropods might then have encouraged some to hunt on dry land. The terrestrial fossil record in Silurian rock shows several kinds of arthropod. These first land animals had already evolved legs and watertight outer skeletons when they were exclusively marine.

The land animals of most interest are those from which humans ultimately evolved: the vertebrates. They are part of the phylum Chordata which possess an end-to-end nerve fibre. *Pikaia* from the Burgess Shale (Figure 3.6) is an early chordate, and the Chordata had evolved long before the Cambrian (Figure 3.7). Cambrian fossils include jawless lamprey-like fish, and fishes became increasingly diverse during the Ordovician and the Silurian. By the Devonian, several orders and families occur in sedimentary rocks that were undoubtedly deposited in freshwater lakes on the fringes of the growing supercontinent of Pangaea.

Some Devonian fishes – aptly described as lobe-finned – developed sturdy fins, rays of which were supported by larger articulated bones. The famous coelacanth, *Latimeria*, is a surviving lobe-finned fish (Book 5, Section 14.4.4). The forms of some Devonian lobe-finned fish skeletons shift with time towards what are clearly animals with a dual life in and out of water; the first amphibians. This evolutionary progression involved the fins (Figure 3.18). The front and rear fins of *Eusthenopteron* and *Panderichthys* have rays, whereas the later amphibians such as *Acanthostega* have limbs without rays to support fin tissue, but they still have tail fins and clearly a dual life (Figure 3.18). In 2005 a remarkable example of a 'missing link' called *Tiktaalik* (an Inuit name), intermediate between fish and amphibian and which has barely any fins, was found in Devonian rocks of Arctic Canada. The changes in fins and limbs shown in Figure 3.18 suggest how evolution led vertebrates onto the land. Note that what became toes developed from a seeming jumble of bones in fish fins, to reach the standard five in Lower Carboniferous fossils.

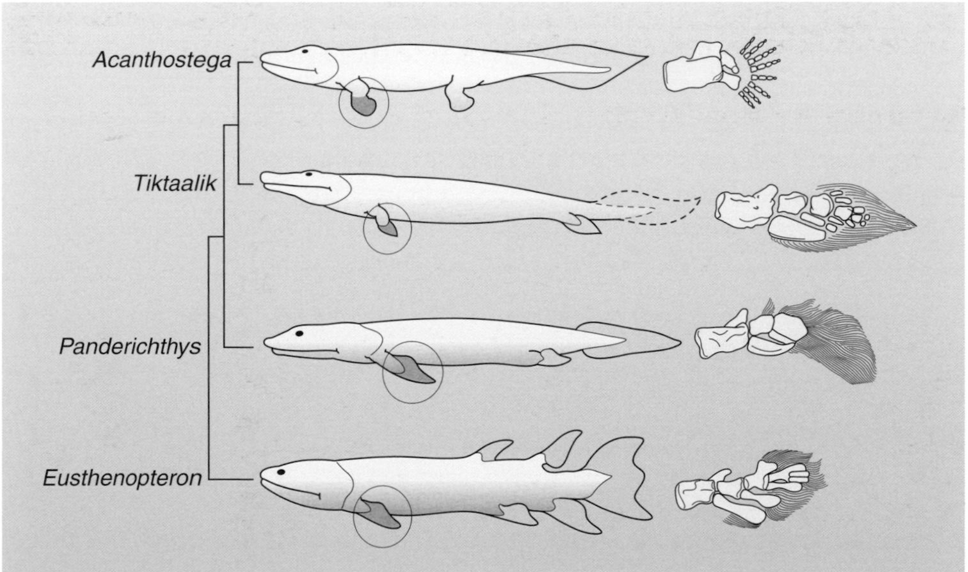

Figure 3.18 The transition from fish to amphibians recorded by Devonian fossil vertebrates shown by changes in body plan (each animal is no more than 0.3 to 1.0 m long). This is an example of a morphological phylogeny, supported by a progression in bones. The shaded areas of limbs and tails signify rays supporting fins. (*Note*: the tail of *Tiktaalik* is drawn with a dashed line as no fossil evidence for it has yet been found.) The connections on the left show a progression (left to right) from older to younger Devonian strata. Details of the forelimbs (on the right) show the progressive development of what were to become toes. The forelimbs are circled on the left. (Forelimbs from Nature Publishing Group. Reprinted by permission from Macmillan Publishers Ltd, http://www.nature.com/index.html)

Another evolutionary change that was needed before four-legged vertebrates could move decisively onto the land was adaptation of the swim bladders of bony fishes to become lungs. Incidentally, this freed what had been gills for later adaptation to other functions, including hearing organs. Amphibians today start life with gills, as in a frog tadpole, and develop lungs as adults (sadly, no Devonian fossil tadpoles are known). Reptiles are born with lungs.

■ What other important adaptation was necessary for reptiles to become permanent land dwellers able to roam the continents?

□ An egg that resisted drying out, which required some kind of shell. Unless they are laid in water, the eggs of amphibians inevitably dry out.

Descendants of the first vertebrates to become land-dwelling had the choice of a host of ecological niches, provided that the environment supported edible plants. The vertebrate body plan is the most complex in the Animal Kingdom, and that complexity provided many opportunities for rapid and varied adaptation. The vertebrates exploited adaptive radiation in a most interesting manner as described in the next section.

3.5 Evolutionary radiations

Figure 3.19 shows the times when vertebrate evolution took major steps by evolutionary radiation. The diagram was constructed from phylogenies based on anatomy (e.g. Figure 3.18), in which the skeletal elements of earlier vertebrate groups can be traced in the bones of newer groups which behaved differently from their ancestors. Few branchings have the clarity of the transition from bony fish to amphibian, but all have sufficient support for palaeontologists to agree on the timing. Molecular genetics is beginning to match relatedness in the genetics of living vertebrates, and this has confirmed the broad evolutionary links (Figure 3.7a). Fossil evidence for evolutionary branchings, such as that in Figure 3.18, helps to calibrate molecular phylogenies by the use of molecular clocks (Section 3.2.1).

To help you spot the important features of the vertebrates' evolutionary radiation, spend a short time studying Figure 3.19, especially changes in the diversity of classes and the branching points.

■ Which of today's classes of vertebrates were in existence by the end of the Triassic Period?

□ Bony and jawless fishes, sharks and rays, amphibians, reptiles *and* mammals had all evolved by about 200 Ma ago. The division among fishes into five classes dates back to the Ordovician.

Question 3.3

Write brief notes (a sentence or two) about the relationships in Figure 3.19 between mass extinctions, vertebrate diversity and evolutionary branching points.

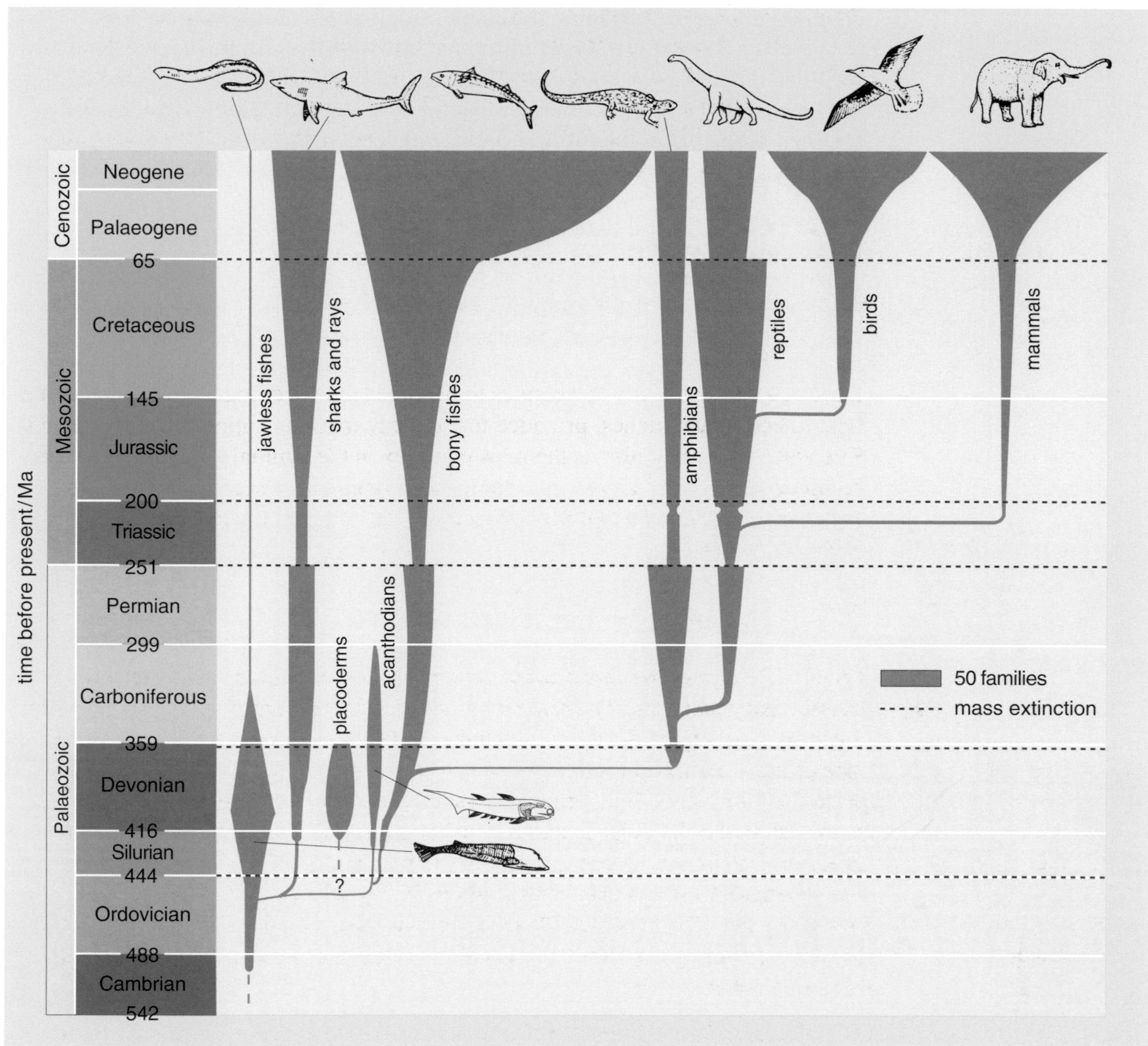

Figure 3.19 Geological ranges of vertebrate classes showing the major evolutionary steps during the Phanerozoic. The changing width of each group roughly indicates how its diversity changed through time, the number of families (see the scale bar) being a useful measure of morphological diversity. The horizontal separation of newly evolved classes from their ancestors (e.g. mammals from reptiles) does *not* indicate large, abrupt change but results from the way the diagram is drawn for clarity. Placoderms are an extinct group of jawed fishes with thick external armour; another extinct group is the slender jawed, spiny fishes or acanthodians.

During the Mesozoic (Middle Triassic) the dinosaurs branched from reptilian stock, which had been decimated by the extinction at the end of the Permian. Interestingly, mammals branched from similar reptiles around the same time, but there the similarity ends. Mammals barely diversified during most of the Mesozoic, while the dinosaurs filled almost every possible land-based niche during the next 150 Ma. Carnivores, herbivores and mixed feeders ranged in size from that of a chicken to the 35 m long *Argentinosaurus* which weighed about 90 tonnes. Discoveries in China of small carnivorous dinosaur fossils with well-preserved feathers confirm that birds evolved from what are generally regarded as truly awesome beasts. Reptiles were not confined to the land during the Mesozoic. Pterosaurs (the 'p' is silent) dominated the skies. Reptiles also returned to the sea in the form of fish-eating ichthyosaurs and plesiosaurs. All this reptilian diversity collapsed at the K–T boundary, to be replaced on an unprecedented scale by mammals and birds.

Comparative anatomy has allowed palaeontologists to reconstruct the evolutionary radiation of mammals (Figure 3.20), aided by many surviving mammalian orders. Their anatomy can be used to backtrack to the skeletal features in possible ancestors, and to identify groups that have no surviving counterparts. However, the evolutionary trail of mammals almost goes cold in rocks older than the K–T mass extinction. The slender threads of relatedness before 65 Ma in Figure 3.20 reflect most Mesozoic mammals having been

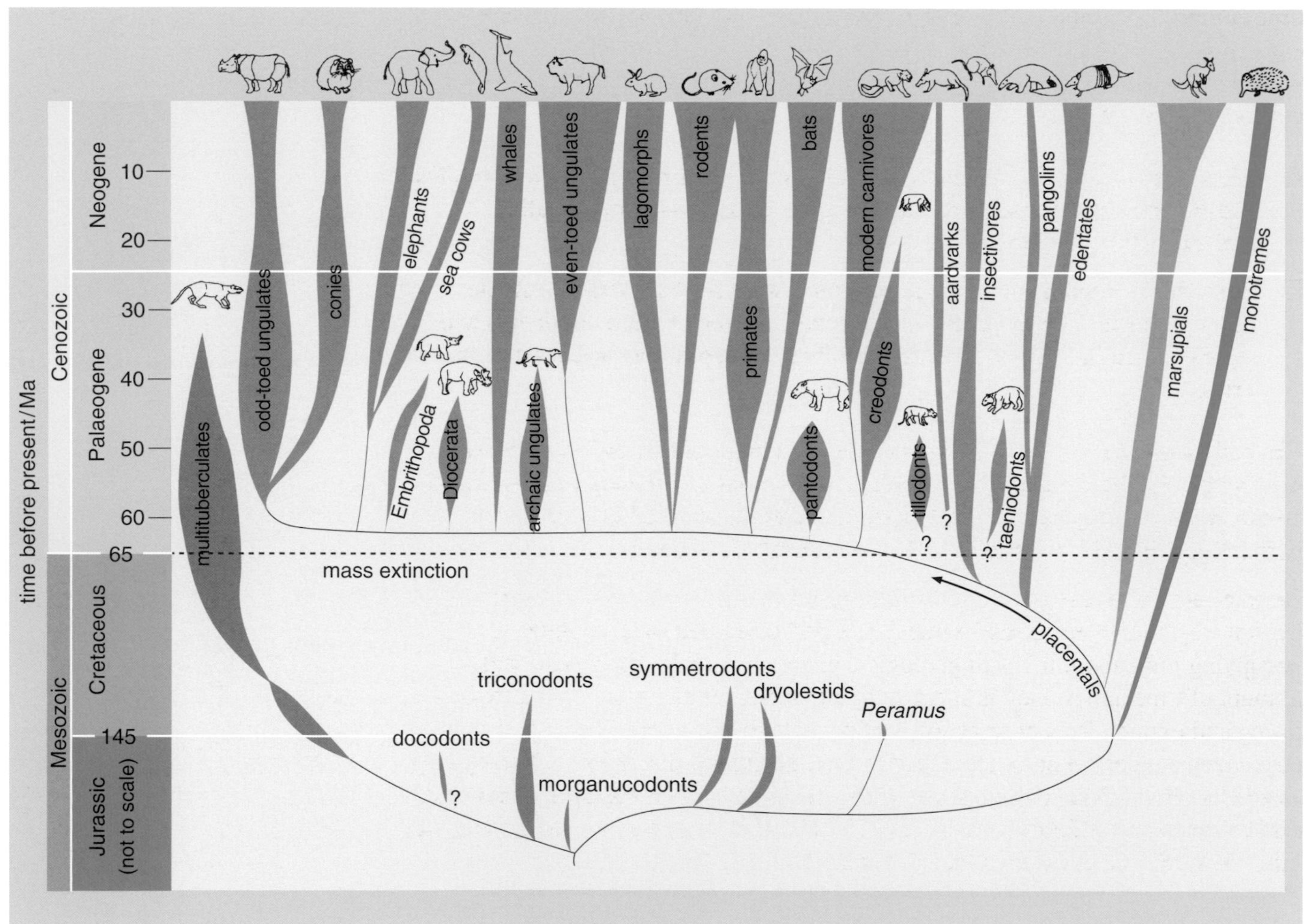

Figure 3.20 Evolutionary radiation of mammals (the divisions are by Linnaean order). Again, the varying width of each order reflects diversity through the number of families.

mouse-sized and difficult to find as complete skeletons. Their division relies mainly on the shapes and distribution of teeth on isolated tiny jaw bones: the names of most orders end in 'odont' (the Greek for 'toothed'). You are not expected to recall all the names of orders!

- ■ What is the most striking feature of the branching pattern in Figure 3.20?
- □ Every order of placental mammals (except for sea cows) appears in the fossil record only a few Ma after the K–T mass extinction.

The simplest explanation for this sudden appearance of diversity may be that branching into more than 20 mammalian orders took place long before 60 Ma, and there simply aren't any fossils, because the creatures were small. That might explain the gap in time between the 'odonts' of the Upper Jurassic and Lower Cretaceous and modern orders. Another approach is to apply the adage 'Nature abhors a vacuum'. With the wiping out of the dominant and highly diverse dinosaur predators and herbivores, many niches were vacant after the mass extinction. Perhaps the seemingly sudden diversification of placental mammals was in response to that. However, there was another important factor, which is covered in Book 2, Section 7.1.

- ■ What was different about land masses between the time amphibians, reptiles and the earliest mammals appeared (Figure 3.19) and the mammalian radiation of the Cenozoic?
- □ From the Devonian until the Triassic, almost all the land was in a single supercontinent – Pangaea. By the Cenozoic, all the modern continents had separated after sea-floor spreading had begun to split Pangaea apart in the Triassic.

The early mammals became divided among and increasingly isolated on seven moving continental masses. They could have diversified independently on each continent by processes such as allopatric speciation, genetic bottlenecks and perhaps genetic drift as conditions changed (Book 5, Chapter 14).

Humans are by far the most interesting species that has ever lived. Despite human origins having formed a minuscule part of evolution as a whole, and occupying only about 0.1% of geological history, a hugely disproportionate amount of time and money is spent studying ourselves and other primates, both living and extinct. Recent re-analysis of primate fossils combined with molecular phylogeny suggests a common ancestor for all primates that lived as long ago as 85 Ma. Such a long evolutionary history helps to explain the considerable differences between lorises, bush babies and lemurs, on the one hand, and all the other living primates on the other (Figure 3.21a).

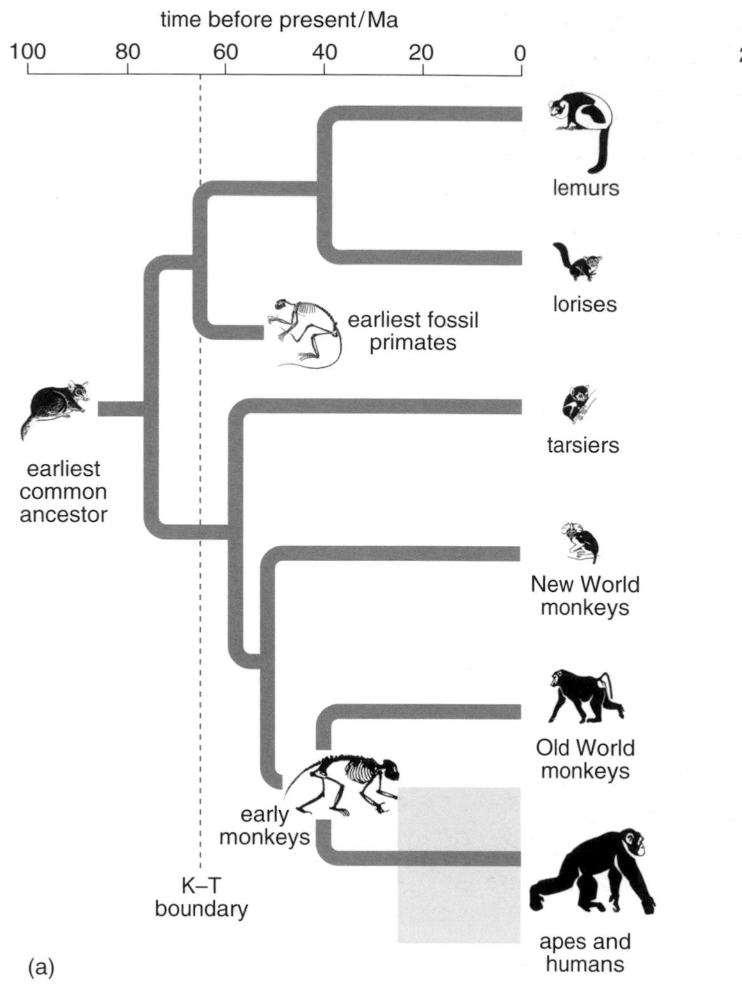
time before present/Ma
100
80
60
40
20
0
lemurs
lorises
earliest fossil primates
tarsiers
earliest common ancestor
New World monkeys
Old World monkeys
early monkeys
apes and humans
K–T boundary
(a)

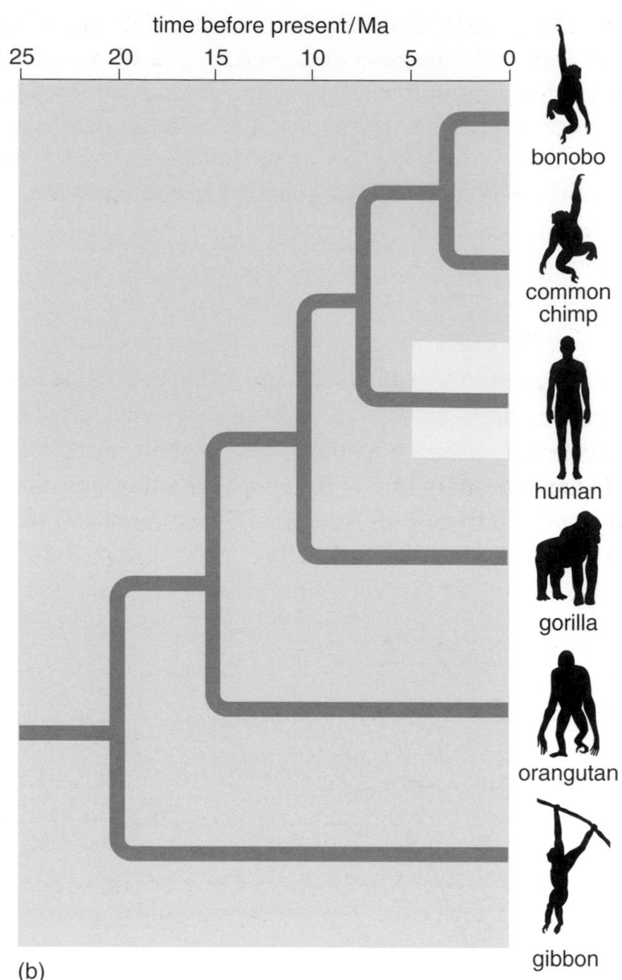
time before present/Ma
25
20
15
10
5
0
bonobo
common chimp
human
gorilla
orangutan
gibbon
(b)

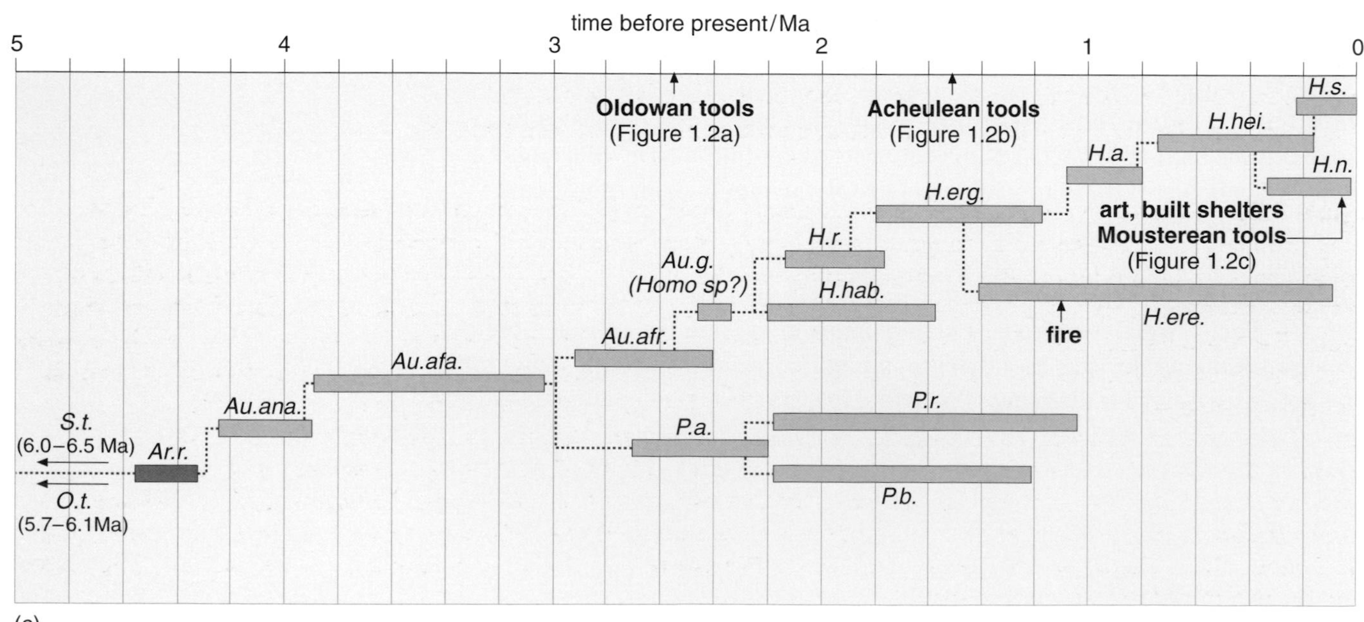
time before present/Ma
5
4
3
2
1
0
Oldowan tools (Figure 1.2a)
Acheulean tools (Figure 1.2b)
H.s.
H.hei.
H.a.
H.n.
H.erg.
art, built shelters
Mousterean tools
(Figure 1.2c)
H.r.
Au.g. (Homo sp?)
H.hab.
H.ere.
fire
Au.afr.
Au.afa.
Au.ana.
P.r.
P.a.
P.b.
S.t. (6.0–6.5 Ma)
Ar.r.
O.t. (5.7–6.1Ma)
(c)

Molecular phylogeny produces a tree of relatedness between living members of the family Hominidae: apes and gibbons (Figure 3.21b). The molecular clock approach suggests that the branching that led to humans and chimpanzees occurred roughly 7 Ma ago, to gorillas at around 10 Ma, orangutans about 15 Ma and gibbons at 20 Ma. Humans, chimps and gorillas are referred to as hominins (members of the tribe Hominini). The questions asked of hominin phylogeny are not the same as for others. They centre on: which creature first walked upright with hands fully freed to manipulate its environment; who made the first tools; and when did consciousness and language arise? That is, they focus on the origin of 'humanness'.

Genetics cannot supply answers to those kinds of question, and understanding our origins depends on a scanty hominin fossil record. Weathering and erosion easily destroy primate remains, despite their moderate size. Fossils older than 1 Ma are extremely rare and, except for a few, consist of little more than teeth and jaw-bone fragments, scraps of the cranium and pieces of long limb bones. Just over a thousand such fossils cover the 6 Ma history of hominin evolution (Figure 3.21c), 700 of which date back only to 1 Ma.

This is not the place either to detail the species of fossil hominins or to discuss current views on how they can be interpreted – Figure 3.21c is but one of many interpretations. Two questions are partially answered by the bones. Fossils of both *Homo rudolfensis* and *Homo habilis* ('Handy Man') are directly associated with rudimentary stone tools, but they were not the first to make them. The first stone tools, unaccompanied by fossil hominins, occur in Ethiopian sediments between 2.4 and 2.6 Ma old. They *might* have been made by the rare *Australopithecus garhi*. If that were proved, those hominins would surely be renamed as the first members of the genus *Homo*.

Fragments of skulls, pelvises and leg and toe bones can give clues to whether or not their former owner walked upright. Figure 1.1 shows clearly that *Australopithecus afarensis* did have a bipedal gait. However, look closely at Figure 1.1, and you may see that in some of the footprints, there is a gap between the big toe and other toes; *A. afarensis* had feet that could grip, and was probably a nimble tree climber as well. Older fossils cannot prove bipedalism conclusively, yet most experts believe *Ardepithecus* had acquired the ability by 4.6 Ma. Debate

Figure 3.21 Primate evolution. (a) The evolutionary branching of the primates. Research on the genetics of living primates and close relatives suggests, surprisingly, that the common Cretaceous ancestor of all primates had similar genes to the modern flying lemurs or colugos of SE Asia. (b) The phylogenetic tree of living members of the family Hominidae, based on DNA. (c) One interpretation of hominin evolution during the last 5 Ma, based on fossils. The known timespan of each species is shown by the bars. The species of *Paranthropus* were similar in some respects to those of *Australopithecus*, but had more rugged skulls and jaws and probably fed on woody vegetation and hard seeds rather than a softer, more mixed diet. (The following abbreviations are used in part (c): *Ar.r.* – *Ardepithecus ramidus*; *Au.afa.* – *Australopithecus afarensis*; *Au.afr.* – *Australopithecus africanus*; *Au.ana.* – *Australopithecus anamensis*; *Au.g.* – *Australopithecus garhi*; *H.a.* – *Homo antecessor*; *H.ere.* – *Homo erectus*; *H.erg.* – *Homo ergaster*; *H.hab.* – *Homo habilis*; *H.hei.* – *Homo heidelburgensis*; *H.n.* – *Homo neanderthalensis*; *H.r.* – *Homo rudolphensis*; *H.s.* – *Homo sapiens*; *O.t.* – *Orrorin tugenensis*; *P.a.* – *Paranthropus aethiopicus*; *P.b.* – *Paranthropus boisei*; *P.r.* – *Paranthropus robustus*; *S.t.* – *Sahelanthropus tchadensis*.) The colours show the extent of the three timespans.

rages about the abilities of the earlier *Orrorin tugenensis* (5.7–6.1 Ma), found in Kenya, and *Sahelanthropus tchadensis* (6.0–6.5 Ma) from Chad. *Sahelanthropus* lived close enough to the time of the last common ancestor of humans and chimps, to possibly be that common ancestor.

Chapter 8 returns to hominins in the context of the environmental conditions that exerted selection pressures and opportunities during their evolution. Those conditions can only be judged for the distant past from the record in sedimentary rocks, the subject of Chapter 5. First, there is a major change of emphasis: all matter in the Earth's surface environment emerged at some stage in the past from the mantle, by way of igneous processes. This is the focus of Chapter 4.

3.6 Summary of Chapter 3

The timing of the emergence of life is highly uncertain. The oldest undisputed fossils occur in 2100 Ma rocks, which are less than half the Earth's age. However, organic compounds that are biomarkers occur in rocks dated at about 3500 Ma, which also contain stromatolites which may have been formed by photosynthesising cyanobacteria that produce oxygen. Together they give a minimum age for the origin of life, as do carbon-isotope studies.

Precambrian life had several dramatic upheavals but, until about 650 Ma, they are revealed by little more than variations in the carbon isotopes in limestones; single-celled life was rarely preserved as fossils. About 2400 Ma ago the surface environment changed profoundly from reducing conditions to oxidising conditions, by the appearance of oxygen in the atmosphere. Prokaryotic cyanobacteria – stromatolite builders – were probably responsible, and made it possible for oxygen-dependent eukaryote cells to evolve.

The first abundant fossils are traces left in sedimentary rocks by large, soft animals – the Ediacaran fauna – towards the end of the Precambrian. True body fossils follow in a rush after 542 Ma; the first organisms with hard parts mark the beginning of the Cambrian. Although in terms of numbers this was an explosive biological development, the molecular phylogeny of animal phyla suggests that there were fundamental evolutionary divisions long before the Cambrian.

Hard parts created intense competition based on 'armour versus arms', but also opened a wealth of ecological niches for suitably equipped animals. This kind of competition established the basic selection pressures for animal diversification, and repeated Phanerozoic adaptive radiations. However, evolution did not run smoothly. The record of animal families shows five sudden plunges in numbers, and numerous lesser mass extinctions. One of these, at the end of the Permian, saw a permanent collapse in the life forms that had dominated the Palaeozoic Era. Their decimation allowed survivors of a minority group of classes and orders that lived in the Palaeozoic to radiate into vacated niches, and create a wide diversity of new ones. This Modern fauna dominated animal life through the Mesozoic and Cenozoic Eras.

The cause of one of the Big Five mass extinctions – the K–T event 65 Ma ago – has two candidates: a major impact and flood-basalt volcanism occurring at the same time. Perhaps they both contributed. Although other mass extinctions in the last 250 Ma seem to coincide in time with other major igneous pulses, details reveal only four flood-basalt events that may have been causal, but one is the largest known, at the end of the Permian. There are other possible causes of the necessary environmental changes for sudden collapses in diversity. However, the only certainty is that mass extinctions occurred repeatedly.

Each mass extinction was followed by adaptive radiation of the surviving faunas. The phylogenies of many groups, especially vertebrates, show signs of the influence of random catastrophes in the history of life. The radiation and evolution of vertebrates also benefited from the colonisation of the land surface by plants, largely after 400 Ma. This transferred the base of a food chain to a previously inhospitable environment for all animals.

Molecular phylogeny, with its provision of a crude 'molecular clock', when applied to vertebrates suggests that primates, including our distant forebears, evolved about 85 Ma ago. Its most powerful influence has been in establishing a rough timing of the common ape ancestor that our more immediate forebears shared with chimpanzees. Along that hominin branch novelties emerged: a permanent upright gait; hands free to manipulate; the invention and development of tools; consciousness and language. None of these attributes is an objective means of establishing phylogeny, but the sole surviving 'twig' is us.

Your study of this chapter involved: comparing information given in figures, diagrams and graphs; describing and interpreting that information, particularly developing generalisations from a wide range of information; summarising and briefly communicating your findings. You have also assessed the quality of data in the context of their level of support for hypotheses.

Chapter 4
Igneous rocks formed from molten magma

Some important rock-forming processes are introduced in this chapter and in Chapters 5 and 6. They also show how you can deduce the processes that formed rocks from particular features in them. Applying such deductions to rocks arranged in a time sequence (Chapter 2) helps us to understand the evolution of geological conditions at places now at the Earth's surface. Geological histories from many places form the basis for reconstructing past geography and plate tectonics, up to global scale. This broad approach has allowed geoscientists to reconstruct a graphic picture of how the Earth has worked throughout geological time.

Deducing processes that involve molten magma are considered first because, ultimately, except for tiny amounts from meteorites, all materials that now form sedimentary and metamorphic rocks emerged from the mantle as constituents of magma. Heat from within the Earth drives convection in the deep mantle, and is responsible for any melting in the upper mantle and crust. The formation of magmas, their emplacement and crystallisation involve igneous processes at divergent and convergent plate margins, and above hot spots within plates (Book 2, Chapters 8 and 9). Older crustal rocks are transformed by chemical reorganisation of their constituent minerals if pressure and/or temperature rise sufficiently. Added to these metamorphic processes is the deformation of rocks by the enormous plate-tectonic stresses to which they may be exposed. Tectonics also directly affects erosion and the supply of materials that end up in sedimentary rocks. (Both of these topics are covered in Chapters 5 and 6.)

Before proceeding, check that you can recall from Book 2, Chapter 5 the means of distinguishing specimens of igneous, sedimentary and metamorphic rocks from differences in their texture.

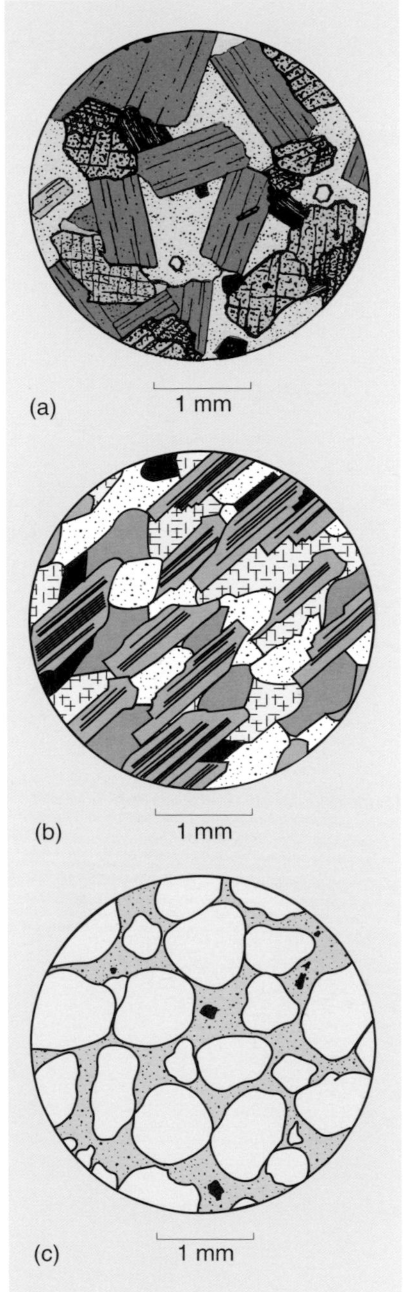

Figure 4.1 Three rock textures seen through a microscope, which are typical of each fundamental division of rocks (Book 2, Activity 5.1). The different shading represents different types of mineral.

■ Describe the shapes of grains and the relationships between the grains shown in the sketches in Figure 4.1. Which sketch represents: (i) a sedimentary rock; (ii) an igneous rock; (iii) a metamorphic rock?

□ (i) Figure 4.1c consists of rounded to angular grains and the spaces between them are filled with smaller grains. It shows a *fragmental* texture, typical of a sedimentary rock (Specimens 2 and 3, the sandstone and limestone in the Practical Kit); (ii) Figure 4.1a shows angular grains that are interlocking and intergrown. Moreover, the grains have no particular orientation; they are randomly oriented. This *random, interlocking crystalline* texture is typical of an igneous rock (Specimens 5 and 6, the basalt and granite, in the Practical Kit); (iii) Figure 4.1b also shows interlocking and intergrown grains, but elongated ones are roughly parallel. This *aligned, interlocking crystalline* texture is typical of a metamorphic rock (Specimen 4, the schist, in the Practical Kit).

You may have seen different rock types at the coast, along road cuttings or in mountains. Without knowing what to look for, you may have been unsure how to distinguish them. In fact, rocks provide more information about their origins than this basic, threefold classification. More varieties in each of the three main categories can be distinguished not only from textures but also from the minerals that rocks contain and give vital clues to how the rocks formed.

In Activities 3.1 and 4.1 in Book 4 you saw the crystal structures of the minerals halite (NaCl), a natural ionic solid, and quartz (SiO_2), a natural molecular solid. In doing those activities, you discovered that the chemical structures of minerals exert controls on their physical properties, which are easily observed. This is the point where you need to expand your knowledge of minerals and the skills needed to distinguish them.

4.1 The minerals in igneous rocks

The dominance in the outer Earth of the elements oxygen and silicon (Book 4, Section 2.1) more or less guarantees that the minerals making up the bulk of the crust and mantle must be based on silicon and oxygen in combination; they will be **silicates** of some kind. Being able to distinguish the main groups of rock-forming silicates from their observable properties will help you to understand processes in the rock cycle that create different kinds of rock. Quartz is a good place to start looking at silicate minerals (Book 4, Activity 4.1). Its basic 'building block' – a SiO_4^{4-} tetrahedron – is involved in all other silicates. Unlike quartz, the other silicates contain elements in addition to silicon and oxygen. Depending on what those elements are, the physical properties of these other silicate mineral groups differ from those of quartz because of the effect of additional elements on their molecular structure. So, a mineral's physical properties give clues to its structure and, in turn, that structure broadly conveys a mineral's chemical composition.

Activity 4.1 Igneous minerals: examining silicates

We expect this activity will take you approximately 60 minutes.

To help you with identifying minerals in Practical Kit specimens of igneous rock, this activity takes you through the structures and some physical properties of common silicates. It involves two computer-based resources: *Minerals Gallery* and *Mineral Properties*. The gallery is on DVD 1 and the properties on DVD 2.

As you work through the four tasks, fill in the rows of Table 4.1 at the end of this activity for each silicate mineral group you examine. The one for quartz is already completed.

The physical property of mineral cleavage (or lack of it) relates to regular arrangements of weak bonding in crystal structures. Ionic crystals of halite (NaCl) have extremely regular alignments of weak bonds, and so possess excellent cleavage in three sets at right angles; they are also soft and will not scratch glass (Book 4, Activity 3.1). Molecular crystals of quartz (SiO_2) have a strong structure that links covalent Si—O bonds in a complex 3D network, based on spiral connections between SiO_4^{4-} tetrahedra and sharing of oxygen atoms between adjacent spirals (Book 4, Activity 4.1). This strength confers on quartz crystals a greater *hardness* than that of glass, and a *lack* of cleavage.

Review Activities 3.1 and 4.1 in Book 4 first, if you can't recall these relationships.

Task 1 Feldspars

Open the computer-based resource *Minerals Gallery*: select feldspar and its structure tab. From the list below 'Explore the feldspar structure', start with the first option.

As well as SiO_4^{4-} tetrahedra, **feldspars** also contain aluminium atoms that bond covalently with oxygen as tetrahedral AlO_4^{5-} groups; note their –5 charge. Effectively, the similarity in size between Si and Al atoms allows aluminium to substitute for silicon, despite its different number of outer-shell electrons. In the feldspar structure this substitution is in a regular arrangement.

Move to the third option (tetrahedra joined by a 'crankshaft').

The charge difference between the SiO_4^{4-} and AlO_4^{5-} tetrahedra changes their arrangement from the spirals of quartz to a *crankshaft*.

Move to the fourth option (large cavities between crankshafts).

Three-dimensional linkage of Si—O and Al—O bonds between the crankshafts in feldspar leaves charge imbalances. These allow atoms of K, Na and Ca into the structure, to balance the charge. These metals bond to AlO_4^{5-} tetrahedra in a weak but regular fashion; such regularly aligned weaknesses define cleavage planes.

Rotate the structure and suggest how many cleavages feldspars might have.

The K, Na or Ca atoms define three marked alignments of weak bonds, two at right angles and one oblique to the others.

Now review the properties of feldspars under its Properties tab. This shows various diagnostic properties of minerals (the computer-based resource *Mineral Properties* explains properties in more detail). Use it to fill in the feldspar row in Table 4.1.

Task 2 Micas

Select mica and its structure tab. Start with the third option in the 'Explore the mica structure' list.

The basic structure of **micas** is very different from the 3D framework of quartz and feldspars. SiO_4^{4-} tetrahedra in micas share Si–O bonds only at the base of each tetrahedron, to create a giant molecular structure that spreads out as a 2D sheet.

Move to the fourth option.

Aluminium also enters the mica structure but, instead of being bonded to four oxygens, each Al atom is shared by six O atoms, to give AlO_6^{9-} which takes on an octahedral (eight-faced) form. In white mica, AlO_6^{9-} octahedra share oxygens with the corners of SiO_4^{4-} tetrahedra to bond the silicate sheets in a 'sandwich'. In dark-coloured micas, iron and magnesium enter the structure, in octahedral combination with oxygen, to join AlO_6^{9-} in the sandwich 'filling'.

Move to the fifth option.

Clearly, with Al, Fe and Mg being able to join with Si and O in the silicate structure of mica, there are several options for charge imbalance and the entry of yet more metals to balance them. In mica, this role is usually filled by potassium atoms, weakly bonded to two adjoining Si–O–Al(–Fe–Mg) 'sandwiches'. It is hardly surprising that micas have one good cleavage; cleaved sheets can be so thin that once they were used as window panes. Thin cleavage sheets are surprisingly strong and flexible along their length.

Now review the properties of micas under the properties tab and fill in the appropriate row in Table 4.1.

Task 3 Pyroxenes

Select pyroxene and its structure tab. Start with the third option.

The structure of **pyroxenes** is based on the linkage of SiO_4^{4-} tetrahedra in zigzag *chains* by Si–O bond sharing. *Note*: only a part of one pyroxene chain is shown.

Move to the fourth and fifth options.

Octahedral groups of Fe or Mg and O balance charge by bonding two chains of SiO_4^{4-} tetrahedra to form 'I-beams'. Some pyroxenes also incorporate calcium in their structure, depending on its availability in the magma.

The chain structure dominates the physical properties of pyroxenes. Although they are hard minerals, the I-beams control two planes of weak bonding and therefore two cleavages at about 90°.

Now review the properties of pyroxenes under the properties tab and fill in the appropriate row in Table 4.1.

Task 4 Olivines

Select olivine and its structure tab. As above, start with the third and fourth options and proceed to the fifth.

Olivine has the lowest silicon content of all the common igneous silicates. There is insufficient silicon for SiO_4^{4-} tetrahedra to link up by sharing Si–O bonds, so the SiO_4^{4-} tetrahedra exist in the olivine structure as isolated groups. Charge is balanced by bond sharing with octahedra of Fe or Mg bonded with O. The linkage between such octahedra and SiO_4^{4-} tetrahedra fills space efficiently to give a strong set of covalent bonds in all directions.

■ Would you expect olivine to be soft and to have cleavage(s)?

□ No, despite its very different composition, olivine is similar to quartz in its multidirectional bonding; it is strong and does not have any cleavage.

Now review the properties of olivine under the properties tab and fill in the appropriate row in Table 4.1.

Table 4.1 Main chemical and physical properties of some common rock-forming silicate minerals.

Mineral	Classification	Composition	Colour	Lustre	Cleavage	Shape	Hardness
Quartz	Silicate (framework)	SiO_2	Mainly colourless – can be coloured	Glassy	None (irregular fracture)	Prismatic	7
Feldspar	Silicate (framework)	Alkali feldspar, $(K,Na)AlSi_3O_8$ Plagioclase, from $NaAlSi_3O_8$ to $CaAl_2Si_2O_8$	Colorless or white, pink red or green	glassy to dull	2	Prismatic	6–6.5
Mica	Silicate (sheet)	Pale (muscovite) $KAl_3Si_3O_{10}(OH)_2$ Dark (biotite) $K(Fe,Mg)_3AlSi_3O_{10}(OH)_2$	brown, black silvery	glassy or pearly	One	Platy crystals	2.5
Pyroxene	Silicate (single chain)	$(Ca,Mg,Fe)_2Si_2O_6$	dk green to black	dull to glassy	2	Stubby Prismatic	5.5–6
Olivine	Silicate (isolated group)	$(Mg,Fe)_2SiO_4$	Pale green to dark	glassy	none	– ''	6.5–7

Before you move on, make sure you check your entries in Table 4.1 with those in the comments on this activity at the end of this book.

Question 4.1

How might you distinguish between the two minerals in each of the following pairs using *one* mineral property that is the most distinctively different between the two (colour, shape, lustre, cleavage or hardness)? (a) Quartz and feldspar; (b) dark mica and pyroxene.

In Section 4.2.2, you will use what you learned in Activity 4.1 to identify some of the minerals in common igneous rocks, and to use them to get a rough idea of the chemical composition of those rocks.

4.2 The diversity of igneous rocks

Book 2, Chapter 4 introduced igneous processes through their best known and most spectacular manifestation – volcanoes.

■ Which types of plate boundary involve igneous processes? Are there any igneous processes that are not obviously related to plate motions?

□ Magmas form beneath divergent plate boundaries to give rise to new oceanic lithosphere and at convergent plate boundaries where old oceanic lithosphere is subducted into the mantle. Magmas also form within plates over hot spots which seem to be associated with mantle plumes rising from far below the base of the lithosphere and not related to plate motion.

Igneous rocks form at divergent plate boundaries from magma newly and directly derived from the mantle. They add to oceanic lithosphere through sea-floor spreading (Book 2, Section 7.3). Those formed at convergent plate margins, intimately connected with subduction, may involve melting of the overriding mantle and, if subduction is beneath a continental margin, the continental crust. Igneous rocks formed at hot spots are new additions to the outer Earth.

In Book 2, Activity 5.1 you compared hand specimens of two different kinds of igneous rock (Specimens 5 and 6: basalt and granite). This involved noting their different grain sizes and other textural features, and comparing their overall colours. Two important points you should have appreciated after completing the activity, are:

- Overall grain size indicates how quickly a magma cooled and crystallised; the coarser it is, the more slowly it cooled, and vice versa.
- The overall lightness or darkness of an igneous rock stems from the relative proportions of light and dark minerals that make up the rock.

Activity 4.2 Basalt and granite: revision of Book 2

We expect this activity will take you approximately 15 minutes.

The aim of this activity is to revise the important visible properties of these rocks.

Safety warning

Read the whole of this section before starting the activity and make sure that you have read the section on 'Practical activities' in the *Course Guide*.

When carrying out practical activities, you should always take care to observe the simple safety precautions highlighted in the course book. Very often, as in the case of this activity, these precautions will seem quite obvious and just a matter of using common sense. However that does not mean that you should ignore the safety instructions. The Open University has a duty to give advice on health and safety to students carrying out any activities that are described in the course. Similarly, *you* have a duty to follow the instructions and to carry out the practical activity having regard for your own safety and that of other people around you. Whenever you do practical activities you should think about the hazards involved, and how any risks can be minimised.

Important safety precautions

Take note of the following safety precautions, which apply to all practical activities:

- Keep children and animals away while you are working, as they may attempt to eat the rock specimens.
- Clear your working area of clutter. Put all food away. Ensure there is nothing to trip on underfoot.
- Always wash your hands thoroughly after a practical activity.
- Any household items used should be thoroughly cleaned before returning them to domestic use.

Precautions when handling rock and mineral specimens from the Practical Kit

Take care when handling the rock and mineral specimens not to touch your eyes. Some rock dust can be an irritant. If you get dust in your eye, wash it out with copious amounts of water for at least 5 minutes. If irritation persists seek medical help.

Equipment needed

Kit items

Rock Specimens 5 and 6

Hand lens

Non-kit items

Ruler marked in millimetres

Large steel nail

Task 1 Distinguishing rock types – rock textures

Examine the basalt (Specimen 5) and granite (Specimen 6) samples. In particular, use your hand lens to look closely at the shapes of the grains that make up each rock and how they are arranged (i.e. the texture of the samples). Also, try to prise out a few grains with the point of the nail. How do you know these samples are igneous rocks?

Task 2 Distinguishing igneous rocks – colour and grain size

(a) Observe the overall appearance side-by-side of the basalt and granite samples, and note particularly their colour and their grain size. Make a note of the ways in which they differ.

(b) Which of your observations – of colour or of grain size – might tell you about differences in the mineral content of the rocks, and which might suggest how the rocks crystallised? Which sample is an extrusive rock, and which is an intrusive rock?

Keep Specimens 5 and 6 to hand for Activity 4.3. Now read the comments on this activity at the end of this book before continuing.

The mainly fine-grained texture of the basalt suggests that it is probably an *extrusive* igneous rock, having cooled and crystallised quickly. (Note that magma sometimes cools so quickly that crystals do not develop and it solidifies as a natural *glass*.) The granite is a typical *intrusive* igneous rock, its coarse grain size signifying slow cooling and crystallisation. The overall colour depends on which minerals make up an igneous rock. The types and proportions of those minerals help subdivide igneous rocks according to the chemical composition of the magma from which they crystallised (see Section 4.2.3).

Useful as they are in deducing how rocks formed, hand specimens are mere samples from large exposures of rock. Field observations of large-scale features provide more information about how a rock formed, the processes involved and sometimes the overall conditions in which they operated.

4.2.1 More clues from igneous rocks

Volcanic cones may be the most familiar forms of extrusive igneous rocks, but they are not the only ones produced by extrusive igneous activity (Book 2, Chapter 4). Moreover, they do not survive erosion once their activity stops. The most common extrusive igneous rocks found in the geological record are those which spread far from the source of eruption. Depending on their chemical composition, magmas vary in their viscosity. Viscous ones cannot flow far as lavas before crystallising, and they tend to produce the classic (conical) volcanoes. More fluid magmas – generally of basaltic composition – move rapidly, even down gently sloping surfaces. The resulting lava flows may extend for many kilometres to form layers. How far they extend and the area which such lavas cover depend on the volume of magma produced during each pulse of activity. The biggest cover tens of thousands of square kilometres and, if many flows pile up, they form the aptly named flood basalts (Figure 4.2a) which you met in Section 3.3.2. The best-known lava flow in the British Isles crystallised from such a basalt flood, and forms the Giant's Causeway (Figure 4.2b). Its peculiar structure of regular, polygonal columns resulted from very regular contraction as it cooled after the lava had solidified.

(a)

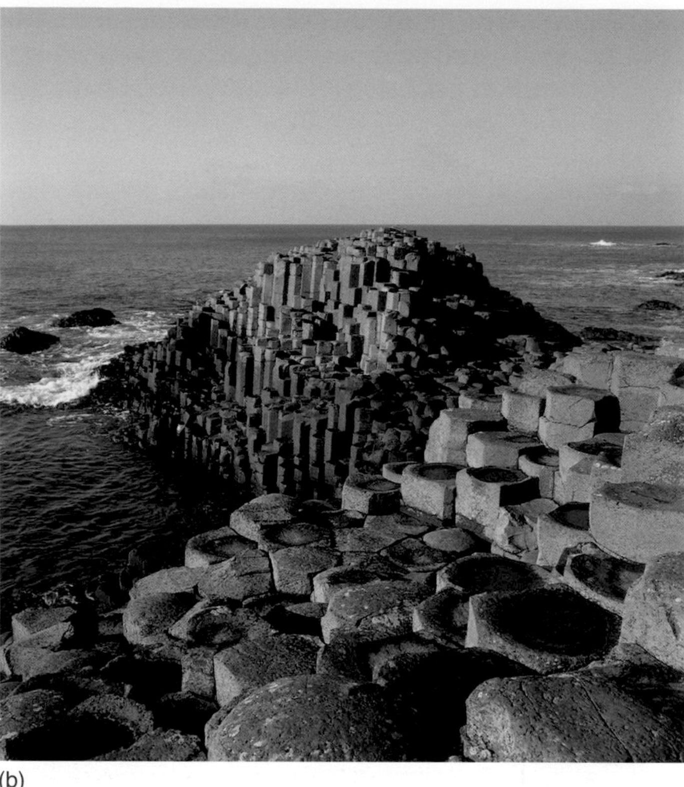
(b)

Figure 4.2 Lava flows produced by fluid magmas. (a) Two kilometres of individual basalt lava flows (each a few metres thick) make up the Simien Mountains in northern Ethiopia. (b) The eroded form of a basalt lava flow at the Giant's Causeway in Co. Antrim, Northern Ireland, which shows polygonal columns formed by shrinkage during cooling.

Many of the lavas that appear in the geological record were erupted on dry land, but some show clear evidence of having erupted beneath water bodies.

■ What special feature characterises sub-aqueous lavas?

□ They contain pillow-like structures (Figure 3.1) which begin to form as water chills the surface of effusing magma to form a skin. This bulges to form the distinctive pillow shape, and then breaks to release another lobe of magma. Instead of a distinct lava flow, the activity is represented by an accumulation of bulbous pillows (Book 2, Figure 7.4b).

Layers of pyroclastic material that fall from clouds of dust and ash released by explosive eruptions may blanket hundreds to thousands of square kilometres, thinning outwards from the centre of an eruption. Looking superficially like sedimentary rocks, volcanic ash layers can be distinguished by their crystals of igneous silicate minerals, and often shards of volcanic glass – magma suddenly chilled after an explosive eruption.

Although volcanic eruptions show clearly that parts of the Earth's interior melt to produce magmas, *where* the magmas form is not so clear from surface observations. Magma must also find a way to the surface somehow, and that too is unclear. To find evidence that suggests how magma moves from its source to the surface, and what happens to magma that did not escape, requires observations from the geological record. Erosion may expose old *intrusive* igneous bodies that crystallised deep within the Earth. Such bodies often cut across older rocks and structures within them, proving that they did indeed form by the intrusion of magma (Section 2.4.1).

Closely packed, vertical **dykes** of basalt are known feeders for the pillow lavas in oceanic crust (Book 2, Section 8.5). In continental crust, isolated dykes cut across older rocks (Figure 4.3). Some dykes occur in eroded volcanoes and suggest that they fed magma to eruptions. A sheet-like intrusion *between* individual layers of older rocks, which lies parallel to the layering is called a **sill**. A few show intrusive relationships in detail (Figure 4.3c), but it is easy to mistake a sill for an interlayered lava flow. Figure 4.3b shows schematically how dykes and sills may be related to one pulse of magma intrusion.

Figure 4.3 Minor intrusive bodies. (a) Dark basaltic dyke cutting across shallow-dipping fractures in a light granite on the island of Lundy, southwest England (the dyke is younger than both the granite and the fractures). (b) Dykes and sills that formed at the same time and intruded older sedimentary rocks. (c) The lower contact of a basaltic sill with sedimentary strata on Salisbury Crags, Edinburgh (the image is about 1.5 m high). Proof of intrusion is visible at the centre where the featureless pale brown basalt cuts across, partly envelopes and has uplifted layered sedimentary rock. This occurrence was one of the first to be recognised as evidence for igneous intrusion, by James Hutton in the late 18th century.

■ Suggest how, apart from local cross-cutting relationships, a basaltic sill could be distinguished from a lava flow with identical composition.

□ One distinguishing feature would be their top surfaces: weathering will have broken down the exposed top of a lava flow, whereas both the top and the bottom of an intrusive sill will be fresh, having formed in contact with existing rocks. Rocks adjacent to hot magma are baked or even metamorphosed. A lava flow would bake only those rocks below it; a sill would affect those above and below it.

Uplift and erosion of many kilometres of overlying rock can expose large igneous bodies that crystallised deep in the crust. These **plutons** (named after the Greek god of the underworld, Pluto) have volumes of tens to thousands of cubic kilometres (Figure 4.4a). At the high temperatures in the deep crust, magma cools very slowly, so that *plutonic* igneous rocks are always coarse grained. Typical plutons cut across older sedimentary rocks, and those of southwest England occur at the surface as irregular 'tors' (Figure 4.4b).

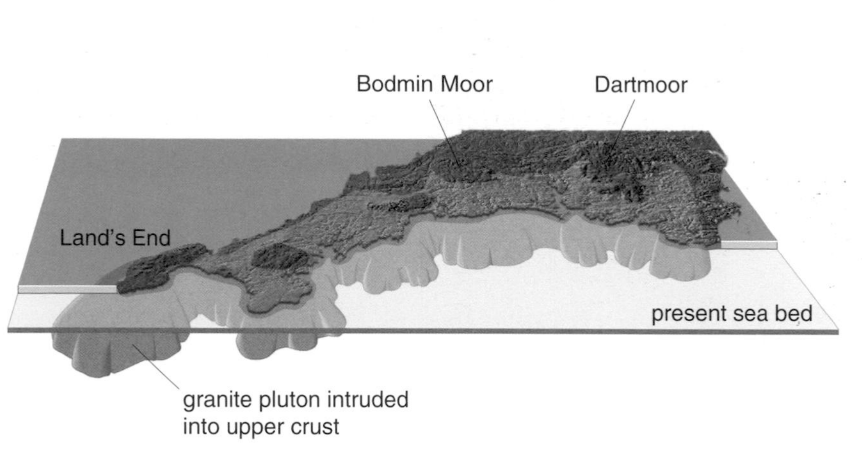

Figure 4.4 The granite plutons of southwest England: (a) showing in 3D how the surface occurrences (red) connect to a much larger body (brown) at depth; (b) exposed near Land's End in a tor.

The mainly fine-grained basalt in the Practical Kit contains a few much larger crystals; a duality of grain size that is known as a **porphyritic** texture. Such a relationship seems to contradict the notion of rapid cooling and crystallisation of extrusive igneous rocks. There is a simple explanation. Often before eruption occurs, large volumes of magma accumulate in a magma chamber (Book 2, Section 4.4), eventually to form a pluton. Entirely molten at first, the cooling magma would slowly start to crystallise. Upward movement of the partly solidified magma would carry some early-crystallising minerals with it. Intrusion of this melt plus crystal mixture at higher crustal levels in thin dykes and sills, or its eruption as lava, would involve more rapid cooling and crystallisation of the molten fraction. The solidified rock would therefore have a finely crystalline part, or groundmass, that envelops the older, larger crystals. Porphyritic igneous rocks (called **porphyries**) thereby carry some important information about the history of the magma before it solidified (Section 4.3).

Question 4.2

Figure 4.5 shows several igneous rocks which formed under different circumstances. Briefly describe the texture of each of them. How and under what circumstances do you think they may have formed?

Figure 4.5 Igneous rocks with different textures and grain sizes (note the different widths of the fields of view): (a) granite (80 mm); (b) feldspar porphyry (containing distinctive crystals of feldspar) (90 mm); (c) rhyolite (70 mm); (d) pumice (100 mm); (e) obsidian (50 mm).

4.2.2 The chemical composition of igneous rocks

Distinguishing igneous rocks, for instance the porphyry from the granite in Figure 4.5, from their different grain sizes and textures is one aspect of classification. Discovering the types and proportions of the minerals in an igneous rock is the basis for classifying rocks according to their chemical composition.

Three of the rocks in Figure 4.5 (a, b and c) are dominated by crystals of quartz, alkali feldspar and plagioclase feldspar; the other two – pumice (d) and obsidian (e) – are glassy and don't contain crystals. Remarkably, although the five rocks look very different, they all have essentially the same chemical composition, i.e. very similar percentages of different elements. Each of them could have solidified under different physical circumstances from the same chemical type of magma.

The chemical differences of igneous rocks frequently relate to how and where magma forms. The basalt and granite in the Practical Kit have quite different grain sizes and so crystallised in quite different circumstances. But are they chemically different?

Activity 4.3 The mineral content and composition of basalt and granite

We expect this activity will take you approximately 15 minutes.

Important safety precautions

Take note of the safety precautions given with Activity 4.2.

Equipment needed

Kit items

Rock Specimens 5 and 6

Hand lens

Non-kit item

Ruler marked in millimetres

Some of the minerals you met in Activity 4.2 are present in the samples of basalt and granite in the Practical Kit. The aims of this activity are to identify the minerals in these rocks and, using the chemical composition of those minerals, to deduce how they contribute to the overall chemical composition of each rock.

Task 1

Examine Specimen 6 with the hand lens; it contains three minerals. Describe each mineral according to its average grain size, shape, colour, cleavage and lustre. Confirm that your observations match the properties of the minerals quartz, feldspar and mica in your completed Table 4.1.

Now examine Specimen 5. The finer grain size makes it more difficult to identify all the minerals. Try to recognise a few large, dark crystals of pyroxene on cut surfaces. On broken surfaces their cleavage planes glint in the light. Long, narrow, grey to white crystals of plagioclase feldspar also show good cleavages. Both minerals also make up much of the dark, fine-grained groundmass, in which the larger grains are set.

Task 2

(a) Note down the chemical formula of each mineral in the granite (see the examples in Table 4.1). Assume that the feldspar content is a combination of alkali feldspar and sodium-rich plagioclase feldspar. (You don't need to remember these particular formulae, but it is important to appreciate which elements occur in the main rock-forming minerals.)

Do the same as above for the basalt. Assume that the plagioclase feldspar is at the calcium-rich end of its composition range.

(b) The chemical formulae for the main minerals in each rock indicate the most abundant elements that are present in the rock. Assume that the granite comprises 30% quartz, 60% feldspars and 10% dark mica, and that the basalt comprises 50% plagioclase feldspar and 50% pyroxene. Try to judge which elements (ignoring oxygen and hydrogen) are likely to be more abundant in the granite than in the basalt, and vice versa.

Now read the comments on this activity at the end of this book before continuing.

Activity 4.3 revealed from their 'blends' of silicate minerals that the basalt and granite samples are chemically very different, as the magmas they crystallised from must have been. In chemical terms, basalt and granite are about as different as you can get among common igneous rocks.

Basalt contains the minerals plagioclase feldspar (the Ca-rich type), pyroxene and sometimes olivine. Pyroxene and olivine are generally dark coloured minerals. Being magnesium- and iron-rich (Fe) silicates, they are often called **mafic** (by adding 'ic') minerals. Igneous rocks containing a high proportion of such minerals therefore have relatively high levels of magnesium, iron and calcium. They are called mafic rocks and usually appear dark. The coarse-grained, mafic igneous rock gabbro (Book 2, Section 8.5.1) has a similar mineral content and composition to extrusive basalt; it is the intrusive equivalent of basalt, and solidified more slowly from a chemically similar magma.

In contrast, **granite** contains the minerals quartz, alkali feldspar and the Na-rich type of plagioclase feldspar, and usually some mica. Pale-coloured feldspars and quartz are called **felsic** minerals (from feldspar, silicon plus 'ic'). Igneous rocks dominated by them are usually pale and called felsic rocks (e.g. Figure 4.5). They contain significantly more silicon, sodium and potassium than mafic rocks. Obsidian glass is a rare exception to that general rule, being felsic but dark in colour; glass can be highly coloured by mere traces of some metals. **Rhyolite** has broadly the same mineral and chemical composition as granite. Being a fine-grained extrusive rock, it is the felsic counterpart to basalt.

Igneous rock compositions range from granites and rhyolites, which are rich in silicon and contain mainly felsic minerals, to gabbros and basalts, which have less silicon and significant amounts of mafic minerals. Variation in the mineral contents of common igneous rocks is the basis for compositional classification. The proportions of different minerals change across Figure 4.6 to signify the

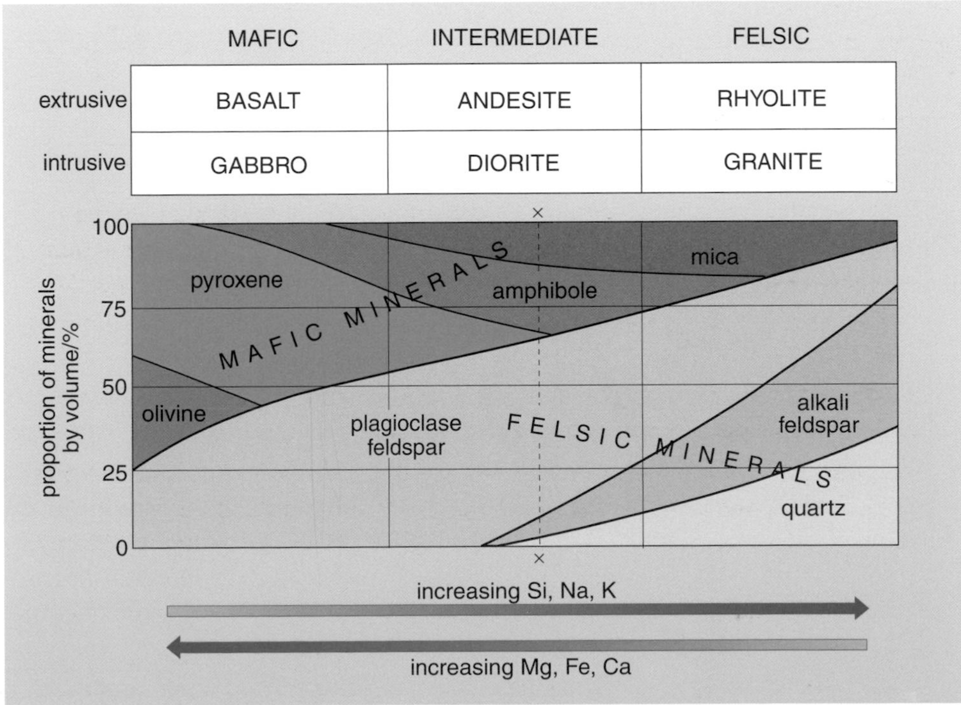

Figure 4.6 Variation in mineral content of common igneous rocks. The vertical axis shows proportions in per cent of minerals (by volume) and the horizontal axis shows the range of rock types. The arrows beneath the diagram show how the content of certain elements varies across the compositional range of common igneous rocks.

typical variation in mineral content of the common igneous rocks. Silicon, sodium and potassium contents *increase* from left (mafic rocks) to right (felsic rocks), while magnesium, iron and calcium contents *decrease*.

The compositions of felsic and mafic rocks in Figure 4.6 bracket those of *intermediate* igneous rocks. Fine-grained intermediate lavas are **andesites** and the coarse-grained plutonic equivalents are **diorites**. The dominant felsic mineral in these intermediate rocks is plagioclase feldspar. The dominant mafic mineral is usually pyroxene or amphibole, a chain silicate containing hydroxyl (OH^-) ions.

The line X–X shows an example of how to use Figure 4.6. The line signifies a particular 'blend' of minerals in an igneous rock: in this case, 2% quartz; 6% alkali feldspar; 54% plagioclase feldspar; 2% pyroxene; 21% amphibole and 15% mica. (You may like to check the percentage values yourself.) The rock represented by X–X is one of a variety of 'blends' constituting intermediate igneous rocks.

■ In Figure 4.6 how much can the percentages vary of: (a) plagioclase feldspar in gabbro; (b) quartz in granite; and (c) pyroxene in diorite?

□ (a) Plagioclase feldspar in gabbro may vary from about 25% to 55%. (b) Quartz in granite may vary from 10% to nearly 40%. (c) Pyroxene in diorite may vary from about 0% to 25%.

Question 4.3

Use Figure 4.6 to answer the following questions.

(a) Which common igneous rocks contain: (i) the highest proportion of quartz; (ii) the highest proportion of mafic minerals and (iii) no alkali feldspar?

(b) How does the mineral content of diorite differ from that of granite?

(c) How do the proportions of chemical elements in diorite differ from those in gabbro?

The classes of igneous rocks are broad and divide up a continuum of chemical and mineralogical compositions in nature. Which geological processes might have produced this diversity of igneous rock? The plate-tectonic context for magmatism (Book 2, Chapter 9) opened new avenues to answering this major geoscientific question.

4.2.3 Igneous activity at plate boundaries

Igneous activity today occurs in five different settings at the boundaries between tectonic plates (Figure 4.7).

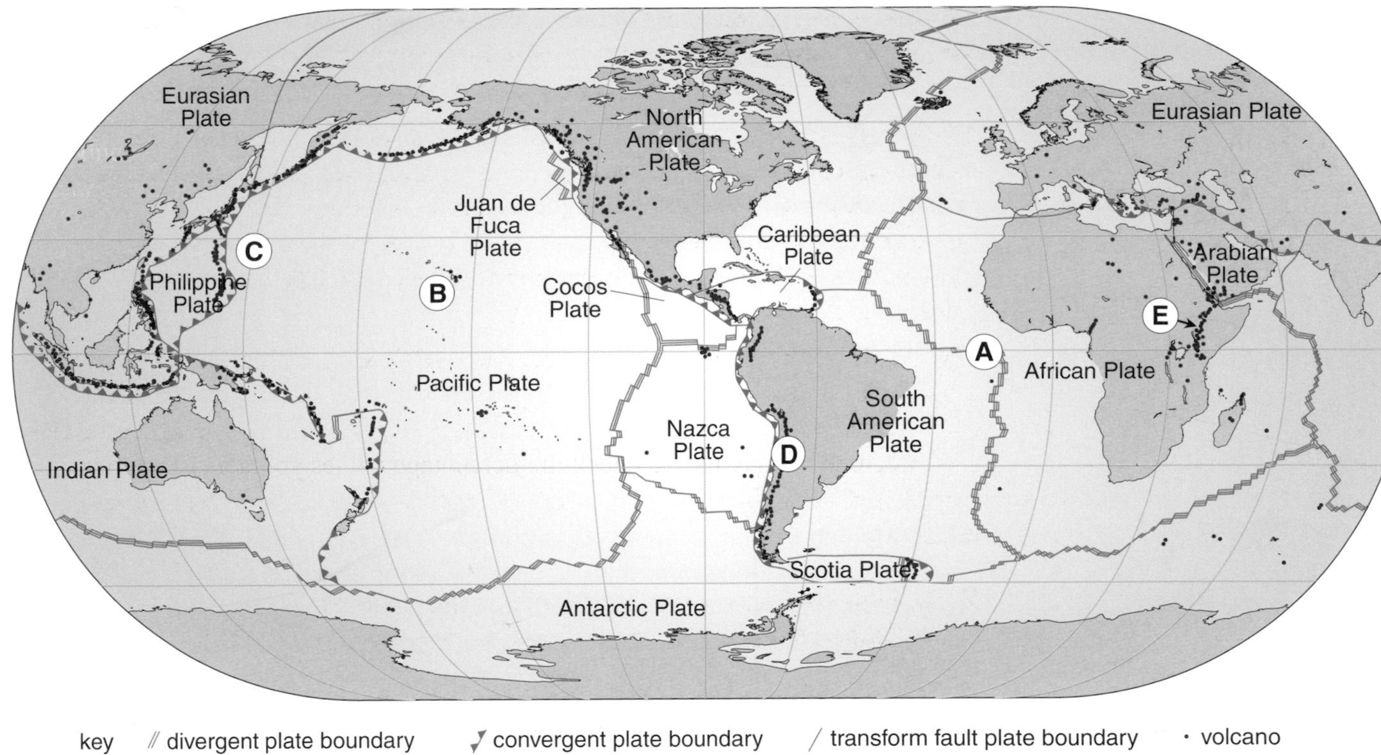

Figure 4.7 Global distribution of active volcanoes in relation to tectonic plate boundaries.

■ Describe the main types of igneous activity in relation to types of plate boundary, for example at locations A–E in Figure 4.7.

□ A is at a *divergent* boundary where magmas emerge from oceanic ridges to add to the oceanic lithosphere. B and E are volcanoes far from plate boundaries. They occur *within* oceanic (B) or continental (E) parts of plates where magmas rise from hot spots in the mantle. C and D are volcanic arcs at *convergent* boundaries where oceanic lithosphere is subducted into the mantle. C has developed on oceanic crust; D on continental crust.

Each site has characteristic kinds of igneous rock. Magmas erupted at divergent plate margins (A) and hot spots (B and E) are mainly basaltic. In both cases only the mantle can have melted to produce the basaltic magma. The mantle is composed of **peridotite** and contains far more Mg-rich olivine (Mg_2SiO_4) than does basalt. Peridotite therefore contains significantly more magnesium and less calcium, aluminium and silicon than magma produced by melting it. The reason for this seemingly odd change in chemical composition will become clear in Section 4.3.

The compositions of magmas erupted at convergent plate boundaries (C and D) are much more variable than those at divergent boundaries or hot spots. Magmas of volcanic arcs range from basaltic to andesitic to rhyolitic. In *oceanic* volcanic arcs (C) the dominant compositions are basaltic to andesitic; in *continental* volcanic arcs (D) they are andesitic to rhyolitic.

- ■ In which type of arc are granite plutons more likely to be present?
- □ In continental volcanic arcs, where rhyolitic magmas are more important.

The diversity of magmas and igneous rocks, particularly in volcanic arcs, stems from two fundamental processes: *melting*, which generates magma (Section 4.3), and *crystallisation*, which forms igneous rocks (Section 4.4).

4.3 Partial melting processes: from rock to magma

Apart from the outer core (Book 2, Section 6.2.3), very little of the Earth is in a molten state. The lithosphere and underlying mantle are solid rock, although the asthenosphere is less rigid (Book 2, Chapter 6). Magma is produced only locally, beneath regions of igneous activity (Figure 4.7). It involves melting of either mantle or crustal rocks.

There are two features of magmas that might seem a little odd. First, they have different compositions from their likely source; for instance, basalt is produced from peridotite (Section 4.1). Second, melting temperatures of individual silicate minerals found in igneous rocks are hundreds of degrees higher than the temperatures of magmas. An example is a quartz crystal that melts at ~1600 °C, yet granitic magma, from which quartz crystallises, forms at around 800 °C.

Phoenician traders first made glass around 2500 years ago after making a discovery that helps to explain the oddity of magmas. They traded what was then a very valuable natural mineral called trona (sodium carbonate), which was used in the ancient world for soap manufacture, preserving and tenderising meat; and in mummification. They found that a mixture of 15% trona and 85% quartz sand melts at a temperature easily attained in a wood fire. The Roman historian Pliny the Elder alleged that this was discovered when Phoenician traders used trona blocks from their cargo as fire stones when cooking on a sandy beach. They were amazed when a hot liquid flowed and then cooled to a hard transparent solid, now called 'soda glass'.

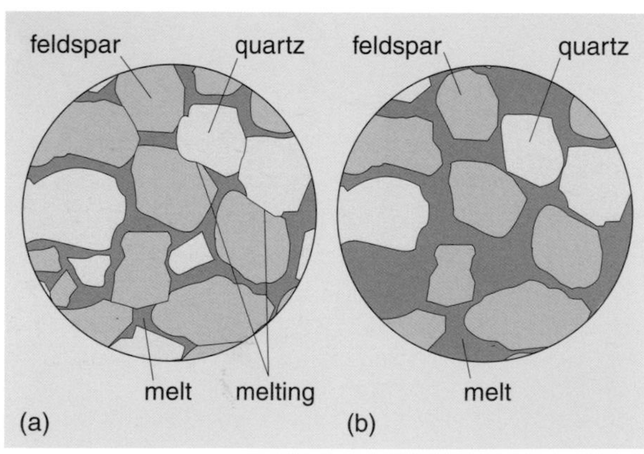

Figure 4.8 Progressive melting in rocks starts at grain boundaries where minerals are in contact: (a) 10% melting; (b) 30% melting.

When heated, trona breaks down to release carbon dioxide gas and solid but highly unstable sodium oxide. At high temperature the bonds that connect silicon and oxygen in quartz molecules vibrate strongly, allowing sodium ions to enter and contaminate the structure. At around 1000 °C the sodium ions so weaken the SiO_2 structure that it breaks down to form a sodium silicate melt. Solidified, this forms soda glass. In rock there is a similar transfer of ions between the different rock-forming minerals as temperature increases.

As the different minerals in a rock are heated, the bonds within their structures increasingly vibrate. The chance of ions breaking free from the silicate molecules is higher at the boundaries of each mineral grain than within their crystalline structure. Therefore, rising temperature increasingly drives ions freed from one mineral to contaminate and disrupt the structure of another. That reduces the temperature at which each mineral will melt, in much the same manner as the formation of soda glass. Melting starts where different mineral grains are in direct contact with one another (Figure 4.8a).

The ion-transfer process also enables several minerals to melt at the same time, although in different proportions according to each mineral's composition. Unlike the melting of single solid compounds, such as water ice or individual silicate crystals, a rock's mineral mixture melts over a range of several hundred degrees Celsius, and the proportion of melt to remaining solid minerals increases as the temperature rises (Figure 4.8b).

Rock begins melting at a temperature depending on the particular mix of minerals in the rock. For instance, felsic minerals with high Si content but with little Fe and Mg (i.e. quartz, feldspars and white mica) melt at lower temperatures than do mafic minerals (i.e. dark mica, amphibole, pyroxene and olivine), which have lower Si and higher Fe and Mg content.

The amount of water present in the rock also plays a role, by reducing the melting temperature of most silicate mixtures. Experiments show that felsic rocks made of a mixture of quartz and feldspars with water-bearing mica, start to melt at between 650 and 800 °C. Mafic rocks composed mainly of pyroxene and olivine start melting at much higher temperatures (1050–1300 °C), partly because olivine and pyroxene don't contain water.

Figure 4.9 shows the order in which common minerals in a rock tend to melt. As a rock is heated up, depending on the minerals it contains, mixtures of mainly felsic minerals melt first. At higher temperatures, mafic minerals start to melt.

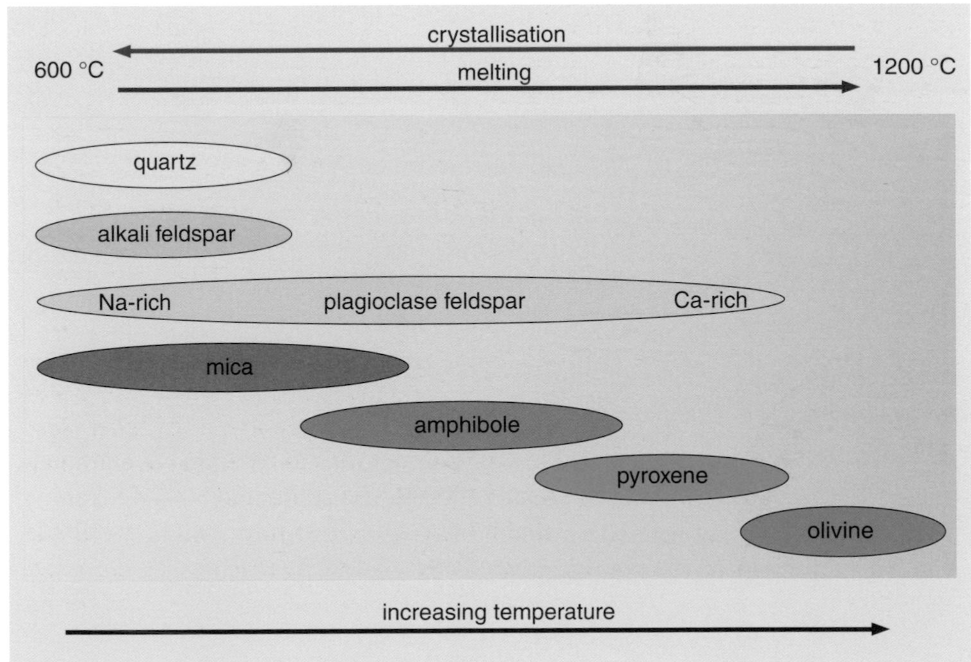

Figure 4.9 Generalised sequence of melting when a rock is heated (and crystallisation when magma is cooled) of common rock-forming minerals with changing temperature. Each mineral has a range of melting temperature.

Question 4.4

Referring to Table 4.2 (in the comments on Activity 4.1) and Figure 4.9, describe how, in general, the composition and internal structure of felsic minerals that melt at lower temperatures differ from those of mafic minerals that melt at higher temperatures.

One felsic mineral does not follow the trend outlined in the answer to Question 4.4. Plagioclase feldspar melts over a wide range of temperatures (600–1000 °C) because its composition varies. The more easily melted variety is sodium-rich ($NaAlSi_3O_8$), whereas the variety which melts at a higher temperature has high calcium, higher aluminium and lower silicon ($CaAl_2Si_2O_8$). It seems that the Si content of minerals, and consequently of rocks, partly controls the temperature at which they begin to melt.

When the mantle's olivine-rich peridotite begins to melt, pyroxene melts along with olivine. At this early stage, however, much less olivine melts than its proportion in the rock might suggest. So the composition of the initial magma is very different from that of the mantle – it is basaltic. The remaining solid mantle becomes even richer in olivine and so needs to reach higher temperatures to continue melting. Should that happen, proportionately more olivine would melt and the magma would become more Mg-rich and poorer in Si. However, complete mantle melting to produce magma of peridotite composition never happens because there is a limit to mantle temperature at a particular depth. This is partly because magmas move from their source and carry heat away quickly. Pockets of magma coalesce to form larger bodies which weaken the surrounding rock structure. Silicate-rich liquids are less dense than the minerals that remain solid, so magma migrates upwards. As a result, an unmelted *residue*, containing more olivine than in the original peridotite, is left behind.

Magmas are therefore produced, not by complete melting, but by **partial melting** of their source rock. This explains how basaltic magma containing higher levels of Si and Ca, but much lower levels of Mg, is produced from peridotite. By this means, partial melting tends to create magmas with more felsic compositions than their sources.

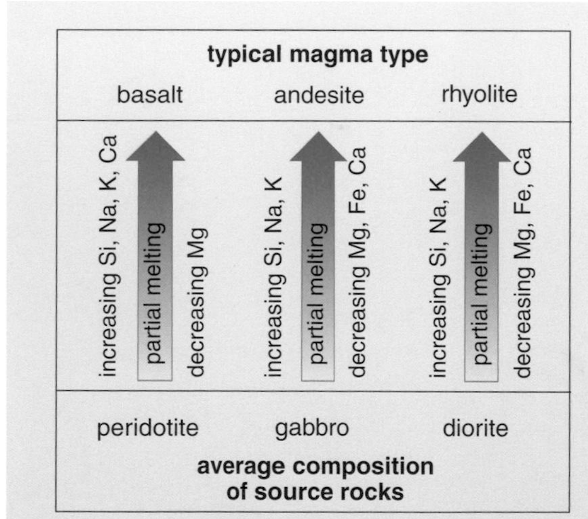

Figure 4.10 Schematic relationships between source rocks and types of magma produced by partial melting, including the resulting changes in chemical composition. Named sources represent average rock compositions. Magmas are usually referred to in terms of the extrusive rocks which form from them, e.g. basalt magma.

■ Referring to Figure 4.9, how might the chemical composition of a magma formed when diorite starts melting differ from the initial rock composition?

□ The felsic minerals of the diorite will tend to melt first, so the initial magma will be more felsic. It will be a magma of granitic (rhyolitic) composition, which is *richer* in Si and the alkali metals sodium (Na) and potassium (K) than the diorite (Figure 4.6).

The melting of any rocks containing both felsic and mafic minerals can be represented in a simplified way, as:

$$\begin{matrix}\text{felsic}\\\text{minerals}\end{matrix} + \begin{matrix}\text{mafic}\\\text{minerals}\end{matrix} \xrightarrow{\text{partial melting}} \begin{matrix}\text{more felsic}\\\text{magma}\end{matrix} + \begin{matrix}\text{more mafic}\\\text{residue}\end{matrix} \quad (4.1)$$

In this way, partial melting of gabbro (equivalent to effusive basalt) can produce a dioritic (andesitic) magma; and partial melting of diorite (roughly average continental crust) can produce a granitic (rhyolitic) magma (Figure 4.10). (*Note*: for simplicity, Book 2 describes continental crust as granitic when, in fact, its average composition is closer to a dioritic or an intermediate composition.)

Melting to produce basaltic magma occurs in the uppermost mantle. Peridotite requires high temperatures to melt, which is one reason why the mantle melts in only three settings: at constructive and destructive plate boundaries and above hot spots. Dioritic continental crust also only reaches temperatures high enough to produce granitic magma under special circumstances: for example, at the base of very thick crust formed during plate collisions (Section 6.3).

4.4 Fractional crystallisation processes: from magma to igneous rock

In the same way as a rock *melts* progressively over a range of temperatures, magma *crystallises* progressively over a range of temperatures when it cools. However, rapid cooling produces rapid crystallisation and a randomly oriented mass of fine-grained crystals, as in volcanic lavas and shallow intrusions. Slow cooling in a large magma chamber deep within the Earth results in gradual crystallisation; crystals grow much larger in plutonic igneous rocks. The first minerals to crystallise are those with higher melting temperatures (Figure 4.9); getting an early start, they often grow large. If the magma erupts before crystallisation is complete, a porphyritic texture forms in the rapidly cooled lava (Figure 4.5b). The large pyroxene and plagioclase feldspar crystals in the Practical Kit basalt probably formed by slow cooling in a magma chamber before eruption.

An important factor in the crystallisation of magma is the order in which different minerals appear.

■ When basaltic magma cools gradually, which minerals are likely to crystallise first?

□ Minerals with high melting temperatures: olivine first, and then pyroxene and calcium-rich plagioclase feldspar (Figure 4.9).

Minerals that crystallise early, individually and together have a different combined chemical composition from that of the magma itself. Progressive crystallisation continually changes the composition of the remaining liquid. If crystals and liquid stay together, complete solidification will produce a rock that is chemically identical to the original magma. However, various processes can separate the magma into different *fractions* before complete solidification. A fraction rich in crystals is dominated by early-formed mafic minerals. The other, liquid-rich, fraction is a more felsic magma with few of those crystals (Figure 4.11). Such **fractional crystallisation** is another means by which chemically different magmas are produced.

How might this separation of crystals and magma occur? Crystals of some early-formed mafic minerals, such as olivine and pyroxene, are denser than basaltic magma and tend to settle under gravity. When this happens, the upper part of the magma becomes liquid-rich and more felsic than the original magma. The lower part becomes more mafic because it contains many olivine and pyroxene crystals. If the liquid fraction has a lower density than surrounding rocks, it rises to form intrusions and volcanic rocks, leaving behind the crystal-rich residue.

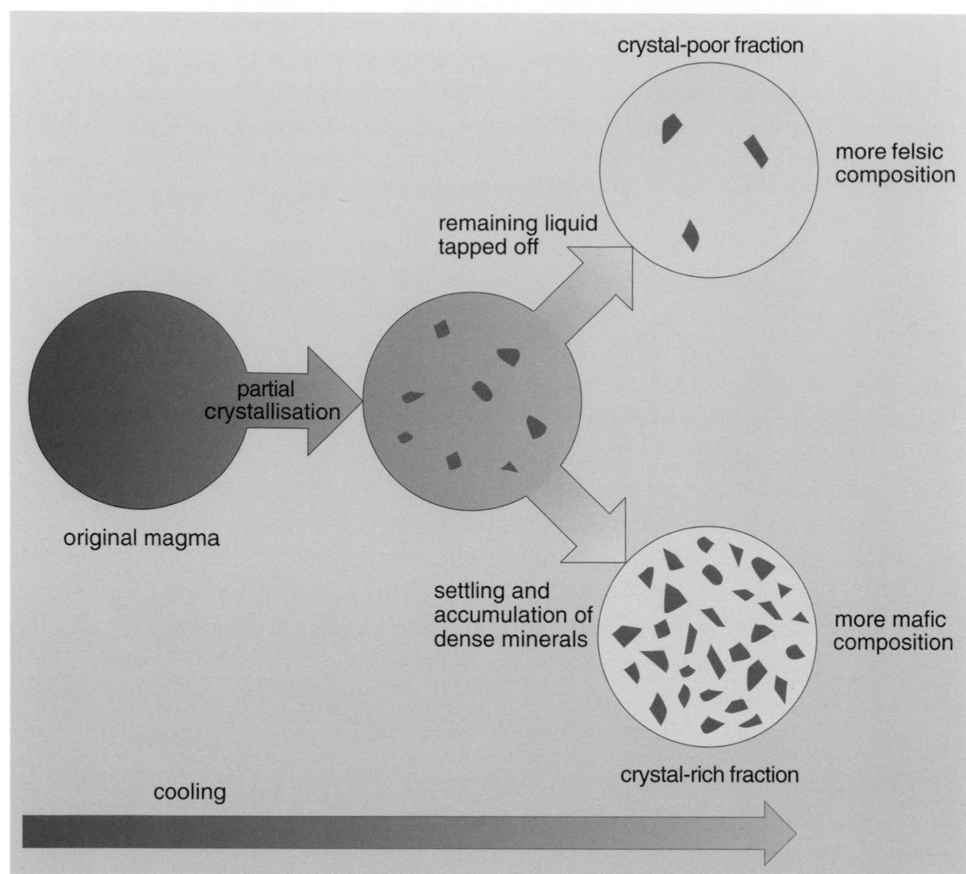

Figure 4.11 Production of different magma compositions by fractional crystallisation. One fraction is rich in accumulated crystals of mafic minerals; the other is a more felsic liquid.

Such fractional crystallisation of a basaltic magma could produce intermediate (andesitic) magma. Subsequent fractionation of that andesitic magma could form felsic (rhyolitic) magma (Figure 4.12). This process helps explain the wide range of igneous rock compositions commonly found in volcanic arcs. Therefore, fractional crystallisation works to 'refine' magma originally derived by partial melting, which itself is already more felsic than its ultimate source.

■ In what kind of igneous body is fractional crystallisation most likely to happen?

□ In a deep magma chamber, which will eventually crystallise completely to form a pluton.

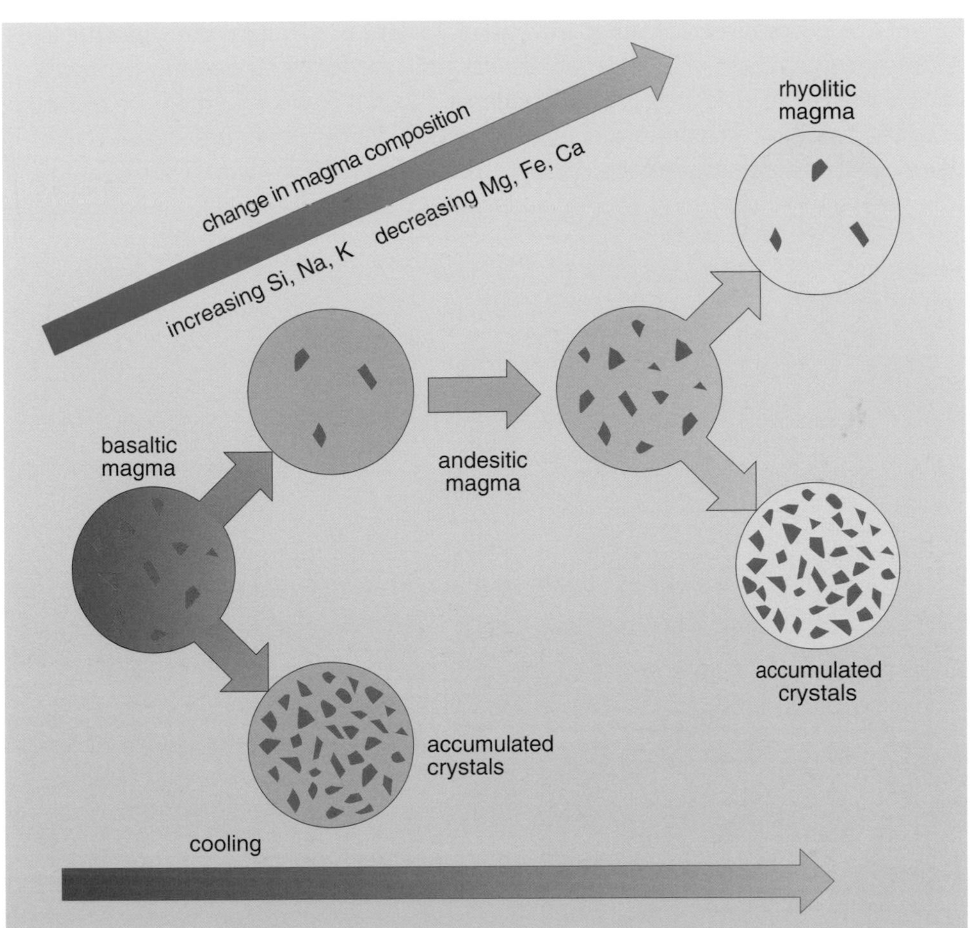

Figure 4.12 Production of progressively more felsic magma as a result of repeated fractional crystallisation. The process may be continuous or occur in stages, as shown.

There is a final point to consider: the *temperature* of different magmas. Felsic minerals melt and crystallise at lower temperatures than mafic ones. As you might expect from that general difference, felsic magmas are much cooler than those of mafic composition. Granitic magmas have temperatures as low as around 700 °C; basaltic magmas emerge at about 1200 °C; andesitic magmas are somewhere in-between.

4.5 Igneous processes and plate tectonic settings

Different magma types occur in different tectonic settings (Figure 4.7). The fundamental processes that produce magmas may account for those differences. The compositions of magmas produced by partial melting depend on the rocks available for melting (Figure 4.10) and the percentage of melting. Fractional crystallisation may produce different magma compositions depending on the starting composition of the magma (Figure 4.12) and the amount of crystallisation achieved by the time the crystals have separated from the remaining melt.

Figure 4.13 summarises types of magmatic activity in different global settings. At mid-ocean ridges, magma is mainly basaltic, produced by partial melting of mantle peridotite at relatively shallow depths. At hot spots, magma is produced by partial melting of mantle peridotite at greater depths. Although basaltic compositions dominate in both settings, other compositions can be produced by fractional crystallisation in shallow magma chambers.

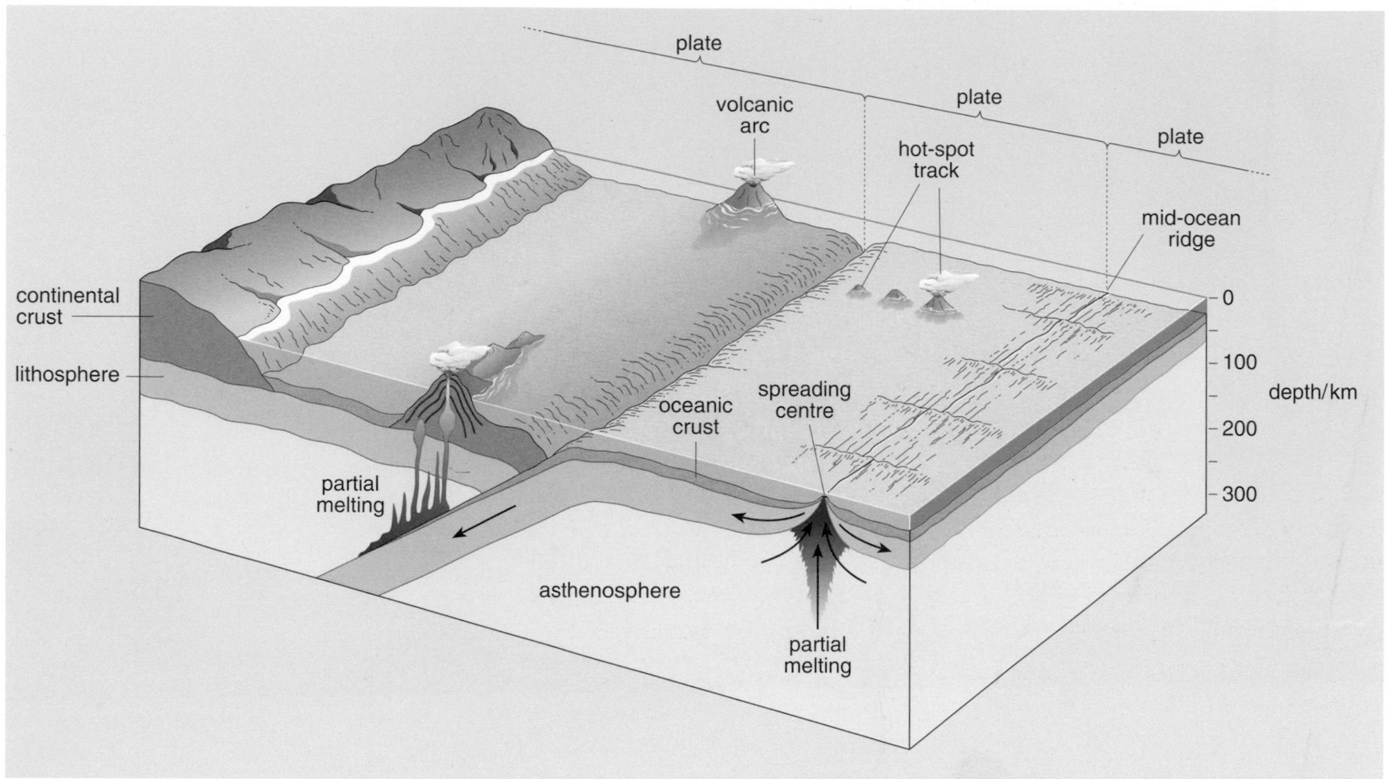

Figure 4.13 Composite diagram showing the typical nature of magmatism in various plate-tectonic settings that correspond with locations A, B and C in Figure 4.7. At a divergent plate margin partial melting of the mantle generates basaltic magma. Partial melting of mantle at a convergent plate margin forms an oceanic volcanic arc from basaltic and andesitic magmas. Basaltic magma generated by partial melting of the mantle at hot spots forms oceanic volcanic islands.

Magmatism in volcanic arcs (Figure 4.13) is more complicated; volcanic rocks there vary in composition from basalt to andesite to rhyolite. Not surprisingly, plutonic intrusions of gabbro, diorite and granite (of equivalent compositions) are exposed in older, eroded arcs. However, in oceanic arcs, basaltic to andesitic magma compositions tend to dominate, whereas more andesitic to rhyolitic compositions occur in continental arcs. Which processes might explain this?

In volcanic arcs, the partial melting of peridotite that generates basaltic magma is assisted by water released by dehydration of subducted old oceanic lithosphere. Andesitic magmas, that are characteristic of oceanic arcs, form by fractional crystallisation of this basaltic magma. In continental arcs (D on Figure 4.7), it is not quite so simple. From Figures 4.10 and 4.12, you can see that andesitic to rhyolitic magma compositions that dominate continental arcs may be produced in one of two possible ways: by partial melting of gabbroic to dioritic source rocks; or by fractional crystallisation of basaltic to andesitic magmas. There might even be a combination of both. Indeed, basaltic magmas that melted at temperatures around 1200 °C do form parts of continental arcs, and must have been produced in the mantle beneath, and continental crust is of dioritic composition – more felsic than the gabbroic crust of oceanic arcs.

- ■ What do you think might happen if hot basaltic magma intrudes dioritic crustal rocks?
- □ If the temperature of the dioritic rocks is raised to more than 600 °C (Figure 4.9), the felsic minerals in them could start to melt, producing a granitic magma.

Intrusion of basaltic magma into the dioritic crust beneath continental volcanic arcs could form rhyolitic magma by partial melting, if sufficient heat was available to raise diorite above its melting temperature. There would also be a good chance, at around the same time, that the cooling of basalt magma in a magma chamber might generate andesitic magma by fractional crystallisation. Another possibility is mixing basaltic and rhyolitic magmas to produce intermediate, andesitic magmas. However andesitic magma might have formed, its fractional crystallisation in crustal magma chambers could also account for rhyolitic magmas. A range of processes can thus account for magmatic complexity in continental volcanic arcs, although methods of telling them apart are beyond the scope of this course. Similar complexities characterise the production of magma at newly formed divergent margins on the continents (E on Figure 4.7).

4.5.1 Clues to ancient igneous processes

You have seen how distinctive types of igneous rock are produced in certain tectonic settings today. So the occurrence of the same rock types in the geological record hint strongly at the presence of equivalent settings in the past. However, the geological record of the most accessible place to study old rocks – on land – may be biased.

- ■ Which are more likely to be preserved in the geological record on land – igneous rocks of volcanic arcs or the ocean floor?
- □ The rocks of volcanic arcs are more likely to be preserved in continental crust, as they are less likely to be subducted than those of the ocean floor (Book 2, Chapter 9).

Volcanic arcs are preserved in the geological record either because they formed along a continental margin that is still active (e.g. the Andes), or because they were tectonically accreted to continents (Book 2, Section 9.4), as seems to be the destiny of the island chains of the western Pacific. More rarely, ocean floor rocks also become accreted onto continents.

Some rocks forming the island of Anglesey off the coast of North Wales include basaltic pillow lavas (Figure 4.14a) together with gabbro and serpentinite (Book 2, Section 8.5). They originated as oceanic crust around 800 Ma ago, and perhaps indicate the site of an ancient convergent plate boundary. North Wales also has a 470-Ma-old range of basaltic, andesitic and rhyolitic volcanic rocks, which probably originated in a continental arc during the Ordovician Period (Figure 4.14b).

(a)

(b)

Figure 4.14 Ancient igneous rocks showing characteristics distinctive of different tectonic settings: (a) 800-Ma-old basaltic pillow lavas on Anglesey, North Wales, which formed as oceanic crust; (b) 470-Ma-old rhyolitic lavas in Snowdonia, North Wales, showing banding produced by the viscous magma having flowed sluggishly. These rocks are evidence of a former volcanic arc.

4.6 Igneous processes in the rock cycle

The crystalline products of magmas – igneous rocks – appear 'fresh and new', literally sparkling. Basaltic magma, and others derived from it by fractional crystallisation, are completely new entrants in the rock cycle. Basalt magmas form by partial melting of mantle peridotite. Except in cases of extreme uplift and erosion in continental collision zones or where oceanic lithosphere has accreted to the continents, mantle rock in bulk never sees the light of day. It participates in the rock cycle through its magmatic products. In this 'second-hand' way the mantle has the most profound effects on the rock cycle, as the ultimate source of the rocky material found at the surface, and the carbon on which life is built. The continental crust itself has grown over four billion years mainly by the accretion of oceanic volcanic arcs (Book 2, Section 9.4.2), made from mantle-derived igneous rocks and their derivatives.

Some magmas, particularly those of granitic composition, may form by melting of the deep continental crust, either through heating by basaltic magma or because of metamorphism (Chapter 6). They are products of a profound recycling of older crustal material, in the form of ancient igneous or sedimentary rocks that have been metamorphosed.

Having crystallised at temperatures as high as 1200 °C and being made up of silicate minerals, most of which don't contain water or hydroxyl ions, igneous rocks that reach the surface are not in equilibrium with their surroundings. Minerals formed at high temperatures are highly prone to weathering, and the resulting debris is a major source of material that ends up in sediments (Chapter 5). In the case of igneous rocks ultimately derived from mantle melting, that material is a new addition to the rock cycle.

Figure 4.15 expresses these fundamental relationships between igneous processes and the rest of the rock cycle. Chapter 5 begins with the surface processes that operate on exposed crystalline igneous rocks to involve them in the 'upper' part of the rock cycle.

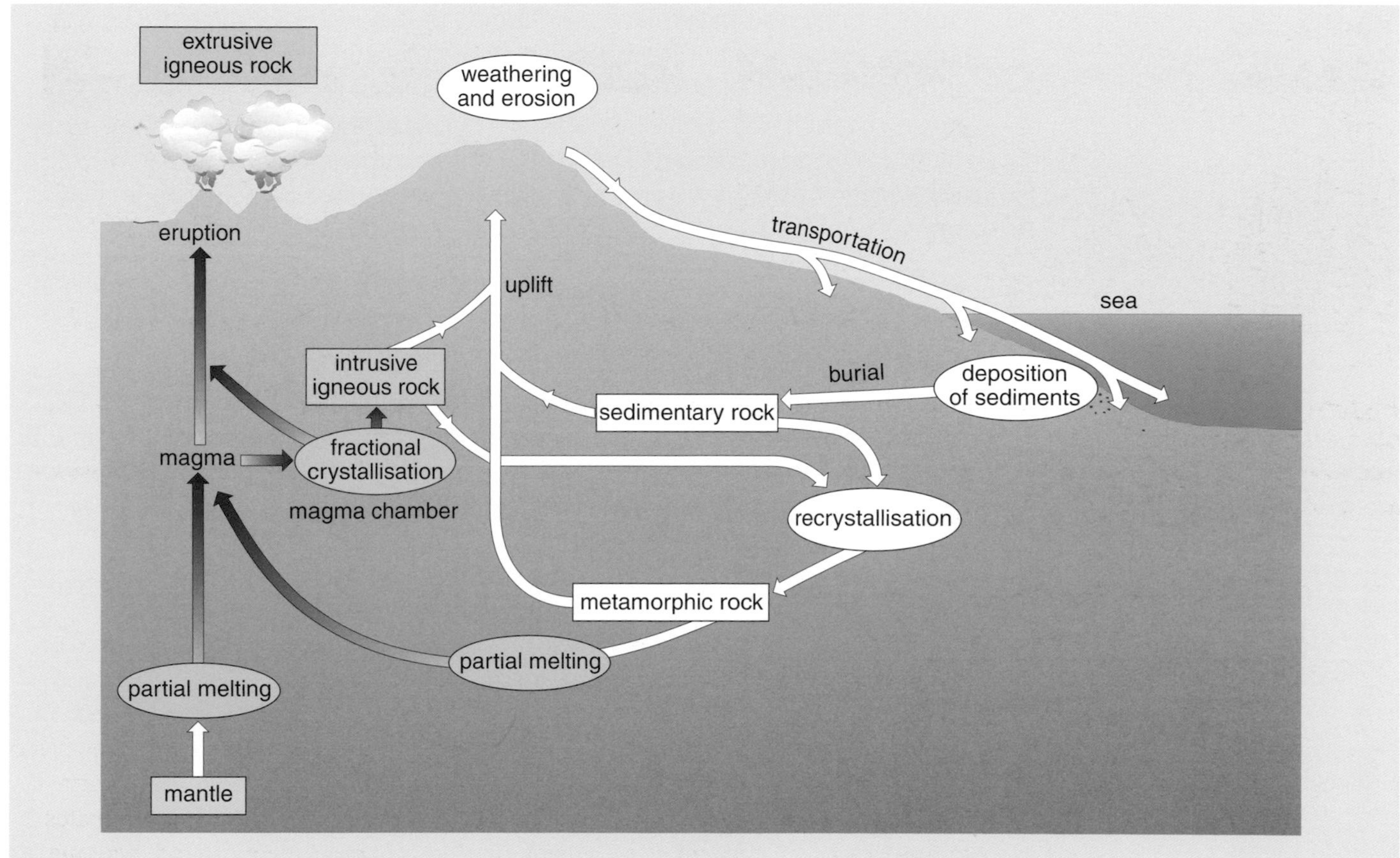

Figure 4.15 Formation and roles of igneous rocks in the rock cycle. This is based on Figure 10.2 in Book 2, with the igneous components highlighted.

4.7 Summary of Chapter 4

Igneous rocks are distinguished by their textures, which feature randomly oriented, interlocking and intergrown crystals.

There is a diversity of igneous rocks because of different magma compositions and crystallisation histories. Usually, large bodies of intrusive rock are coarse-grained; layers of extrusive rocks are fine-grained. Magma chambers form plutons; offshoots during the upward rise of magmas form sheet-like dykes and sills.

The fundamental differences in magma composition are often reflected by the presence of different minerals in igneous rocks. Mafic rocks (such as gabbro and basalt) are rich in mafic minerals (especially pyroxene). Felsic rocks (such as granite and rhyolite) are dominated by felsic minerals (especially quartz and feldspar). The amounts of mafic and felsic minerals are more equally balanced in intermediate rocks (such as diorite and andesite).

Magmatic activity today is concentrated at mid-ocean ridges, over hot spots and along volcanic arcs, both in oceanic settings and along continental margins.

Partial melting produces magmas that are more felsic in composition than their source rock. Fractional crystallisation produces magmas that are more felsic in composition than the original magma.

Partial melting and fractional crystallisation processes operating in different circumstances account for the production of different types of igneous rock in different tectonic settings. Peridotite mantle partially melts to produce basaltic magma beneath mid-ocean ridges, island hot spots and volcanic arcs. The partial melting of peridotite mantle and dioritic crust beneath continental arcs, with subsequent mixing of magmas and fractional crystallisation, together produce a range of igneous rocks, including andesites and rhyolites.

Particular associations of igneous rock types in the geological record can help to reveal past plate-tectonic settings.

Your study of this chapter involved: comparing information given in diagrams and graphs, and by rock hand specimens and the minerals in them; describing and interpreting that information; applying it more widely, and summarising your findings. You have also applied concepts about magma-related processes to explain variations in igneous rocks, including their relationships to global tectonic processes.

Chapter 5
Sedimentary rocks – records of changing environments

Igneous processes are mostly hidden at depth, except where magmas erupt. Discovering what the deeper processes might be involves interpreting evidence preserved in old igneous rocks. Yet there are not many fundamental igneous processes that form and transform magmas. By comparison, processes that create accumulations of sediment are extremely varied. However, since they operate at the surface, you can see and understand some of them in action: sand or pebbles shifting on a beach; sand, gravel and silt accumulating by the roadside after heavy rain; muds settling in an estuary or a tidal river; fine sand blowing over coastal dunes. Many, but not all, modern sediments are accumulations of fragmentary material derived from exposed older rocks of all kinds. They result from weathering and erosion, and then the transport and eventual deposition of the liberated materials (Book 2 Section 5.2.2). Sedimentary processes span the entire planet, from the highest mountains to the deepest ocean floor, and cover a great range of environments.

Sedimentary rocks exposed in cliffs, for example, are usually neither loose nor soft; somehow sediments become hardened (Section 5.4). Their origin as unconsolidated sediments usually shows clearly in their fragmental texture (Figure 4.1c). In moderately extensive exposures, another characteristic feature of sedimentary rocks stands out: usually they show some kind of layering. These layers can have developed on a range of scales, from millimetres to tens and, rarely, hundreds of metres. Some represent marked changes in the style of deposition which may produce sedimentary rocks of different kinds (Figure 2.9), often after a break in deposition. These constitute beds or strata (singular, stratum) which may also vary in thickness. Each bed often consists of several thinner layers of the same kind of rock. Figure 5.1 gives a flavour of the variety of sedimentary layering. As discussed in Section 2.2, beds are usually laid down as widespread, almost horizontal layers (Figure 2.9) in response to gravitational force. Yet the finer layers that make up a bed may have been deposited at a marked angle to the horizontal (Figure 5.1b).

From these examples (and others you may have seen), you will be aware that there is a wide diversity of sedimentary rocks. Before discovering what these rocks can reveal about the environments in which they formed, you first need to appreciate what they are made of and understand how to classify them.

(a)

(b)

(c)

Figure 5.1 Field exposures of different kinds of sedimentary rock (vertical extent of image in parentheses). (a) Beds of rounded cobbles and pebbles, separated by beds of sand (2 m). (b) Beds of sand, in which minor layering is at an angle to the horizontal (20 m). (c) Beds of fine-grained silt and mud (40 cm).

5.1 Sedimentary materials

Although some sedimentary rocks form by chemical means (Section 5.3.2), most are made of discrete grains. The sizes of these grains span a vast range, from the finest of wind-blown dusts, measured in micrometres, to house-sized blocks moved by tsunamis, floods, glaciers, or landslides. Different size ranges are given familiar names (Figure 5.2). Muds (including clay and silt) feel smooth when squeezed between fingers and are very fine-grained. Sands feel gritty and are granular. Pebbles are grains larger than peppercorns; cobbles are larger than a tennis ball; and boulders are larger than a football. Granular sediments are classified primarily in terms of the grain-size ranges shown in Figure 5.2.

Few materials on Earth are more familiar or common than soil. So some simple but informative tests on a soil sample will be a good introduction to sediments and sedimentary processes.

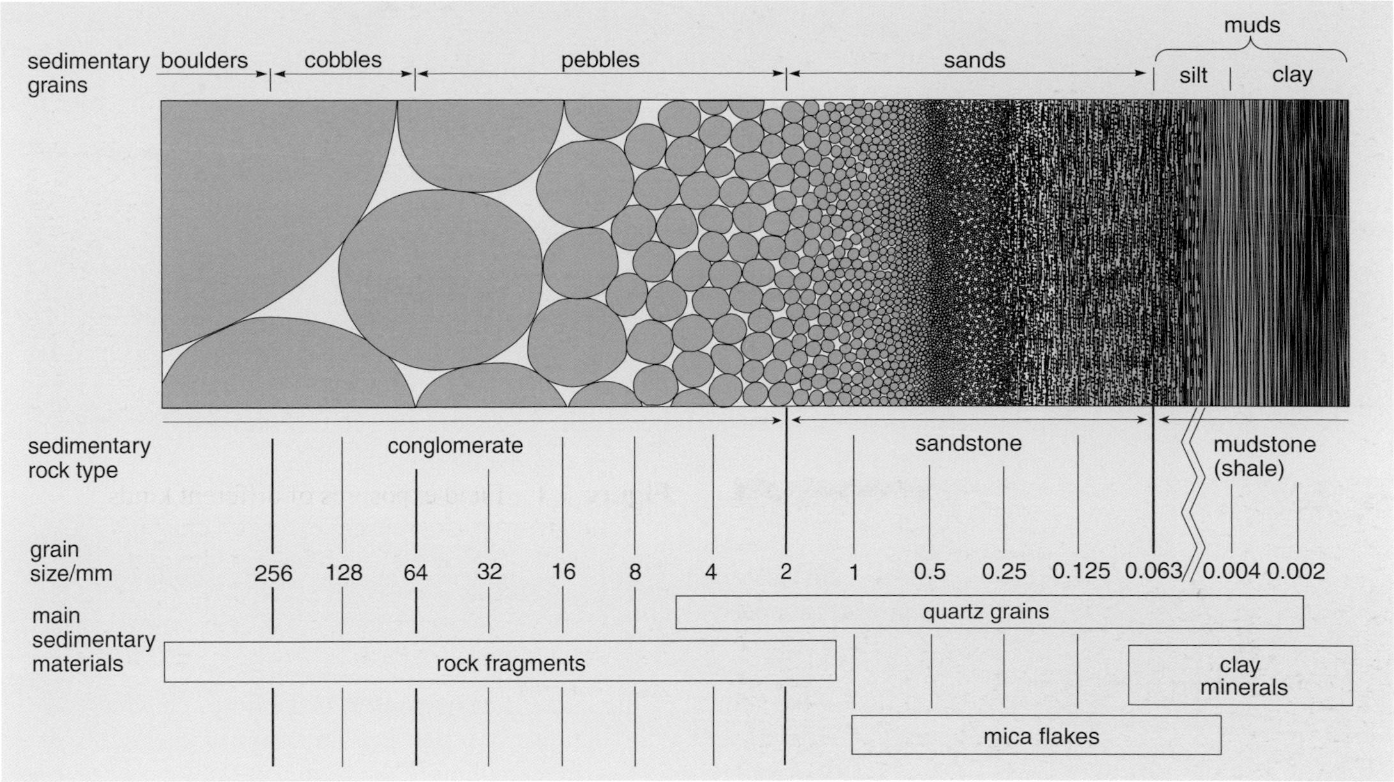

sedimentary grains: boulders | cobbles | pebbles | sands | muds (silt | clay)

sedimentary rock type: conglomerate | sandstone | mudstone (shale)

grain size/mm: 256 128 64 32 16 8 4 2 1 0.5 0.25 0.125 0.063 0.004 0.002

main sedimentary materials: rock fragments | quartz grains | mica flakes | clay minerals

Figure 5.2 Classification of sedimentary materials and corresponding rock types according to grain size. Typical materials found in sediments are also indicated. Note that the scale is not linear; successive divisions represent a halving of grain size, with a break between 0.063 and 0.004 mm.

Activity 5.1 Examining sedimentary materials in soil

We expect this activity will take you approximately 60 minutes (spread over 24 hours).

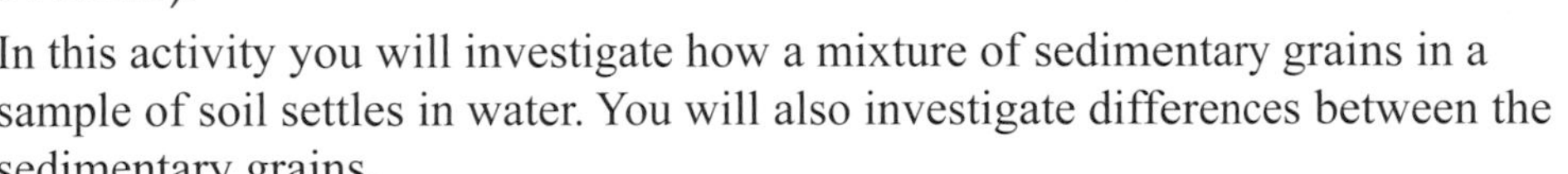

In this activity you will investigate how a mixture of sedimentary grains in a sample of soil settles in water. You will also investigate differences between the sedimentary grains.

Important safety precautions

Take note of the safety precautions given with Activity 4.2.

In addition, you should note the following precautions which are specific to this activity:

- Soil can contain harmful microorganisms. You are strongly advised to cover any cuts and abrasions with plasters and to wear rubber gloves when collecting and handling the soil. As with any practical work, wash your hands when you have finished, using a bactericidal soap if you handled samples without gloves.

Equipment needed

Kit item

Hand lens

Non-kit items

Clear glass jar with a tight-fitting lid

Old spoon and fork

Ruler marked in millimetres

Paper tissues

Sufficient garden soil to fill about one-third of your glass jar

Task 1

First, collect a sample of soil and break it down with a spoon. Remove any large stones (>10 mm), leaves, roots, worms and other organic debris. Fill a jar to a depth of about one-third with soil, topping up with water to about three-quarters full. Let the soil soak and break up for some time (up to an hour if it is dry).

Tighten the lid and shake the jar vigorously for about a minute. Then let the jar stand, and observe what happens for a few minutes.

Record your observations, noting especially what sort of material you see settling in the jar and the condition of the water. Then leave the jar to stand for at least two hours (preferably overnight).

Task 2

After the jar has been standing for at least two hours, make notes on what you can see in the sediment at the bottom. Describe any variations in the grain size (use the terms in Figure 5.2), or in the colour of the sediment. Is the water clear?

Draw a sketch of the jar and its contents, with labels based on your notes.

Task 3

Taking care not to disturb the sediment, pour off the water.

Use a spoon to sample different layers of sediment, from top to bottom – four or five samples will be sufficient. Scrape off the top layer, and retain a small amount of sediment on a tissue. Then excavate another layer and retain some, and so on until you have a sample of material from the very bottom. Be sure to make a note of the order of the samples.

Examine the samples closely with the hand lens, noting the size, shape and colour of the grains present at each level. (*Hint*: for the coarsest grains, it will help to clean any fines from them by carefully adding water to them in a saucer and swirling it for a few minutes with a fork.)

Now look at the comments on this activity at the end of this book.

Activity 5.1 showed that you can distinguish individual sediment grains in terms of three features: shape, size and mineral composition. The same three features distinguish the grains in sedimentary rocks.

- *Grain shape:* shape can vary from very angular to well-rounded (you will learn more about this in Activity 5.2). A hand lens reveals the shape of sedimentary grains of sand-size or larger. A high-powered microscope can reveal the shapes of finer grains.
- *Grain size:* **mudstones** and **sandstones** are named according to their grain sizes (Figure 5.2). A rock containing grains larger than 2 mm is a **conglomerate** if the grains are well-rounded, but a **breccia** if the grains are angular; the reason for this difference will become clear later.

- *Composition:* any material that can survive weathering, erosion, transport and accumulation – rocks, minerals and the hard parts of organisms – may become a sedimentary grain. Pebbles and larger grains are usually made of rock fragments. Sand grains are mostly composed of minerals (especially quartz) or the broken shells of organisms. Muds contain very fine grains, especially clay minerals, but also silt (mostly fine quartz) and organic matter. However, many minerals found in igneous rocks, such as olivine, pyroxene and feldspars, occur only rarely in sediments; you will see why in Section 5.2.1.

The processes that form and shape grains operate at the Earth's surface, and so can be observed directly. The character of sedimentary grains therefore conveys information about the origins of the sedimentary rocks that contain them. Added to that is the form of the layers in which they are deposited (Section 5.3).

5.2 Sedimentary processes

In the upper part of the rock cycle weathering and erosion break down all kinds of existing rocks, including older sedimentary rocks (Figure 5.3). These processes liberate fragmentary material, which is transported until it settles out under gravity and is deposited as sedimentary layers.

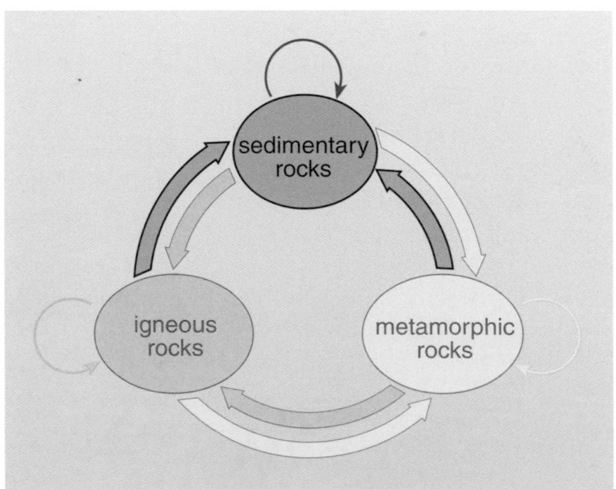

Figure 5.3 Formation of sedimentary rocks in the rock cycle. The three bold arrows indicate the routes through which sedimentary rocks can be formed from any kind of rock by weathering, erosion, transportation and deposition.

Most sediment grains are transported across the land surface by flowing water, strong winds and glaciers (Book 2, Section 5.2.2). Once sediment reaches the sea, shoreline wave motion and tidal currents carry materials, as do gravity-driven flows of sediment–water slurries where seabed slopes are steep. Some organisms create sediment particles by secreting hard parts from ions dissolved in water. Intact or as broken fragments, such organic material may mix with inorganic grains in a sediment. Where they are the only kind of grain, such organically derived grains are buried and form limestones (Section 5.3.3). There are also sediments which are not fragmental, having formed directly from dissolved ions by chemical means (Section 5.3.2).

5.2.1 Surface rocks and the weather

Existing rocks break down to yield fragments that end up in sediments through several weathering processes, which can involve both physical and chemical processes. Rocks disintegrate and decompose when they are exposed to solar heat and cold, rain and surface water, chemicals exuded by plant roots, and even an atmospheric gas – carbon dioxide – dissolved in water.

Physical weathering directly breaks rocks into fragments but geological processes that affected solid rock far beneath the surface can also help. When rocks are buried or formed at depth, pressure tends to compress them – not much, but enough to cause them to crack when the pressure is released. This is demonstrated in a spectacular and dangerous fashion in deep mines. In active mine workings the newly exposed rock sometimes explodes spontaneously in a rock burst. Erosion and uplift very slowly shift rocks that were once deeply buried to the surface, so their compression is released imperceptibly. Yet that still produces cracks, called **joints**, which you will see in one form or another in any exposure of solid rock. Joints allow water to penetrate deeply into exposed rock.

■ What happens if water in cracks freezes?

□ When water solidifies, it expands (by about 9%). Ice forming in cracks and joints therefore exerts a force tending to wedge the rock apart.

A burst water pipe in winter makes us uncomfortably aware of the magnitude of that force. It is also responsible for breaking up road surfaces in winter. Figure 5.4 shows the result of this simple process on jointed rock exposed on a mountain top; this is the result of year-in year-out, day-and-night freezing and thawing, possibly over several thousand years.

Figure 5.4 Slabs of rock on a mountain top broken apart by frost action. Note the skyline, which shows how the accentuation of vertical joints by ice forming in them produces the typical jaggedness of cold mountainous areas – the slabs in the foreground have toppled from the area of exposed rock. (The person just above the patch of snow on the left shows the scale.)

■ Which other physical process might result in expansion and contraction?

□ When solids are heated they expand slightly and they contract as the temperature falls.

Heating and cooling also produces forces in rock, directly at the surface. Solar radiation can heat rock to uncomfortable temperatures, even in climatically frigid areas such as Antarctica. Radiation emission from the surface at night cools the rock. So, on a 24-hour basis, thermal expansion and contraction continually stress the rock. This occurs throughout exposed rock. Each kind of mineral responds differently to heating and cooling. So, differential forces act at boundaries between different minerals, particularly in coarse-grained rocks. Eventually the forces begin to split the minerals from one another, allowing water to seep along the grain boundaries. Freezing and thawing then liberates grains of each of them.

■ Which property of minerals is likely to assist breakage?

□ Some minerals have one or more cleavage planes; the planes of weakness within their crystal structure that allow them to break apart more easily.

Easily cleaved minerals, such as mica, feldspar and calcite, are more susceptible to breakage by physical weathering processes than quartz, which has no cleavage planes.

Physical weathering, by breaking rocks into fragments, increases the exposed surface area of different minerals so that they become more susceptible to chemical attack.

Two processes dominate **chemical weathering**: the action of acids and oxidation, which often operate together. Rainwater is slightly acidic, because it dissolves carbon dioxide:

$$\underset{\text{rainwater}}{H_2O(l) + CO_2(aq)} = \underset{\text{acidic solution}}{H^+(aq) + HCO_3^-(aq)} \quad (5.1)$$

The pH (Book 4, Chapter 11) of rainwater is not particularly low (5.2–6.5) but that is sufficient to attack many minerals chemically. Stronger acids are produced by vegetation, particularly when it decays in the soils of the humid tropics. However, there is another potent and widespread source of hydrogen ions. Crustal rocks contain on average about 0.04% sulfur. That is not very much but, since sulfur cannot enter silicates, it forms sulfide minerals in its own right; the most common being iron sulfide or pyrite (FeS_2) (you can view this in the computer-based resource *Minerals Gallery*). Pyrite is present in many rocks but usually in tiny amounts. However, its effect on chemical weathering can be dramatic because it readily oxidises when exposed to water containing dissolved oxygen:

$$\underset{\text{pyrite}}{2FeS_2(s)} + \underset{\text{oxygen}}{7O_2(aq)} + \underset{\text{water}}{2H_2O(l)} = \underset{\text{iron ions}}{2Fe^{2+}(aq)} + \underset{\text{sulfuric acid}}{4H^+(aq) + 4SO_4^{2-}(aq)} \quad (5.2)$$

The reaction is exothermic (Book 4, Section 9.2) and proceeds spontaneously when pyrite is exposed to oxygen. Once they reach the surface, rocks containing pyrite and those nearby are exposed to highly acidic conditions because of this vigorous reaction.

The most 'pristine' minerals to encounter surface conditions are the silicates in igneous rocks. Some are more prone to chemical attack by hydrogen ions than others. Quartz resists because of its strong framework structure (Book 4, Chapter 4). Olivine and pyroxene have structures containing metal atoms bonded weakly to their isolated and chained silicate tetrahedra (Section 4.1) and are particularly susceptible to chemical weathering. Feldspars and micas fall somewhere in between. They are less stable than quartz because a variety of metal atoms weakly connect the silicate tetrahedra in their framework and sheet structures respectively but they are more resistant than mafic minerals.

Igneous minerals are stable when igneous rocks crystallise at very high temperatures (Chapter 4), and most of them are anhydrous, i.e. contain neither water nor hydroxyl ions. When they meet the cool, wet, acidic conditions of the Earth's surface, all except quartz are unstable and eventually succumb to chemical attack. During weathering, hydrogen ions help to break free their loosely bonded metal atoms. When this happens their structures collapse to form clay minerals, which are hydrated aluminosilicates (e.g. kaolinite or 'china clay' – $Al_4Si_4O_{10}(OH)_8$) with a mica-like, platy structure that is stable under acid conditions. A good example is the breakdown of alkali feldspar ($(K,Na)AlSi_3O_8$) by acidic water:

$$\text{alkali feldspar(s)} + \underset{\text{acidic rainwater}}{H_2O(l) + H^+(aq)} = \text{kaolinite clay(s)} + \underset{\text{soluble ions}}{Na^+(aq) + K^+(aq)} + \underset{\text{silica}}{SiO_2(aq)} \quad (5.3)$$

The end products are the hydrous clay mineral kaolinite, along with K^+ and Na^+ ions and SiO_2 dissolved in water. Much the same happens to olivine and pyroxene, plagioclase feldspar and micas. The products are various clay minerals and dissolved metal ions, according to the igneous mineral's composition.

■ Alkali feldspar is a major constituent of granite, along with quartz and mica. If the chemical weathering of granite proceeds to completion, which solids remain?

□ Just quartz and clays remain.

When quartz-free igneous rocks – that is, most intermediate and all mafic varieties (Figure 5.5) – are completely weathered in this way, almost the only solids left are clays. Exposed rocks in the cool climate of northern Europe are often quite fresh (Figure 5.5a). In contrast, rock exposures in the humid tropics are often almost completely weathered (Figure 5.5b).

(a)

(b)

Figure 5.5 Effects of climate on the chemical weathering of granite: (a) an exposure in cool, wet southwestern England; (b) an exposure in a hot, humid part of Africa.

■ How might high rainfall and high temperatures influence chemical weathering reactions such as Equation 5.3?

□ Intense tropical rainfall provides copious amounts of acidic water. High temperature encourages abundant vegetation, whose rapid decomposition produces more acidity, and heat speeds up chemical reactions (Book 4, Chapter 10).

Chemical weathering is more rapid in warm, wet, tropical climates than in more temperate ones, and extremely slow to non-existent in cold climates. Indeed, rock can be weathered to depths of tens of metres in tropical climates.

The end products of the weathering of igneous rocks are:

- physically broken rocks and chemically stable minerals, mainly quartz
- newly formed clay minerals which are stable at the surface
- soluble ions.

Note that, although quartz is the most stable common mineral, small amounts of silica (SiO_2) do enter solution as a result of chemical weathering of other minerals (Equation 5.3).

This weathered mixture is more easily picked up by an agent of transportation than simply cracked, fresh rocks. Its exposure to flowing water, wind or, in frigid conditions, a glacier leads to mechanical removal or **erosion**. Once charged with moving debris, each transporting agent can become a means of eroding unweathered rock. Pebbles carried in rivers, sand grains carried by strong winds and fragments jutting from the base of a moving glacier can pound, blast and scrape more debris to wear away the surfaces over which they pass. The transported fragments are also broken down as they move along, to become smaller and more rounded.

Rates of erosion vary immensely, partly depending on topography because gravity is the dominant force in water and glacial erosion. Erosion can slowly wear away rocks over long periods of time, or it may be associated with sudden, catastrophic events. You may have witnessed the scouring of a river bank during a flood, the collapse of a sea cliff by storm-wave action, or rock debris sliding down a steep slope after heavy rain.

5.2.2 Sediment transport

Whether sedimentary grains can be transported or not depends partly on the energy supplied by the transporting medium so that grains can be moved.

■ What form of energy is this and on which properties of the transporting medium does it depend?

□ It is energy due to movement, or kinetic energy (E_k) (Book 3, Chapter 3):

$$E_k = \frac{1}{2}mv^2 \qquad (5.4)$$

Kinetic energy varies with the speed of movement (v) and the mass (m) and, therefore, the *density* of the transporting medium.

A grain's resistance to motion, which varies with its shape, size and density, also governs transportation. The video sequence *A Story in Sand* (Activity 5.2) shows what happens when sediment, containing a range of grain sizes, is dropped into flowing water. The larger grains settle to the stream bed, their mass being too great for them to be transported. Under the influence of the water current, smaller grains roll or bounce along the stream bed, and very small grains are picked up and carried along in suspension.

Activity 5.2 Sedimentary grains, transport and sorting – a story in sand

We expect this activity will take you approximately 60 minutes.

Important safety precautions

Take note of the safety precautions given with Activity 4.2.

Equipment needed

Kit items

Rock Specimen 2

Hand lens

Non-kit item

Large steel nail

First, watch the video sequence *A Story in Sand* on DVD2. It shows how physical and chemical weathering of granite, in a humid climate, produces grains available for transport by water and wind; and the types of sediment that these processes deposit. Make notes based on the questions in Task 1.

The rest of the activity involves making deductions about the origins of sediments and sedimentary rocks (including the sandstone sample from your Practical Kit) from simple observations and measurements.

Task 1

(a) Which processes break down exposed rocks to produce sediment grains?
(b) What are the three ways in which grains move downstream in flowing water?
(c) How do typical river sediments differ from typical beach sediments?
(d) How do the shape and surface texture of wind-blown grains differ from grains deposited by water?

a) wind, rain, temp
b) rolling, bumping, carried in stream
c) Coarser
d) wind blown rounder smoother, duller, oxidised

Task 2

Draw a histogram (as demonstrated in *A Story in Sand*) to describe the grain-size distribution of a sample of sand. (The sieving data for this sediment are given in Table 5.1.)

First, calculate the total mass of sediment, and then express the mass retained by each sieve as a proportion of the total mass, in per cent (enter your results in Table 5.1).

On Figure 5.6 plot a histogram showing the grain-size distribution of this sample of sand, using the mass percentages that you entered in Table 5.1. The height of each vertical bar on the histogram should correspond to the mass percentage in a particular sieve. By convention, each bar should be drawn to the left of the sieve size it represents. For example, the bar for the 0.5 mm sieve should be drawn

Table 5.1 Grain-size data from a sieving experiment with a sand sample.

Sieve size/mm	Mass in sieve/g	Proportion of total mass/%
4	1.0	2%
2	1.4	2.9
1	4.8	10.1%
0.5	7.1	14.9
0.25	14.5	30.4
0.12	9.4	19.7
0.06	7.3	15.3
pan	2.2	4.6
total	47.7	

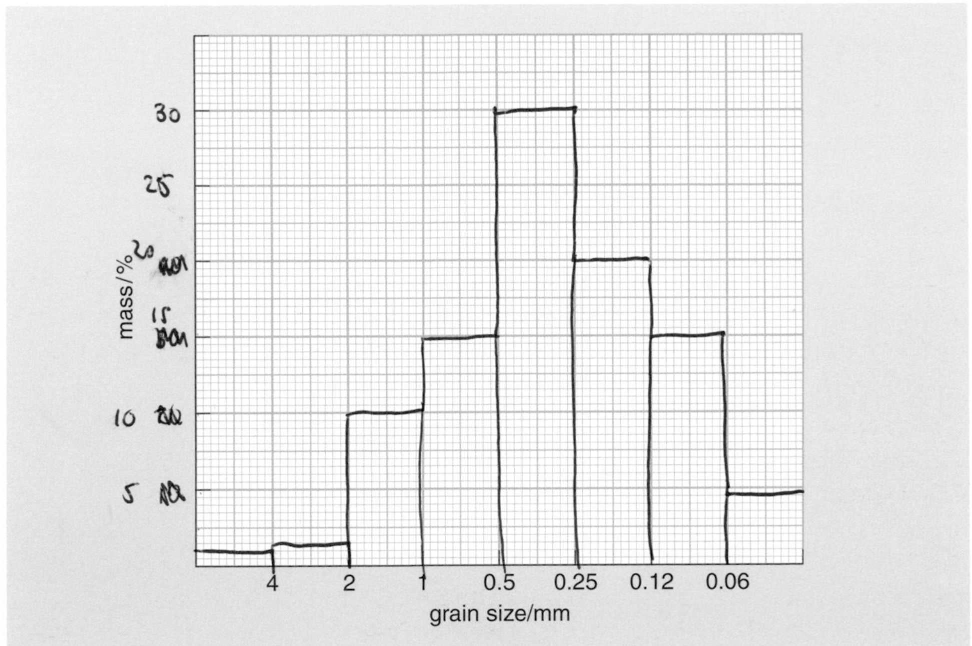

Figure 5.6 Graph paper for plotting a histogram of the sieving experiment data in Table 5.1.

between 0.5 mm and 1 mm. This is because the 0.5 mm sieve retains all grains with sizes between 0.5 mm and 1 mm (the size of the grains that just pass through the next largest sieve).

Is the sediment sample well-sorted or poorly sorted?

Task 3

Histograms represent visually the grain-size distribution in a sediment. Different environments of deposition result in different forms of distribution; in the video sequence you saw histograms of desert sand and beach sand.

(a) From your notes on the video, suggest which histogram in Figure 5.7a corresponds to the grain-size distributions for river, beach and desert dune sands, and explain why.

Cumulative frequency distribution diagrams (as you saw in *A Story in Sand*) are an alternative means of representing sediment grain-size data.

(b) Which cumulative frequency distribution diagram in Figure 5.7b matches which histogram in Figure 5.7a?

Task 4

The video sequence showed sand grains from a beach and from a desert.

Try to scrape some grains from the sandstone sample (Specimen 2), first with a fingernail, then using a steel nail.

How difficult is it to remove grains from the sandstone compared with the igneous samples (Activity 4.2)? Why do you think that is?

Prise several grains onto millimetre-squared graph paper (Figure 5.6), and use your hand lens to examine them.

What kinds of grain can you see, and roughly what is the range of grain sizes present? (You will use this information in Section 5.2.3.)

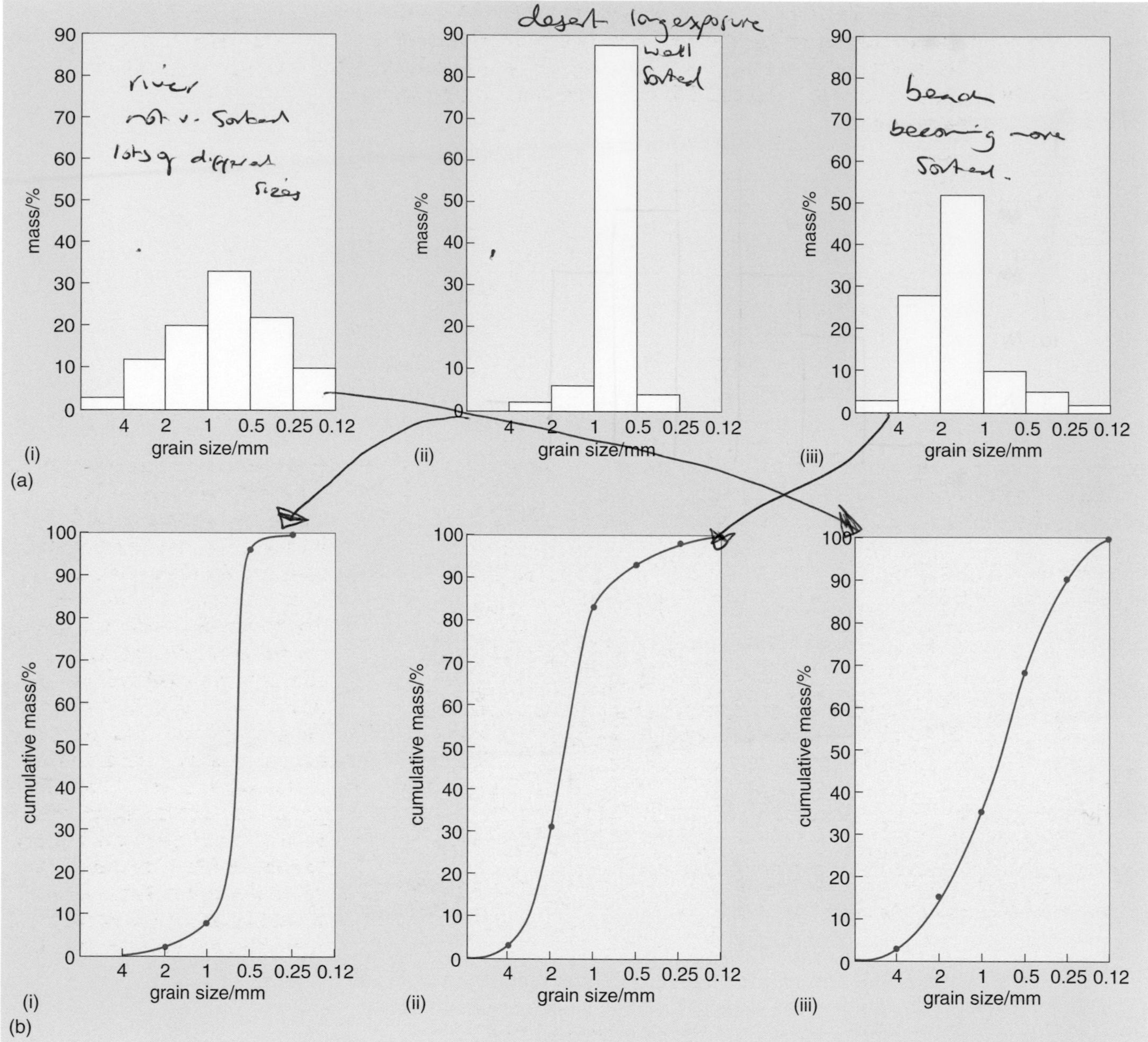

Figure 5.7 (a) Grain-size histograms for three sedimentary environments. (b) Cumulative frequency distribution diagrams, featuring equivalent sediment grain-size distributions to those in part (a). Note that grain sizes in the histograms decrease from left to right.

Now look at the rock through your hand lens, and describe the shape and the arrangement of the grains.

What medium would have transported them?

Place a few drops of water on the surface of the rock.

What happens to them, and what does that suggest about the rock? (Make a note for use in Section 5.4.)

Now look at the comments on this activity at the end of this book.

Activity 5.2 showed that the ability of wind or flowing water to pick up, transport and deposit sediment grains depends largely on both the speed of the flowing medium and the grain size of the material. The behaviour of different grain sizes with varying speed of flow is shown in Figure 5.8. This graph is explained in some detail in the video sequence *A Story in Sand*.

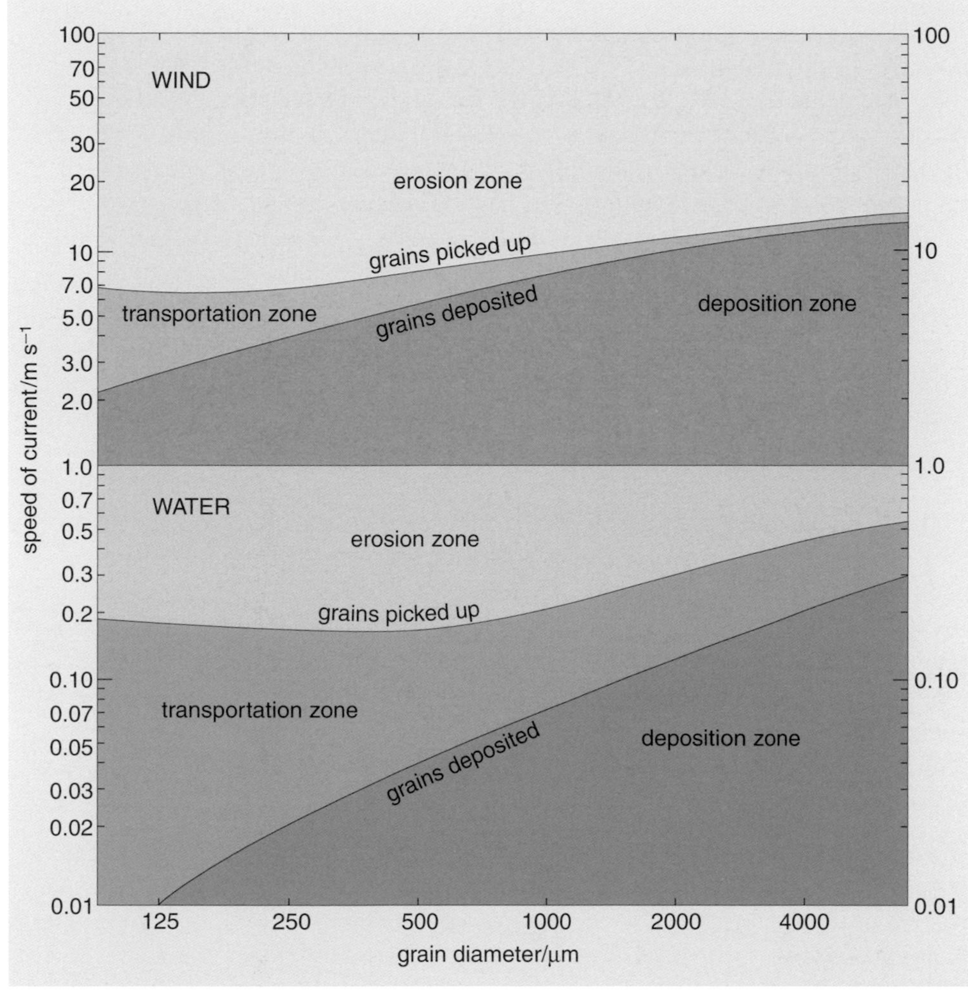

Figure 5.8 The behaviour of different-sized sediment grains at varying speeds of flow for wind and water. In both cases, the boundaries of the erosion zone, the transportation zone and the deposition zone (see text) were derived experimentally under controlled conditions of flow using sediment grains of uniform density. Note that the scales on the axes are not linear: on the horizontal axis, each division corresponds to a doubling of grain size; on the vertical axis, each major division corresponds to a factor of ten increase in the speed of current. These forms of scaling allow a wide range of flow rates and grain sizes to be shown.

The main points to appreciate from the blue part (lower part of the figure) of Figure 5.8 relating to *water* transportation are:

- Flowing water picks up grains of a particular size only if the speed of flow exceeds that of the upper curve. The slope of the curve for grain diameters above 500 µm shows that the speed (and thus kinetic energy, Equation 5.4) of the water current must increase to pick up larger grains. The erosion zone above this curve, therefore, describes conditions under which static grains of a particular size can be picked up and moved.
- Grains that have already been picked up can continue to be transported at speeds of flow lower than those required for pick-up (the upper curve). If the flow speed of a particular grain size drops to the lower curve, the flow can no longer transport the grain and it settles. The transportation zone is between these two curves.
- Grains do not move at all at flow speeds below the lower curve. Material of a particular grain size, transported at higher speeds of flow, is deposited when the flow speed drops to the lower curve – this defines the deposition zone.

■ From Figure 5.8, at what speed of water current would 1 mm diameter sand grains be picked up and at what speed would they be deposited?

□ A flow of more than $0.2\ m\ s^{-1}$ would be required to pick up 1 mm (i.e. 1000 μm) sand grains; but they would not be deposited until the flow speed had dropped to about $0.07\ m\ s^{-1}$.

While sedimentary grains are being transported in water they are exposed to both physical abrasion and chemical attack. The chemical decomposition of rock fragments during transport is much the same as in chemical weathering (Section 5.2.1). Reactive minerals (e.g. alkali feldspars) form clay minerals and dissolved ions (Equation 5.3), while resistant quartz is liberated. Inevitably, transported grains collide with each other and the stream bed. The viscosity of water cushions the impacts, so rock fragments tend to become rounded by abrasion, rather than broken by impact. The larger and more massive the grains, the more kinetic energy they have. Consequently, large grains tend to become rounded more readily than smaller ones. You could verify this by examining pebbles and sand in a river bed or on a beach.

5.2.3 Sediment deposition

Figure 5.8 and Activity 5.2 showed you that sedimentary material is deposited when transporting currents slow down sufficiently. Where does this usually occur? In rivers, the downhill movement of water and its sedimentary load involves their gravitational energy being transformed into kinetic energy (Book 3, Section 5.2). On steep slopes, where flow rates are high – a high-energy environment – only coarse material is deposited. As the slope decreases, the flow speed lessens, so that progressively finer grains are deposited in environments which have decreasing energy. Eventually, only very fine grains are left to be deposited in low-energy environments.

High in a river system, deposits in these environments are transient; erosion will eventually remove them. Thick sequences of sediments can accumulate and remain in lowland areas or on the sea floor if the crust subsides, because of either tectonic activity or the mass of sediment, to create sedimentary basins.

The 'degree of sorting' can be used to describe and characterise certain types of sediment, as in the video sequence *A Story in Sand*. It describes the extent to which the grains deposited are of a similar size. Thus a well-sorted deposit (Figure 5.9a) contains a narrow range of grain sizes, whereas a poorly sorted deposit contains a wide range of grain sizes (Figure 5.9b); the corresponding, histograms of well- and poorly sorted sediments are also given. Figure 5.8 helps explain why such sorting occurs. The lower curve gives the size of grains deposited at a particular speed of water flow. The curve rises steadily, so there is a direct link between the speed of the current and the size of grains deposited; the result of this is sediment sorting.

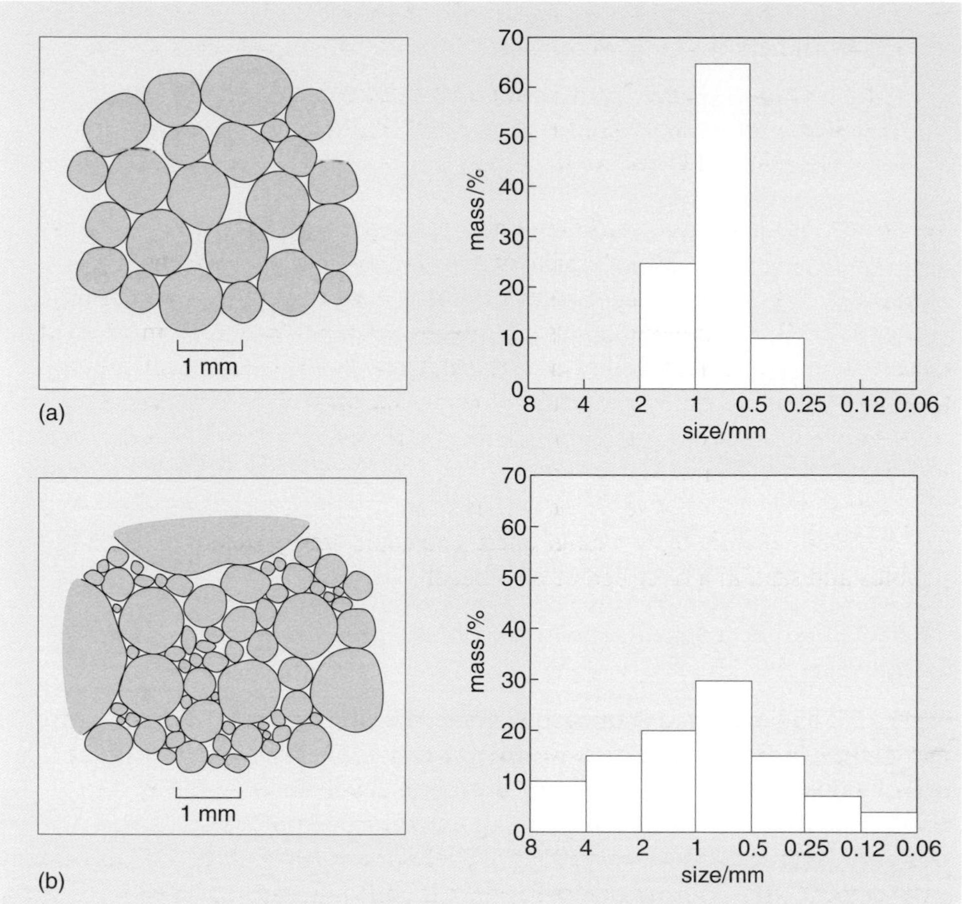

Figure 5.9 Schematic representation of (a) well-sorted and (b) poorly sorted sediment grains with histograms of their grain-size distributions. Note that grain sizes in the histograms decrease from left to right.

What might produce good sorting? According to Figure 5.8, a rapidly flowing current can pick up and carry a range of grain sizes. If the current *gradually* slows, all the picked-up grains continue to be transported until a speed is reached when the coarsest material is deposited. Finer material is still carried onward. So, when speeds of flow drop slightly – because either slopes flatten or there is a reduction in the volume of flow – a narrow range of grain sizes is deposited. If the speed of flow continues to decrease steadily, grains of successively smaller size are deposited, but grains deposited at one place at a particular time will have a narrow size range and be well-sorted. In contrast, if a rapid flow subsides abruptly, a wide range of grain sizes are deposited all at once, creating a poorly sorted sediment. Thus, the measured degree of sorting of a sediment gives information about the way it formed, especially about the conditions of flow that transported and deposited it.

■ Grains from the Practical Kit sandstone vary in size. Is it a well-sorted or a poorly sorted sandstone? What does that indicate about the conditions of deposition?

□ In most samples, 0.5–1 mm grains are common, but grain size ranges from <0.1 mm to about 2 mm in diameter. The sandstone is only moderately well-sorted and must have been deposited under somewhat variable flow conditions.

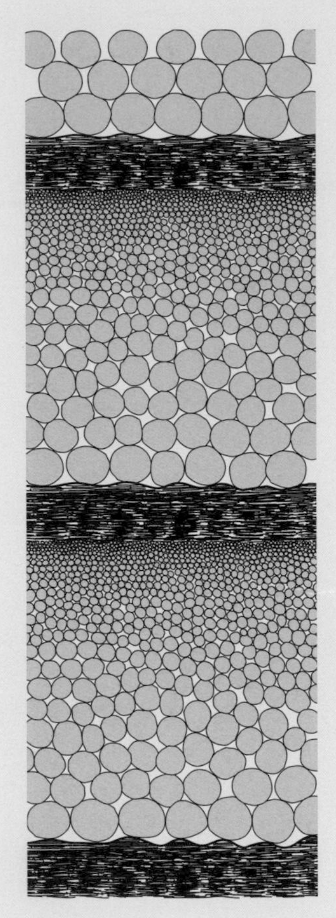

Figure 5.10 Graded beds resulting from deposition as flow speeds repeatedly decline. Successive graded beds are often separated by an eroded surface, reflecting the increase in flow that precedes deposition of the next graded bed.

■ A rapidly flowing river carrying a range of sediment grain sizes enters the sea. What happens to the sediment?

□ The flow speed suddenly slows. As in Activity 5.1, a range of grain sizes begins to settle at once. Coarse grains settle out first and then progressively finer material builds up on top. In still water, all the grains eventually settle.

A rock bed produced in this way will look rather like the sediment that accumulated after you stopped shaking the jar in Activity 5.1. The grain size varied with height but, at any particular level in the jar, the sediment was fairly well-sorted. The gradual change in grain size from the bottom to the top of the bed is called **graded bedding** (Figure 5.10). How does this 'grading' of grains happen?

The answer comes from Book 2 (Section 14.1). Two forces affect every grain: one from gravity acting downwards; the other from the resistance of the water (its viscosity) acts upwards. The smaller the grain, the greater this resistance is, and the result is that smaller grains fall more slowly than larger grains. The difference is profound over the natural size range of sedimentary grains. That is why mud-sized sediment remains suspended in stagnant water, even after several days.

The upwardly decreasing grain size in graded bedding can help geologists work out the time order in which beds were deposited. In Section 6.2 you will see that rock strata are sometimes completely overturned by tectonic activity.

Question 5.1

How does weathering in hot, humid climates differ from that in cold, wet climates? What kind of weathering would you expect on the Moon?

Question 5.2

How does weathering affect granite? Explain the effects of physical and chemical weathering on the main minerals of granite (Specimen 6 in the Practical Kit), and write down the main products of weathering.

5.3 Sedimentary deposits as environmental indicators

As well as the movement of fluids, many other influences, such as climate, biological activity and topography, create a huge diversity of depositional environments. Environments dominated by water, wind and ice each deposit distinct types of sediment, but conditions associated with water are the most diverse. They include rivers and lakes; beaches and deltas; shallow seas and the deep ocean floor. Studying sediments being deposited today plays a crucial part in recognising and making deductions about their ancient equivalents in the rock record – thus providing the keys to understanding past environments.

This section considers three very different sedimentary environments to illustrate the most important concepts used in understanding sedimentary rocks. They involve the transportation of fragmentary material by wind; the crystallisation of salts from water; and the extraction of soluble material from seawater by marine organisms.

5.3.1 Desert sands

By definition, a desert is an environment in which very little lives, because it is a dry, barren wilderness (which could be hot or cold). The most familiar deserts are where winds create storms of sand and dust, and form sand dunes.

■ What implications does the lack of water have for weathering and for erosion in such a desert?

□ Lack of water inhibits chemical weathering and the release of soluble ions (nutrients), and the formation of clay minerals (vital components of fertile soils). Physical processes dominate desert weathering. With sparse vegetation there are few roots to bind together fragments of rocks and minerals and little shelter by leaf and branch cover from transporting agencies, so as to resist erosion.

Physical weathering in hot deserts is dominated by extreme temperature changes that cause expansion and contraction of rock surfaces and individual mineral grains. Daytime solar radiation may heat rock surfaces to over 80 °C. Lack of night-time cloud cover allows temperatures to plummet, often to well below 0 °C. Layers of rock flake off, and they break down to particles rich in one mineral or another. There is evidence that dew, which can penetrate grain boundaries, speeds up this physical weathering.

Rock and mineral fragments exposed in deserts are very prone to being eroded and transported by wind, an additional factor being their dryness. Moist material is held together by pore water, as you will have seen in garden soil after rain, or in beach sand when the tide is going out. After heavy rain from rare storms, water runs off the land surface rapidly to cause flash floods, which have intense erosive power. Such floods easily erode and transport desert sediment to flat ground, in isolated but spectacular episodes. Strong winds are much more frequent. Although air is 1000 times less dense than water, winds can move large quantities of loose, dry sand grains from the sediments occasionally shifted by flash floods.

■ A water current of over 0.2 m s^{-1} can pick up 1 mm quartz grains (Figure 5.8). How much faster must the wind travel to pick up the same grains?

□ A wind travelling at more than 10 m s^{-1} (or 36 km h^{-1}), at least 50 times as fast as the minimum water current, would be required. A similar factor applies across a wide range of grain sizes.

Once picked up, dust grains (less than 0.01 mm in diameter) can be carried by a light wind, but it takes a brisk wind to carry sand grains, and pebbles are rarely moved even by very high winds. Dust picked up in suspension may be transported many thousands of kilometres (Section 2.1.1).

Wind transports grains, as water does, in three ways (Figure 5.11): suspended in the air; by rolling surface grains along; and by bouncing so that sand grains, lifted and propelled by the wind, then fall and hit other grains, triggering them to bounce too (you saw this in the video sequence *A Story in Sand*). In windy conditions, the last process may lift sand grains as high as 2 m above the ground, producing a sand blast capable of wearing away both other grains and rock surfaces. It also stings if you walk with bare legs across a dry sandy beach on a very windy day.

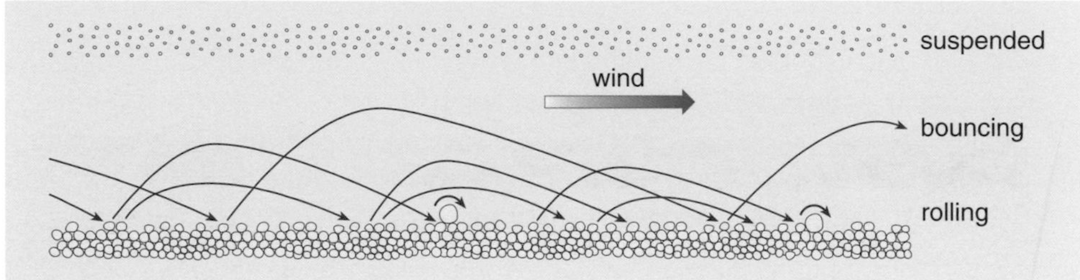

Figure 5.11 The movement of sand by wind. Bouncing often involves grains propelled by the wind knocking other grains into the air as they fall.

Air is far less viscous than water, so does little to cushion impacts between wind-blown grains. Repeated impacts produce well-rounded grains with finely pitted surfaces – often described as a 'frosted' appearance – a particular characteristic of desert sands (as you saw in the video sequence *A Story in Sand*). In contrast, sand grains worn down in water are never so well rounded and they look glassier; they are not pitted because of cushioning by the water around them. Desert sands consist mainly of quartz, the most resistant of the common minerals. Lacking cleavage, quartz fragments resist being smashed by impacts, whereas cleaved minerals easily split into increasingly fine particles. Sand grains in deserts are generally too large to be carried away in suspension but are small enough to be transported by high winds through bouncing or rolling.

■ Would you expect sand from a desert dune to be well or poorly sorted?

□ It will probably have a fairly narrow range of grain size. Small grains are carried far away in suspension, while large grains are left behind, even if they do roll a little. Only the narrow range of grain sizes that can bounce (Figure 5.8) contribute to a dune, so it will be well-sorted.

Sedimentary rocks in the geological record that contain well-sorted, well-rounded and frosted grains of quartz sand are most likely to have formed under desert conditions. However, these characteristics are not sufficient to *prove* deposition by wind, because desert sand grains could be picked up by flowing water and redeposited. Consequently, additional indicators are needed to confirm deposition by wind under arid conditions.

Wherever there is abundant dry sand that wind can move, and if strong winds blow frequently, the moving sand builds up wave-like features on a range of scales from small ripples (tens of centimetres) to dunes up to 100 m high (Figure 5.12a and 5.12b). Figure 5.12c shows how a simple sand wave develops on an uneven surface. On the slope facing the wind, grains shift to the wave crest, beyond which they build up in the sheltered conditions of the wave's lee side. Periodically, the accumulation of grains collapses so that sand slides down the lee side of the feature, to form sloping layers. Whenever the wind blows strongly, more sand is shifted from the windward side of the wave and over its crest, to be added layer by layer to the lee side. In this way, the wave itself advances slowly downwind.

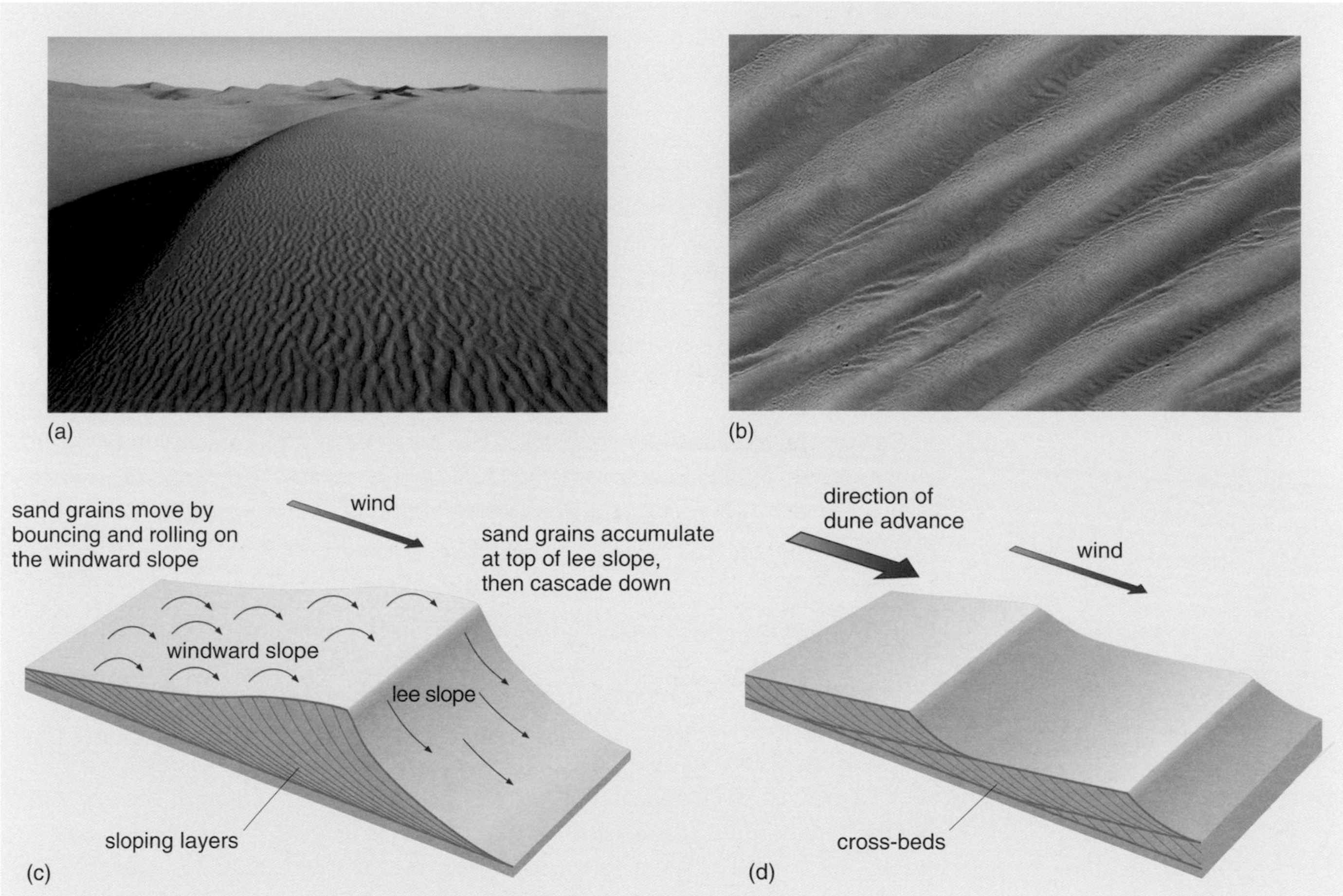

Figure 5.12 Wind-blown sand: (a) ripples on dunes in Death Valley, California, USA. The foreground is about 5 m across; (b) dunes of several scales superimposed on giant linear dunes in the Empty Quarter of Saudi Arabia, viewed from satellite. The image is 15 km across. (c) Movement of a sand wave and the formation of sloping layers of sand. (d) Formation of a series of cross-bedded layers when a wave is overridden by another. Note that the main beds are nearly horizontal. The inclination of the layers between them does not result from tilting but from deposition on a slope. (Part (b), an image from the *Quickbird* satellite, courtesy of DigitalGlobe.)

Before long, another sand wave advances to ride up the windward side (Figure 5.12b). It may partially erode a previous series of layers. Eventually, a series of beds, each made up of dipping layers, becomes preserved. This creates a sedimentary structure known as **cross-bedding**, whose scale can range from centimetres in migrating ripples, to tens of metres in the case of dunes. Water currents also produce moving sand waves, but the resulting cross-bedding is usually on a smaller scale, with cross-bedding that dips at significantly shallower angles than in desert dunes.

■ Re-examine Figure 5.1, and decide which image is of a sedimentary rock that probably formed as a wind-blown dune.

□ Figure 5.1b shows horizontal beds about 1 m thick, each made up of dipping layers a few centimetres thick. This cross-bedding is typical of sedimentation in wind-blown dunes.

Another feature of ancient desert deposits is their colour. The lack of vegetation and decaying organic material in deserts, combined with their dryness, results in air filling the spaces between sand grains. As a result, desert sediments experience highly *oxidising* conditions (Book 4, Chapter 8). The iron content of ferromagnesian minerals (i.e. those containing iron and magnesium) is partly in the form of Fe^{2+} ions. During chemical weathering these ions may enter aqueous solution, if conditions are reducing. Although chemical weathering is very slow in deserts, when unstable ferromagnesian minerals do break down, their iron content is rapidly oxidised to highly insoluble Fe^{3+}. Its combination with oxygen to form small amounts of fine-grained hematite (Fe_2O_3) gives desert sand grains a distinct red-orange hue. It is the combination of redness and evidence of wind-blown sediments that truly signifies desert conditions in the past.

Desert sandstones are an example of **red-beds**, which are important indicators of oxidising conditions in the past (Book 2, Section 7.2). Waterlogging in sediments deposited on land (called terrestrial sediments) under humid climatic conditions creates *reducing* conditions. Many such sediments containing preserved, unoxidised organic matter maintain reducing conditions long after their deposition. Oxidised Fe^{3+} minerals do not form in them. Instead, reduced Fe^{2+} commonly forms fine-grained iron sulfide (pyrite, Fe_2S), which gives the rocks a grey to black appearance. (Note that modern weathering of such rocks in humid conditions results in the oxidation of pyrite to form Fe^{3+} hydroxides, giving their exposed *surfaces* a yellow-brown to orange colour.)

As you saw in Section 3.4, vegetation appeared on the land surface only after about 430 Ma ago, and only became prominent during the Lower Carboniferous (350 Ma). Organic matter was rarely, if ever, preserved in earlier terrestrial sediments, irrespective of the climate in which they formed. So, many terrestrial sandstones older than 430 Ma were easily oxidised to form red-beds; thus a red sediment is *not* a universal indicator of desert deposition. The environment under which red-beds formed has to be deduced from the kinds of sedimentary structures in them. In Chapter 7 you will meet examples of red-beds that feature strongly in the geological history of the British Isles.

5.3.2 Evaporites – crystalline sediments

The soluble ions released by chemical weathering are predominantly Na^+, K^+, Ca^{2+}, Mg^{2+} and HCO_3^- (Equation 5.1). They are transported at very low concentrations in rivers (freshwater) eventually to reach the sea. In seawater, such dissolved materials amount to about 3.5% by mass, forming a salty solution in which Na^+, Mg^{2+}, SO_4^{2-} and Cl^- ions are the most important (Table 5.2). You might expect that the continuous addition of soluble material to the oceans would lead to a steady increase in the concentrations of salts in seawater over time, but this is not the case. In fact, a more-or-less steady state is maintained, and concentrations are constrained by natural processes.

Table 5.2 Typical concentrations of dissolved ions in natural waters.

Dissolved ion	Concentration in river water/mg litre^{-1}	Concentration in seawater/mg litre^{-1}
Na^+	7	10 770
K^+	2	380
Ca^{2+}	15	410
Mg^{2+}	4	1 290
HCO_3^-	56	140
SO_4^{2-}	11	2 650
Cl^-	18	19 500

Note: concentrations in river water are extremely variable.

Rates of evaporation in hot climates are high, especially from bodies of shallow water, which heat up quickly. Evaporation increases the concentration of salts in aqueous solution, until the water becomes *saturated* (Book 4, Chapter 11) and can hold no more dissolved salts in solution. Further evaporation causes dissolved salts to crystallise, forming **evaporite** deposits. These are mined for raw materials used in the chemical industry, and for winter road treatment in the case of common salt. These salts include halite (NaCl or 'rock salt'), and the less soluble salt gypsum ($CaSO_4.2H_2O$), which is used to make plaster, and potassium salts which are vital in fertilisers. (The $.2H_2O$ in its formula signifies that gypsum contains water in its structure.) Such deposits form in several different environments, including the following:

- Enclosed inland basins in arid regions into which rivers flow intermittently, such as the Great Salt Lake, Utah, USA (Figure 5.13a). The trapped water evaporates and the dissolved salts eventually crystallise to form salt flats.
- Shallow coastal lagoons in hot areas, where evaporation is high and salts crystallise (Figure 5.13b). Restricted access to the open sea allows the intermittent inflow of seawater to replenish the supply of salts.
- Coastal mudflats along arid shorelines, such as the Persian Gulf, where water evaporates from tidally exposed mud, in which salts crystallise as it dries out. Seawater replenishes the supply of salty water by seepage into the muds.

(a)

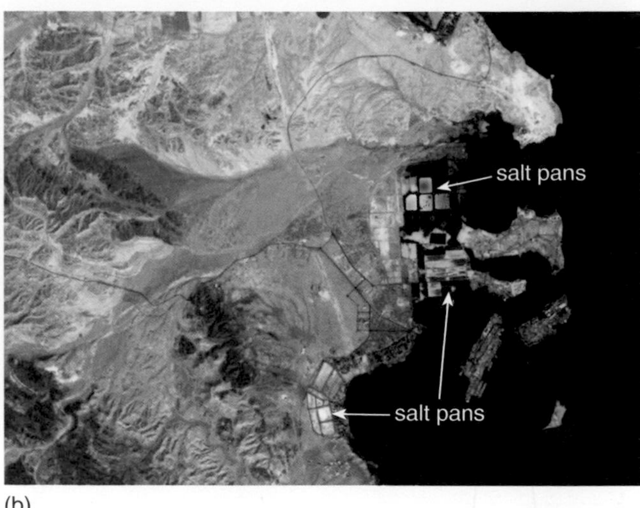

(b)

Figure 5.13 Products of natural evaporation. (a) The salt flats of the Great Salt Lake, Utah, USA. (b) By creating artificial lagoons on arid coasts, seawater can be evaporated to produce a variety of salts commercially. This is a view from space of such salt pans on the Red Sea coast of Eritrea, northeast Africa.

Evaporation forms sedimentary rocks which are not fragmentary but are made of intergrown crystals; an exception to the generalisation that sedimentary textures are fragmental. However, evaporites are usually distinguishable as sedimentary deposits by their layering, and are often associated with red-beds. Rock salt and gypsum deposits are also key indicators of arid climatic conditions in the geological record.

5.3.3 Limestones

Many groups of marine organisms take up calcium (Ca^{2+}) and hydrogen-carbonate (HCO_3^-) ions dissolved in seawater to produce shells or skeletons composed of calcium carbonate (calcite). When these organisms die, both whole and broken hard parts accumulate on the sea floor. When sufficiently abundant they form **limestone** deposits containing fragments that are clearly organic in origin (see Kit Specimen 3). Animal groups such as bivalves, brachiopods, echinoids, corals and foraminifera are often found in limestones. Even marine phytoplankton produce calcium carbonate; for example, the calcite plates of tiny coccolithophores (Book 1, Figure 7.5a) which form the bulk of Cretaceous Chalk deposits of western Europe.

Clay and silt suspended in seawater inhibit the growth of many carbonate-producing organisms, so limestones tend to indicate deposition in clear water, away from supplies of land-derived sediment. The most productive marine environments for limestone formation today are shallow, tropical or subtropical seas, between about 30° N and 30° S of the Equator. There, reef-building organisms such as corals are common (you met these in Activity 2.2). By analogy, many ancient limestones were formed in warm, tropical seas that were clear and shallow.

Many animals that secrete hard parts made of calcite are subject to predation, despite their defences. Predators digest the soft parts but excrete calcite as ground-up fragments and mud. This debris also contributes to the formation of limestone, as does fine carbonate material produced by the erosive action of waves and currents on dead remains.

■ Imagine a bed of limestone formed almost completely of fine-grained calcium carbonate, which is now a hard rock. What inference can you make about the strength of currents that were active when the bed was deposited and about the proximity at that time to sources of land-derived sediment?

□ The limestone must have accumulated in quiet, low-energy conditions where currents were not strong enough to remove the carbonate mud. There was probably no nearby source of land-derived sediment because this would have introduced material such as clay minerals and quartz.

■ Examine Kit Specimen 3, the crinoidal limestone. What evidence is there that currents involved in its deposition were stronger than those depositing the muddy limestone discussed here?

□ This limestone contains small fragments of broken and haphazardly arranged crinoid stems and plates, some of which exceed 5 mm in size. The currents required to break up and move these sizeable crinoid fragments were certainly far stronger than those that deposited only fine carbonate muds.

Question 5.3

What are the main indicators of arid desert conditions in ancient sandstones?

Question 5.4

Which sedimentary processes are important in maintaining the natural balance of salts in seawater?

5.4 From sediments to sedimentary rocks

If sedimentary deposits form as loose sands or soft muds, how do they become hard rocks, such as the sandstone in the Practical Kit?

Material between the sand grains in Specimen 2 holds it together. The sandstone absorbs water, so this material does not fill spaces inside the rock completely; it merely coats and loosely bonds the grains, so that they can be dislodged (Activity 5.2). The limestone (Specimen 3) holds together much better.

The conversion of loose or soft sediments into sedimentary rocks results from several processes of lithification (Book 1, Section 7.4.3), which can start soon after deposition. Many sediments are deposited by water and, even when desert sandstones are buried, underground water eventually occupies the spaces between the grains.

■ What happens to the water filling the spaces between sediment grains when more and more sediment is loaded on top?

□ The weight of overlying sediment tends to press the sediment grains closer together, driving the water out from between them.

Muddy sediments may contain up to 60% water when they are deposited, much of which is expelled by **compaction** to form a mudstone. If the mud contains platy clay minerals, compaction and de-watering may align them (Figure 5.14a), making a rock that is easily split into thin layers; a form of mudstone commonly called shale. Coarser sediments, such as sands, do not compact much during burial because their grains pack together tightly when first deposited, whether in air or under water.

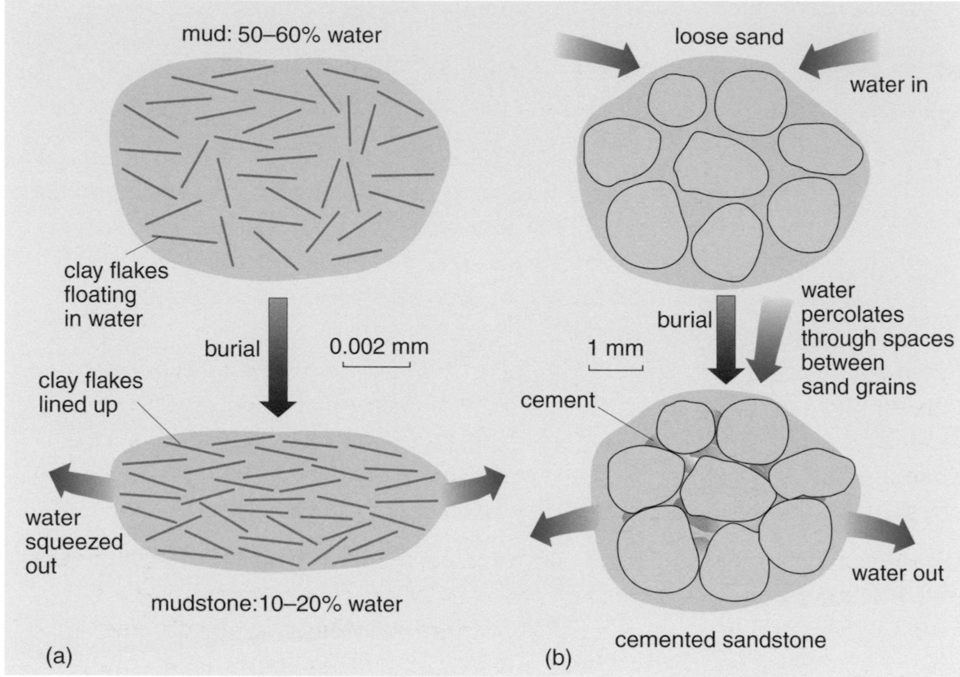

Figure 5.14 Lithification of sediments: (a) burial compacts muds; (b) percolating water precipitates cement between sand grains.

Water between the grains in buried sediments may dissolve material, such as calcite, from the surrounding mineral grains themselves. If minerals are precipitated from the resulting solution in the spaces between the grains (Figure 5.14b), they hold the grains together. This process is called **cementation**. It is the main way in which sandstones and especially limestones are lithified. Interestingly, the weathering of feldspars releases some SiO_2 to solution in natural waters (Equation 5.3). If this precipitates as quartz in the spaces between grains, it forms a particularly strong cement. An analogy for cementation is what happens to damp grains of sugar; on drying out they form a hard lump. The whole process takes much longer in rocks.

Since most sedimentary rocks are lithified after burial, they are normally exposed only when they return to the surface through erosion or earth movements. However, earth movements can also force sedimentary rocks many kilometres deep into the Earth. There they encounter high temperatures and pressures, and may eventually completely recrystallise to become metamorphic rocks (Chapter 6).

Question 5.5

Match the following rock types to an appropriate description from the list below: (i) mudstone; (ii) conglomerate; (iii) limestone; (iv) evaporite; (v) breccia: (*Hint*: each of (a) to (g) may be used once, more than once, or not at all.)

(a) Contains rounded grains of quartz sand

(b) Contains a high proportion of clay minerals

(c) Contains large angular rock fragments

(d) Contains interlocking crystals of water-soluble minerals

(e) Contains layers of sandy and muddy sediment

(f) Contains rounded pebbles cemented by quartz

(g) Contains remains of shelly organisms in fine-grained carbonate mud.

5.5 Summary of Chapter 5

Sedimentary deposits are formed by the processes of weathering, erosion, transportation and deposition at the Earth's surface. Once they are converted to rocks, they are usually distinguished from other rocks by their fragmental texture and by their layering. The size of sedimentary grains provides a means of classifying them into muds, sands, pebbles, cobbles and boulders.

Weathering involves the disintegration and decomposition of rocks by exposure to the weather, surface waters and organisms. Physical weathering opens up cracks, breaking down rock into smaller fragments. Chemical weathering involves the breakdown of unstable minerals (e.g. feldspars) by acidic waters to form new, more stable minerals (e.g. clays) and soluble products (e.g. metal ions and silica); resistant minerals (e.g. quartz) are liberated. Erosion is the physical removal of rocks and minerals and the wearing away of rock by debris carried by flowing water, wind and ice.

The size of sedimentary grains picked up and transported by water or wind depends on the energy of the flowing medium (its density and speed of flow). Wind speeds need to be about 50 times greater than water speeds to pick up grains of similar size. Whether or not sediment is eroded, transported or deposited is mainly determined by its grain size and the speed of flow. Materials deposited under a narrow range of flow conditions have a narrow range of grain sizes and are well-sorted. Wind-blown sands are particularly well-sorted. A gradual change in grain size through a bed is known as graded bedding; the upward decrease in grain size reflects a declining speed of flow.

Desert sandstones typically contain well-sorted, well-rounded, finely pitted and reddened grains in quite steeply sloping layers which indicate formation as a result of wind action in an arid environment. Evaporite deposits such as rock salt and gypsum also indicate arid environments where salts have crystallised by evaporation of shallow or enclosed saline waters. The accumulation of calcium carbonate shells or skeletons of organisms produces limestone, which is often indicative of warm, clear marine waters. The observation of depositional processes in modern sedimentary environments provides a means of identifying ancient environments from sedimentary structures in rocks.

During burial, sediments are lithified by compaction and/or by cementation to form sedimentary rocks such as mudstones, shales, sandstones, conglomerates and limestones.

Your study of this chapter involved: comparing information given in diagrams, graphs and computer-based learning resources, including data that you have plotted as histograms; describing and interpreting that information; applying it more widely, and summarising your findings. You have also applied concepts about sedimentary processes to explain variations in sedimentary rocks in terms of various surface environments. By performing a simple experiment, you have developed new insights into your own surroundings, i.e. soil.

Chapter 6 Metamorphic rocks and deformation – heat, pressure and force

Large-scale processes in the rock cycle (Figure 6.1) transform the rocks' environment so that they encounter very different conditions. For example, a plutonic igneous rock, having crystallised at depth, reaches the surface after uplift and erosion of overlying rocks. The plutonic rock then begins to contribute to the production of sediments. Conversely, sedimentary burial or compressive tectonic forces may move rocks that were at the surface to deep within the crust. The most extreme cases occur when lithospheric plates converge. This deforms and thickens continental crust to form mountain belts, and oceanic crust in subduction zones descends deep into the mantle (Book 2, Section 8.6). Conditions in the crust may also change without any significant deformation, when hot magmas rise, intrude and heat up older rocks that would otherwise be much cooler. This chapter looks at the processes of metamorphism and deformation that transform rocks when temperature, pressure and tectonic forces rise significantly.

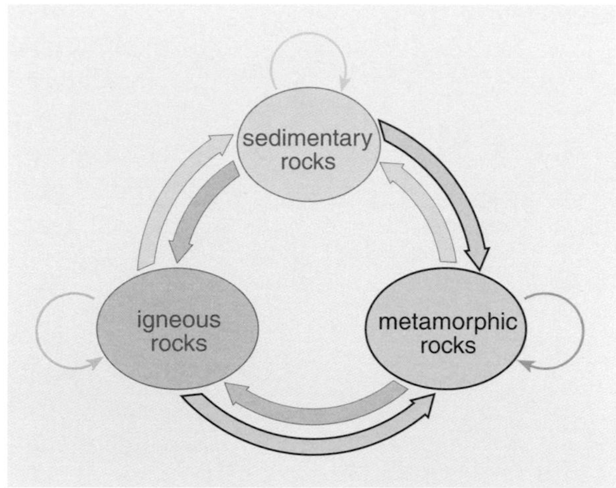

Figure 6.1 Formation of metamorphic rocks in the rock cycle. The three bold arrows indicate the routes of formation of metamorphic rocks by burial and crystallisation under heat and pressure.

Metamorphic rocks have distinctive textures: interlocking crystals; platy minerals showing clear alignment (Figure 4.1b); other minerals sometimes arranged in bands. Such textures indicate that crystallisation happened in the solid state (Book 2, Section 5.2.3), under the influence of deforming forces. Metamorphic changes occur when mineral structures reorganise themselves in response to temperature and pressure changes in their physical environment. Increased vibration of bonds in mineral structures, caused by rising temperature, encourages elements to leave one structure and enter another that is more stable under the new conditions. This results in the growth of new minerals or recrystallisation of old ones, yet the overall chemical composition of the rock remains unchanged. Metamorphic reactions are very different from familiar chemical reactions in aqueous solutions. In comparison with laboratory experiments, solid-state metamorphic reactions are very slow.

Minerals deep underground encounter far higher temperatures and pressures than at the Earth's surface. If you went down a mine shaft, you would notice that the rocks become hotter the deeper you go. On average, the temperature in the continental crust increases by about 25 °C for every kilometre of depth. This increase is a result of the Earth being heated internally, mainly by the decay of naturally radioactive isotopes, and losing this geothermal heat from the surface. The pressure increases with depth because rocks have to support the weight of those above. The pressure in rock increases by about 1000 times that of the atmosphere at the Earth's surface for every 3.5 km of depth.

Atmospheric pressure at sea level is 1×10^5 Pa (Book 1, Section 5.1).

South African gold mines penetrate as deep as 4 km below the surface. At such depths temperatures at the rock face may exceed 100 °C. The pressure on the rocks at the bottom of the deepest South African mine is about 1200 times the atmospheric pressure, or 1.2×10^8 Pa. So, where mining exposes deeply buried rock to atmospheric pressure in the mine workings, huge forces build up in the rock, sometimes sufficient to exceed its strength, when it explodes into the excavation as a 'rock burst'.

Metamorphic conditions can be represented on a graph of pressure versus temperature (Figure 6.2), where the vertical axis shows pressure increasing *downwards*, as it does beneath the Earth's surface. The rate at which rock temperatures increase with depth is termed the **geothermal gradient**. The 'typical' geothermal gradient of Figure 6.2 (~25 °C km^{-1}) is the average beneath tectonically stable continental regions that lack magmatic activity; as beneath much of northern Europe today. In volcanically active areas, the geothermal gradient can reach hundreds of degrees per kilometre. Conversely, where cold oceanic lithosphere is subducted at convergent plate boundaries faster than it can heat up as it descends, the geothermal gradient is lower than normal. So, there is a wide range of pressure and temperature conditions under which metamorphism can occur within the crust.

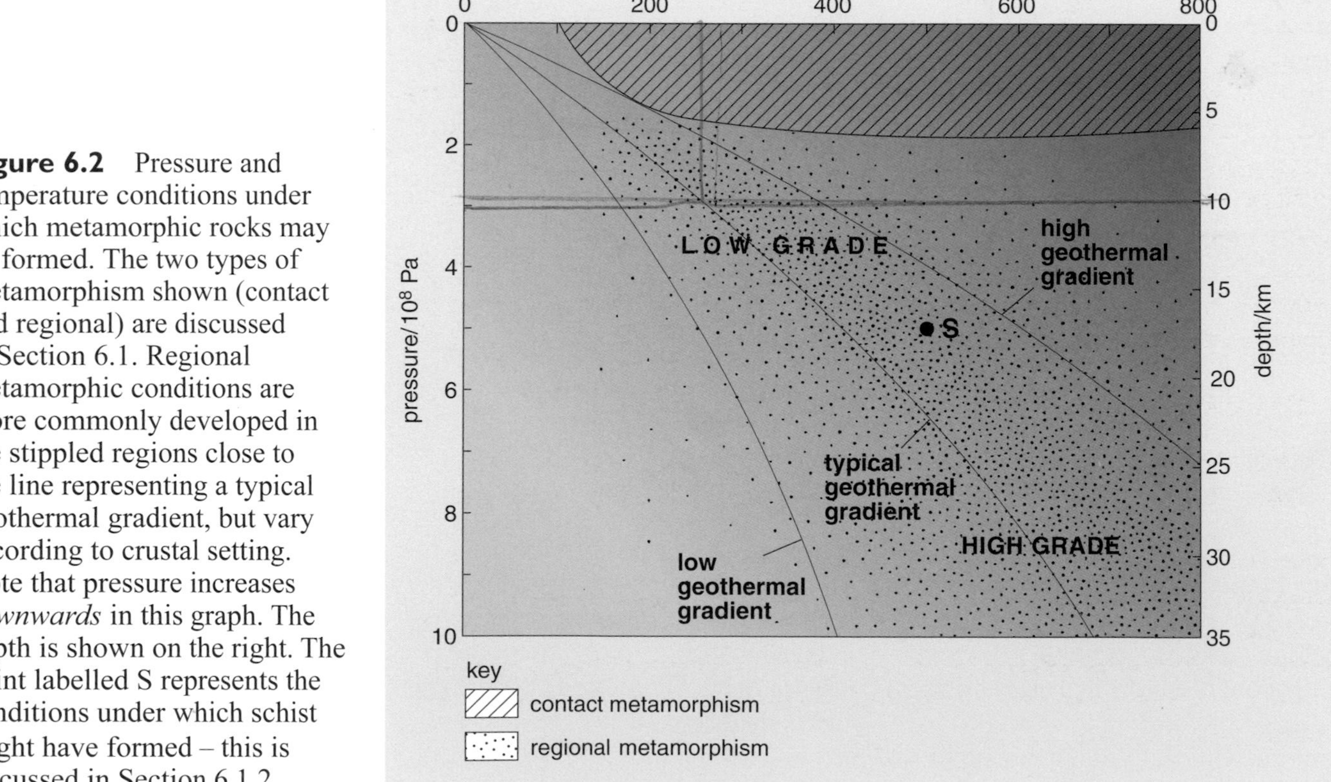

Figure 6.2 Pressure and temperature conditions under which metamorphic rocks may be formed. The two types of metamorphism shown (contact and regional) are discussed in Section 6.1. Regional metamorphic conditions are more commonly developed in the stippled regions close to the line representing a typical geothermal gradient, but vary according to crustal setting. Note that pressure increases *downwards* in this graph. The depth is shown on the right. The point labelled S represents the conditions under which schist might have formed – this is discussed in Section 6.1.2.

The conditions under which metamorphism occurs, and the rocks that form as a result, are generally described in terms of **metamorphic grade**. Thus, both the metamorphic conditions of high temperature and high pressure, *and* the metamorphic rocks produced by them, are called *high grade*. Correspondingly, both the conditions of low temperature and low pressure, and the resulting rocks, are called *low grade* (Figure 6.2).

6.1 New rocks for old

Since drilling is possible down to only about 10 km depth, directly sampling the effects of metamorphism on rocks deep in the crust is impossible. Metamorphism has barely begun 10 km down (Figure 6.2). However, tectonic activity, uplift and erosion may have gradually raised metamorphic rocks from a range of depths (up to 70 km) to the Earth's surface, to reveal minerals that have grown and stabilised under various combinations of temperatures and pressure. Remarkably, the remains of sedimentary structures, such as cross-bedding (Section 5.3.1), show that some metamorphic rocks originally formed as sediments at the Earth's surface. Somehow, they were transported downwards beneath great thicknesses of rock before returning to the surface again.

Earth movements, by uplifting and subsidence, are mainly responsible for moving rocks around the rock cycle (Figure 6.1). Divergent tectonic forces may result in subsidence, to allow thick sequences of sediments and extrusive igneous rocks to build up in depositional basins; the progressive burial of older layers makes them more prone to metamorphism. A more effective process occurs where lithospheric plates converge and squeeze together to form mountain belts, as happened to form the Alps and the Himalaya (Book 2, Section 8.6). Most mountain belts contain large areas of rocks affected by metamorphism. Developed on a regional scale, this is called **regional metamorphism**. The more erosion wears down mountains, the greater the extent of metamorphic rocks exposed at the surface. The stippling on Figure 6.2 shows the more common conditions of regional metamorphism, but there are other environments in which metamorphism may occur.

■ How might rocks near to the Earth's surface get very hot?

□ They may come into contact with magma at temperatures between 800 and 1300 °C.

Rocks in contact with magma can be heated sufficiently for metamorphic changes to occur on a scale of centimetres to metres at the base of lava flows or around sills and dykes, and on a scale of hundreds of metres to kilometres around plutons. Metamorphism of this kind is called **contact metamorphism**, and usually involves *high* temperatures but *low* pressures (the *high* geothermal gradient in Figure 6.2).

■ Why should contact metamorphism be more extensive around plutons than below lavas or around sills and dykes?

□ Plutons contain much larger volumes of magma and therefore provide much more heat to be dissipated during cooling. The heat spreads further and the source stays hot for longer.

Sedimentary mudstones containing clay minerals are particularly susceptible to contact metamorphism. Hydrous clay minerals form at the Earth's surface and become unstable when temperature increases. Heating dehydrates them to produce new minerals containing less water. At shallow depths, where plutons cool more rapidly, temperature rises are usually short-lived. Shallow contact metamorphic rocks therefore don't have long to crystallise and are usually finer grained than regional metamorphic rocks. Since contact metamorphism happens under *static* conditions, the resulting metamorphic rocks don't develop aligned crystals; they may *appear* to be igneous but closer examination often reveals signs of the rock's previous 'incarnation'. For instance, preserved sedimentary layering and structures indicate a sedimentary rock that has been changed by contact metamorphism.

Rocks of the oceanic lithosphere at convergent plate margins slide down subduction zones to depths greater than 70 km. Old oceanic lithosphere has a *low* geothermal gradient (Figure 6.2). So, high pressure dominates metamorphic change in subduction zones and it happens at low temperatures. Contact and subduction-zone metamorphic rocks are uncommon, so the rest of this section focuses on products of regional metamorphism.

6.1.1 Metamorphic 'cookery'

In a very crude sense, the ways in which heat and pressure metamorphose rocks are similar to what happens when a cake is baked. A cake comes out of an oven after cooking with a constitution and texture quite different from the mixture that went in. Similarly, metamorphic rocks end up with different textures (and usually different minerals). To continue the analogy, when a cake comes out of the oven, its texture gives clues to the conditions in the oven. A charred lump suggests the temperature was very high for some time; a soggy mass shows it was too low for the ingredients to react.

Metamorphism involves chemical reactions between mineral 'ingredients' in the starting rock. In the case of sedimentary rocks, water also participates in these reactions. The result is a solid mixture of *new* minerals. Just as different ingredients produce different kinds of cake, different metamorphic rocks develop according to the 'blend' of mineral constituents in the starting rocks. For example, the metamorphism of limestone (mainly calcite) produces marble; sandstones (mainly quartz) transform to quartzites; and basalts change to amphibolites (mainly amphibole and plagioclase feldspar), all under similar ranges of temperature and pressure. In the first two cases, the starting rocks contain only a single mineral, so there is no reaction; a single mineral merely recrystallises to form an interlocking mass. In the third case, the anhydrous minerals olivine, pyroxene and feldspar in the basalt react with each another and with water to form the new mineral amphibole (a hydrated chain silicate of mafic composition) plus some recrystallised feldspar.

Textures and new minerals in metamorphic rocks give visible clues to the temperature and pressure of their formation, and to the original rocks before metamorphism, as you will see in the next activity.

Activity 6.1 Comparing metamorphic rocks

We expect this activity will take you approximately 30 minutes.

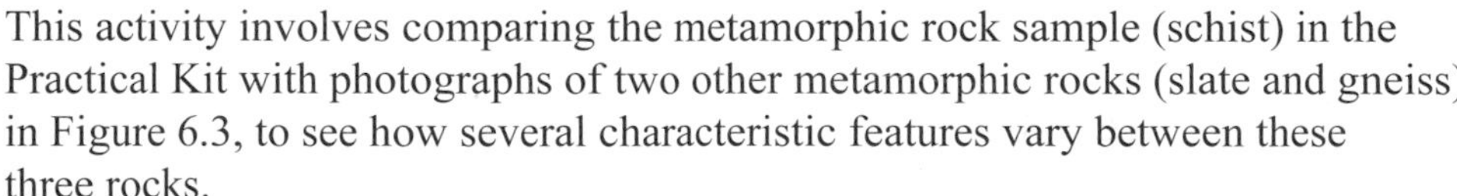

This activity involves comparing the metamorphic rock sample (schist) in the Practical Kit with photographs of two other metamorphic rocks (slate and gneiss) in Figure 6.3, to see how several characteristic features vary between these three rocks.

Important safety precautions

Take note of the safety precautions given with Activity 4.2.

Equipment required

Kit items

Rock Specimen 4

Hand lens

Non-kit item

Ruler marked in millimetres

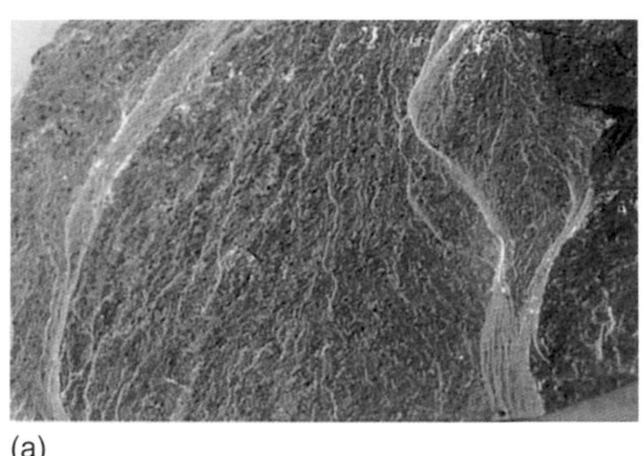

(a)

(b)

Figure 6.3 Examples of metamorphic rocks (with width of field of view): (a) slate (60 mm); (b) gneiss (70 mm).

■ What features could you use to distinguish the three rocks?

□ Their appearance, in terms of colour, grain size and how the grains are arranged (texture), and their mineral content.

Task 1

Use Table 6.1 to record your descriptions of slate, gneiss and schist. *Note*: wetting the cut surface of Specimen 4 will reveal the mineral grains more clearly. When comparing grain sizes, take into account the scales of the photographs.

You may not be able to recognise all the minerals present in these rocks, especially the slate, but you should recognise some of the minerals in the schist and the gneiss. Compare your completed Table 6.1 with the table in the comments to see whether you missed anything important.

Task 2

Look at the characteristics you listed in Table 6.1, particularly the grain size and the texture. In what order would you put these three rocks based on a systematic gradation in these two features?

Table 6.1 Comparison of the properties of slate, gneiss and schist.

Property	Slate	Gneiss	Schist
Grain size	Small < 0.1 mm	0.5 mm	1 mm
Colour	White + grey bands.	White + black	light + dark grey bands + pink minerals. Circles.
Texture	Platy.	Platy granular.	Platy
Minerals		mica + feldspar.	mica.

Now look at the comments on this activity at the end of this book.

6.1.2 Changes with metamorphic grade

Activity 6.1 showed that the textures and mineral contents of the typical metamorphic rocks – slate, schist and gneiss – are quite different. However, they are not due to differences between the compositions of the original rocks from which they were formed by metamorphism. Surprisingly perhaps, the slate, schist and gneiss all began as soft mudstones, with essentially the same overall proportions of elements. Their distinctive mineral and textural characteristics developed under different metamorphic conditions; i.e. under different *grades* of metamorphism.

The **slate** is the lowest grade metamorphic rock in the group and would have formed typically at 200–350 °C and 5–10 km depth. The **gneiss** (pronounced 'nice') has the coarsest grain size and formed under high-grade conditions, typically at temperatures of 550–700 °C and a depth of 20–35 km. The **schist** (pronounced 'shist') has an intermediate grain size and might have formed under the conditions represented by point S in Figure 6.2.

■ What temperature and pressure conditions does point S in Figure 6.2 represent?

□ A temperature of 500 °C and a pressure of 5×10^8 Pa.

Schists typically form at temperatures of 350–550 °C and depths of 10–20 km ($3–6 \times 10^8$ Pa pressure). The textures of the three rocks differ according to the way their minerals are arranged and their grain size, both of which vary with metamorphic grade.

Slate (Figure 6.3a) can be cleaved into thin parallel flakes with smooth surfaces, hence its use in roofing. Cleavage in rocks originates differently from that in minerals, which is a result of their crystal structure. Slate can be cleaved because of the parallel alignment of very fine-grained metamorphic mica flakes. This aligned growth of platy minerals is a response to compressive tectonic forces (Figure 6.4). Tectonic compression generally operates in a roughly horizontal direction as a result of lithospheric plate movements, distinct from the pressure caused by the weight of overlying rocks.

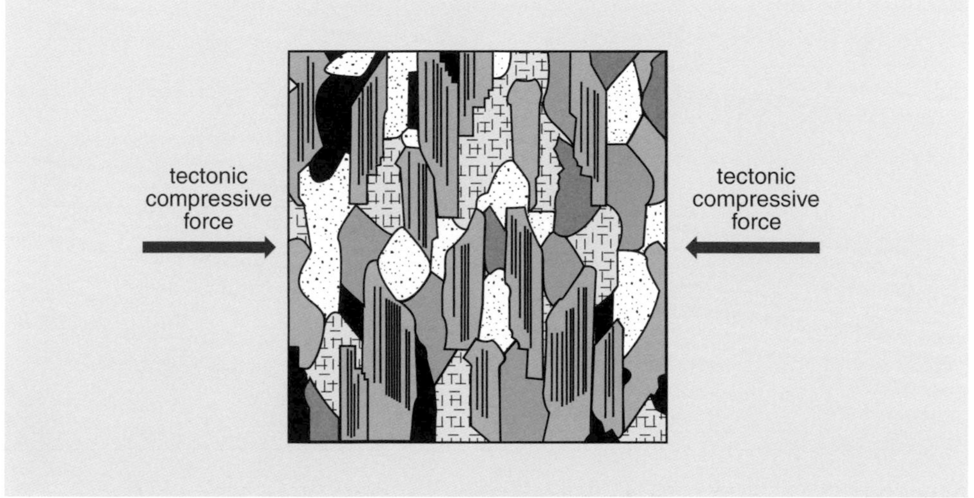

Figure 6.4 Mineral alignment (greatly magnified) developed during metamorphism at right-angles to the direction of tectonic compression.

The schist has shiny, but somewhat crinkly, surfaces made of easily recognised mica flakes. At this coarser grain size, the unevenness is caused by platy crystals having grown around other, granular minerals. Individual mineral grains are visible, even without a hand lens; there are flakes of dark and pale mica, grains of glassy quartz and pinkish brown garnet (see the computer-based *Mineral Gallery*).

Gneiss contains even coarser mineral grains, arranged in more or less parallel bands (Figure 6.3b). It contains much less mica than schist. The pale mica (muscovite), breaks down at the high temperatures of gneiss formation, with the loss of water vapour, to form alkali feldspar, in the following, simplified metamorphic reaction:

$$\text{muscovite mica (s)} + \text{quartz (s)} = \text{alkali feldspar (s)} + H_2O \text{ (l)} \qquad (6.1)$$

Along with quartz, alkali feldspar (Activity 4.1) forms blocky crystals, unlike the thin plates of mica it replaces. As a result, gneiss (Figure 6.3b) is a more granular rock, and not as easy to split as schist. Instead, it contains rough bands containing different proportions of quartz, feldspar and the dark mica, biotite.

■ At even higher temperatures, what might happen to gneiss?

□ It might start to melt and form magma.

At very high temperatures (700–1000 °C), rocks such as gneisses may partially melt to produce magmas and hence igneous rocks. This melting of metamorphic rocks, which were once igneous or sedimentary rocks, closes a major loop in the rock cycle (Figure 6.1).

So, at increasing temperatures of metamorphism, minerals that become unstable break down to form new, more stable minerals. Clay minerals, which were stable at low temperatures, are converted into micas at low metamorphic grades and, at high grades, micas are converted into feldspars. Also, with increasing metamorphic grade, less hydrous minerals replace hydrous ones, thus releasing water (Equation 6.1). High pressures also affect mineral stability, tending to favour the formation of minerals with dense, compact structures, such as garnet (*Minerals Gallery*).

Figure 6.5 summarises the progressive change, both in grain size and in the arrangement of mineral grains, in rocks formed from mudstone or shale at increasing grades of metamorphism.

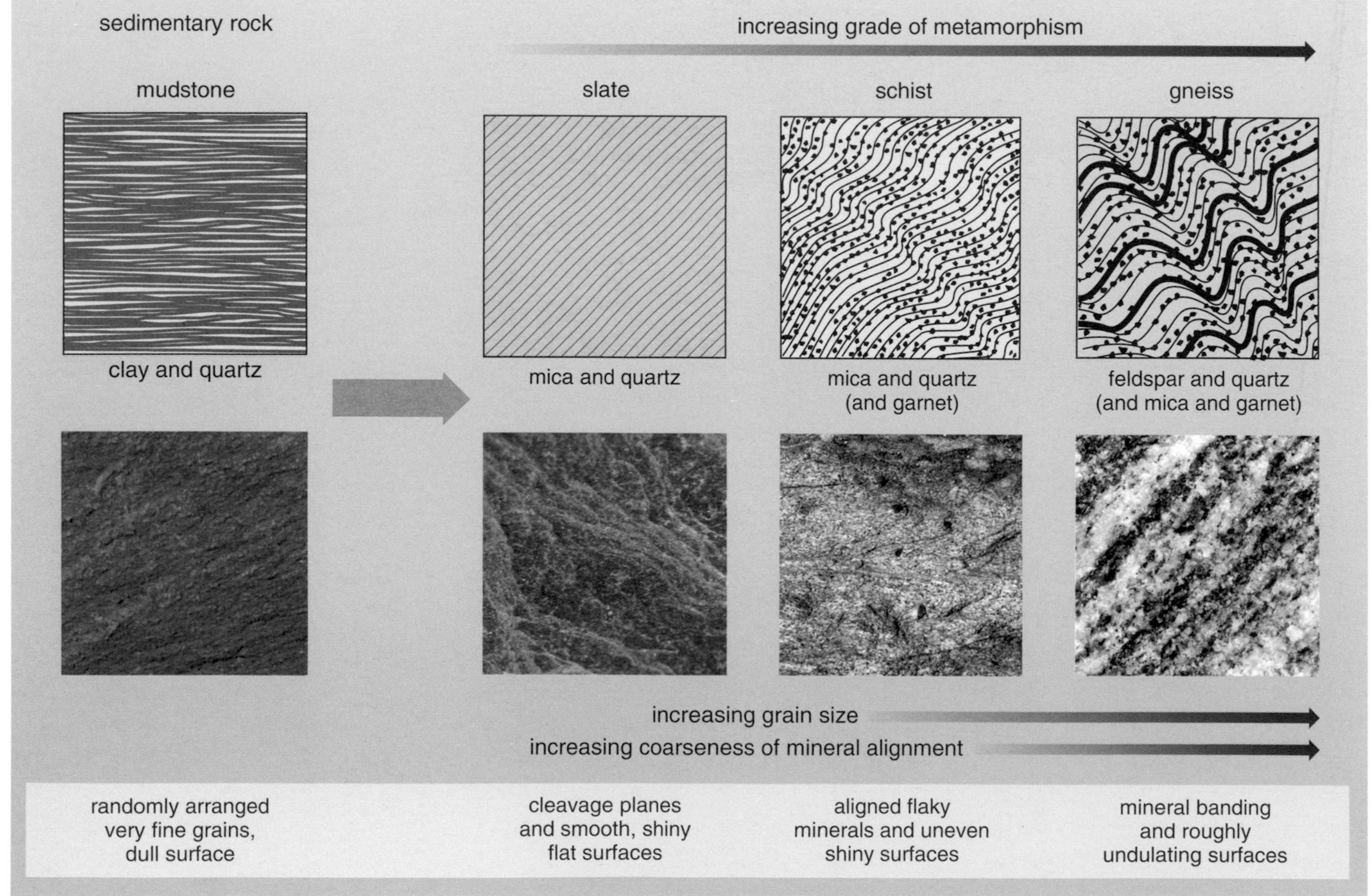

Figure 6.5 Variation in metamorphic rock textures and minerals with increasing grade of metamorphism, as developed from a mudstone or shale. The minerals in brackets occur in small amounts.The images of actual rocks each cover about 5 cm.

Metamorphic mineral alignments form during periods of compression, but do not necessarily coincide with the increases in temperature or pressure that encourage other metamorphic minerals to grow. The relationship between metamorphic minerals and tectonically related alignments provides clues to the relative timing of both (Section 2.4.1). Figure 6.6 shows such an example.

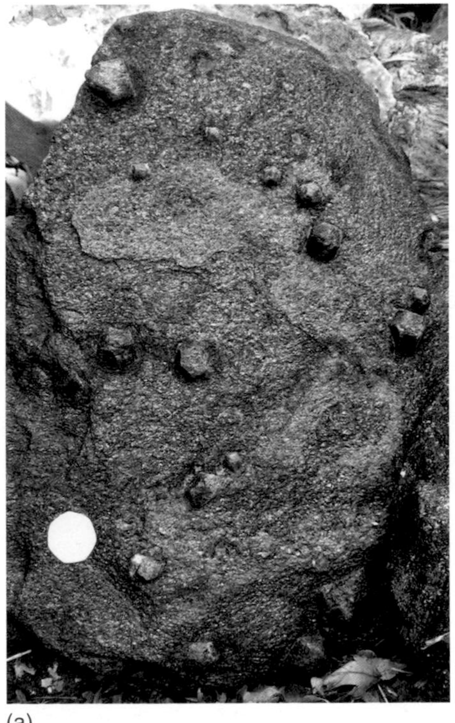

(a)

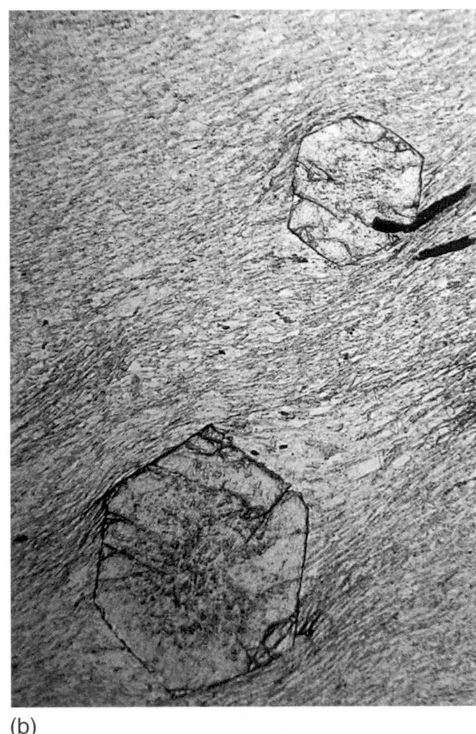

(b)

Figure 6.6 Garnet crystals set in a mica-rich schist: (a) hand specimen; (b) microscopic view (15 mm wide) of a thin, transparent slice.

■ Examine the relationship between the pink garnet crystals and the mineral alignment in the schist shown in Figure 6.6b. Which developed first: the garnets or the alignment?

□ The garnets show well-developed crystal faces that cut across the aligned minerals, so the garnets grew *after* the alignment had formed.

The pervasive mineral alignments seen in slate, schist and gneiss are typical of regional metamorphism. They develop in the original rocks as they are moved into crustal environments with different pressure and temperature. This occurs most commonly during the tectonic compression associated with plate collision and mountain building. By contrast, *contact* metamorphic rocks are formed by simple, static recrystallisation and normally do not exhibit mineral alignment. However, new minerals sometimes grow over the original textures. Figure 2.12b shows spots of new minerals which have grown across fine layering in a siltstone (you can also see occasional rounded quartz grains).

6.2 Rock deformation

Earth movements may buckle once fairly flat-lying sedimentary strata, to form a variety of contorted shapes (Figure 6.7). Metamorphic rocks, formed deep within mountain belts, commonly show these effects of deformation. The scale varies from microscopic, involving mineral banding (Figure 6.7a), to beds in a cliff face (Figure 6.7b), to a vast scale, visible only from the air (Figure 6.7c). Other structures form when movements in the Earth break rocks apart.

Figure 6.7 Deformation features on a variety of scales: (a) microscopic folding of mica flakes in a thin, transparent slice of rock (2 mm across); (b) folded sedimentary beds exposed in a road cutting (5 m across); (c) aerial photograph of large-scale folding of sedimentary rocks of different kinds (5 km across).

Deformation results from any process that causes an object to *change its shape* – by breaking, bending, stretching, or squashing – when a force is applied. A tectonic force directed towards a fixed object produces *compression*; when operating in the opposite sense it produces *tension.*

Materials respond differently to deformation. Grip one end of a French bean, pull the other end and it breaks. Pull on a piece of dough and it stretches and thins before breaking. These are different responses to tension: the bean pod exhibits **brittle deformation**; the dough responds by **plastic deformation**.

Experiments can demonstrate the effects of rock deformation, or geologists can infer the nature of deformation from structures in the rock. Figure 6.8a shows the results from an experiment to compress rock between the jaws of a mechanical press. Figure 6.8b shows how layers of rock in natural exposures have failed under tension.

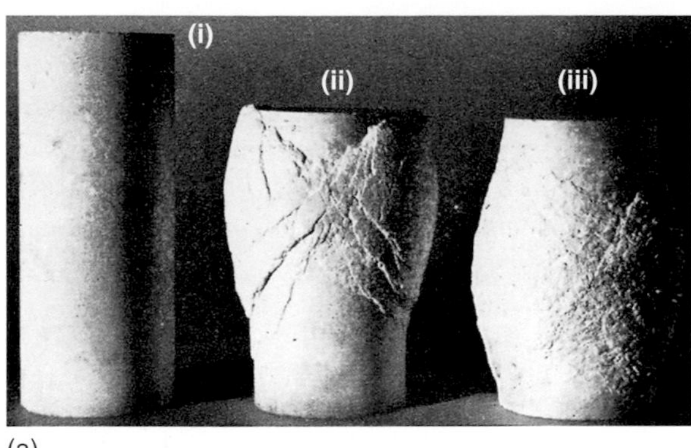

(a)

(b)

(c)

Figure 6.8 Simple deformation. (a) Results of an experiment showing the effect of compression on cylinders of marble under different conditions: (i) undeformed marble; (ii) deformation at low temperature; (iii) deformation at high temperature. (b) and (c) Two different results of tension forces that operated along rock layers: (b) thinning under plastic conditions; (c) fracturing during brittle deformation.

■ Examine the experimental results in Figure 6.8a. How can you tell which of (ii) and (iii) shows the outcome of plastic compression and which shows brittle compression?

□ The marble cylinder in (iii) has thickened by just bulging, its shape having developed by plastic deformation. Specimen (ii) has thickened by brittle fracturing, which allowed broken parts of the cylinder to move past each other.

It should now be clear how the rock layers in Figure 6.8b and 6.8c responded to tension: those in Figure 6.8b thinned to produce a 'neck' while deforming in a plastic manner; those in Figure 6.8c broke in a brittle fashion and moved past each other.

These two kinds of behaviour seem puzzling; rocks tend to smash when hit with a hammer, and are much stronger than dough or a bean pod. What determines whether they deform in a brittle manner or in a plastic manner? If you try to bend a toffee bar on a hot day, it will almost certainly bend. If you chill it in the freezer and try again, it will be more likely to break. So, the extent to which the deformation is plastic or brittle depends not only on the character of the material itself but also on its temperature; *increasing temperature increases plasticity*.

Here is another experiment that you might try. Place a hard toffee bar in the refrigerator, one end hanging over the edge of a tray, the other held in place with a weight. After a few days you will see that the bar has bent; it behaves plastically. Remove the bar and hit it sharply with a hammer (take care if you try this yourself); it will easily break in a brittle manner. This demonstrates the way in which something deforms depends on the rate of deformation: *fast-acting forces tend to result in brittle behaviour; slow-acting forces encourage plastic deformation.*

- ■ Given that temperature increases with depth in the Earth, roughly where, in relation to the Earth's surface, would you expect brittle deformation and plastic deformation to occur?
- □ Brittle deformation tends to occur near to the Earth's surface where rocks are cooler; plastic deformation is more likely to occur at considerable depth, where rocks are hotter.

On an even larger scale, the lithosphere behaves in a brittle fashion, whereas the asthenosphere acts as a plastic solid (Book 2, Section 8.1).

6.2.1 Faults

Brittle rocks can fracture because of either compression or tension (Figure 6.8). If a fracture surface shows signs of *dislocation* (that is, where once continuous rock layers no longer line up across the fracture), it is a fault and was probably once the site of earthquakes (Book 2, Section 3.2). Brittle fractures without associated dislocation – joints – are common in all rocks. If you can see a sense of displacement across a fracture surface (Figure 6.9), you can tell whether compression or tension caused the displacement: compression moves rocks closer together; tension moves rocks further apart.

Question 6.1

(a) Which fault in Figure 6.9 formed by tension and which formed by compression? (*Hint*: look at the mudstone bed on either side of each fault.) Draw arrows parallel to the ground surface in Figure 6.9a and 6.9b to show the directions of horizontal movement.

(b) Draw a vertical line downward from point A on Figure 6.9a and 6.9b. Imagine these lines represent boreholes. How would the sequence of rocks in each borehole differ?

(c) The trees in Figure 6.9a and 6.9b were the same horizontal distance apart before the faulting occurred. How has their separation changed in each case as a result of tension and of compression?

Compression faults result in the *repetition* of layers; tension faults locally *omit* layers from the original sequence. This is related to crustal *shortening* and *extension*, respectively.

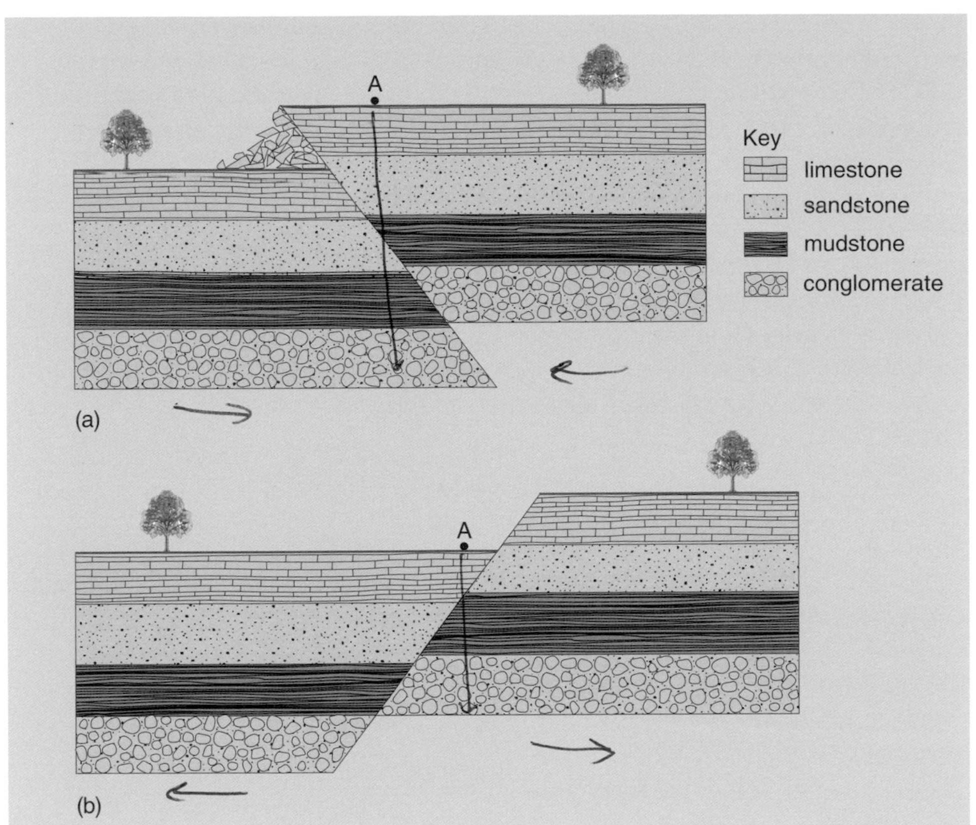

Figure 6.9 Dislocation of rock strata by faulting: examples of faults produced by tension and compression.

6.2.2 Folds

The plastic behaviour of rocks under compression results in bending or bulging, to give **folds**, rather than faults (Figure 6.10). Folds (and faults) are most easily detected in sedimentary and metamorphic rocks containing layers or aligned

(a)

(b)

(c)

Figure 6.10 Simple folding of rock layers by compression deformation. (a) An open fold in Cumbria reflects a little shortening. (b) A tight fold in North Devon reflects much greater shortening. (c) An overturned fold in metamorphic rocks near Aberdeen resulted from extreme compression and plastic behaviour sustained over as much as a million years.

minerals. Fold shapes differ according to the strength and plasticity of the rocks; the amount of compression and overall shortening; and the rate of deformation. A little shortening produces an open fold (Figure 6.10a), whereas greater shortening may produce a tight fold (Figure 6.10b), rather like a concertina. In cases of extreme compression, overturned folds may develop, in which part of the rock sequence is turned upside-down (Figure 6.10c). In such cases, the deformation may have taken as long as a million years, allowing the rocks to behave in a plastic fashion. Faster movements on the same scale may achieve the same immense shortening by the development of brittle thrust faults (Figure 6.9a is a small example of a thrust fault). When rocks are strong but brittle, as they generally are at low temperatures, they tend either to fracture or to form simple open folds. When more plastic, especially at high temperatures, rocks tend to form tight, intricate fold patterns.

6.3 Mountains and metamorphic belts

Crossing large areas of the continents are linear regions of crust containing rocks which have been strongly deformed. They formed as mountain belts, some of which still remain, such as the Alps and the Himalaya. Such belts usually contain rocks transformed by regional metamorphism that deep erosion has exposed. Together, processes of regional deformation and metamorphism constitute an **orogeny** (from the Greek *oros* for 'mountain' and *genic* for 'producing'). Folding and faulting of the rocks within these linear belts indicate large-scale compression.

■ At what kind of plate boundary might this compression have occurred?

□ At a convergent plate boundary, especially where subduction of the ocean floor has caused continents to collide (Book 2, Section 8.6).

Mountain belts form during continent–continent collision because the continental crust is too buoyant to be subducted (Book 2, Section 8.6). The collision deforms sediments that were deposited between the converging continents, as well as the continents themselves (Figure 6.11). The compression results in thickening of the crust. Note also from Figure 6.11 that continental crust above the subduction zone thickens as a result of magma intrusion during the formation of a volcanic arc. A good example of **crustal thickening** is the crust that was deformed when India collided with Asia. The continental crust beneath the Himalaya and the Tibetan Plateau extends down to about 70 km, compared with a thickness of about 35 km for crust beneath most of the continental surface.

The additional mass of mountains raised up by crustal thickening during collision orogenies (e.g. the Tibetan Plateau is an average of 5 km high) depresses the mantle beneath (Figures 6.11c and 6.12a), even though the crust is not as dense as the mantle. Why does this happen and what are its implications?

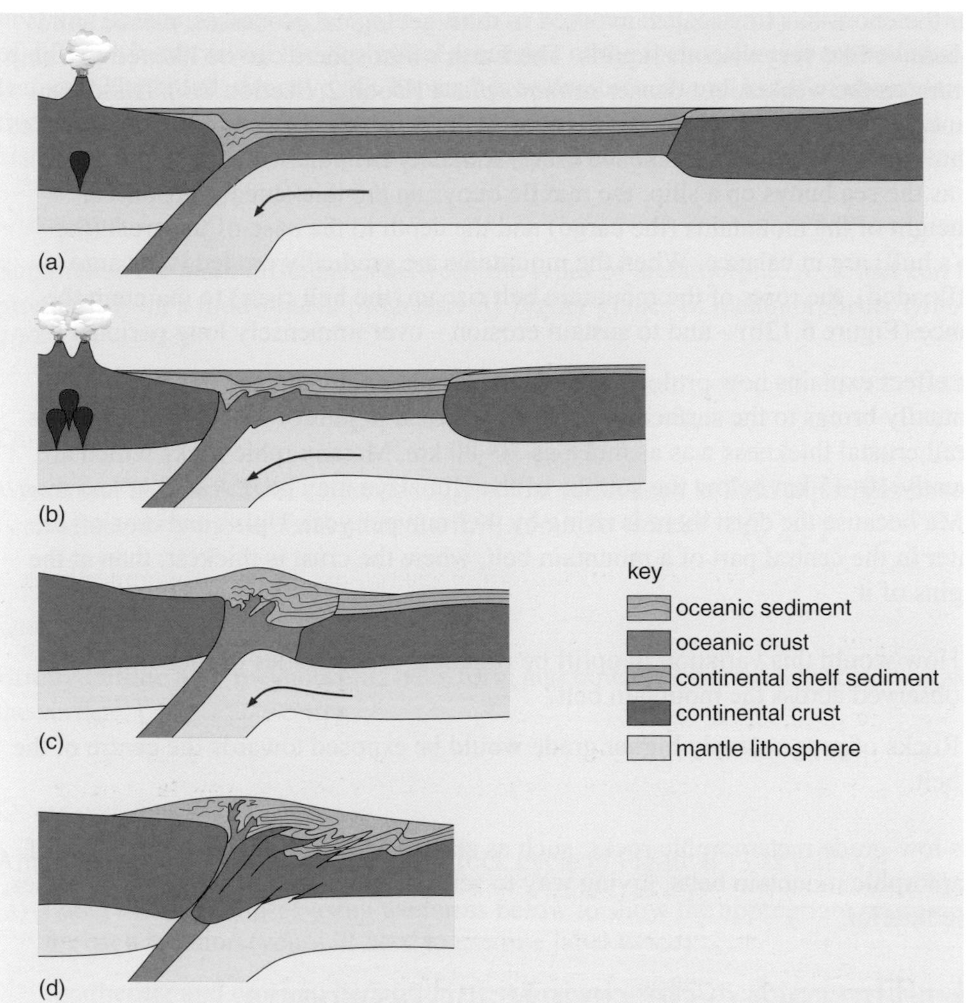

Figure 6.11 Formation of a mountain belt by the collision of continents carried on converging lithospheric plates. (a) and (b) Converging continents, showing magmatic addition beneath a volcanic arc above a subduction zone. (b) and (c) Sediments deposited between the approaching continents begin to deform close to the subduction zone. (d) Crustal thickening as a result of continental collision. (*Note*: the figures are not to scale.)

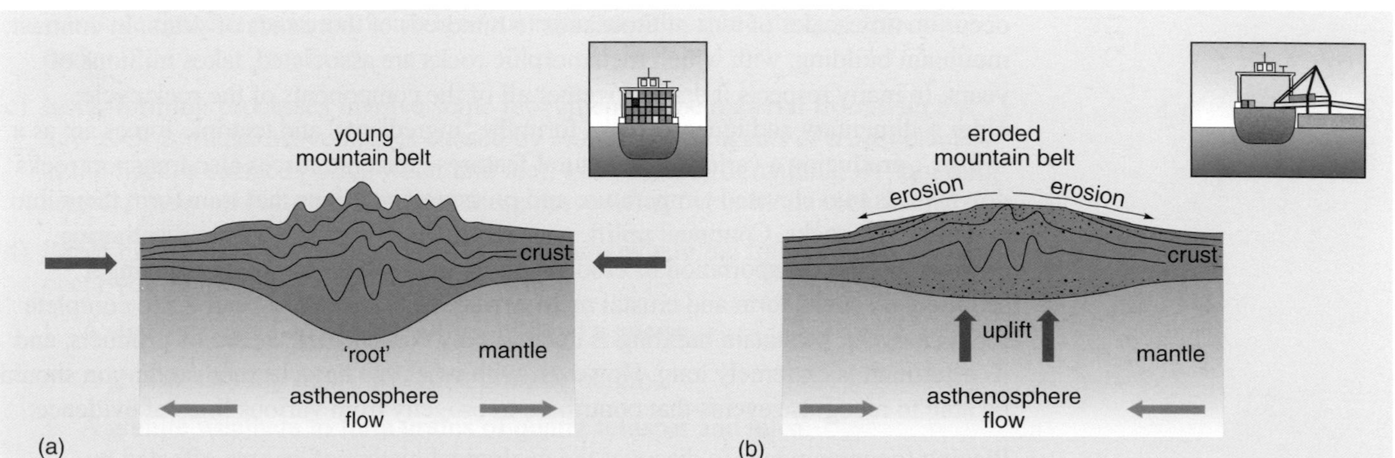

Figure 6.12 Evolution of a mountain belt: (a) compression during mountain building causes crustal thickening which displaces the asthenosphere away from the mountain belt; (b) subsequent buoyant uplift and erosion of the mountain belt brings metamorphic rocks to the surface when the asthenosphere moves back as the load is reduced. The insets show how a ship's hull is analogous to the 'roots' of the mountain belt. Note that the container ship in (b) has offloaded most of its deck cargo.

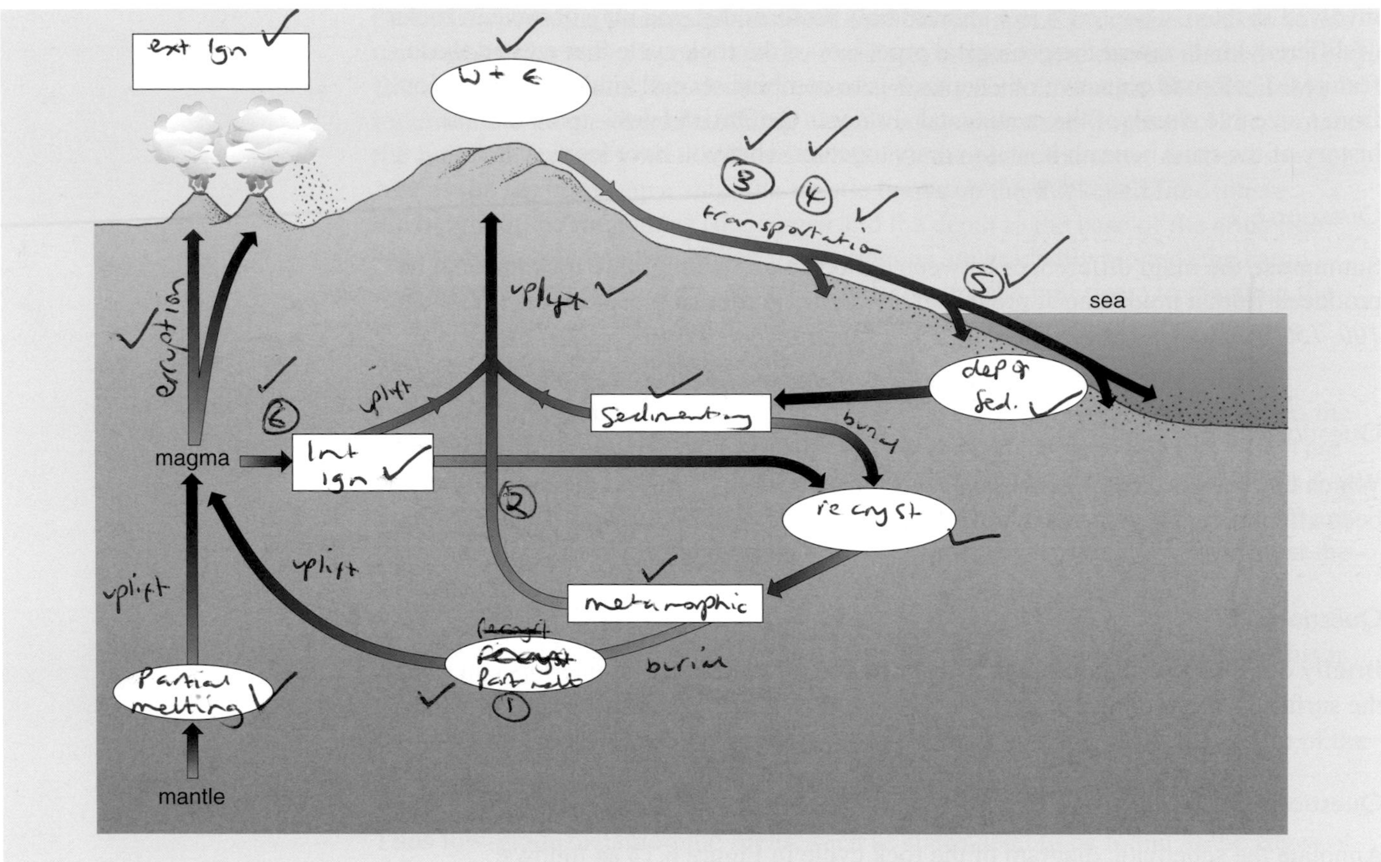

Figure 6.13 Schematic diagram of the rock cycle (for use with Question 6.5).

6.5 Summary of Chapter 6

Metamorphic rocks form deep in the Earth's crust where older rocks respond to the prevailing temperatures and pressures by growing new minerals through reactions between solid, pre-existing minerals. Different geothermal gradients in different tectonic settings create conditions that form a wide range of metamorphic rocks. The concept of metamorphic grade describes both the conditions and the rocks produced by them.

Igneous intrusions bake the older rocks adjacent to them, generally at low pressure. Such contact metamorphism is a local, static process that produces no alignments of the new minerals. Regional metamorphism affects much larger areas to produce rocks containing aligned crystals or bands of minerals formed by recrystallisation during tectonic compression. During regional metamorphism, mudstone transforms to slate, schist and gneiss, in order of increasing metamorphic grade. With increasing temperature, hydrous minerals break down and less hydrous minerals become stable. With increasing pressure, denser minerals become stable.

Either tension or compression associated with movements in the Earth may deform rocks. Those remaining cool near the surface tend to be brittle and usually deform by fracturing, or by simple folding. Deeper down, higher temperatures make rocks more plastic and folding is more complex. Very long periods of sustained, directed pressure encourage rocks with a brittle response to rapid deformation to deform in a plastic manner.

Tectonic compression and crustal thickening result in linear mountain belts at convergent plate boundaries, especially where continents collide. Uplift and erosion of thickened crust allows belts of regional metamorphic rocks formed by an orogeny to rise slowly to reach the Earth's surface.

Your study of this chapter involved: comparing information given in figures, and by rock hand specimens and the minerals in them; describing and interpreting that information; and summarising your findings. You have also applied concepts about metamorphic and deformation processes to explain features shown by metamorphic and deformed rocks, including their relationships to internal and tectonic processes.

Chapter 7
Geology of the British Isles: perpetual change

Study note

Several place names in the British Isles are referred to in the text. If you are unfamiliar with them, an annotated map is supplied as a computer-based resource.

In this chapter you will use some of the skills and knowledge you gained earlier in this book to assess some key geoscientific observations that helped to unveil the remarkable history that shaped the crust beneath the British Isles. Four approaches are involved:

- establishing a sequence of events in relative time
- interpreting maps showing where rocks occur at the surface and extend beneath it
- assessing the conditions which produced rocks and the structures in them
- reconstructing past environments.

The aim is to give you a 'feel' for how history on the grand scale is pieced together in the context of local, regional and global geography and plate tectonics of the past. At several points in this chapter you will need access to computer-based resources.

7.1 Geological observations in time and space

Geologists have developed broad ideas about the relative timing of major events in the Earth's history from observations at unconformities (Section 2.4). An unconformity represents a gap in time, when weathering and erosion stripped the surface down, often after an orogeny (Section 6.3 and Figure 6.12). A surface of unconformity was once the landscape or seabed upon which sediments began to accumulate once uplift and erosion stopped, and often that surface was almost flat. Observations of the rocks below and above an unconformity provide a 'before and after' visualisation of geological events that affected an area. Three profoundly significant unconformities break up the geological history of the British Isles.

7.1.1 The vestige of a beginning

The oldest unconformity in the British Isles is limited to a small area of the Highlands of northwest Scotland, where several isolated, steep-sided mountains rise above a low-lying but irregular surface spangled with lakes (Figure 7.1).

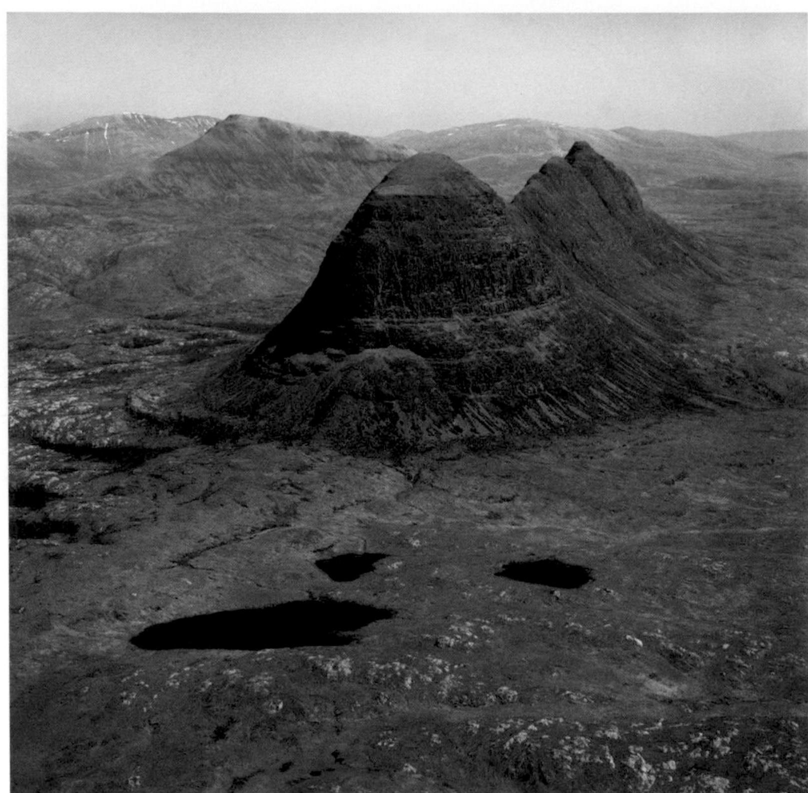

Figure 7.1 Aerial view of the distinctive mountain Suilven in Sutherland, Scotland, looking towards the northeast.

■ Which kind of rock makes up Suilven (Figure 7.1): igneous, sedimentary or metamorphic?

□ The prominent horizontal layering suggests that the rocks are probably sedimentary in origin. The mountain in the background – Canisp – shows similar layering.

The topography surrounding Suilven is 'knobbly' and its few exposures of rock show no clear layering. From an aerial view it is not possible to suggest the kind of rock that lies beneath this lower part of the landscape. An abrupt change in slope marks the base of the mountain, and tracing the slope change suggests that it too is roughly horizontal. The base of Suilven is a major geological boundary. A few kilometres to the north a roadside cutting exposes that boundary. Figure 7.2a shows a very sharp, horizontal contact between layered upper rocks and apparently featureless but hard ones below.

■ Briefly describe the upper rocks in Figure 7.2a, from the more detailed view in Figure 7.2b.

□ Apart from the white patches of lichen, the rocks are reddish brown. There are coarse fragments in some of the layers and cross-bedding is present.

(a)

(b)

Figure 7.2 Exposures near Suilven. (a) A major geological boundary exposed by blasting in a nearby road cutting. (b) Close-up of the upper rocks in (a). Note that the pale patches in both photographs are lichens growing on the rock surface.

(a)

(b)

Figure 7.3 The rocks in Figure 7.2b: (a) hand specimen; (b) microscopic view, about 7 mm across, of a thin, transparent slice of (a). The cloudy, pale yellowish grains are alkali feldspar; the clear ones are quartz.

These observations confirm that the upper rocks, which form the mountain Suilven, are sedimentary. They are beds of sandstone and conglomerate, laid down by a moving fluid, hence the cross-bedding. Locally, they are known as the Torridonian Sandstones. Were they deposited by water or by wind? If by water, was it on land or are these marine sediments? A closer look at a hand specimen and down a microscope (Figure 7.3) helps answer these questions.

Question 7.1

After looking at the hand specimen and thin, transparent slice in Figure 7.3, answer the following questions.

(a) (i) Is the upper rock well or poorly sorted? (ii) Are the grains well or poorly rounded? (iii) Were these sedimentary rocks deposited in a high- or low-energy environment?

(b) In what kind of environment was the rock deposited: by wind in a desert; by water on land; on a beach? (If you need a reminder of transport and sorting, refer back to Activity 5.2.)

(c) Were the grains in the upper rock exposed for long to chemical weathering?

The Torridonian Sandstones were deposited by flowing water and are red-beds (Section 5.3.1), indicating oxygen-rich conditions when they formed. The cross-bedding (Figure 7.2b) is typical of the many-channelled streams which today flood across flat ground at the foot of most large mountain ranges. Yet Torridonian Sandstones contain neither animal nor plant fossils, and therefore probably pre-date the colonisation of the land surface. Radiometric dating of rare minerals that grew while fine-grained Torridonian sediments were being lithified dates them between 1200 and 1000 Ma.

The rocks beneath the unconformity, which form the low-lying, 'knobbly' ground in Figure 7.1, are generally coated with lichens and often hidden by vegetation and peat as their terrain is poorly drained. As so often in the British Isles, these rocks show best when exposed on the seashore (Figure 7.4).

(a)

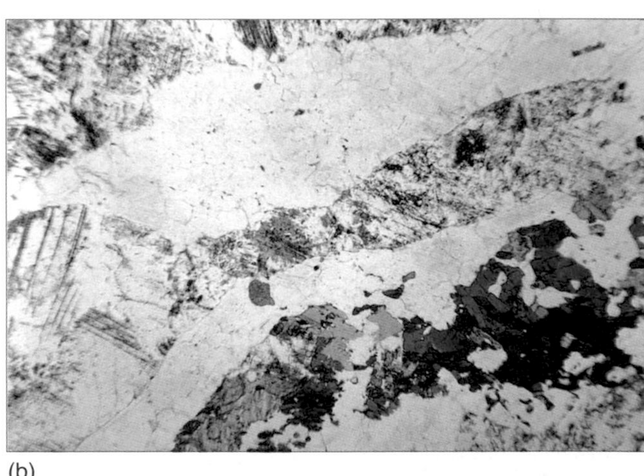

(b)

Figure 7.4 The lower rocks in Figure 7.2a. (a) A fresh shoreline exposure of the lower rocks in Figure 7.2a, about 2 m across. (b) A microscopic view, about 5 mm across, of a thin, transparent slice of (a). It contains clear quartz; white and cloudy feldspar; green amphibole; and the grey mineral slightly below centre is garnet.

These lower rocks are texturally very different from those above the unconformity.

■ Are the lower rocks in Figure 7.2a (shown in Figure 7.4) igneous, sedimentary or metamorphic? Once you have decided, suggest a name for the rock type.

□ They are banded and coarsely crystalline, i.e. metamorphic. They are an excellent example of a gneiss (see Activity 6.1).

■ From Figure 7.4 and the information in its caption, suggest the chemical composition of these gneisses in terms of what you learned in Section 6.1.2.

□ They contain roughly equal numbers of mafic and felsic bands. The felsic bands are quartz and feldspar, i.e. roughly granitic, whereas the mafic bands contain a lot of amphibole, i.e. roughly basaltic. So, overall, they are of intermediate or roughly andesitic composition.

These Lewisian gneisses – so-called because they make up most of the Hebridean island of Lewis – form the continental crust beneath northern Britain. Dating of zircons (Section 2.5) shows that the Lewisian formed originally as andesitic igneous rocks between 2800 and 3000 Ma ago – they are Europe's oldest rock formation – and were metamorphosed at around 2600 Ma. The last major deformation to affect them occurred around 1800 Ma ago. So, the unconformity beneath the Torridonian Sandstone therefore records a period between 600–800 Ma during which there is no sign that sediments were deposited or that magmas formed in what is now northern Britain. Instead a mountain range made of thickened continental crust was slowly eroded down.

The later geological record of the British Isles is much more complete. The next step in its division involves a second unconformity, where the immensity of geological time first dawned on one of the founders of the geosciences.

7.1.2 Witness to orogeny

Lawyer and physician James Hutton (1726–1797), who lived in Edinburgh during the late 18th century, was a keen observer of his surroundings. On one excursion along the coast of southeast Scotland he was confronted by the rock exposures shown in Figure 7.5, now known widely as Hutton's Unconformity. In Figure 7.5a, the geologists are sitting just above the unconformity on the upper rocks which dip gently northwards. The lower rocks, beneath the unconformity are different, and you may be able to trace the unconformity from right to left as a fairly sharp line on the picture.

(a)

(b)

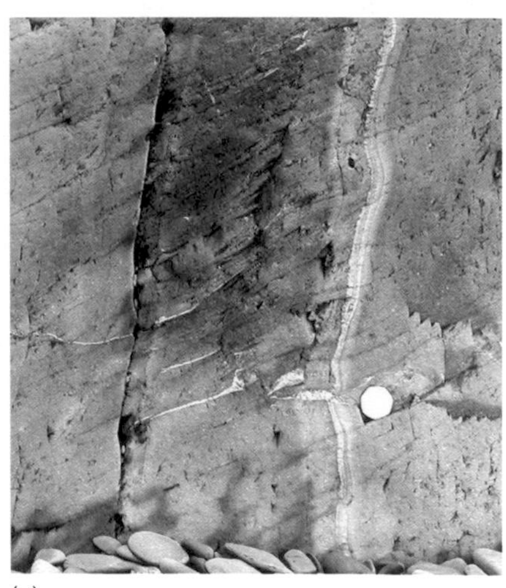
(c)

Figure 7.5 Siccar Point on the Berwickshire coast of Scotland: (a) Hutton's Unconformity, looking eastwards; (b) the upper rocks in close-up; (c) the lower rocks in close up – the coin is 30 mm across.

Activity 7.1 The Siccar Point unconformity

We expect this activity will take you approximately 15 minutes.

The aim here is to deduce the steps in the geological evolution of southeastern Scotland from the relationships and other features at Siccar Point by studying Figure 7.5 and referring, if necessary, to earlier chapters.

Task 1

The upper rocks in Figure 7.5a are about 380 Ma old (Upper Devonian). They are shown in close-up in Figure 7.5b. Describe them and suggest an environment in which they may have formed (*50–100 words*).

Task 2

The lower rocks in Figure 7.5a contain fossil trilobites (which you looked at in Activity 2.2) and are about 420 Ma old (Upper Silurian). They are shown in close-up in Figure 7.5c. Describe them and suggest an environment in which they may have formed (*50–80 words*).

Task 3

Suggest a sequence of tectonic and surface processes that would account for the unconformity (*50–100 words*).

Now read the comments on this activity at the end of this book.

The unconformity at Siccar Point signifies that between 420 and 380 Ma southern Scotland experienced an orogeny and then erosion of the resulting mountain belt. By the time the surface of southern Scotland had been reduced to an almost flat plain, erosion had not penetrated to a depth in this area where regional metamorphism had occurred during the orogeny. James Hutton was the first to realise the implications of unconformities, and for this reason is numbered among the 'fathers' of geology.

Through the rest of the Devonian and the succeeding Carboniferous Period, most of southern Scotland, England and Wales experienced almost unbroken sedimentation. In northern Scotland, there are no Carboniferous sedimentary rocks. That absence can be explained by the continued rise of the mountain belt in northern Scotland where erosion unloaded the lower crust and asthenosphere (Figure 6.12). This 'passive' behaviour was interrupted at the end of the Carboniferous Period (~300 Ma) by orogenic events in southern Ireland, South Wales and southwestern England, to produce a third fundamental unconformity.

7.1.3 The desert of Avalon

One possible location for King Arthur's mythical domain of Avalon is southwest England in Devon or Cornwall. The third unconformity which helps to divide the geological history of the British Isles is best exposed there, close to the South Devon coastal resort of Torquay (Figure 7.6).

(a)

(b)

Figure 7.6 (a) Permian rocks resting unconformably above more steeply dipping Devonian rocks near to Torquay in southwest England. The unconformity is about two-thirds of the way up the cliff, beneath the conglomerate, and marked by its angular discordance with the tilted beds below it. Although it is not obvious, the lower rocks dip at about 50° away from the viewpoint. (b) Modern boulder beds laid down by a torrent in Death Valley, California, USA.

In this case, the upper rocks in Figure 7.6a are of Permian age, about 270 Ma old. They are red conglomerates containing large, rounded boulders; this is clear evidence of very high-energy transportation by water and deposition on land under the oxidising influence of the atmosphere. Crude bedding in the conglomerates dips gently towards the right. Figure 7.6b shows a modern analogy for their probable environment of deposition: boulder beds deposited on the floor of Death Valley by torrents that drain occasional heavy rainfall from the surrounding mountains.

The rocks beneath the unconformity are layered on a scale of tens of centimetres and are fine-grained mudstones and siltstones. Their layering dips more steeply than that above the unconformity. They are Devonian, roughly the same age (~380 Ma) as the upper rocks at Siccar Point (Figure 7.5a). Despite their red coloration by Fe^{3+} oxide, these are not terrestrial sediments. They contain fossil brachiopods and other marine animals, and were deposited on a deep sea floor to the south of the Devonian land surface that covered the rest of Britain. They are red because they were exposed at the land surface and weathered before being covered by the Permian conglomerates. The unconformity at the base of the Permian elsewhere in southwest England rests on similar deep-water marine mudstones and siltstones that are Carboniferous in age, and also on the granites shown in Figure 4.4.

Although slightly disturbed occasionally by far-off orogenies, much of the record of the British Isles for the following 270 Ma is one of continual sediment deposition, with one dramatic episode of volcanic activity (Section 7.2.5). The rocks take the general form of a simple 'layer cake' in which the principle of superposition shows the upwards passage of time and events. Activity 7.2 reveals changing environments in southwest England through the first 50 Ma of this relatively quiet period, during the Permian and Triassic Periods.

Activity 7.2 A geological field trip

We expect this activity will take you approximately 60 minutes.

You will need to view and work through the computer-based activity *A Geological Field Trip*.

This interactive activity simulates three field visits to Permian, Triassic and lower Jurassic rocks that are exposed in southwest England. While using it you will learn how to record observations in note form and as geological sketches. You may find it useful to refer back to Chapter 5, especially Activity 5.2 and Section 5.3.1.

The field techniques covered by this activity are used widely by geologists. The first step is to get a general, broad view of an exposure from around 10–50 m, to see how the various parts are related. Then you can move in to examine specific features of interest in more detail, and to look at hand specimens of the rocks. Hand specimens help to identify particular rock characteristics (such as texture and the minerals present), which in turn will help you identify the rock type and the conditions under which it formed. A final look at the exposure from a greater distance again often enables you to see additional features which you missed at first. In practice, field studies involve repetition; a lot of prowling around rocks.

Field notebook pages recording observations at each site provide an essential summary of the main features exposed there and their interpretation. Typically, a notebook will also include annotated sketches illustrating particular features. Of course, photographs will show detail that is impossible to draw, but a simple sketch is a vital reminder of your main geological observations.

Task 1

Visit the sites in order of decreasing age of the exposed rocks, starting at Dawlish with Permian rocks that occur just above the conglomerates in Figure 7.6a. Then go on to Budleigh Salterton, and finally visit Aust Cliff.

At each locality you should make notes on what you see in the notebook pages that follow; the headings on the left will give you an indication of what to look for. (You should look at the Main view, the Close view and then the Rock specimen screens.) When you have completed each locality, check your notes against information that is given by working through the Notebook section. *Don't worry if you miss some of the details* – it takes time to understand which features are important and to be able to recognise them in a new situation. You will probably see more if you repeat each visit; then you can add any details that you missed.

Notebook pages

Locality: Dawlish, Devon	**Description**
Rock age: Upper Permian (~255 Ma) Rock characteristics Colour: Texture: Grain shape: Grain size: Grain composition: Features: Rock identification:	red. granular up to 2cm grains beds Fragmentary texture. Sandstone layering. faults through

Locality: Budleigh Salterton, Devon	**Description**
Rock age: Middle Triassic (~240 Ma) Rock characteristics Colour: Texture: Grain shape: Grain size: Sorting: Features: Rock identification:	large pebbles, rounded up to 25cm. pinkish grey. Conglomerate fragmentary texture poor sorting bands of fine grains + conglomerate

Locality: Aust Cliff, Avon (focus on upper part of cliff)	**Description**
Rock age: Upper Triassic to Lower Jurassic (~220–200 Ma) Rock characteristics Colour: Texture: Grain size: Grain composition: Sorting: Features: Rock identification:	brown/gray. + white bands. mud top section - gray + white large pieces/fragments diff [illegible] medium sorted. med section - red, swirled white fine grain lower section - white stone no grain visible

Task 2 Producing a geological sketch from a photograph

After studying the 'sketches' sections at each locality, and noting the guidance on drawing sketches, try sketching part of the cliff at Dawlish, shown in Figure 7.7a. (The top and bottom of the sketch have been started for you in Figure 7.7b.) You might be wondering 'Why make a sketch, when I have a photograph of the cliff?' The point is that nature is 'messy', mixing geological features with vegetation (the many plants on the cliff), manufactured objects (the fence), and products of recent sediment deposition (beach sediments). A sketch should *emphasise* and *simplify* the features in the rocks, to bring out geological relationships, by omitting non-geological detail.

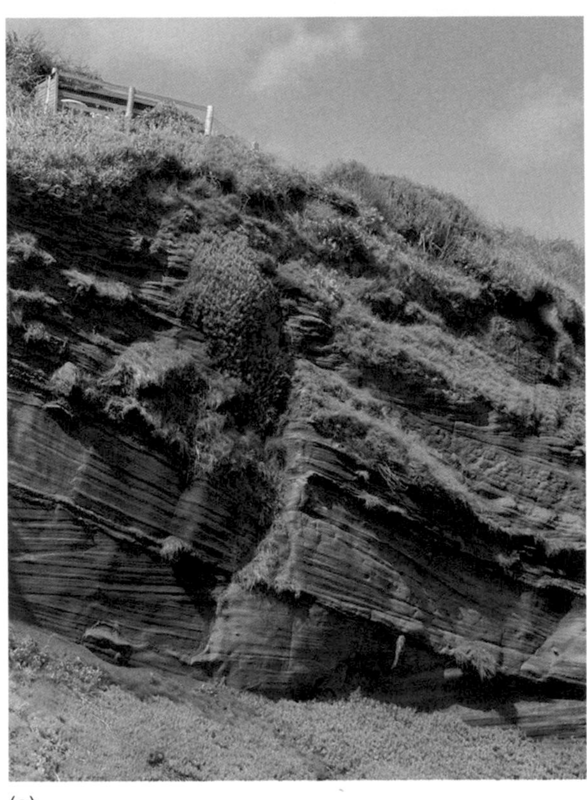

(a)

(b)

Figure 7.7 (a) View of the cliff face at Dawlish. (b) Space for a sketch of the cliff face shown in part (a).

Now look at the comments on this activity at the end of this book.

Figure 7.6a and Activity 7.2 illustrated isolated exposures of sedimentary rocks whose short periods of deposition are separated from each other by tens of millions of years. However, they reveal that each short interval witnessed very different environments in the Lower Permian to Upper Triassic as follows.

- At the start of the Permian, what is now the Torquay area (Figure 7.6a) experienced torrential floods that deposited conglomerates immediately above the unconformity. It probably lay at the foot of rapidly eroding mountains made of deformed Devonian and Carboniferous marine sedimentary rocks. Erosion of the mountains also exposed undeformed granite plutons that had intruded those earlier sedimentary rocks (Figure 4.4). Fragments of these granites occur in the Permian conglomerates, so the granites are older than Permian but younger than the Carboniferous rocks of the area, and the deformation. Radiometric dating shows that granite intrusion took place between 293–273 Ma.
- At Dawlish, red desert dune sandstones of Permian age overlie the same conglomerates as seen at Torquay, showing that the area was dry, highly oxidising and windy during the Permian.

- The Middle Triassic conglomerates of Budleigh Salterton show a return to torrential transport of debris being eroded from the remaining mountains of southwest England. Their red coloration indicates continued hot, oxidising conditions.
- Aust Cliff exposes lower red mudstones deposited under low-energy conditions on land, which probably had become quite flat by Upper Triassic times. The red-beds are abruptly succeeded in the upper part of the cliff by fine-grained, green-grey mudstones and limestones, which contain abundant marine fossils of Lower Jurassic age. Either the crust had subsided locally or sea level had risen globally, to inundate what had been land for at least 60 Ma.

Other Permian and Triassic exposures in southwest England fill in the time gaps, to show a continuous history of changing environments from 270 to 200 Ma. However, in the same way as human history records different sequences of events in different areas, so geological history has a geographic dimension. Because modern environments of many kinds (e.g. deserts, rain forests and bare mountains; coral reefs, deep sea floor and tidal coasts) make up the global picture, a similar environmental diversity probably characterised the geological past, whatever the overall global climate. One aim of studying geological history is to reconstruct the **palaeogeography**, to see how that relates to evidence for plate tectonic influences and how it changed through time. Section 7.3 introduces this wider dimension, including the arid Permian Period in the British Isles, and then how local palaeogeography can be seen in a global context.

Generally, observations of the kind you made in Activities 7.1 and 7.2 are recorded in a field notebook, each visited locality warranting its own record. Many records spread over wider geographical areas provide information that can be expressed on a map, but one that is different in many respects from those you may be familiar with. A geological map expresses the kinds of rock, and rocks of different ages, lying immediately below the land surface, sometimes to be exposed where soil and vegetation have been stripped away by erosion, as in Activity 7.1. Published geological maps contain a vast amount of information, simply because even the small area represented by a standard 1:50 000 topographic map may contain rocks of many different kinds that span tens or even hundreds of million years. Yet, given a few basic observations, it is not difficult to begin working out events in Earth history from the features that geological maps show.

7.2 Geological maps: charts of Earth history

Study note

To study this section fully you need to view detailed digital images (supplied as a computer-based resource) of some of the figures.

As well as observations of rocks and their relationships on the ground, much more familiar observations of the environment help in constructing geological maps. Rocks vary greatly in the way they respond to erosion. Some are more resistant than others and tend to form higher, more rugged ground. As a general rule, sedimentary rocks are much less resistant than crystalline igneous and metamorphic rocks. Among sedimentary rocks, beds of sandstone and limestone tend to form escarpments and ridges, whereas finer-grained siltstones and mudstones are picked out by erosion to form low ground between upstanding, tougher sedimentary rocks (Figure 7.8). The older a sedimentary rock is, the more likely it is to have become strongly lithified (Section 5.4) through cementation by carbonates and quartz precipitated from waters that have percolated through when it was buried by younger sediments. Older sequences of sedimentary rocks, subject to deeper burial, also have a greater chance of being deformed by folding and faulting during orogenies.

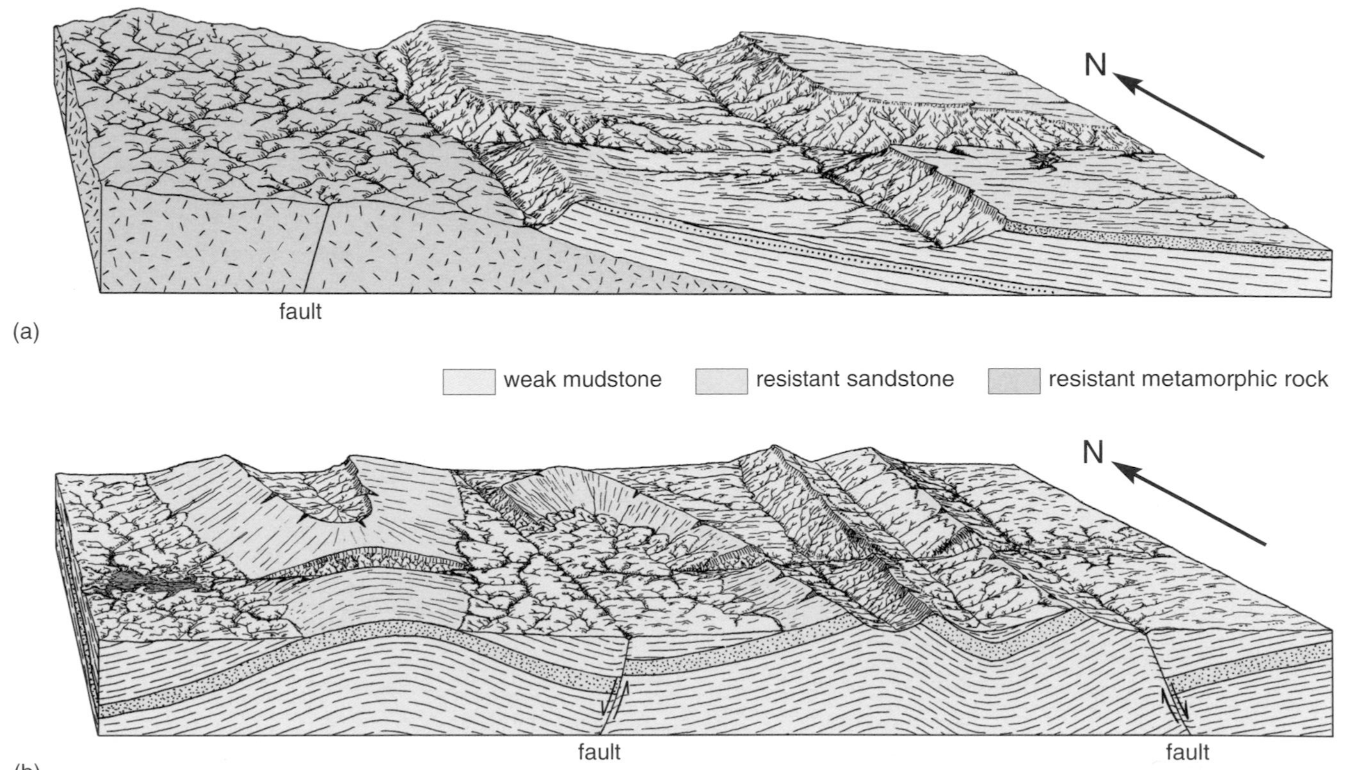

Figure 7.8 Three-dimensional sketches of how underlying geology may control surface topography and the trends and patterns of streams flowing across it. (a) Simply dipping sequence of sedimentary rocks overlying crystalline rocks. (b) A folded and faulted sequence of sedimentary rocks.

Figure 7.8a shows in 3D how beds of sedimentary rocks that are simply dipping beneath the surface are picked out according to their resistance: more resistant beds form escarpments, while less resistant ones are etched out to form vales. Also shown are the minor streams that tend to flow on such a landscape. On the left there are older crystalline rocks that the sedimentary rocks had once buried beneath an unconformity. By resisting erosion uniformly, the crystalline rocks control landforms that have no particular orientation, except where faults occur. Being products of repeated earthquakes, faults shatter the rocks they cut through and become weak zones which erosion may etch out (Book 2, Figure 3.3) to create clear linear elements in the landscape.

Figure 7.8b shows more complicated landforms which may form when erosion has cut through a folded sequence of sedimentary rocks. Steeply dipping resistant beds tend to form linear ridges rather than the more irregular escarpments that develop on horizontal or gently dipping strata. Alternating resistant and softer strata pick out the effects of folds on the topography as broad curved features.

Topographic features controlled by the underlying geology are best identified from far away, using images and other data captured by Earth-orbiting satellites.

Figure 7.9 shows topographic elevation across the British Isles given a 3D appearance by computer-generated 'illumination' from the west. Study it for a few minutes, looking for evidence of escarpments formed by gently dipping sedimentary strata, sharp straight lines that may be major faults or ridges controlled by steeply dipping sedimentary strata, and curved linear features that may outline large folds. The areas to focus on are outlined. The features will be clearer if you view the enlargeable digital images of those areas of Figure 7.9.

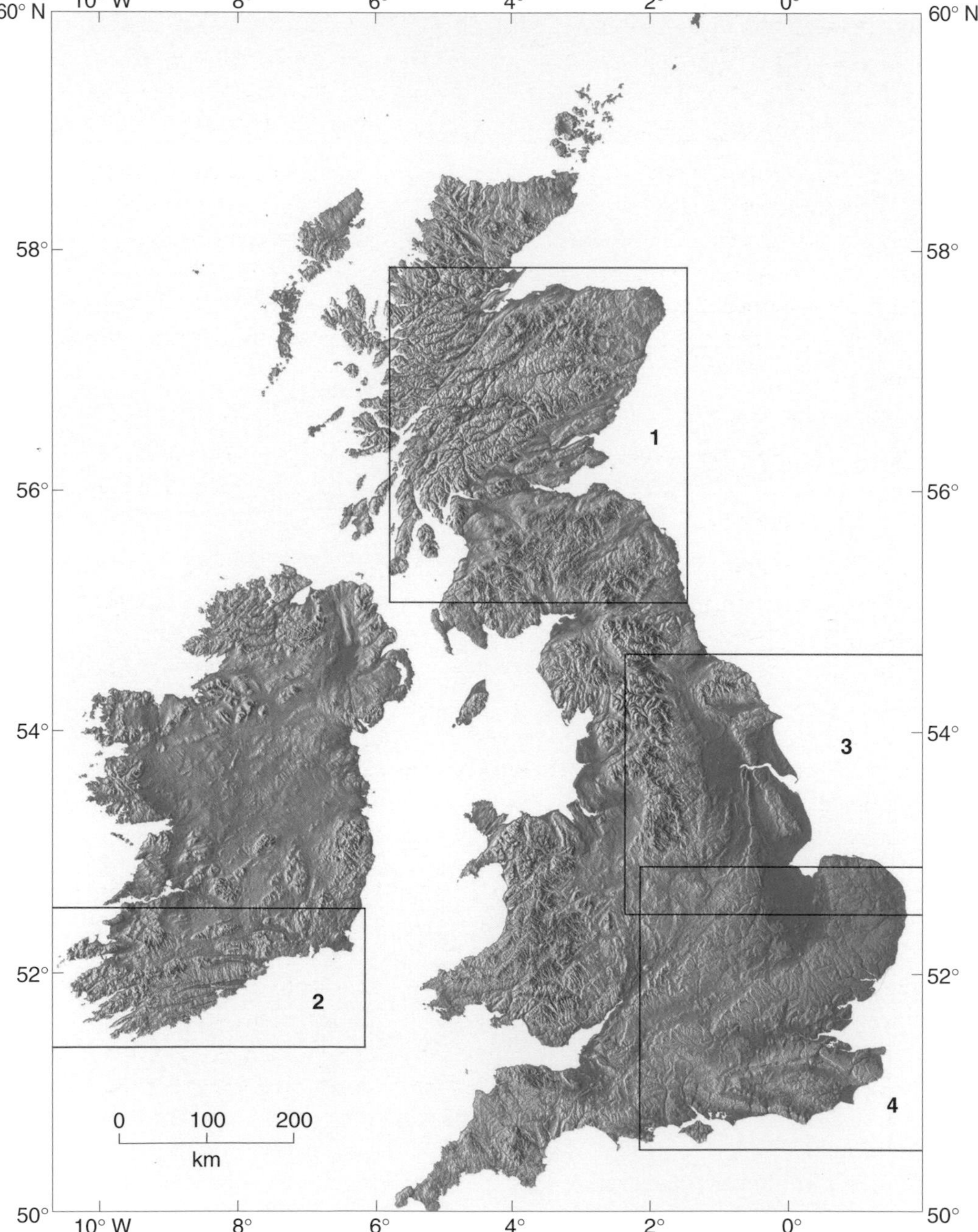

Figure 7.9 The topography of the British Isles measured by radar from a satellite and shaded by 'illumination' from the west – the topography is exaggerated so that features are easier to see. The colour coding ranges from greens for low elevations through browns to grey at elevations greater than 500 m. Concentrate on areas 1–4 which are shown by black outlines. You are encouraged to use the enlargeable digital images – see the course website for details.

Some of the clearest linear features are in Scotland (area 1). One stretches NE–SW between Inverness and Fort William and marks the line of the Great Glen Fault – a transform fault (Book 2, Section 8.2) which was active between 400 and 300 Ma. Another is the straight southern edge to the Scottish Highlands, running ENE–WSW from Stonehaven to just north of Glasgow. This is the Highland Boundary Fault which was formed by tensional tectonic forces. To the south of it the crust beneath the Scottish Midland Valley has dropped by more than one kilometre. It too began forming around 400 Ma ago, and is still occasionally active. About 80 km SSE, a series of thin, sharp lines mark the northern limit of the hills in southern Scotland. This is the Southern Uplands Fault, against which the crust dropped down to the north.

Southernmost Ireland (area 2) shows other linear features in 'batches' of short, roughly parallel ridges and valleys that trend WSW–ENE. These features are controlled by sedimentary strata that dip steeply into the Earth. Some resist erosion and form ridges, while others that are less resistant define valleys.

The east of England (area 3) is very different. There are no sharp linear features and the topography is quite gentle and at low elevations. However, it is possible to trace a series of broad tracts of slightly higher land that trend roughly N–S and have west-facing escarpments. Each is underlain by a resistant sedimentary stratum that dips gently eastwards (similar to Figure 7.8a). Some of the escarpments can be traced to the southwest of area 3, where they swing around to trend NE–SW.

Now shift your focus to southeast England (area 4). There are features in the topography that outline a strange, crudely elliptical shape, cut through by the Channel in the east. The features seem to have been bent and, as you will see in Section 7.2.1, so they have.

Despite the possibilities presented by space technology, such as that used to make Figure 7.9, mapping rocks still involves field observations and data recording. In a small, densely populated area, such as the British Isles, geologists have examined nearly every surface rock occurrence, and then plotted on a map the boundaries between occurrences of different types and ages of rock, helped by rock-related topographic features. The resulting geological maps look stunning because of the colour scheme needed to signify where rocks of different types and ages occur at the Earth's surface.

Figure 7.10 is a highly simplified geological map of the British Isles. The top eleven coloured divisions in its key correspond to sedimentary rocks that were laid down during the Periods of the Phanerozoic, and to older (542–1000 Ma), non-fossiliferous sedimentary rocks of Precambrian age (Figure 2.15). Four enlargeable digital versions of Figure 7.10 are available which superimpose the geology on the topographic image in Figure 7.9 (see the course website for details of where to find them). They cover the four study areas shown in Figure 7.9 and will help you to appreciate how geology controls landforms.

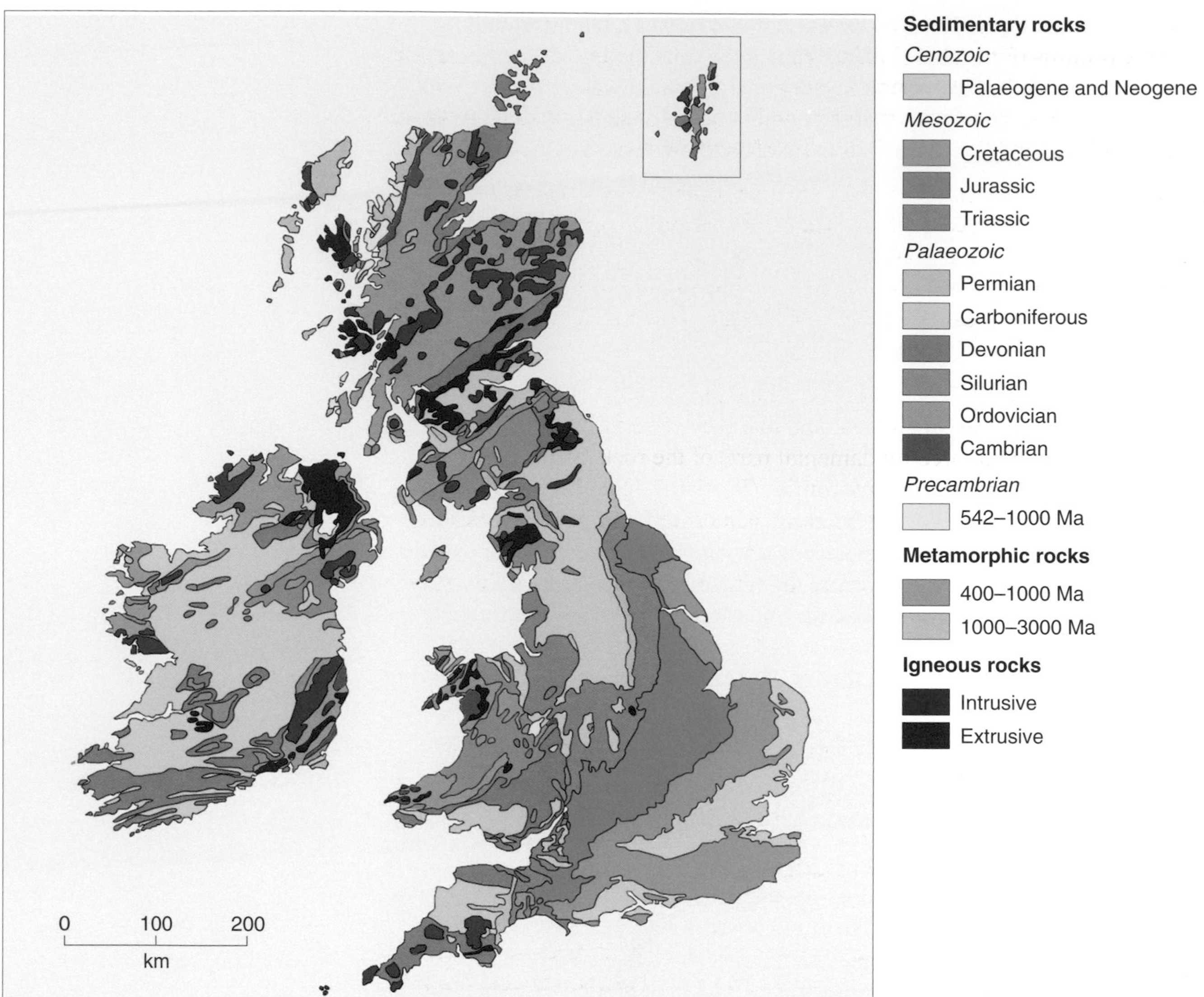

Figure 7.10 Simplified geological map of the British Isles. Each division includes a very wide range of different kinds of sedimentary, metamorphic and igneous rocks. Digital versions combining geology with the topography of Figure 7.9 are available for the four study areas in Figure 7.9.

■ Which parts of the British Isles are dominated by sedimentary rocks?

□ They are most abundant at the surface in the southern two-thirds.

Below the sedimentary divisions there are two rock groups signifying that they were greatly transformed by regional metamorphism. One group of metamorphic rocks formed during orogenies between 400 and 1000 Ma (Section 7.1.2); the other group formed at various times between about 1000 and 3000 Ma (Section 7.1.1).

■ Where do each of these metamorphic divisions occur at the surface?

□ That between 400 and 1000 Ma dominates northern Scotland and northwestern Ireland, whereas the older group occurs in northwestern Scotland and the Hebrides, and in small patches in the west and southeast of Ireland.

Regionally metamorphosed rocks of the younger division also occur in the southern two-thirds of the British Isles, but only in small areas. Their key colour shows as a narrow belt in the promontory of southeastern Ireland. Follow its trend to the northeast across the Irish Sea, and you will discover it again in the island of Anglesey and the Lleyn Peninsula of North Wales.

The final division is into intrusive and extrusive igneous rocks. The two distinctive key colours reveal that the British Isles is dotted with evidence for the intrusion and extrusion of magmas. Note, however, that sedimentary rocks of Carboniferous and younger ages are barely, if at all, interrupted by igneous materials. The igneous rocks are not divided by age to keep this map simple (that detail will appear in Figure 7.16).

The geological map of the British Isles confirms the immense timespan represented by rocks in this small area, and that they were assembled by processes operating in all three fundamental parts of the rock cycle. This section uses two fundamental unconformities (Section 7.1) in the British Isles to introduce you to understanding and 'reading' geological maps. An unconformity separates younger and structurally simpler rocks above it from the more complicated geology formed by older events. The later of these unconformities (Section 7.1.3) is a useful and easily understood starting point.

7.2.1 Above and below the Permian unconformity

Permian and Triassic sedimentary rocks extend continuously from southwest England to the Midlands, where they split into two belts that extend to North West and North East England (Figure 7.11a). There are isolated exposures elsewhere. Permian and Triassic terrestrial red-beds lie above a major unconformity, and they are important markers representing arid tropical conditions, which deposited sediment on top of eroded mountains.

Figure 7.11a shows only the main occurrences of sedimentary rocks of Permian and Triassic age, including the area in southwestern England which you studied in Activity 7.2. To simplify matters, it groups all older rocks beneath the Permian unconformity as a single unit and younger rocks on top of the Permian and Triassic red-beds as another. The more rugged landscapes of northwestern Britain are mainly underlain by rocks which are older than Permian. The line separating the older (brown) rocks from the Permian and Triassic, is where the Permian unconformity occurs at the surface (more about that in Section 7.2.2). The younger (Mesozoic and Cenozoic) rocks occur mainly in the dominantly lowland areas of eastern and southeastern England; the exceptions are three large patches of Cenozoic igneous rocks in Northern Ireland and the Inner Hebrides. Figure 7.11b adds the younger Mesozoic and Cenozoic sedimentary rock divisions. The roughly parallel swathes of colour show where each division – Permian, Triassic, Jurassic, Cretaceous and Cenozoic – occurs at the surface.

Display the enlargeable, digital version of Figure 7.10 (area 3) to examine eastern England at full resolution. Bands of colour superimposed on the topography correspond to Mesozoic and Cenozoic rocks. (Refer to Figure 7.11b for the Permian, Mesozoic and Cenozoic colour divisions.)

Figure 7.11 (a) Map showing the occurrence of Permian and Triassic sedimentary rocks, and younger and older rocks. (b) Map of sedimentary rocks that are Permian and younger. Note that the blank areas in both maps are igneous rocks of various ages (see Figure 7.16).

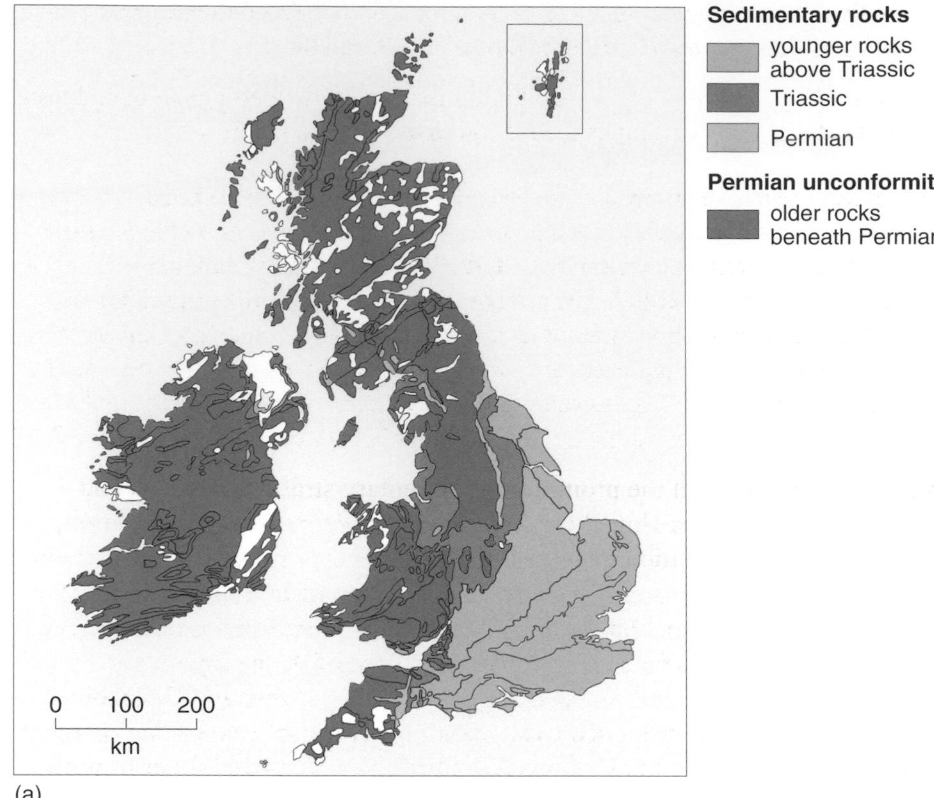

(a)

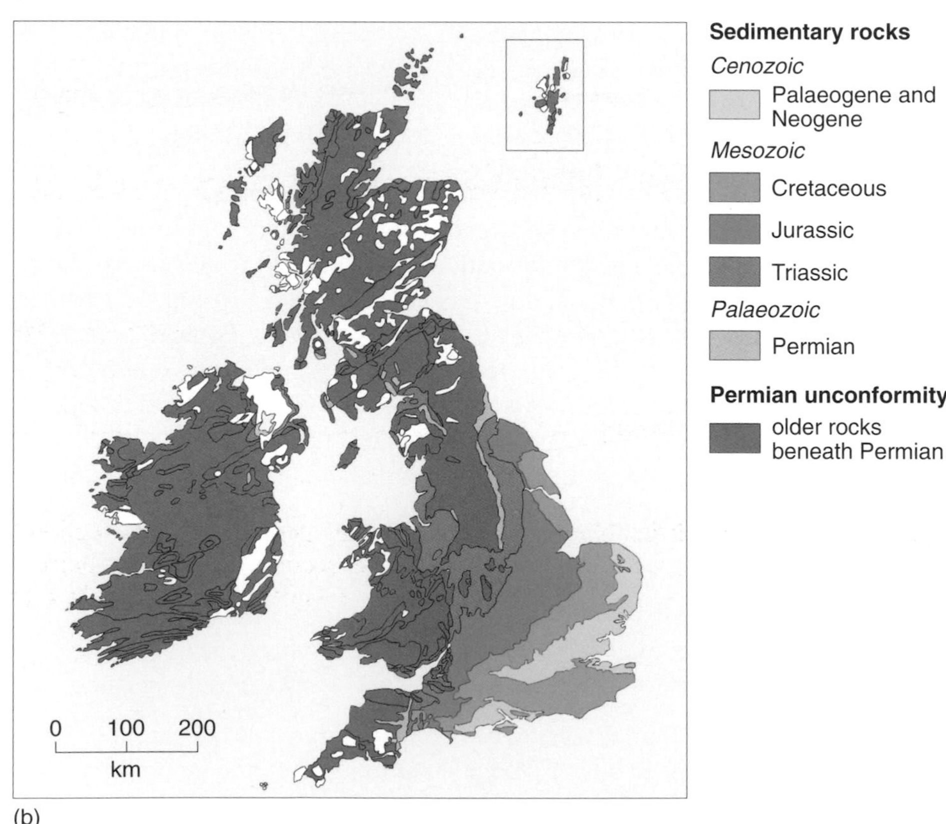

(b)

■ Are there any topographic features that seem to be related to the geological divisions younger than and to the east of the Permian?

□ Several long escarpments trend roughly parallel to the geological boundaries, whose steep 'well-lit' slopes face towards the west to northwest.

These escarpments are controlled by resistant Jurassic and Cretaceous limestones, including the Cretaceous Chalk that underlies the downlands and wolds of southeastern and eastern England. Resistant Jurassic sandstones underlie the hills in Cleveland. The roughly coincident patterns of land forms and geological Periods show that the underlying geology has a major influence on the landscape. Travelling eastwards from Triassic rocks progressively moves to younger Jurassic, then Cretaceous and finally Cenozoic sedimentary rocks, as William Smith discovered in the late 18th and early 19th centuries (Section 2.2.1).

Smith also found that all the prominent sedimentary strata of Permian and younger ages in this area sloped or *dipped* at a few degrees to the southeast, from the Midlands towards London – Figure 7.8a can help you visualise this. This dip was imposed by regional tilting of the crust, after deposition of the youngest Cenozoic rocks, and results in strata of each Period descending eastward beneath the surface, to be hidden by those of the next younger Period (Figure 7.12a). Their dip also suggests that Mesozoic and Cenozoic sedimentary rocks once extended over areas further to the west of their present exposures. The erosion which followed the tilting has removed them from the former western extents.

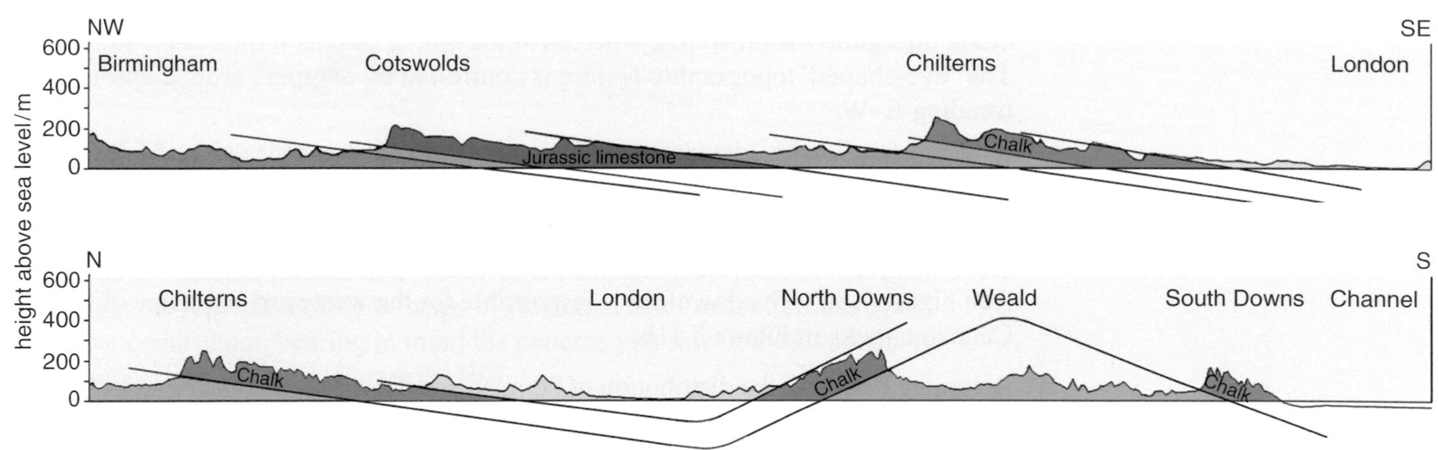

Figure 7.12 (a) Simplified NW–SE topographic and geological cross-section from Birmingham to London. (b) Simplified N–S topographic and geological cross-section from the Chilterns to Brighton. (*Note*: the vertical scales of both sections are greatly exaggerated, so the angles appear much larger than they are in reality.)

(a)

(b)

Figure 7.14 (a) Large folds in Carboniferous muddy marine sediments in North Devon, England. (b) Undeformed horizontal beds of Carboniferous limestones resting unconformably on vertical Silurian mudstones at Horton, North Yorkshire, England.

Question 7.2

From what you learned about regional fold structures in Section 7.2.1, suggest an explanation for the distribution in Figure 7.13 of Carboniferous rocks for about 150 km north of Birmingham (ignore the small occurrences in the south).

Much of central Ireland comprises almost horizontal Carboniferous and Devonian rocks. In Scotland, the Midland Valley has Carboniferous rocks flanked to the north and the south by older Devonian rocks; a pattern that suggests a broad ENE–WSW-trending downfold. Further north, in Scotland, the Devonian occurs alone to form an eastern fringe around the Scottish Highlands. Interestingly, from Birmingham to the border of Scotland there are no Devonian rocks beneath the Carboniferous. During that Period, northern England was probably an upland area.

7.2.3 Getting to the roots: beneath the Devonian unconformity

In general, the older rocks are, the more likely it is that an orogeny has affected them. Except for its southernmost parts, the crust beneath the British Isles was extensively deformed before the Devonian during the **Caledonian Orogeny**. The 100 Ma preceding the Devonian unconformity saw the creation of the crustal mass that now underpins the whole British Isles. Evidence for that bold conclusion comes from rocks in the more rugged west and northwest.

Figure 7.15a highlights rocks that are older than the Devonian. The colour scheme shows a clear division between a northern block dominated by regionally metamorphosed rocks, and one exposed patchily to the south that consists mainly of sedimentary rocks ranging from Cambrian to Silurian in age (542 to 416 Ma). The Devonian unconformity at Siccar Point (Section 7.1.2), and throughout England, Wales and southern Ireland, signifies mountain building to the *south* of the Scottish Midland Valley which occurred between 420 and 380 Ma ago, during a southern phase of the Caledonian Orogeny, followed by intense erosion.

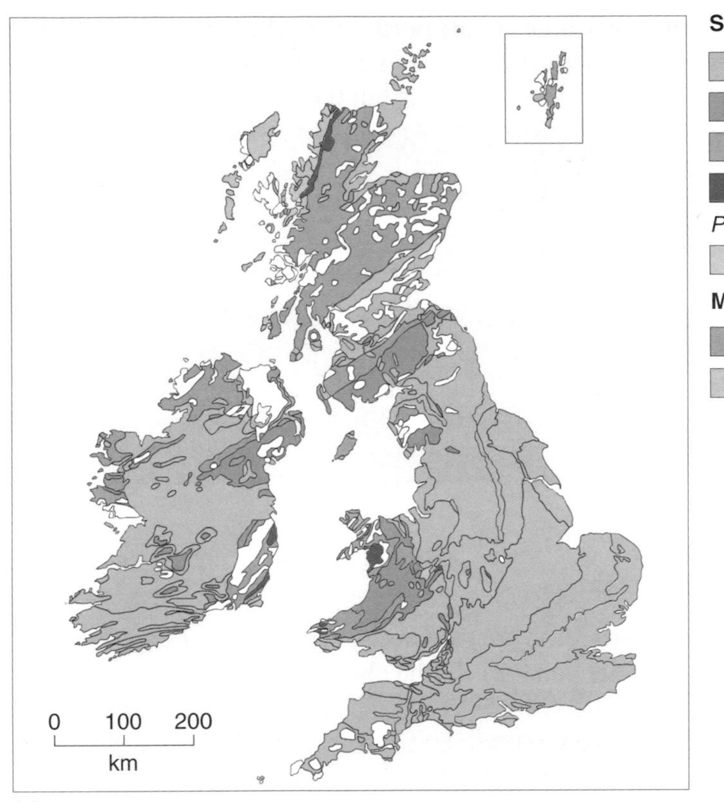

(a)

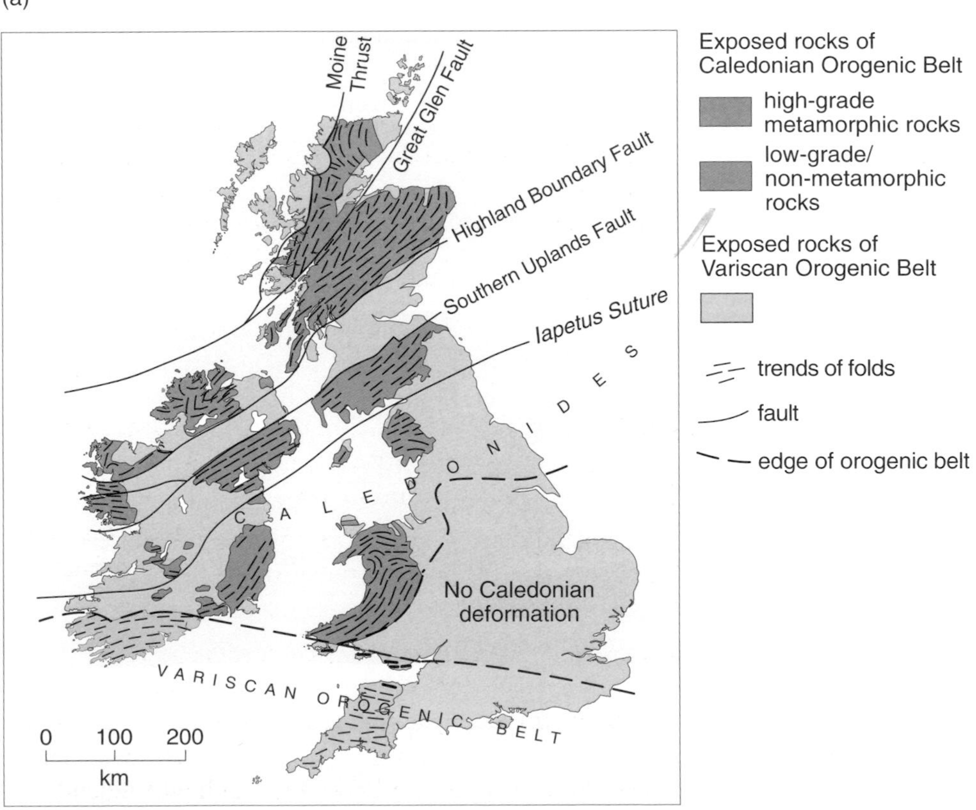

(b)

Figure 7.15 (a) Map showing the distribution of pre-Devonian rocks from 415 to 3000 Ma old, and the area of younger rocks resting on top. The blank areas are igneous rock of various ages (see Figure 7.16). (b) Map showing the major faults and alignments of folds in the orogenic belts of the British Isles. The grey areas are where almost undeformed rocks occur at the surface.

Three geologically quite different blocks of pre-Devonian crust underpin the region (Figure 7.15).

1 The Caledonian metamorphic complex of northern Scotland is made predominantly of highly metamorphosed, 1000–1510 Ma sedimentary rocks. They are underlain by even older (1800–3000 Ma) high-grade metamorphic rocks exposed in northwestern Scotland (Figure 7.15a). This block is made of very old continental materials.

2 The Scottish Southern Uplands are made of marine Ordovician and Silurian sedimentary rocks resting on oceanic crust no older than the Lower Ordovician (~490 Ma).

3 England, Wales and southernmost Ireland formed partly as a volcanic arc, but the pre-Devonian Palaeozoic rocks in places rest on Precambrian sedimentary, igneous and metamorphic rocks (you need to look closely at Figure 7.15a, as the number of occurrences are small), so some older continental crust is present there too.

Some evidence points to a fourth block, an oceanic volcanic arc – now deep beneath the Scottish Midland Valley – separating blocks 1 and 2. Huge faults mark the main boundaries (Figure 7.15b), except that separating 2 and 3, which is hidden by younger rocks. As you will discover, that is the most important of the boundaries.

So many different tectonic settings with similar ages are unlikely to have developed near to each other. Resolving this seemingly strange 'alliance' involved using a simple technique – roughly equivalent to a compass needle frozen during those times.

A compass needle lines up with the Earth's magnetic field to show the direction to the north magnetic pole. What is less obvious is that if you turn a compass on its side, so that the magnetised needle can swing about in a vertical plane, the angle at which it settles is different depending on the latitude. At the magnetic poles it hangs vertically, but at the Equator it settles in a horizontal position. At latitudes in between, the angle is approximately equal to the latitude.

The Earth's field magnetises iron oxide minerals formed when igneous rocks crystallise and cool. That locks into the rock both the direction to the magnetic poles and the rough latitude *at the time of their crystallisation* (Book 2, Section 7.3.1). Tiny fragments of magnetised minerals also line up in this way as they settle with other grains to form sediments. Assuming that the Earth's axis of magnetism has always been as it is now, the place of formation of igneous and sedimentary rocks can be located from measurements of their ancient magnetisation.

The results for pre-Devonian Palaeozoic rocks in the blocks that now make up the British Isles, and for those on other continents, are surprising. Figure 7.17 shows the positions of blocks in the Lower Ordovician and at the end of the Silurian. About 480 Ma ago (Figure 7.17a) the blocks that now constitute the British Isles were scattered far and wide across the **Iapetus Ocean** (Iapetus was the father of the Greek god Atlas, from whom the name of the Atlantic Ocean is derived). By about 410 Ma (Figure 7.17b) all the blocks constituting the British Isles, the Baltic area and North America had collided to form a large continent – eventually part of northern Pangaea. This was achieved by sea-floor spreading, together with subduction of oceanic lithosphere beneath oceanic volcanic arcs.

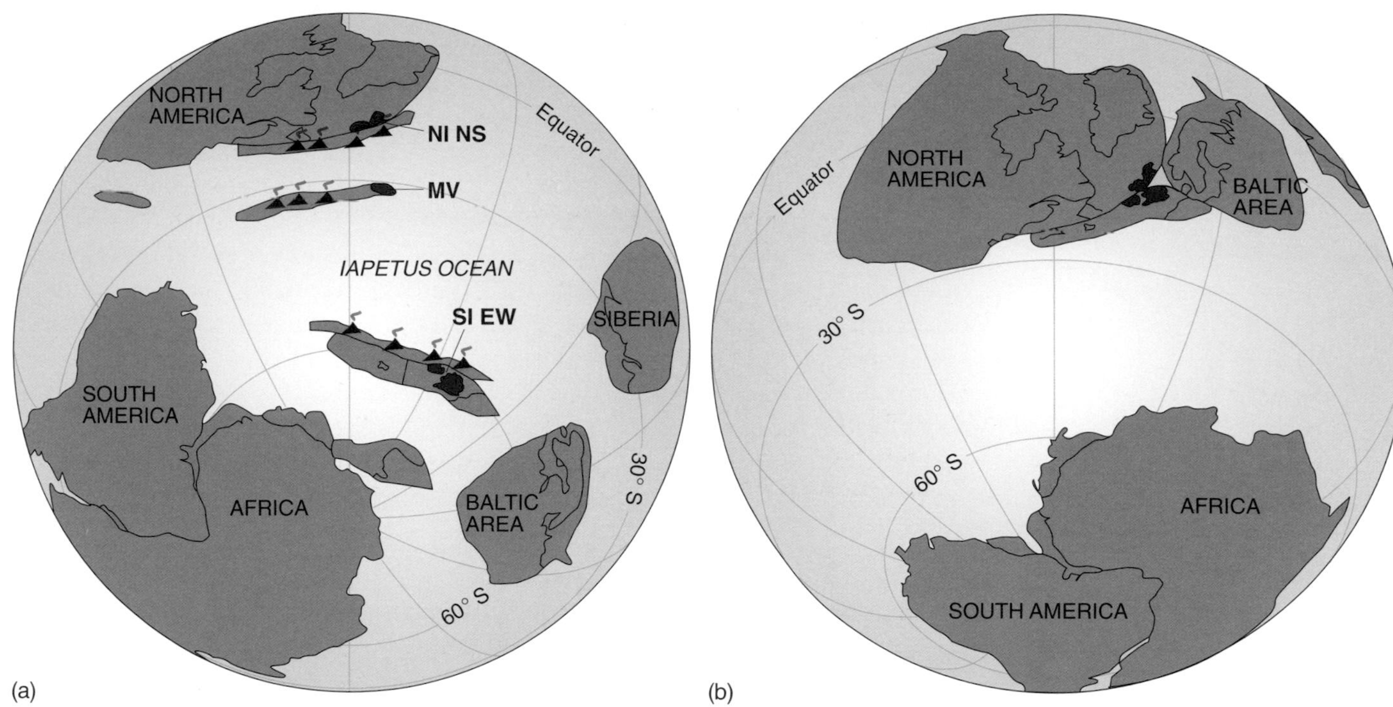

Figure 7.17 Reconstructions of the possible distribution of continental masses at two stages in the Palaeozoic Era. Both show the Southern Hemisphere of the time. (a) In the Lower Ordovician (480 Ma), continental crust now beneath the British Isles (shown in red) was in two pieces on either side of the Iapetus Ocean. Subduction zones are marked by volcano symbols (blue triangles). (b) By the end of the Silurian (410 Ma), the Iapetus Ocean had closed to drive the Caledonian Orogeny and unite the crust under the British Isles. NI = Northern Ireland; NS = northern Scotland; MV = Scottish Midland Valley; SI = southern Ireland; EW = England and Wales.

The addition of ancient magnetic measurements to the evidence used in Book 2, Section 7.2 to reconstruct Pangaea and chart the opening of the oceans that split it apart after 200 Ma reveals global geography back to almost a billion years ago. You can see the results in the computer-based resource *Plate Motions Through Time*, which forms part of Activity 7.3.

Activity 7.3 How Pangaea was made – plate motions through time

We expect this activity will take you about 30 minutes.

View the animation of global palaeogeographic evolution in *Plate Motions Through Time* frame by frame from 600 to 240 Ma. At this scale it is not possible to show all the details of the crustal slivers that make up the British Isles (Figure 7.15b). Instead, the northern and southern parts are shown in blue and red, respectively.

Describe in about 500–600 words the changes in the global distribution of continental crust during this time. Note in particular the changing positions of the two main parts of the British Isles crust, relative to one another and to latitude.

Note: the terms Early and Late are used in the animation with reference to Periods; these terms are interchangeable with Lower and Upper. The Proterozoic Eon is the last part of the Precambrian.

Now read the comments on this activity at the end of this book.

7.3.2 Removing the wrinkles

The line of the Variscan Orogeny in Figure 7.15b extends into Europe, and a similar zone runs all the way down the eastern side of North America. That line marks where two massive continents collided to create Pangaea at the end of the Carboniferous. The British Isles then lay well within the supercontinent: a landlocked region extending roughly from 15 to 25° N of the Equator, similar to the present range of the Sahara desert. So the results of your brief exploration of Permian and Triassic rocks (Activity 7.2) are not surprising; the area was arid desert affected by occasional flash floods and the development of wind-blown sand dunes. However, it was not a monotonous surface of continuous desert sedimentation. Large tracts are devoid of Permian rocks (Figure 7.11) having been uplands subject to continual erosion. Surface occurrences of Permian sedimentary rocks (Figure 7.11), together with cores from boreholes where they are hidden beneath younger rocks, provide evidence for different environments.

Permian rocks throughout southwest England and the Midlands are essentially the same: sheets of debris eroded from the Variscan mountains and the remaining Caledonian mountains, together with dune fields of sand winnowed out by the wind. In northwest England and southwest Scotland the same association prevails, but with the addition of a thin bed of limestone and evaporites; a sign of a short-lived inundation by a shallow sea prone to evaporation.

The Permian in northeastern England is different (Figure 7.18). Just above the unconformity there are sands with dune cross-bedding (Figure 7.18A), but their top surface is full of burrows. The burrowing organisms were tiny brachiopods (*Lingulella*, Book 5, Figure 1.2) which signify marine inundation of the desert. The next bed (Figure 7.18B) is finely laminated shale containing exquisitely preserved fossil fishes. That a shallow sea covered northeastern England for most of the Permian is clear from the succeeding thick fossiliferous limestones (Figure 7.18C). That sea extended across northern Europe to the foot of the Ural Mountains in Russia. It was neither deep nor always connected to true oceans, for across that vast area the limestones are interlayered with thick beds of evaporite salts. Figure 7.19 is an artist's impression of how the British Isles region might have appeared from space during the Permian.

Much the same desert conditions dominated the Triassic, but relentless erosion gradually wore down the Variscan and Caledonian mountains, to deposit terrestrial Triassic sediments more widely than Permian ones (Figure 7.11a). Triassic sedimentation gradually filled the shallow sea, which retreated eastwards. As the surface became flatter, the energy of transportation decreased so that soft mudstones dominate the Triassic of the British Isles. Beds of evaporites in the mudstones indicate that much deposition was in ephemeral lakes (the lower part of Aust Cliff in Activity 7.2). Northern Europe at the end of the Triassic had become almost flat as a result of erosion and sediment deposition. A global rise in sea level easily inundated huge tracts (as recorded by the top of Aust Cliff in Activity 7.2). However, those parts of the crust most affected by the Caledonian and Variscan Orogenies were still not completely flat.

■ Suggest a reason why mountain belts linger for immense timespans.

□ Thickened crust beneath mountain belts 'bobs up' as erosion unloads their low-density roots (Figure 6.12).

Figure 7.18 Signs of the Permian desert and tropical sea in northeastern England. Working quarry exposing three Permian sedimentary rocks – A, B and C. The arrows point to the base and top of the central unit (B). A – cross-bedded dune sands, overlain by B – finely layered mudstones (containing fossil fishes) and C – rubbly reef limestones.

Figure 7.19 Reconstruction of landscape in the area of the British Isles during the Upper Permian, as would be seen from a satellite.

For the next 140 Ma sea level rose globally, eventually standing 200 m above present levels during the Cretaceous, to flood vast areas of continental crust. Shallow marine sediments or those of estuaries and deltas covered most of the southern British Isles during the Jurassic and Cretaceous Periods. These seas extended continental shelves, in many cases right into continental interiors.

■ How might the expansion of shallow seas have influenced the marine biosphere?

□ An increased area of sunlit shallow water would have boosted photosynthesis by phytoplankton and expanded the base of the food chain.

The Jurassic and the Cretaceous Periods were biologically very productive, which transformed the carbon cycle in two important ways. During the Jurassic, huge 'blooms' of marine phytoplankton supported increased animal populations. Moreover, the accumulation of dead plankton in muddy sediments periodically overwhelmed the biosphere's ability to oxidise carbohydrates to CO_2 and water. Deep ocean water then lost its oxygen content so that organic-rich muds could accumulate, thereby burying carbon. These oxygen-starved events steadily removed CO_2 from the atmosphere, and laid the chemical basis for the generation of rich reserves of oil and gas by the later burial and heating of the black mudstones (Figure 7.20a).

(a)

(b)

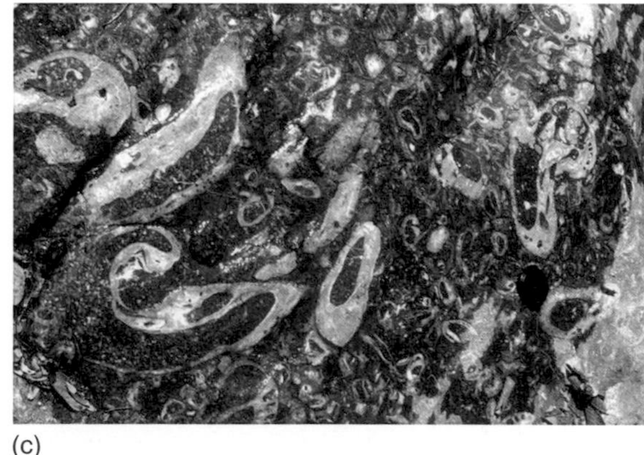

(c)

Figure 7.20 (a) Hydrocarbon rich Jurassic mudstones in Dorset. (b) Chalk cliffs of the Kent coast. (c) Cretaceous limestone from Croatia crammed with fossils of large, colonial molluscs.

During the Cretaceous, calcium carbonate plates of phytoplankton (coccolithophores, Book 1, Figure 7.5a) accumulated in unimaginable numbers on the floors of shallow seas. This formed the thick chalk limestones, now in the white cliffs either side of the Channel (Figure 7.20b). Sustained by increased phytoplankton, animal life in the shallow Jurassic and Cretaceous seas increased in both numbers and diversity. Calcite-secreting corals, brachiopods, molluscs and echinoids thrived, to produce reefs in suitable areas or accumulated as ground-up debris to form other kinds of limestone (Figure 7.20c). Free-swimming animals benefited too, the most common being ammonites, whose rapid evolution and widespread distribution allow the intricate relative time division of the Jurassic and Cretaceous. The seas also swarmed with fish and marine reptiles, such as ichthyosaurs and plesiosaurs, which the anoxic deep-water muds of the time could preserve exquisitely.

Section 3.3.3 broadly charted the increase in diversity of the Modern marine fauna during the Mesozoic. That evolutionary burgeoning continued to the present, despite decimation by the K–T mass extinction. You should now be able to see that modern animal diversity is not solely a product of biological acceleration, perhaps driven by some 'special' genes that survived the devastation at the end of the Permian. It was partly made possible by plate tectonics driving the accretion of continents and rise in sea level which vastly increased the area of shallow seas: two global *inorganic* processes. After Pangaea broke up into smaller continents, moist air from the seas could penetrate larger areas of land, thereby enlarging and diversifying potential habitats for terrestrial evolution.

■ With such a surge in biological productivity and the burial of organic carbon and carbonate, what would you expect to have happened to the late Mesozoic climate?

□ The burial of organic carbon and carbonate would have drawn carbon dioxide from the atmosphere into long-term storage, so you might expect the greenhouse effect to have lessened and global cooling to have resulted.

In fact, the opposite happened: the GMST (global mean surface temperature; Book 1) peaked during the Cretaceous. Herds of dinosaurs seasonally roamed great forests at polar latitudes. The only plausible explanation for such a paradox is that igneous activity released CO_2 more rapidly than carbon burial was withdrawing it. As you will see in Activity 7.4, sea-floor spreading, subduction and continental drift were extremely active during the late Mesozoic. So, igneous activity of all kinds would have been much more extensive and voluminous than it is today.

Activity 7.4 The break-up of Pangaea – plate motions through time

We expect this activity will take you about 30 minutes.

Look at the computer-based animation of global palaeogeographic evolution in *Plate Motions Through Time* frame by frame from 240 Ma to the present. This activity covers the period during which modern ocean floors formed, and you may want to refer to the ocean floor age map in Book 2 (Figure 9.7) to check the evidence for initiation of break-up in different places.

(a) Describe the timing of separation of each of the modern continents from one another, and times when there were major continent–continent collisions (*about 300–400 words*).

(b) Describe the evidence for sea-level change during the Mesozoic and Cenozoic (*about 200–300 words*).

Now read the comments on this activity at the end of this book.

7.3.3 Great tension in the early Cenozoic

The lull in tectonic and magmatic activity in northern Europe throughout the Mesozoic was rudely interrupted in the British Isles during the early Cenozoic (53–63 Ma). Volcanic and plutonic igneous rocks of this age define a narrow zone that runs from the Hebrides southwards to the island of Lundy in the Bristol Channel (Figure 7.16). Sea-floor spreading had been driving North America away from Africa to form the Central Atlantic since 200 Ma (Activity 7.4). Yet the North Atlantic did not develop in the Mesozoic, except as a shallow seaway to the early Arctic Ocean. Around 63 Ma a massive linear burst of volcanism almost cut the British Isles in two. It involved the effusion of lava to cover the Inner Hebrides and Northern Ireland with kilometre-thick flood basalts. As well as the volcanoes in the northwest, a swarm of basaltic dykes running NNW–SSE cut through much of the region as magma followed cracks opening in the crust. The crust beneath the British Isles was being pulled apart. Then, as suddenly as it began, the rifting and volcanism stopped.

This 10 Ma pulse of within-plate igneous activity extended well beyond the British Isles. The then-adjacent region of East Greenland was covered by even more flood basalts. Together, the two centres represent the influence of a hot spot (Book 2, Section 9.2) which developed beneath the still-united northern Europe and Greenland. The hot spot eventually formed Iceland, where it is still active today, as part of the Mid-Atlantic Ridge.

Since 55 Ma, the Earth has gradually become a much cooler planet than it was during the Mesozoic Era. By 34 Ma, Antarctica developed a polar ice cap for the first time since the Permian; Greenland acquired one about 10 Ma later. By 2.5 Ma, the Northern Hemisphere entered the climate instability that periodically forced ice caps down to the latitude of the British Isles, to which their present landscapes owe a great deal. Section 2.1 introduced some details of the last such cycle. Cenozoic global cooling had profound effects on the surface part of the rock cycle, and played a role in shaping human evolution, which lies at the heart of Chapter 8.

Question 7.3

Cretaceous and Cenozoic sedimentary rocks in southeastern England (Figures 7.10 and 7.12b) are affected by folds trending roughly E–W. Was there an episode of mountain building elsewhere in Europe which might explain the tectonic forces that buckled these rocks? If so, where did it happen, what was the tectonic event to which it probably related, and roughly when did it take place? You will need to review the later parts of the animation in Activities 7.3 and 7.4, concentrating on Europe.

7.4 Summary of Chapter 7

Evidence from the earliest continental crust beneath the British Isles indicates that the northern part of the region began to form about 3 billion years ago. For the last billion years the region's evolution involved a uniquely diverse range of processes. Rocks of all kinds accumulated almost continuously for the first half of that time, but on what were widely separated continents.

At 500 Ma, the region's southern part was a small continental mass about 60° south of the Equator. The northern part was at a latitude of about 15° S, at the edge of a large continent dominated by modern North America. Between them lay the Iapetus Ocean, whose closure involved subduction and andesitic volcanism in several arcs. Progressive collision of the two continental masses caught up the volcanic arcs and created the Caledonian mountain belt. By 400 Ma (Lower Devonian), the British Isles' crust had become a unified whole, as part of a large North American continent.

The Devonian erosion of Caledonian mountains deposited thick red sandstones, which everywhere lie with profound unconformity on the older, more complex rocks. The large continent drifted northwards, to straddle the Equator during the Carboniferous. Tropical conditions supported huge rainforests, whose debris accumulated to form coal seams between the muds and sandstones of Upper Carboniferous coastal swamps in northern Europe. At the end of the Carboniferous, closure of another ocean in the south united nearly all continental crust during the Variscan Orogeny.

Erosion of the Variscan mountain belt and sediment deposition produced another great unconformity, at the base of Permian strata. Permian and Triassic dune sands indicate arid desert conditions over part of the region. A shallow sea inundated low-lying areas to deposit limestones similar to modern barrier reefs. Periodically the sea dried up to produce thick evaporite deposits. The rise in sea level in the Jurassic covered much of the region, to deposit limestones, shales and sandstones. The Upper Cretaceous sea level was so high that few areas of land remained in northern Europe. Chalk deposits, composed mainly of the tiny calcite plates of phytoplankton, blanketed much of the British Isles.

The last volcanism to affect the British Isles was in western Scotland and Northern Ireland from 63 to 53 Ma. The region then lay above a mantle plume – now located beneath Iceland – which flooded either side of the North Atlantic with basaltic lavas. The linear trend of the igneous rocks suggests that the crust almost separated to initiate sea-floor spreading. However, the British Isles drifted away from the mantle plume and volcanism stopped. The North Atlantic then opened to the west of Ireland to develop into the ocean of today.

In this chapter you have brought the skills that you developed in earlier chapters to bear on understanding the geological evolution of a large segment of continental crust – that beneath the British Isles. In doing so you have developed skills needed to interpret geological maps and the information that they contain about the 3D distribution of different kinds of rock, and the relative timing of tectonic, sedimentary, igneous and mountain-building events. It has involved you with many highly informative maps, observing, recording and interpreting field evidence. Through use of computer-based learning resources, you have addressed the geological evolution of a region in terms of global processes, and written substantial accounts of your deductions.

Chapter 8
Belonging to the Earth system

In Chapters 2 to 7 you met some new concepts but, equally important, you developed some new skills, especially those used to make deductions from observations of various features in rocks on many scales. Many of the concepts are developed from Book 2, with insights added from other areas of science (Books 3, 4 and 5). Interpreting features in ancient sedimentary, igneous and deformed metamorphic rocks depends largely on what can be observed or inferred about processes in the rock cycle and the Earth system today. You have repeatedly seen how *processes of the present are a key to those of the past*. In fact, without that underpinning principle of the geosciences, it would be impossible to reconstruct the history of the Earth and its life, or to understand other planets.

The other overarching outcome is an awareness that not only do all the physical, chemical and biological processes operating at and above the Earth's surface today form an interwoven whole, they interacted similarly in the past as well. Moreover, the surface part of the Earth system has responded to tectonic events linked to processes deep in the crust and throughout the mantle, in the context of the rock cycle. There has even been at least one instance of a major extraterrestrial influence.

Flood basalts formed above narrow plumes that rose through the mantle, perhaps from the core–mantle boundary, influenced some mass extinctions, especially the biggest 251 Ma ago (Section 3.3.2). A massive meteorite impact is deeply implicated in the K–T mass extinction, in the aftermath of which mammals radiated explosively to their present dominance. Less spectacular but just as important connections have involved steady but slow plate movements that drove continents and volcanic arcs together to make supercontinents, and then to split them up into drifting fragments. An obvious outcome would have been shifts in local climate as individual continents changed their latitude or became locked in the interior of a larger supercontinent. Yet changing configurations of land and oceans would also have transformed the circulation of both air and ocean water, to have a long-term effect on global climate through shifts in the water cycle and the transfer of solar heat.

Tectonic change has had other profound influences. The break-up of supercontinents (Figure 8.1a) combined with a rise in sea level, increases the area of greatest biological productivity: shallow seas over continental shelves. This encourages photosynthesising organisms, with two outcomes for the carbon cycle (Book 1, Chapter 7). Firstly, an excess of photosynthesis over metabolism higher in the food webs leads to the burial of unconsumed dead remains, and the carbon that they contain. After many animal groups evolved hard parts made of calcium carbonate (~542 Ma), increases in overall biological productivity in the oceans have also involved burial of their shelly remains. Second, burial of carbon in these two forms ultimately draws down CO_2 from the atmosphere, thereby checking or reducing the greenhouse effect.

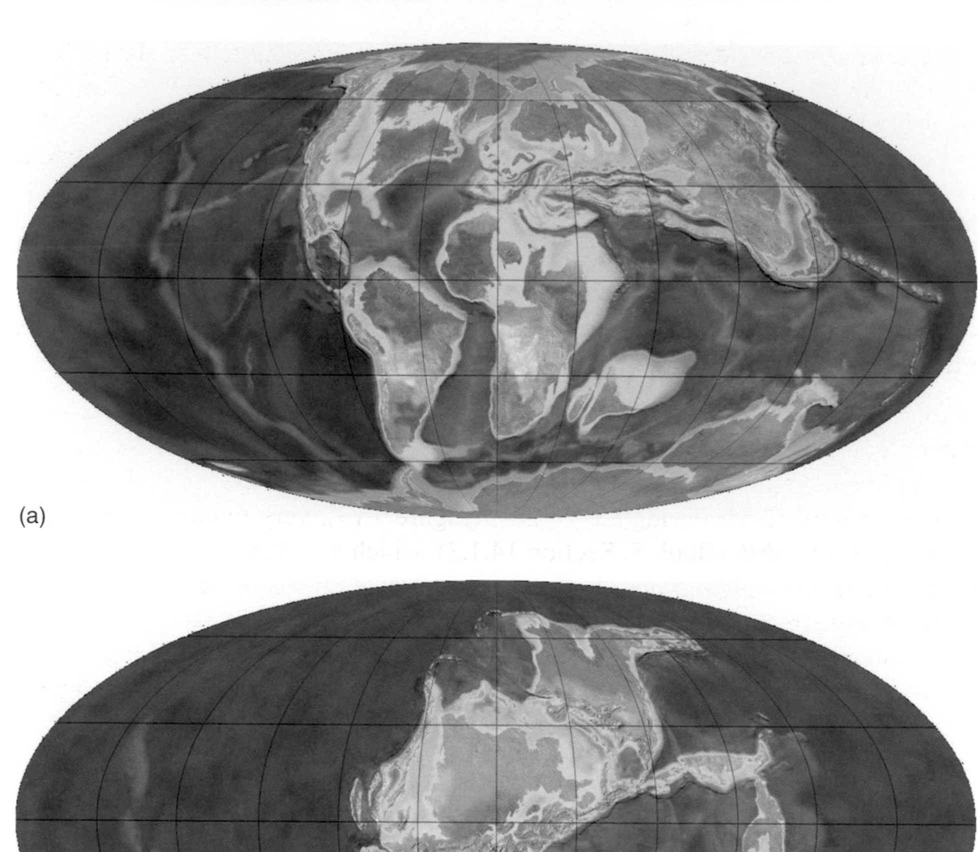

Figure 8.1 Continental configurations that favoured a reduction in atmospheric CO_2 by carbon burial. (a) An increase in shallow seas on continental shelves in the Cretaceous, resulting from the break-up of Pangaea. (b) The spread of land plants in tropical regions of Pangaea during the Carboniferous, and the mountain belts which shed sediment to bury dead plant matter. Both figures correspond to reconstructions in the computer-based resource *Plate Motions Through Time*, at (a) 90 Ma, and (b) 300 Ma.

A unique third influence on the carbon cycle began when Pangaea formed fortuitously after plants had begun colonising the land (Section 3.4). The many collision orogenies involved in constructing the supercontinent threw up widespread mountain belts (Figure 8.1b). Their weathering and erosion shed great volumes of sedimentary debris to form deltas and swamps on which the burgeoning plant life took hold. A combination of expanding terrestrial photosynthesis and accumulating sedimentary debris helped to bury vast amounts of carbon on land, eventually to form coals. So efficient was this means of 'pumping' the greenhouse gas CO_2 from the air, that the Earth, especially the Southern Hemisphere (Figure 8.1b) became locked in probably the longest ice age in the Earth's history; about 80 Ma of Carboniferous and Permian time.

There are many other examples of linkages between all parts of the Earth system. In concluding this book, we will examine a few of them that have a bearing on us, starting with influences on human evolution.

8.1 Human evolution on a changing planet

Humans and our immediate hominin ancestors appeared half a billion years after the first complex animals appeared as fossils, including the first recognisable chordate, *Pikaia* (Figure 3.6c), and perhaps a billion years since chordates split from other deuterostomes (Figure 3.7). Geoscientists have few clues to reasons for those early phylogenetic shifts, apart from evidence for repeated rises and falls in the global biomass and at least three Precambrian ice ages extending to the tropics. Yet, the sequence of events that led to ourselves can be visualised from that far back in time – earlier developments from prokaryotes to the first eukaryote are less well defined. Branching among chordates during the Palaeozoic involved two decisive steps: the transition from fishes to amphibians, and then to reptiles (Figures 3.18 and 3.19). However, that was only possible after plants had established themselves as the base for terrestrial food webs. The formation of Pangaea may have influenced this colonisation, but massive magmatism and then continental break-up were even more influential for vertebrate evolution on land.

Terrestrial reptiles were badly hit by the mass extinction at the end of the Permian when flood basalts erupted in Siberia. Yet mass extinctions open up the possibility of adaptive radiation, once conditions permit biological recovery; in this case, it was delayed by 50 Ma during the Triassic (Figure 3.19). Very reduced populations undergo *genetic drift* (Book 5, Section 14.1.3), which may have focused the evolution of surviving reptiles along paths that would otherwise have been absorbed in much larger populations. Eventually, Pangaea began to break apart. Terrestrial vertebrate populations thereafter became increasingly isolated on drifting continents, to evolve in increasingly independent ways. However, at some time in the Upper Triassic, mammals had already split from their reptilian ancestors, and were evolutionary passengers of continental drift.

Placental mammals appeared in the late Mesozoic Era. Sparse fossil evidence (early mammals were small and fragile) and molecular phylogeny suggest that the earliest primates were among them. That rarity changed rapidly in the wake of the K–T mass extinction, which wiped out mammals' main competitors – the dinosaurs. This left many vacant niches on ecologically and climatically diverse drifting continents. Together with the anatomical advantages of placental mammals, this broader set of conditions allowed their explosive diversification in the Cenozoic (Figure 3.20). Primates diversified too, in Africa, Asia and South America. It was in Africa where the decisive evolutionary event happened, around 7 Ma ago, with the branching that led to humans and chimpanzees.

Think for a moment about the environmental contexts for the major evolutionary steps summarised in the previous three paragraphs.

■ What is common to all of them?

□ They all relate to *geological* influences on a global scale, whether slow reorganisation of lithospheric plates or sudden catastrophic events.

Although living processes may have had a feedback effect on climate and other surface processes, and through them on sedimentary processes, they cannot have influenced mantle convection and magmatism. An element of chance has played a major role in evolution, including at least one 'throw of the dice' from elsewhere in the Solar System. It is difficult to argue for any predetermined path towards life as it is today. Chance may have operated among living organisms too. The basic human bilaterian body plan was laid down about 1 billion years ago. If early evolutionary experiments among metazoan animals had not resulted in a chordate body plan that survived, the only deuterostomes would have been on the line to sea urchins. In this respect, the late-Precambrian Ediacaran fauna are instructive (Section 3.2). Virtually none of those bag-like and quilted soft animals survived into the Phanerozoic.

Much the same might be said for the emergence of the Eukarya as a whole, the split between Archaea and Bacteria, and life being based on complex nucleic acids. Little is known about the timing of these most fundamental developments. Such knowledge as there is, stems from living organisms and a lot of speculation. Book 8 returns to the subject of the earliest life and its origins. From hereon the focus is on one of the outcomes of the often chaotic course of the terrestrial biosphere – ourselves – and on how we have interacted with our surroundings.

8.1.1 A geological and phylogenetic split

An ability to walk on two legs must have characterised the beings that were on the line leading to fully modern humans. The prerequisite for hands able to fashion tools is not having to use them in walking. For an ape ancestor adapted to life in trees to evolve such strange behaviour needed an environment with few trees, rather than dense forest in which all other living apes are found. The East African terrestrial sediments containing the *Ardepithecus* and *Australopithecus* fossils in Figure 3.21c show evidence for a highly seasonal, dry–wet climate. Their environment was very like today's savannah grasslands dotted with trees. East Africa was not always so seasonal, and sediments older than about 10 Ma suggest a continent-wide, humid tropical rainforest. So what caused the change?

A belt of highlands with linear systems of depressions and lakes extends from the shores of the Red Sea to Malawi 6000 km to the south (Figure 8.2). This East African Rift System separates the western rainforests and eastern savannahs of

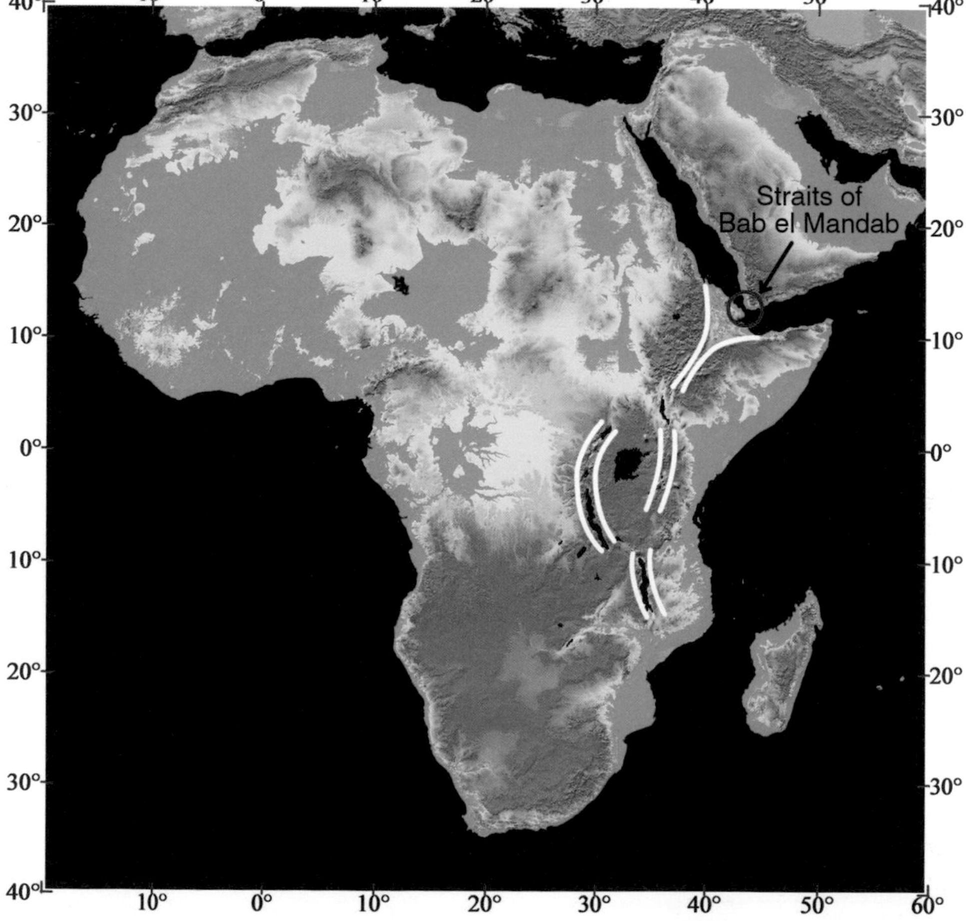

Figure 8.2 The topography of Africa as if illuminated from the northwest to give the illusion of relief. The colour coding shows variations in topographic elevation: green = <1000 m; yellow = 1000–2000 m; brown = 2000–3000 m; grey = >3000 m. The rifts are shown as thick white lines.

tropical Africa. The rift system is tectonically active, thinning the crust beneath the linear depressions. A divergent plate margin is slowly forming. More heat from the mantle flows through the rifts than elsewhere in the continent, so they are volcanically active. This extra heating also buoys up the crust beyond the rifts to form the N–S highlands which rise to 4 km above sea level. The majority of hominin fossils, which piece together the anatomical side of human evolution, occur in sediments deposited in the plains and lake beds of the rift valleys.

In the tropics, the general global pattern of winds is from the northeast and the southeast, north and south of the Equator respectively.

■ Once it had formed, how would the East African Rift System have influenced wind patterns?

□ It runs across the air flow, so would have disrupted it.

Water vapour evaporated from the ocean surface reaches continental interiors only by winds. So once it formed, the East African Rift system would have disrupted patterns of rainfall. Figure 8.3 shows models of the forest and grassland cover resulting from air and moisture movements over tropical Africa with (a) its present topography and (b) without the East African Rift System.

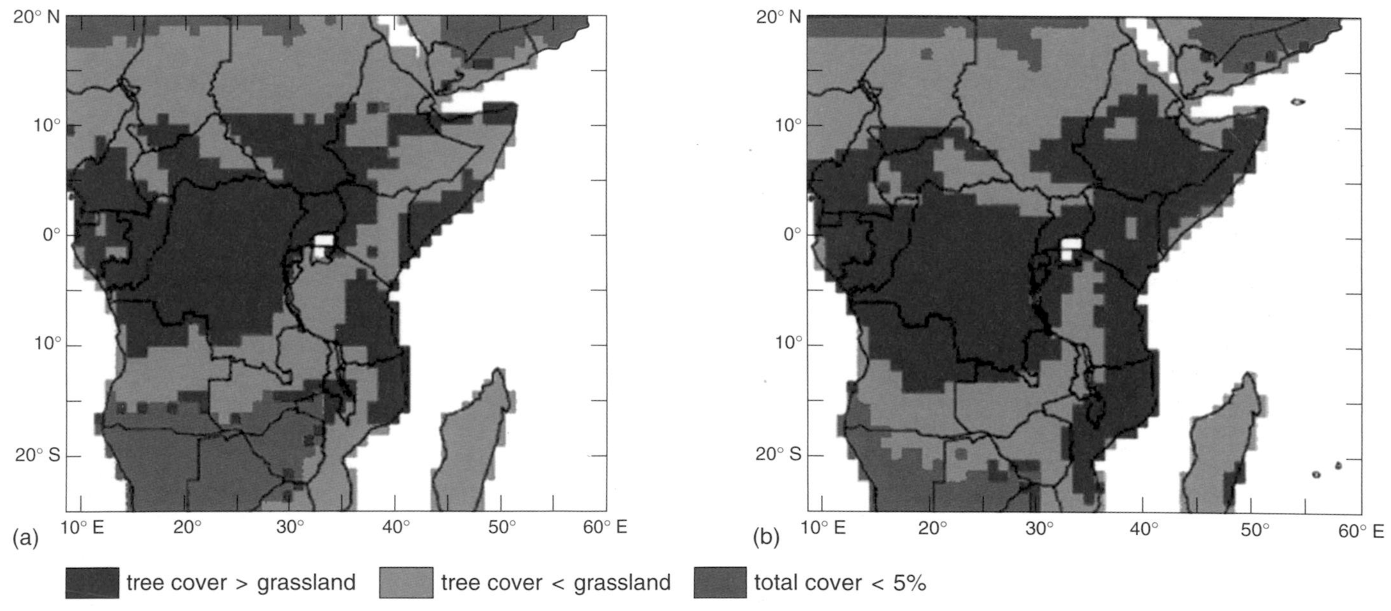

Figure 8.3 Simulation of the vegetation cover of tropical Africa, based on models of air flow and moisture transport: (a) with the present topography; (b) without the East African Rift System.

■ From Figure 8.3, what were the likely effects of the East African Rift System on vegetation patterns in tropical Africa?

□ What had been a continuous belt of forest in East Africa, linked to the rainforest of West Africa (Figure 8.3b), was broken up into isolated patches by the spread of grasslands along and to the east of the Rift system (Figure 8.3a).

Tectonic processes linked to events in the mantle probably underlay shifts in climate and vegetation patterns exactly where hominin evolution took place.

Sea-floor sediment cores in the Arabian Sea off East Africa show an increase in grass pollen over that of trees around 7 Ma ago, roughly when major uplift began to raise the East African Rift flanks. That timing is also within the range of estimates of the separation of chimpanzee and hominin branches in primate molecular phylogeny (Figure 3.21b).

Evidence from the floor of the Arabian Sea shows a further expansion of East African grasslands after 3.5 Ma, at the time of *Australopithecus afarensis*; the species to which the famous Ethiopian fossil called 'Lucy' belongs (Figure 8.4). From 3.0 to 2.6 Ma, wind-blown dust in sea-floor sediments shows increased aridity in East Africa, roughly coinciding with two hominin developments. Australopithecines split into two groups: *Paranthropus aethiopicus* having extremely heavy jaws and chewing muscles, adapted to survival on tough plant material when necessary and, a more 'dainty' species, *A. africanus* (Figure 8.4). The other development was the appearance in Ethiopia of the first stone tools (Figure 1.2a), although signs of their makers do not accompany them. Fossils of the first human species (*Homo habilis*, Figure 1.2a) appear at about 2.2 Ma in association with much the same rudimentary stone tools. Cut marks on animal

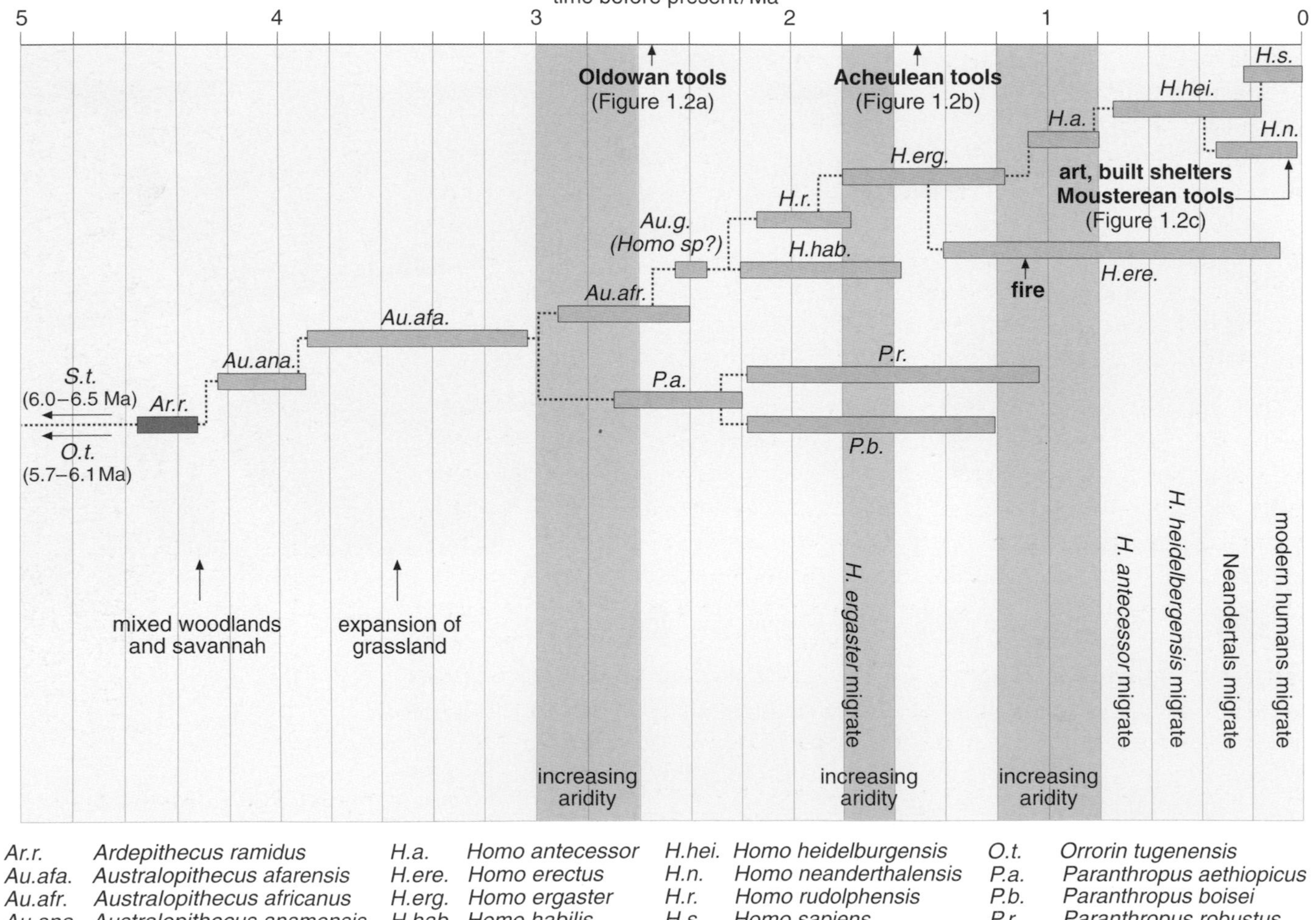

Figure 8.4 Hominin evolution and climate change in East Africa.

bones, associated with *H. habilis*, indicate that meat was a regular part of their diet, and that they used the tools to get it. Around that time, the global climate began to fluctuate wildly (Figure 8.5).

Oxygen-isotope records for benthic foraminifera in ocean-floor cores (Section 2.1.3) extend back into the Cenozoic. They provide evidence for the onset and progress of large-scale glaciation. Although other evidence shows that Antarctica had a substantial ice cap from about 35 Ma, there are no signs of one in the Northern Hemisphere until about 2.5 Ma. In Section 2.1 you examined proxy data for aridity, high-latitude air temperature and ice-cap volume, and found that the last 140 ka preserved a warm–frigid–warm and moist–arid–moist global climate cycle. Such cycles recorded by the proxy ocean-floor $\delta^{18}O$ for volume of ice extend back beyond 2.0 Ma (Figure 8.5).

■ Do the fluctuations shown in Figure 8.5 reveal any signs of regularly repeated cycles?

□ There are repetitions of cold and warm episodes, but it is difficult to determine their pace exactly because no two are identical.

Taking the low $\delta^{18}O$ values in Figure 8.5 as indicators of warm periods, it is possible to pick out roughly one major warming every 100 ka, going back to 1 Ma ago. Before then, the frequency increases to around every 40 ka (particularly clear from 1.2 to 1.5 Ma). The full reasons for repeated glacial cycles are beyond the scope of this book. However, computer analysis of the patterns links them to cyclical changes in the Earth's rotation and orbit around the Sun because of gravitational effects on the Earth by other planets. Recalling that increased glaciation is associated with increased aridity (Section 2.1.1), early humans in Africa faced the selection pressures of extreme drought roughly every 40 ka and then every 100 ka. As well as the increased duration of cold, arid periods, the glacial maxima became distinctly more severe after 1 Ma.

The hominin fossil record is so scanty that evidence for climate change affecting human evolution is circumstantial. An intriguing aspect of the fossil record is that modern humans are not the first hominins to have spread out of Africa. The first was *H. ergaster*, who reached China 1.8 Ma ago, to become the widest-ranging species the land surface had ever seen. Their descendants, *H. erectus*, survived in South East Asia until about 20 ka. The first hominins known to have set foot in Europe – *H. antecessor* – did so during a warm period around 700 ka, and left stone tools and remains of butchery in river sediments deposited on England's east coast. Similar migrations brought *H. heidelbergensis* and the Neandertals to Europe around 500 ka and 250 ka respectively. Neandertals lived in Europe through at least one glacial maximum and survived until around 30 ka, just before the last one.

Once equipped with tools, humans conferred on themselves the ability to live across a wide range of latitudes and survive considerable differences in climate and habitat. That several human species migrated far beyond Africa well before *H. sapiens* did is unquestionable. Exactly what drove those distant relatives' migrations and when they took place remain uncertain. Once members of our species began their conquest of the world, they left not only abundant physical traces but also molecular signatures in the DNA of their living descendants. These have become a means of timing and tracing human migration and colonisation in growing detail.

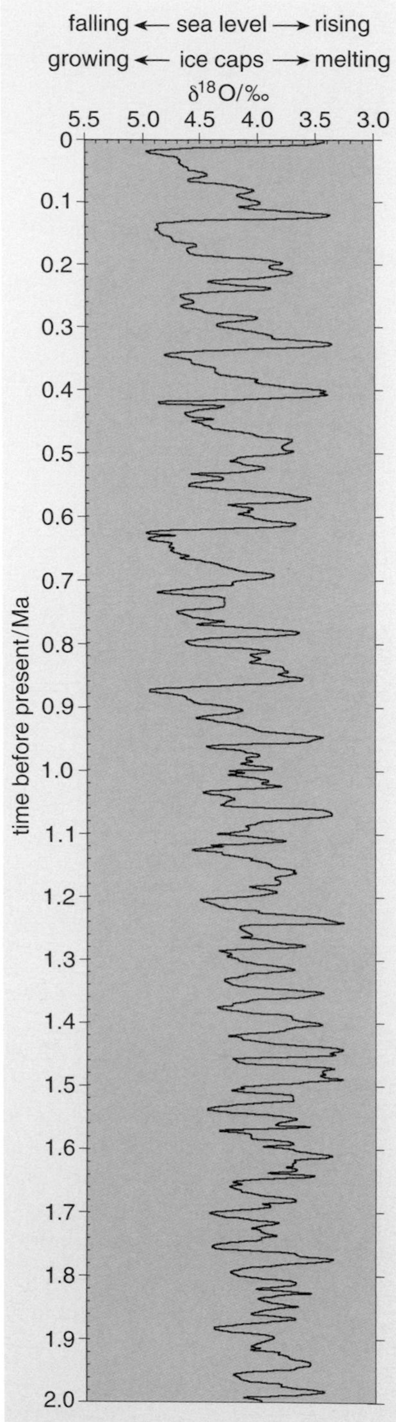

Figure 8.5 Variation in the oxygen-isotope composition of deep-water foraminifera shells in ocean-floor sediments, going back to 2 Ma ago. The fluctuations in $\delta^{18}O$ represent increases (to the left) and decreases (to the right) in the mass of ice in continental glaciers.

8.2 Populating the planet

Archaeology shows that fully modern humans arrived in Australia 60 ka ago, and there are signs of their presence in India around 72 ka. Theirs was the first permanent migration of fully modern Africans. The erratic cooling and drying of global climate since the moist warmth of 120 ka had been under way for 50 to 60 ka by the time people reached Australasia. Their movements were not at the best of times.

The fall in GMST after 120 ka made Africa an increasingly arid continent. The African sedimentary record shows that the great lakes in the East African Rift System dried up (Lake Victoria only began to refill 12 ka ago), deserts spread and the western tropical rainforests shrank to far less than their present size. The pressure on African people to migrate in order to survive would have grown inexorably. Africa is virtually an island continent, so to leave would not have been easy. Even today only water from wells makes it possible to leave through the deserts of the Middle East, and those deserts would have been far larger at that time. Yet there is one place where a route was possible. At the southern end of the Red Sea, Arabia is visible from Africa, 25 km across the straits of Bab el Mandab.

■ What might have allowed people an easier means of escape across the Red Sea than swimming or rafting 25 km?

□ As ice built up on land so sea level would fall, to expose more of the continental shelf.

The divergent plate margin of the Red Sea ends just north of Bab el Mandab, and much of the sea floor there is shallow. The further sea level fell, the narrower the straits became. Figure 8.6 shows the results of converting the oxygen-isotope data from deep-sea sediment cores to sea level for the last 140 ka.

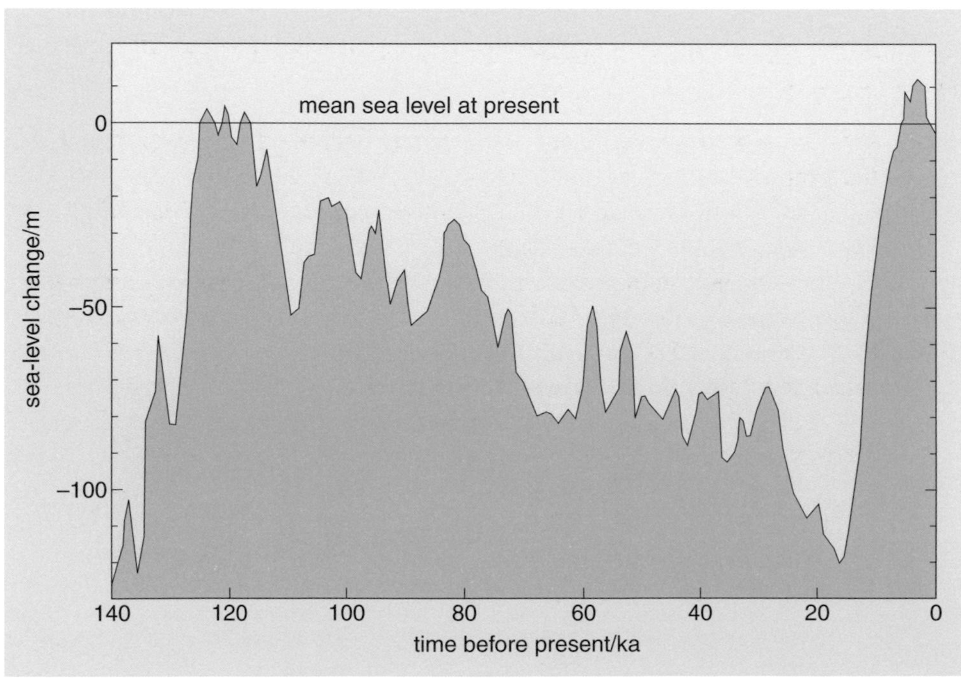

Figure 8.6 Fluctuations in global sea level during the last 140 ka, relative to sea level at present. Estimated from the oxygen-isotope record of bottom-dwelling foraminifera preserved in sea-floor sediment cores.

■ When were the easiest times to cross Bab el Mandab?

□ Figure 8.6 shows several falls in sea level of up to 50 m between 120 and 80 ka. After 80 ka, sea level declined to 80 m below present, maintaining that level for ~8 ka until 60 ka, when there was a sudden 20–30 m rise. The last glacial maximum at 18 ka would have been the easiest time to cross but, by then, humans spanned large areas of Eurasia and beyond.

A fall in sea level of 80 m would have shrunk Bab el Mandab to less than 5 km dotted with small islands. Crossing to Arabia opened up a coastal route around the whole of southern Asia, the Persian Gulf being completely dry. Note that seafood would have been easily obtained along the shores.

The starting points, routes and timing of human migrations can be assessed by comparing neutral mutations or markers in short sections of mitochondrial DNA (mtDNA) and Y-chromosome DNA (Y-DNA). Descendants of individual women or men respectively, in whom the markers first appear, would inherit copies of the marker. Occurrence of the markers among living people spread around the globe, tracking their ancestors' migrations and liaisons between different groups. From the present abundance of the markers in different local populations, it is also possible to backtrack to *where* the mutation may have occurred. Using the molecular clock approach, *when* the mutations occurred can be estimated too.

Linked with radiometrically dated archaeological finds, this genetic approach roughly charts much of the prehistory of fully modern humans. Between 30 and 50% of modern people in southern Pakistan carry the earliest mtDNA marker of non-African origin. A woman living in that area between about 70 and 75 ka hosted the mutation. The first 80 m fall in the level of the Red Sea is the most likely event to have allowed an exodus from Africa to start. Using the modern location and abundance of later mutations superimposed on the earliest helps to chart human migration (Figure 8.7).

The major 'milestones' of fully modern human's activities on the continents, shown on Figure 8.7, are as follows:

1 195–150 ka: modern humans descend from an African female, probably in the Rift Valley
2 After 80 ka: a small band of people crosses Bab el Mandab at a period of low sea level
3 ~80–75 ka: a marker mutation arises that is carried by all non-African people
4 ~75–60 ka: modern people move into South East Asia and China, meeting earlier *H. erectus* and Neandertal-like populations
5 ~60 ka: first entry to Australia and New Guinea
6 ~46–50 ka: modern people migrate to Europe and meet the Neandertals
7 ~40 ka: migration into Central Asia
8 ~22–25 ka: humans cross the Bering Straits, which were exposed at the last glacial maximum
9 ~15–19 ka: earliest signs of human occupation of the Americas
10 ~12.5 ka: earliest evidence of human habitation in Chile.

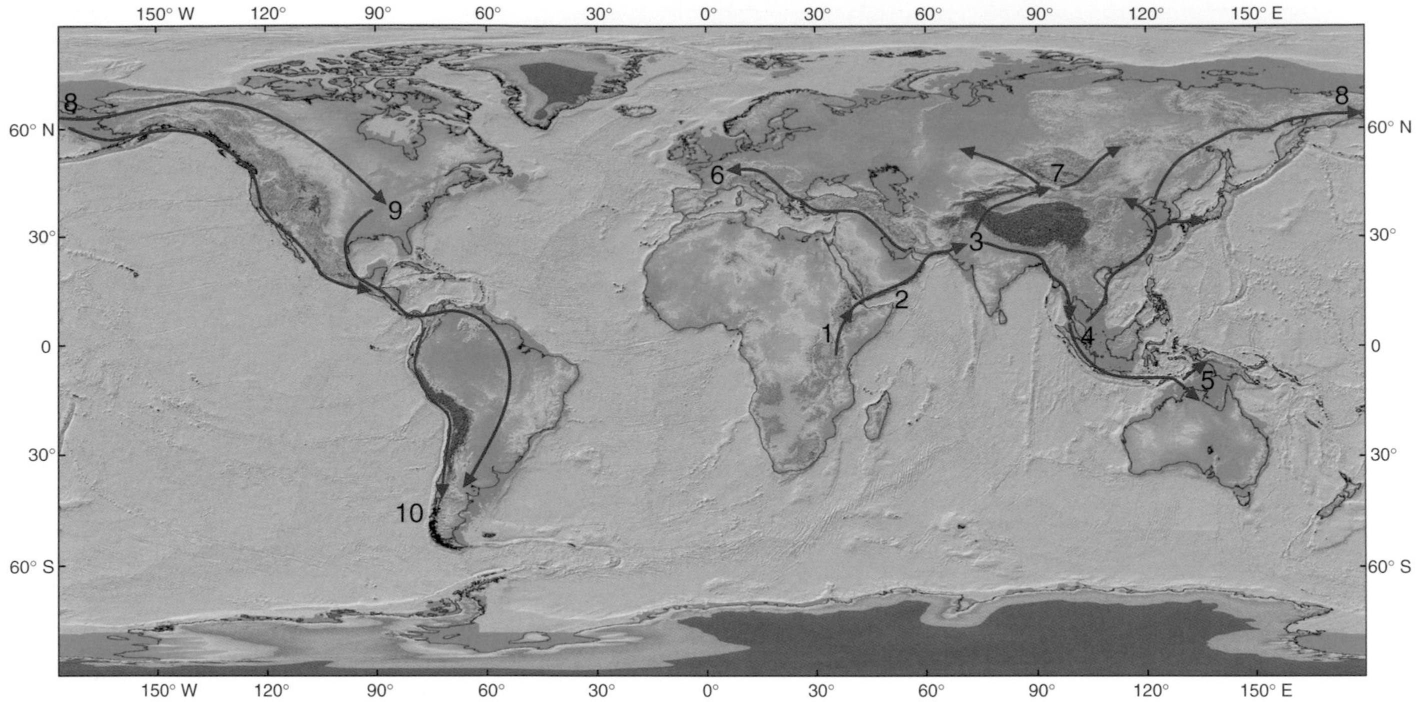

Figure 8.7 The likely routes of major human migrations during the last glacial period, shown on a topographic map that shows the land distributions at the last glacial maximum. At that time (18 ka ago) sea level was 120 m lower than at present, and what are now shallow seas had become dry land. Numbers refer to major events deduced from patterns of DNA mutations in modern populations. Colours range from green at elevations close to sea level through yellow and brown to red at elevation above 4000 m.

Falls in sea levels of more than 50 m created a world with huge areas of coastal flats as the continental shelf was exposed. The Indonesian archipelago became an extension of South East Asia, almost linking it to combined Australia and New Guinea; the Bering Sea between North America and Eurasia formed a land bridge and many other changes are noticeable in Figure 8.7. At the last glacial maximum it was possible to walk from Africa to the southern tip of South America.

8.3 Technologies that changed the world

In the hands of small groups of forager-hunters, stone tools and less durable artefacts of wood and fibre may not seem environmentally threatening. But did humans have any noticeable effects on natural ecosystems between 2.2 Ma and the start of historic times? The fossil record and modern plant communities provide surprising clues. The rate of extinctions at the genus level among large mammals (>45 kg body mass) that were potential prey for human hunters changed from a steady 10–20 Ma^{-1} to >100 Ma^{-1} after 2 Ma ago. Controversy continues about whether this selective mass extinction had a human cause or stemmed from climate changes since 2 Ma. (No one disputes the accelerated extinction resulting from human activities over the past few centuries.) The extinctions varied according to time and place (Figure 8.8).

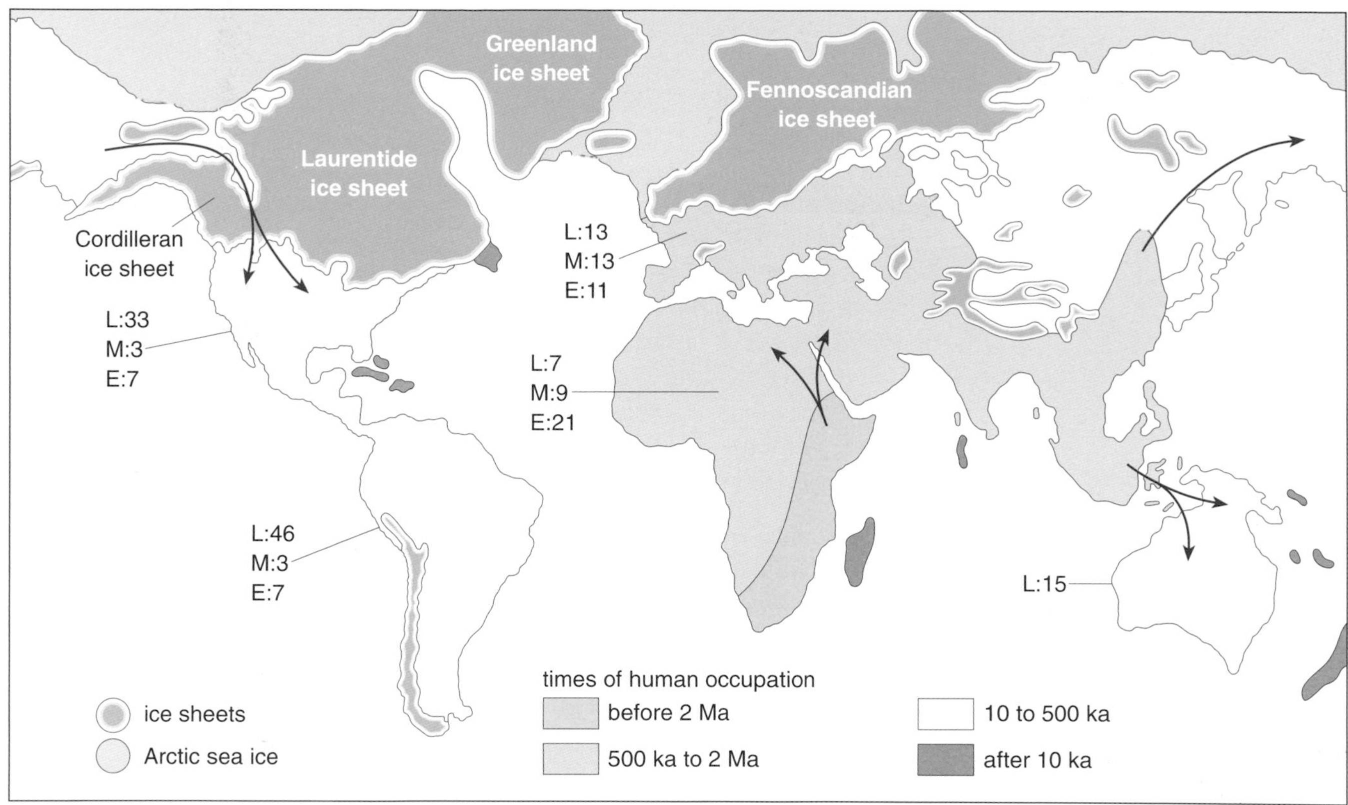

Figure 8.8 The map shows the distribution of ice on land and floating on the sea, and coastlines when sea level was about 130 m lower than at present during the last glacial maximum (18 ka). Age ranges of extinctions of large mammal genera (>45 kg) relative to time of first occupation by humans are divided into: early (E, 700 ka–2 Ma); middle (M, 100–700 ka); and late (L, after 100 ka), with the numbers of extinctions at the genus level during each period. Arrows show continent-to-continent migration routes.

The clearest support for a human cause of the extinctions comes from the Americas and Australia, where extinctions rose dramatically in the last 100 ka. In Australia, large marsupials disappeared shortly after human occupation around 60 ka. The connection with humans seems even clearer in the Americas, where the bulk of the late extinctions followed signs of human occupation after the last glacial maximum. In both cases, the fully modern human colonisers were well-equipped hunters. No such conclusions can be drawn from Eurasia, which humans entered as early as 1.8 Ma. In Africa, most extinctions occurred in the early period. Although humans then were equipped with sharp-edged stone tools (Figure 1.2), there are no signs of spear points; perhaps there were wooden spears. An alternative view is that the early African extinctions accompanied climatic drying after glacial cycles began.

The other sign of a change with a possible human connection is the dominance of African and Australian savannah trees by fire-resistant species. Some researchers attribute this to grass and scrub being burned to drive game and make animals more easily seen; a method used today by surviving forager-hunters. In marine sediment cores off Australia wood ash shows a clear increase and pollen proportions change after 60 ka; about the time of first human colonisation.

■ What effects would the spread of agriculture have left after its invention about 10 ka ago?

□ Land clearance would reduce the amount of natural grass and woodland cover.

The onset of agriculture appears in pollen records from lake-bed sediments in different areas as a sudden decrease in the proportion of tree pollens relative to those of weeds. More surprising are the otherwise unexplained rises in the CO_2 content of air bubbles in Antarctic ice at 8 ka and 5 ka, which have been ascribed to forest clearance and burning, and the start of rice cultivation respectively. Rice fields are waterlogged for part of the growing season and release large amounts of methane, which is quickly oxidised to CO_2 in the atmosphere. Although controversial, this may point to a significant influence on the greenhouse effect long before industrial releases of CO_2.

Starting with the Bronze Age (roughly between 5.5 and 3.2 ka), the last 5000 years of human culture has become increasingly one of metal use. The technologies used to extract metals from their ores (Book 4, Chapter 8) rely on a special part of the rock cycle, which concentrates metals far above their normal levels in rock. Working even the most concentrated ores requires far more rock to be excavated than the mass of metal produced. Figure 8.9a gives an idea of the extent to which humans now intervene in the Earth system to extract physical resources.

Both archaeological and modern civil engineering show up clearly from space (Figure 8.9b and 8.9c) and involve shifting vast amounts of soil, sediment and rock. What is mainly hidden is another outcome of metal-using cultures. Felling trees to clear land and tilling it with iron ploughs remove natural protection against erosion; soil pours off the land, especially in densely populated upland areas (Figure 8.9d). It is estimated that 7.5×10^{13} kg y^{-1} of human-induced erosion occurs globally at the outset of the 21st century, compared with a natural rate of 2.1×10^{13} kg y^{-1}, estimated from the mass of sediments deposited over the last few thousand years. If correct, this human influence is greater than natural rates of mass movement over the land by the ice sheets during the last glacial period.

The latest development in the use of metals is making machines, including means of transportation. Vastly more energy is needed by an industrial economy than that available from muscle power alone. Industry turned first to coal and soon after to petroleum, both products of the Earth system at special times during the geological past. Both mark periods when global photosynthesis exceeded global metabolism for millions of years. Coal formed in tropical swamps at times, especially the Carboniferous, when erosion and sediment transport rapidly buried carbon in the form of wood tissue. Petroleum is an outcome of marine processes that starve bottom water of oxygen, so that dead organic matter is not oxidised on the sea floor. Instead it accumulates in clay-rich muds to form a source for petroleum through heating during burial. Both coal and petroleum reserves are legacies of tens to hundreds of million years of geological processes. In energy terms, they store past solar energy in chemical form.

Figure 8.9 Human movement of material. (a) The world's largest earth mover: the Krupps Bagger 288, a bucket-wheel reclaimer used to surface-mine coal. (b) The 4-ka-old pyramids of Giza, Egypt. (c) Beach resort on an artificial island on the Persian Gulf shore of Dubai. (d) Soil erosion in South Dakota, USA.

Burning these fossil fuels reverses the ancient reduction of water and carbon dioxide to organic C, H, O-containing compounds (with oxygen as a by-product) by oxidation back to CO_2 and H_2O. At the time of writing (2007), the annual output of CO_2 by human activity (>7 Gt of carbon-equivalent) is about 100 times more than that emitted by all the world's volcanoes (~0.08 Gt y^{-1}). As you saw in Book 1, this is now recognised as a major contributor to the greenhouse effect that contributes to global warming.

Although always part of the Earth system, some human activities now rival natural geological processes in magnitude and rate. Currently, the greatest concern is our massive influence on the carbon cycle. It should be clear to you that parts of the Earth system operate over timespans far greater than those of human affairs. Geoscientists have to take a long-term view, in which the two to three centuries since the Industrial Revolution may seem trifling. However, what would happen if global warming caused by burning fossil fuels went on for several more centuries? There is probably enough coal in the ground for that. The Greenland ice cap contains enough water to raise global sea level by about 7 m if it melted. Melting all the ice on Antarctica would add an extra 60 m.

The full circumstances of the sudden cooling and warming that recurred throughout the last 120 ka are not yet certain (Section 2.1.2). The last major warmings were around 14.5 and 11.5 ka. They melted the huge ice sheets covering large areas of North America, northern Europe and northern Asia. Each rise in GMST took place over a few centuries at most – as did sudden coolings. One 'unthinkable' future scenario is that uncontrolled global warming, fuelled by society's release of CO_2, may eventually cause both ice caps to melt. For hundreds of million years before 35 Ma ago, neither polar region had a major ice cap. Today's world without them would look like Figure 8.10. Consider it for a while, in terms of where modern population density, capital investment and agriculture are high.

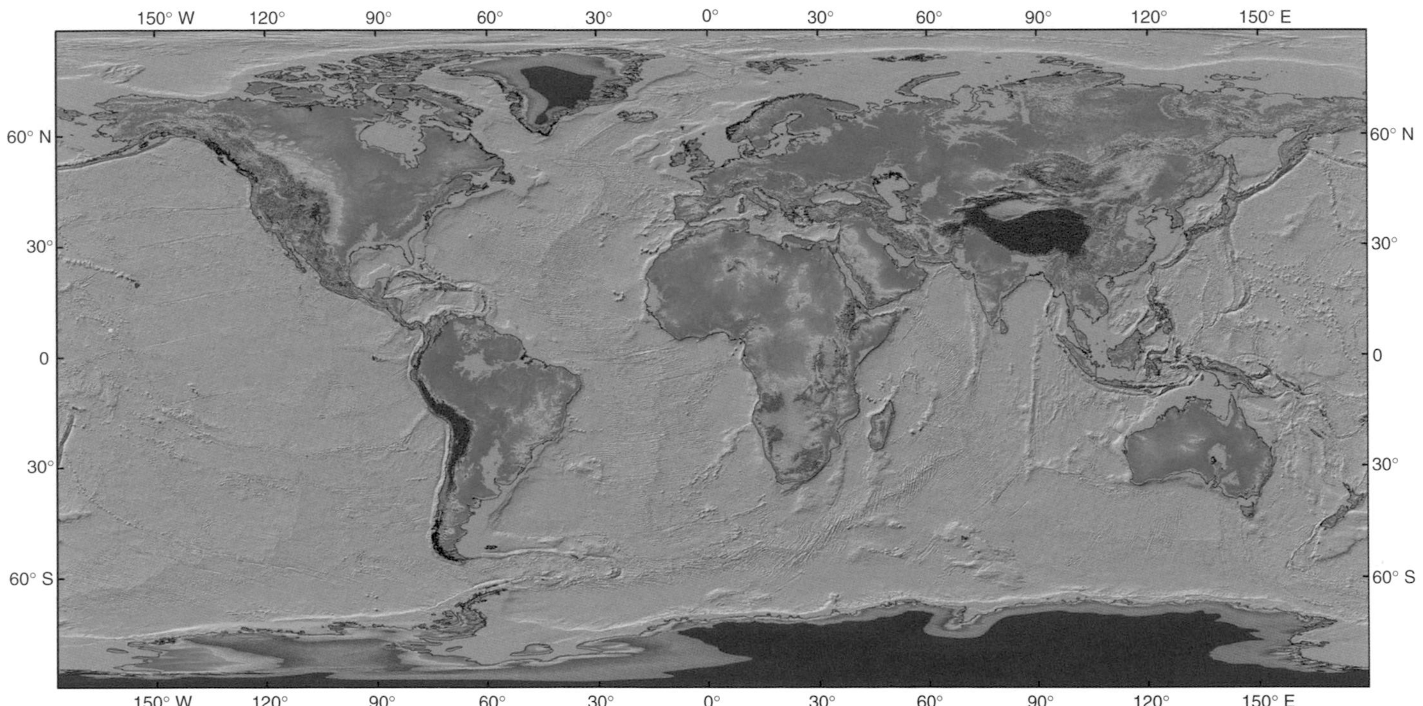

Figure 8.10 How land masses would look if sea level were to rise by 67 m, which would occur if the Greenland and Antarctic ice caps melted completely. Colours range from green at elevations close to sea level through yellow and brown, to red at elevation above 4000 m.

Chapter 9
An overview of Book 6

By covering aspects of the biosphere, hydrosphere and atmosphere, as well as the solid Earth, this book has re-engaged you with material from the earlier books. You should now understand more deeply the links that are inherent in the Earth as a complex system, which were introduced in Books 1 and 2. A good example is the way in which living evolutionary processes are closely bound up with long-term and sudden changes in the non-living environment. This covers, among many other effects, climate change and the curious evolution of hominins that led to us. Yet this book's main aim was to introduce you to the means of understanding the Earth processes that operated in the ancient past, partly from simple field observations of rocks and partly from data that the Earth's materials yield when analysed in a laboratory.

The key scientific concepts covered include: relative and absolute ages; the use of stable isotopes of oxygen and carbon; radiometric dating; glacial and interglacial cycles; the stratigraphic column and geological timescale; the broad course of biological evolution; mass extinctions; processes involved in forming sedimentary, igneous, metamorphic and deformed rocks; geological maps and the plate tectonic evolution of the British Isles.

You have undertaken a wide range of practical activities, including extracting information from plots of oxygen and carbon isotopes against time; looking at the fundamental features of fossil organisms; exercising your skills in using maths and graphs in the context of radioactive decay and dating; discovering the characteristic properties of rock-forming minerals; revising the features of igneous, sedimentary and metamorphic rocks; extracting information from geological maps and topography; and tracing the evolution of the British Isles in the context of plate tectonics. In short, you have swept across the huge range of subjects covered by the geosciences, and probably feel that your mind has been boggled. You need not worry about remembering all of this material. However, we expect you to have made sense of most of what you read and to now understand how all the strands of science are interwoven in nature, and always have been.

As in Book 5, you have extended the communications skills you developed in Books 1 to 4. You have learned how to compile field notes and draw simplified sketches of geological relationships.

By now, you should be well-versed in linking the material you have studied and the activities you have engaged in with the course learning outcomes. There is no formal requirement here for you to record your progress in that context but, if you found that useful in earlier books, set aside a little time to do it for this book.

The history of processes in the Earth system and the materials they produce, including organisms, can be deduced from examining those materials. That scrutiny may be in the field, looking at relationships in exposed rock and at hand specimens of rock and fossils. Laboratory analysis of collected materials adds insight, as does compiling and correlating information for different geological times from many parts of the world. Geological maps are a vital means of visualising the geographic variations in processes on all scales, and seeing how different rocks relate to one another in 3D and in the dimension of time. This is predominantly practical science, although it does involve an essential element of abstract thought. Book 7 completely reverses this approach, with theory dominating observation. Minerals, rocks and even planets occupy the 'medium' size scales of the Universe, as do the laws governing them. Book 7 is about the smallest and the largest scales of both objects and natural laws, in which all is not necessarily as it might seem to be.

Answers to questions

Further comments on the answers are given in square brackets [...].

Question 2.1

You might have found the wealth of information in Figure 2.3 overwhelming. If you did, the following description of the general trends should show that there are clear underlying patterns within the data, and help you to see them for yourself. For about 5 ka after 110 ka, dust levels (and therefore aridity) remained high, although erratic, before a roughly 5 ka period of decreased dust and aridity (and therefore increased humidity). Humidity declined (aridity increased) until 90 ka, followed by a brief increase in humidity, then a rapid increase in aridity to mark a very arid period from 87 to 84 ka. For about 6 ka climate became more humid again, to be followed by drying from 78 to 74 ka. Thereafter, the climate of the Northern Hemisphere was dominantly arid except for some short-lived episodes of increased humidity. A 55 ka long predominantly dry period ended very rapidly about 15 ka ago, when dust levels became close to the low values of modern times.

Question 2.2

(a) The mean $\delta^{18}O$ for the last 10 ka is about –35‰, corresponding to around –31 °C.

(b) The lowest recorded $\delta^{18}O$ is about −44‰; extending the straight line in Figure 2.4 gives a lowest mean surface air temperature at the site of about −44 °C.

(c) That minimum was reached about 22 ka ago.

(d) Around 115 ka, Greenland was somewhat warmer (about –26 °C) than over the last 10 ka, as it was in two other periods around 120 and 130 ka, although these were separated by significantly colder periods.

Question 2.3

(i) Shallow sea floors are subject to tidal currents and storms, and even tsunamis (Book 2, Section 3.1.2). Sea level may rise or fall globally as a result of the growth and melting of ice caps (there are other reasons, beyond the scope of this book), or locally because of tectonic deformation of the crust. (ii) On land there may be changes in the flow of water because of seasonal climatic conditions, in the short term, or continental drift across global climate zones in the long term. After rain storms, rivers may erode where they normally deposit sediment, and even shift their course. Climate change can affect vegetation cover. This will slow the supply of sediment when the vegetation becomes dense, and will expose more sediment to flowing water and wind if there is little vegetation. There are so many possibilities for change, you probably thought of other means.

Question 2.4

Fossil B is the only organism without symmetry (the specimen used in making Fossil C is too complex and incomplete to tell for sure), and the rest are all bilaterians.

Question 2.5

The lower layered rocks (C) were deposited and then folded by a tectonic event (G). After the folding, magma cut through the layered rocks and across the folds, to form a large igneous intrusion (A). Erosion wore down the mountains that had formed during the tectonic event. That left the surface (D), maybe as a plain or a marine erosion surface, which defines an unconformity. Sediments (F) then accumulated above the unconformity. At a later stage, another tectonic event fractured and displaced all the older rocks along a fault (Ef). The last geological event represented by rock was another injection of magma that cut across the fault and all other features to form a narrow igneous intrusion (B). Since then, erosion has produced the present land surface. [*Note*: because the section does not show a relationship between the granite intrusion A and the unconformity, their ages relative to one another are uncertain, but both are older than the fault and the basalt intrusion.]

Question 2.6

The half-life of ^{235}U is 704 Ma. From Table 2.4 in the comments on Activity 2.3, a D/P value of 3.0 corresponds to 2.0 half-lives. For the ^{235}U to ^{207}Pb decay scheme, that is equivalent to an age of 2.0×704 Ma = 1408 Ma. Thus the zircon, and hence the granite, are 1400 Ma old, to two significant figures.

Question 3.1

The Cambrian Explosion shows as a rise to about 100 families but the rate of increase was hardly explosive, having taken 40–50 Ma. In the later Cambrian and through much of the Ordovician there is a steady increase which stops abruptly at the end of that Period, when the number of families falls. The rest of the Palaeozoic Era shows only a slow overall increase in the number of families, with some ups and downs. Around 250 Ma ago, at the close of the Permian Period, there was a sudden, major reduction of about 200 families. Numbers recovered slowly through the Triassic and Lower Jurassic, and then began to climb through the rest of the Mesozoic Era to reach 1300 by its end. Once again, an Era closed with a sudden fall in diversity, which grew rapidly again through the Cenozoic Era to a level of about 2400 families today.

Question 3.2

(a) Massive objects travelling at high speed have high kinetic energy (Book 3, Section 3.1). Impacts happen quickly, so the power (rate of energy conversion; Book 3, Section 4.3) involved is enormous. The transformation of kinetic energy to other forms of energy can do a lot of work (Book 3, Section 4.1). The impact would have excavated rock, involving immense heat, to spray molten rock into the atmosphere. [You might also have considered tsunamis had the strike been in the ocean, and gases released by vaporisation of seawater or water contained in rocks on land.]

(b) In comparison, even the greatest volcanic upheavals represented by flood basalts are slow, low-power events. They more than make up for that by the sheer mass of material released, including gases, especially CO_2 and SO_2. Each basalt flood would involve a renewed pulse of gas that convection could transfer to the stratosphere.

Question 3.3

Mass extinctions are associated with:

- Upper Ordovician: fishes branched around this time, jawless fishes diversifying afterwards to a maximum in the Devonian.
- Upper Devonian: placoderms became extinct; amphibian diversity reduced. Thereafter, jawless fish decline; little diversification of fishes; amphibian families increase; reptiles branch in Carboniferous.
- Upper Permian: major fall in diversity for all surviving classes; afterwards, overall vertebrate diversity remains low.
- Upper Triassic: reduction in diversity of amphibians and reptiles; recently evolved mammals came through. All classes except amphibians increase diversity afterwards, reptiles and bony fishes most of all. Birds branch from reptiles in Upper Jurassic.
- K–T: only reptile diversity suffers major decline. Subsequently, they, amphibians and sharks and rays increase family numbers slightly; bony fishes, birds and mammals diversify explosively during Cenozoic.

Question 4.1

(a) Both quartz and feldspar are light-coloured, often colourless or white to pale grey (sometimes feldspars are pale pink – the green variety shown is rare). Both are quite hard and may have a glassy lustre and form prismatic crystals; it is not easy to tell them apart using any of these properties. However, cleavage should give the answer; quartz shows none, whereas feldspar shows two. A mineral's cleavage controls the way in which it fractures. Consequently, broken feldspar crystals will show flat surfaces that reflect light almost like a mirror. Quartz will break irregularly, usually along curved surfaces in a similar fashion to glass (note that this often gives small broken quartz crystals a somewhat 'greasy' lustre).

(b) Both dark mica and pyroxene can be black. They also show cleavage, but the two cleavages in pyroxene are poor compared with the single perfect cleavage in micas. In fact, mica's cleavage is so good that it reflects light extremely well, which is something of a give-away! Apart from being similar in colour, pyroxene and dark mica are different in all their other physical properties; for instance, mica is soft enough to scratch with your fingernail.

Question 4.2

(a) Granite is composed of large crystals, arranged randomly. It crystallised slowly from magma, deep in the crust.

(b) Porphyry consists of large crystals, formed first during slow cooling at depth, and set in a later, fine-grained groundmass. The groundmass solidified rapidly after the magma was erupted or intruded as a sill or dyke, when cooling speeded up.

(c) Rhyolite is fine-grained throughout. It is difficult to distinguish individual crystals. It crystallised quite rapidly on eruption at the Earth's surface.

(d) Pumice is a rough-textured rock but few, if any, individual grains are visible. In fact, the solid material is a glass and the roughness is caused by innumerable bubbles. On eruption, the magma released gases while the magma chilled to form glass; pumice is solidified magma froth.

(e) Obsidian looks like glass, and so it is. Very rapid cooling solidified the magma faster than silicate minerals could crystallise. All parts of the rock are the same composition as the original magma.

Question 4.3

(a) (i) Granite and rhyolite contain the highest proportion of quartz. (ii) Gabbro and basalt contain the highest proportion of mafic minerals. (iii) Gabbro and basalt do not contain alkali feldspar.

(b) Diorite may contain pyroxene; granite does not. Diorite contains more plagioclase feldspar and amphibole than granite; granite contains more alkali feldspar and quartz than diorite.

(c) Diorite contains more silicon, sodium and potassium, but less magnesium, iron and calcium than gabbro.

Question 4.4

Quartz, alkali feldspars and pale mica (all felsic minerals) are rich in Si and have complex framework or sheet structures made of connected SiO_4 tetrahedra. Magnesium- and iron-rich silicate minerals (mafic minerals) contain less Si, so have quite different, and somewhat simpler, structures: olivine is based on separate SiO_4 groups; pyroxene's is based on SiO_4 chains.

Question 5.1

In hot, humid regions, chemical weathering is rapid, whereas in cold, wet regions it is very slow, but physical weathering, through repeated freezing and thawing (frost shattering), is much more important. Water is essential for chemical weathering – without it rocks are not decomposed – and it plays a major role in physical weathering. Although there are extremes of temperature on the Moon that can cause some physical shattering, in the absence of water there is no chemical weathering of lunar rocks.

Question 5.2

Granite is a coarse-grained rock, composed mainly of feldspar, mica and quartz crystals. Physical weathering breaks down the rock into smaller fragments and may release individual mineral grains. Chemical weathering decomposes unstable minerals such as feldspar and mica, forming stable clay minerals and soluble metal ions (e.g. Equation 5.3); it also liberates resistant quartz grains.

Question 5.3

Arid desert conditions are indicated in ancient sandstones by the presence of well-rounded, well-sorted quartz grains, with pitted (or 'frosted') surfaces, as a result of wind transportation, and a red surface coating of iron oxide, resulting from oxidising conditions.

Question 5.4

Chemical weathering provides a steady supply of soluble ions, especially Na^+, K^+, Ca^{2+}, Mg^{2+} and HCO_3^-. These ions are removed from seawater by: (i) the crystallisation of salts, extracting Na^+ and Ca^{2+}, especially during the formation of evaporites; and (ii) the growth of marine organisms responsible for many limestones, which 'lock away' Ca^{2+} and CO_3^{2-} ions in calcium carbonate.

Question 5.5

(i) Mudstone = (b); (ii) conglomerate = (f) and also (a); (iii) limestone = (g); (iv) evaporite = (d); (v) breccia = (c).

[*Note*: the descriptions are *appropriate* to the rocks given, but do *not* represent definitions of those rocks. For example, not all conglomerates contain pebbles in a quartz cement.]

Question 6.1

(a) Figure 6.9a represents compression; the mudstone to the right of the fault has moved leftwards to override the mudstone on the left. Figure 6.9b represents tension; the mudstone on the right has moved to the right, away from the mudstone on the left. In the case of the compressional fault, horizontal movements were towards one another, and away from one another for the tensional fault. Directions of movement are shown in Figure 6.14.

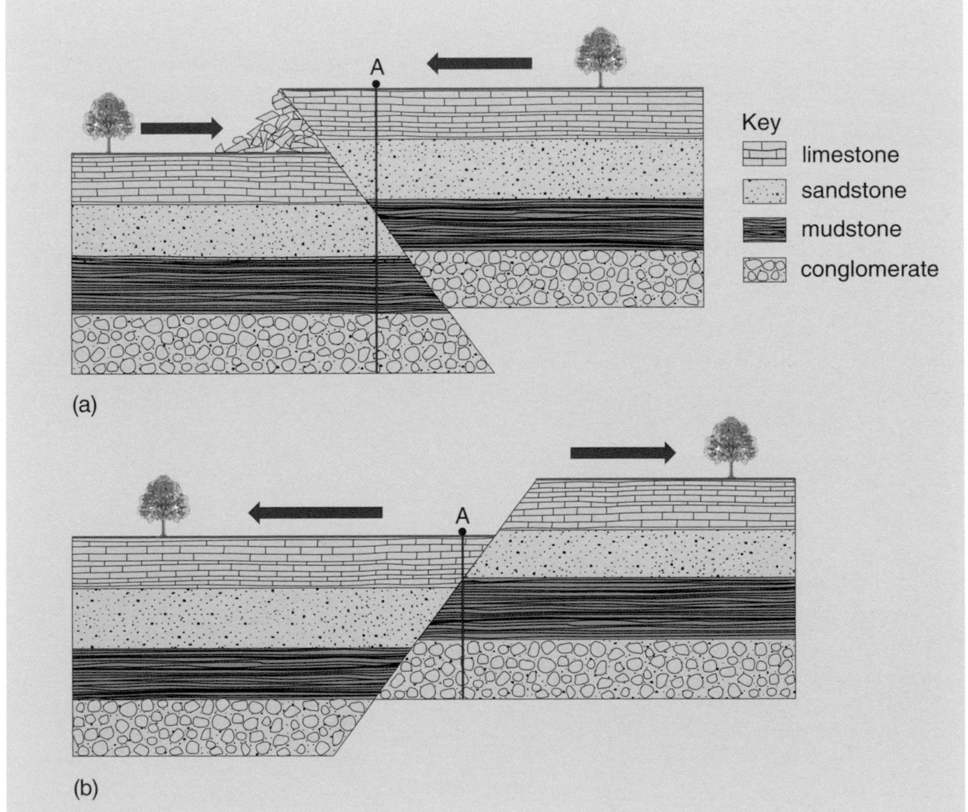

Figure 6.14 A repeat of Figure 6.9, with arrows to show the direction of horizontal movement.

(b) The sandstone and the mudstone are *repeated* in the sequence in Figure 6.9a, whereas the sandstone is *missing* from the sequence in Figure 6.9b.

(c) The separation of the trees in Figure 6.9a is less than in Figure 6.9b; therefore, compression results in overall *shortening* and tension results in overall *extension*.

Question 6.2

Mudstone is converted to slate, to schist or to gneiss at progressively higher grades of metamorphism. The rocks produced at higher grades are increasingly coarse-grained. The minerals formed are progressively more anhydrous (like feldspars and garnets) as water is liberated when hydrous minerals (like clays and micas) break down. The texture changes from the smooth, even texture of a mudstone with fine clay mineral grains to that of: slate, with very fine-grained aligned mica flakes, allowing the rock to split into thin flakes along smooth, perfectly parallel surfaces; schist, with roughly aligned, coarser-grained platy minerals, so that the rock splits along uneven, roughly parallel surfaces; and gneiss, with crude mineral banding and fewer platy minerals, so it does not split as easily.

Question 6.3

The presence in rock exposures of folds and faults, formed in response to either compression or tension, are signs of movements in the Earth. The presence of regional metamorphic rocks with visible metamorphic minerals and textures formed at considerable depth also demonstrate that burial and uplift had taken place as a result of tectonic activity.

Question 6.4

Metamorphic belts are formed by regional metamorphism of pre-existing rocks encountering high pressures and temperatures during mountain building, which generally involves collision and crustal thickening at convergent plate boundaries. Erosion of mountains and the buoyant uplift of thickened crust are largely responsible for raising metamorphic belts to the surface and exposing their interiors.

Question 6.5

Figure 6.15 shows a completed version of the rock cycle.

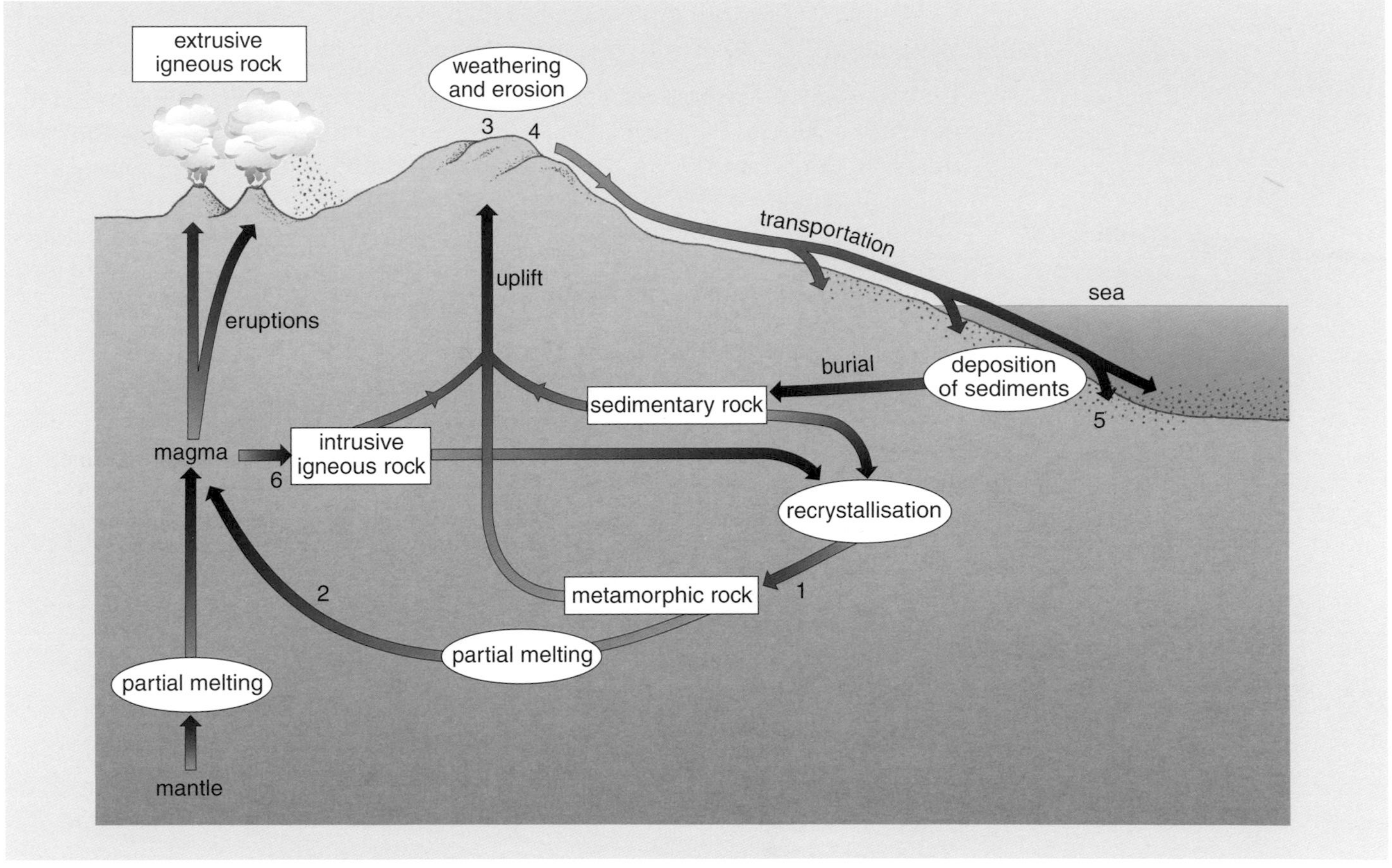

Figure 6.15 The completed rock cycle.

Question 7.1

(a) (i) The microscopic view shows a large range of grain sizes, from pebbles around 3 mm to fine sand grains of 0.1 mm and perhaps smaller in size – therefore, it is poorly sorted. (ii) The grains range from moderately to poorly rounded, the smaller ones being angular. (iii) Whatever the environment in which they were deposited, the pebbles indicate it was high energy.

(b) The sediment's poor sorting rules out an origin as a wind-blown dune sand or on a beach. The most likely environment was water flowing on land.

(c) Because the rock contains feldspar grains, the influence of chemical weathering in liberating grains to be transported must have been minimal (the presence of feldspar also suggests rapid transport in water).

Question 7.2

The irregular but roughly N–S trending belt of Carboniferous rocks coincides with the uplands of the Pennines. It is surrounded to the east, west and south by younger sedimentary rocks occupying lowland areas. This is most easily explained by a broad upfold trending N–S along the line of the Pennines.

Question 7.3

From around 90 Ma, the animation shows Africa slowly moving towards Europe. The seaway between them was clearly experiencing the tectonic effects, developing a series of slivers of land in the frames for 65 and 50 Ma. At some time between 50 and 20 Ma, the two continents collided, to form the Alps. In fact, that major orogenic event began around 30 Ma ago, to form the E–W mountain belt. The structures in southeastern England are parallel to that trend, and affect both Cretaceous and Cenozoic rocks, so they are the outermost ripples of the Alpine Orogeny.

Comments on activities

Activity 2.1

The warmest temperatures between 65 and 90 ka occurred at about 69, 74, 83 and 88 ka, being separated by colder periods of various durations. These periods of relative warmth are associated with periods of reduced dustiness when humidity in the Northern Hemisphere had risen. The colder periods are all associated with low ice conductivity and therefore increased dustiness; the Northern Hemisphere was more arid at these times. Aridity and reduced temperatures are closely associated. [*Note*: it is not possible from this evidence to say whether there is a cause–effect relationship.]

Activity 2.2

Table 2.3 Completed Table 2.1.

Fossil	Symmetry	Segmented?	Coiled?	Made of plates?	Other features
A	Bilateral	Yes	No	No, segments may be mistaken for plates	Body divided three ways, both along and across
B	None	No	No	Possibly	Lines radiating from centre of polygonal features
C	None	Yes (?)	No	Yes	Stem and branching 'arms'
D	Bilateral	No	Yes	No	Frilled pattern on shell
E	Bilateral – through both shells	No	No	No	Two unequal shells
F	Bilateral	No	No	Yes	Knobs, holes and plates radiate from apex; arranged in fives

Figure 2.16 shows sketches of all the fossils, labelled to pick out features that you may have observed, but may not have understood.

Fossil A is the shell of a **trilobite** (genus *Acaste*). At the front end there are crescent-shaped bumps which are compound eyes, like those of a fly, made of many lenses. They are visible through the hand lens. There is a tail, and a segmented trunk separates the two extremities; this would have been articulated in life, as in a woodlouse. The bilateral symmetry is across the animal's long axis.

Trilobites are bilaterians and a class within the phylum Arthropoda, which also includes classes of which crabs, lobsters, insects, spiders and scorpions are members. The trilobites became extinct about 250 Ma ago and are believed to have been exclusively marine.

Fossil B is a colony of a **coral** (genus *Acervularia*) made up of several individual animals' hard parts, whose mutual growth has forced their skeletons to assume straight walls. Each depression is roughly at the centre of an individual animal's skeleton, which includes radiating vertical plates. Corals can reproduce asexually, by 'budding', and several large corallites show evidence of that.

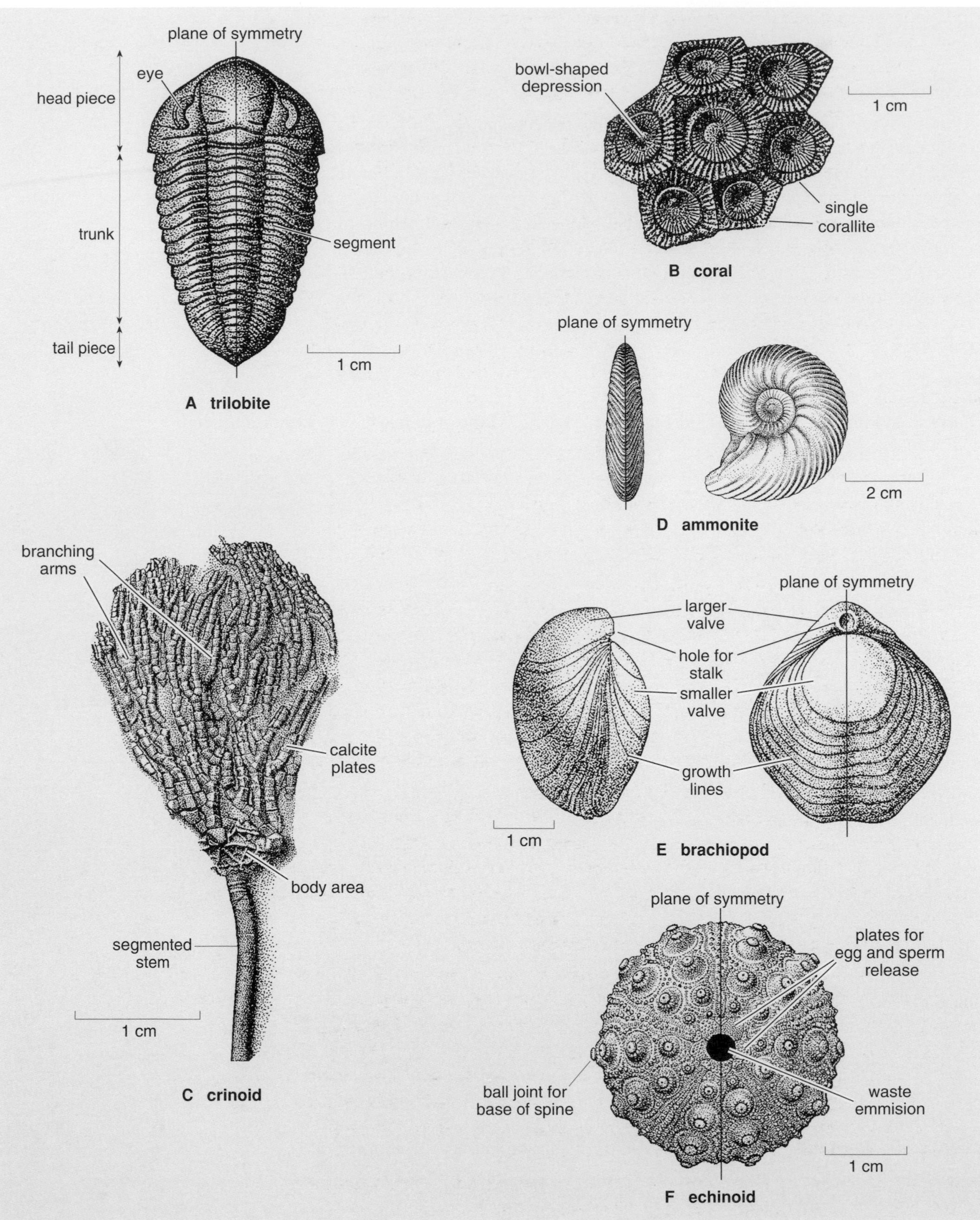

Figure 2.16 Labelled sketches of the Practical Kit fossils A–F.

Corals show no symmetry and are not bilaterians. They are a class (Anthozoa) in the phylum Cnidaria, which also includes jellyfish and sea anemones. All living cnidarians are exclusively marine. Many modern corals depend on algal cells living in their soft tissues for some of their food supplies (they are also filter feeders). This restricts such corals to clear shallow water that light can penetrate to allow the algae to photosynthesise. Most modern corals are also restricted to warm tropical to subtropical seas. (There are also rare, deep-water corals living at high latitudes.)

Fossil C is perhaps the most difficult. Is it an animal or is it a plant? In fact, it is an animal that adopted a fixed mode of life: a **crinoid** (genus *Gissocrinus*) whose mouth, anus, respiratory and reproductive organs are at the top of a long segmented 'stem' fixed to the seabed. Radiating from the mouth area are five segmented arms (one is missing from the specimen), which branch in a regular way. Figure 5.5 in Book 2 shows a reconstructed crinoid. In modern crinoids, the arms bear small tube-like structures which gather and transport food items down the arms to the mouth area. Modern crinoids are exclusively marine.

It is not possible to judge whether the fossil shows symmetry. In fact, the arrangement of its five arms does display symmetry similar to that of Fossil F. Crinoids are bilaterian, and a class of the phylum Echinodermata, along with sea urchins and starfish. Incidentally, much of rock Specimen 3 in the Practical Kit is made of segments from broken crinoid stems. The plates that make up the skeletons of many echinoderms are made of large calcium carbonate crystals.

Fossil D is an **ammonite** (genus *Quenstedtoceras*). Essentially an ammonite shell is a coiled tube, divided into chambers by internal walls – you may have mistaken these for segments. The animal itself would have lived in the outermost of the chambers, the rest being abandoned as the animal grew. The other chambers were gas-filled and acted as a means of achieving neutral buoyancy. The walls separating chambers differed in complexity from species to species. Where they meet the outer shell shows up as an intricately frilled line (Book 5, Figure 1.3). Ammonite evolution also developed various ridges and keels on the shells, probably to stabilise motion through water.

Each side of the coiled shell is a mirror image of the other, so ammonites were bilaterians. Their closest modern relatives are *Nautilus* (Book 5, Figure 1.3) and squid, and like them, ammonites are members of the class Cephalopoda, part of the phylum Mollusca. Ammonites differ from coiled gastropods, such as the winkle, by having sealed chambers. All living cephalopods are exclusively marine. Ammonites disappeared from the fossil record at 65 Ma.

Fossil E is a **brachiopod** (genus *Cererithyris*). Having two shells, you might think it is related to bivalves, such as the common mussel. The difference lies outwardly in the type of bilateral symmetry: brachiopods have unequal shells, but each has mirror-image symmetry. Bivalve shells are usually mirror images, but each is asymmetrical. The fundamental difference, however, lies inside the shells. Bivalves feed and respire through siphons connected to a gut. Brachiopods have skeletal features within the shell cavity which carry tentacles covered with hair-like cilia for extracting suspended food particles from water.

Another variety of bilaterian, brachiopods are so anatomically different that they warrant their own phylum (Brachiopoda). They are exclusively marine.

Fossil F is probably the most familiar, being an extinct sea urchin or **echinoid** (genus *Hemicidaris*). It is made up of interlocked plates, each bearing a 'ball joint' for a spine and several pores attached to the living creature's tube feet. The plates are arranged in five bands radiating symmetrically from the top to the base of the body. Only the top is preserved by the replica, which is where the echinoid's reproductive organs and anus are situated.

Despite most parts being arranged in fives, a line drawn along and beyond any one of the fivefold divisions separates an echinoid into two mirror images. They are bilaterians like us. All living echinoids are exclusively marine.

Activity 2.3

Task 1

Table 2.4 shows the results for (a) and (b), which are plotted in Figure 2.17.

(c) The black (solid line) graph (Figure 2.17) for atoms of the parent isotope shows numbers of atoms decreasing rapidly for the first few half-lives, and then the decrease in numbers slows until only one is left. Since there is no such thing as 'half an atom', all atoms of the parent isotope have decayed by the eleventh half-life. In reality, the number of atoms of even a rare isotope in a small sample of a mineral will be enormous, and some will still exist after a great many more than 10 half-lives. The red (dashed line) graph for atoms of the daughter isotope is an exact mirror image of that for its parent.

Table 2.4 Completed Table 2.2.

Time/days	0	3	6	9	12	15	18	21	24	27	30
Half-life/n	0	1	2	3	4	5	6	7	8	9	10
Atoms of parent isotope/P	1024	512	256	128	64	32	16	8	4	2	1
Atoms of daughter isotope/D	0	512	768	896	960	992	1008	1016	1020	1022	1023
D/P ratio	0	1	3	7	15	31	63	127	255	511	1023
D/P ratio by Eqn 2.7	0	1	3	7	15	31	63	127	255	511	1023

Task 2

Table 2.4 shows that the values of D/P calculated by using Equation 2.7 are the same as by simple division. The latter is equivalent to using measurements by a mass spectrometer of both parent and daughter isotopes in a sample.

Figure 2.17 shows the plot of D/P changing with time in blue (dotted line); again, it is a mirror image of the decay curve for the parent isotope.

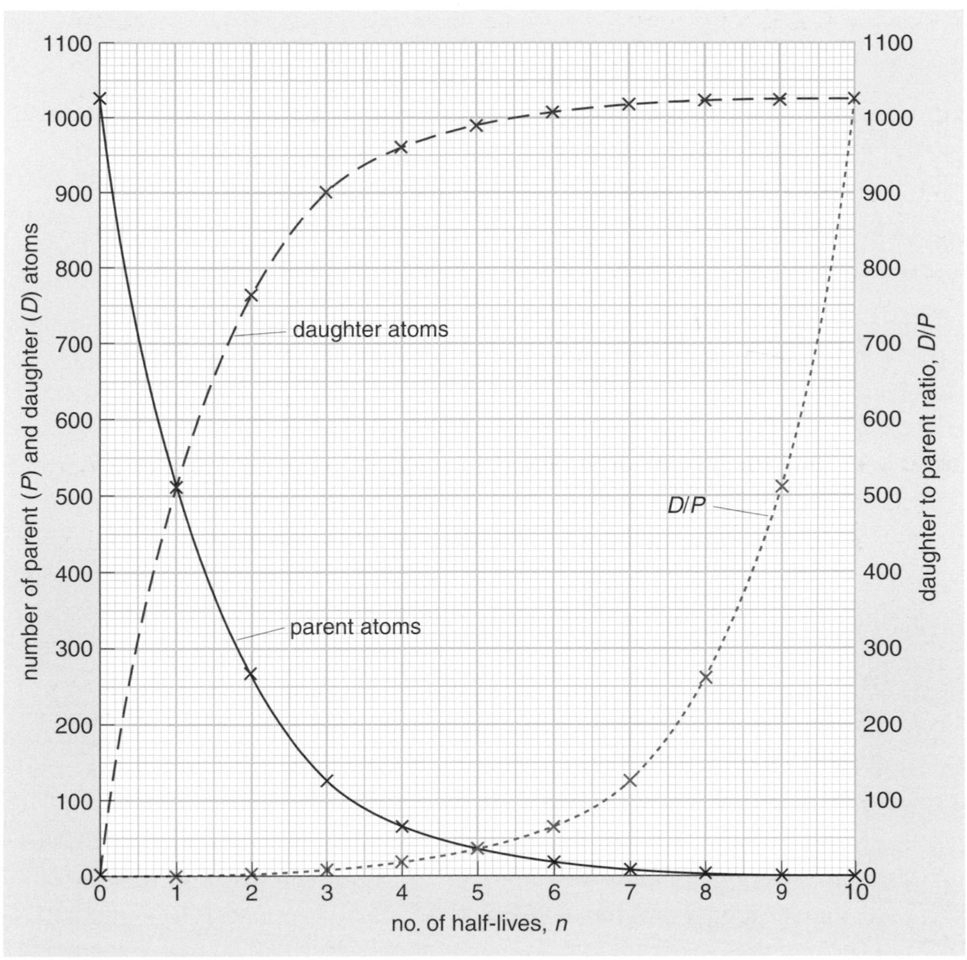

Figure 2.17 Plots from Task 1 (a) and (b) and Task 2 on Figure 2.14. The black (solid) line shows the change in the number of radioactive parent atoms with time (Task 1a); the red (dashed) line shows the change in the number of daughter atoms with time (Task 1b) and the blue (dotted) line the change in the daughter to parent ratio (D/P) with time (Task 2).

Activity 4.1

Table 4.2 Completed Table 4.1.

Mineral	Classification	Composition	Colour	Lustre	Cleavage	Shape	Hardness
Quartz	Silicate (framework)	SiO_2	Mainly colourless – can be coloured	Glassy	None (irregular fracture)	Prismatic	7
Feldspar	Silicate (framework)	Alkali (K,Na)$AlSi_3O_8$ Plagioclase, from $NaAlSi_3O_8$ to $CaAl_2Si_2O_8$	Mainly white – can be pinkish	Glassy to dull	Two good	Prismatic	6–6.5
Mica	Silicate (sheet)	Pale (muscovite) $KAl_3Si_3O_{10}(OH)_2$ Dark (biotite) $K(Fe,Mg)_3AlSi_3O_{10}(OH)_2$	Silvery (muscovite) or brown to black (biotite)	Pearly	One perfect	Tabular	2.5
Pyroxene	Silicate (single chain)	$(Ca,Mg,Fe)_2Si_2O_6$	Dark green to black	Dull to glassy	Two at 90°	Stubby prismatic	5.5–6
Olivine	Silicate (isolated group)	$(Mg,Fe)_2SiO_4$	Pale to dark green. Weathers reddish brown	Glassy	None	Stubby prismatic	6.5–7

Activity 4.2

Task 1

Grains do not break away easily from Specimens 5 and 6, nor do broken surfaces tend to pass around grains, as is common in many sedimentary rocks. In fact, where the rock is broken, some individual grains reveal cleavage planes of mineral crystals. Characteristically for igneous rocks, the individual grains in both basalt and granite are crystals held together tightly, being intergrown and interlocking, so they are irregular in shape.

Grains in the granite sample are randomly oriented and randomly distributed. This is characteristic of an igneous texture, rather than that of a metamorphic rock (a tendency for interlocking crystals to be aligned, or to be arranged in a banded structure). A few flat crystals in the basalt sample may show some alignment, but that does not affect the entire sample as it would in a metamorphic rock. In the basalt (Specimen 5) a few flat crystals became aligned because the magma was *flowing* before it became completely solid (see Section 4.2.1).

Task 2

(a) The basalt is very dark throughout; the granite is generally paler, but more variable in the colour of its constituent grains (white, grey and black). Much of the basalt is fine-grained, most crystals being too small to measure by eye, but some (long thin ones and broad chunky ones) are up to 10 mm long. The granite, by contrast, is coarse-grained throughout, most grains being 2–5 mm across, and a few up to 20 mm.

(b) The overall colour of a rock depends on its mix of different minerals. Almost all of the minerals in the basalt are dark grey or dark green to black (although there are some paler crystals on and close to weathered surfaces). By contrast, most of the minerals in the granite are white or pale grey, only a few being black.

The grain size depends on the rate of cooling during crystallisation; an indication of the way crystallisation occurred (Book 2, Activity 5.1). Thus the mainly fine-grained basalt cooled rapidly as an *extrusive* rock and crystallised at the Earth's surface. (The few larger crystals in the basalt are explained in Section 4.2.1.) The coarse-grained granite cooled slowly as an *intrusive* rock, crystallising deep beneath the Earth's surface.

Activity 4.3

Task 1

The three types of mineral in granite have the following properties, which match consistently with those in Table 4.2 in the comments on Activity 4.1:

Quartz: grey, glassy, irregular, 1–4 mm diameter, no cleavage.

Feldspar: white, more box-shaped, 2–10 mm across, with reflecting cleavage planes.

Mica: black (some silvery) flakes, 1 mm across, shiny surfaces, which represent cleavage planes.

Task 2

(a) The chemical formulae for the main minerals in granite and basalt are as follows.

Granite:	alkali feldspar	$(K,Na)AlSi_3O_8$
	plagioclase feldspar (Na-rich)	$NaAlSi_3O_8$
	quartz	SiO_2
	dark mica (biotite)	$K(Fe,Mg)_3AlSi_3O_{10}(OH)_2$
Basalt:	plagioclase feldspar (Ca-rich)	$CaAl_2Si_2O_8$
	pyroxene	$(Ca,Mg,Fe)_2Si_2O_6$

(b) On the basis of the proportions of these minerals and their compositions, granite will contain more potassium (K, in alkali feldspar and dark mica) and sodium (Na, in alkali feldspar) than the basalt. Silicon (Si) is present in all the silicate minerals but granite contains 30% quartz (SiO_2) whereas basalt does not contain any, so silicon must be more abundant in granite. Basalt will contain more calcium (Ca, in plagioclase feldspar and pyroxene). There is abundant pyroxene (50%) in the basalt, so it will contain much more iron (Fe) and magnesium (Mg) than granite. The dark mica (10%) is the only mineral in the granite containing iron and magnesium.

Activity 5.1

Task 1

The soil (a mixture of sediment grains) begins to settle as soon as the water comes to rest. The largest grains settle almost immediately, and obvious but smaller grains soon after. The finest grains need a few hours to settle from murky water.

Task 2

The types of grain will depend on the nature of your soil sample. Some soils are stony or sandy, others are muddier. The following description is of a fairly typical soil.

Larger grains at the bottom of the jar are succeeded by layers of progressively finer material. The coarsest material contains pebbles (>2 mm). Immediately above it is sand (<2 mm, >0.063 mm). The next grains are just visible but not easily measurable. The finest material at the top is too fine to see with the unaided eye.

If the soil has a high organic content, there will be fragments floating on or suspended in the water.

Figure 5.15 is a simple sketch, with labelling conveying the important information in the description above. Your diagram, and the way it is labelled, will differ from this one because your soil is different, but you should check that you have labelled the important features.

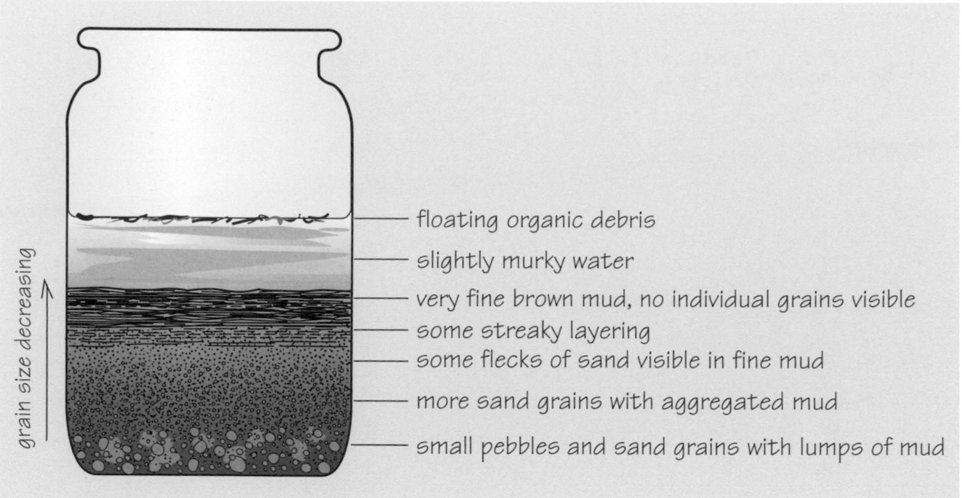

Figure 5.15 Sketch of settled sediment in a jar.

Task 3

The topmost sediment is like sludge and feels slimy. It is probably clay- to silt-sized mud (4–63 μm) and the grains cannot be seen using the hand lens. Below that are increasingly coarse sands. The coarsest material may include rounded or angular pebbles made of rock and/or mineral fragments. Some of the sand-sized grains may be recognisable minerals. Translucent glassy grains of quartz are common in soil. Pale-coloured but opaque grains of feldspar or silvery flakes of mica sometimes occur. There may also be dull, dark-coloured grains of unidentifiable minerals – probably iron minerals or bits of charcoal.

Activity 5.2

Task 1

(a) Physical and chemical weathering break down exposed rocks to produce sediment grains.

(b) Grains move downstream by rolling, bouncing or in suspension.

(c) River sediments typically contain a wide range of grain sizes and minerals. Beach sediments contain a much narrower range of grain sizes and fewer minerals, and quartz frequently dominates. The range of grain sizes expresses the degree of sorting in the sediment; the narrower it is, the better sorted are the grains.

(d) Wind-blown grains are normally well-rounded and their surfaces are very finely pitted. Grains deposited by water are more angular and have a glassy appearance.

Task 2

The calculated mass percentages for each sieve are shown in Table 5.3.

Table 5.3 Completed version of Table 5.1.

Sieve size/mm	Mass in sieve/g	Proportion of total mass/%
4	1.0	2.1
2	1.4	2.9
1	4.8	10.1
0.5	7.1	14.9
0.25	14.5	30.4
0.12	9.4	19.7
0.6	7.3	15.3
pan	2.2	4.6
total	47.7	100.0

The histogram for these data is shown in Figure 5.16. Because the sand is distributed over a large number of sieves, this histogram represents a poorly sorted sediment.

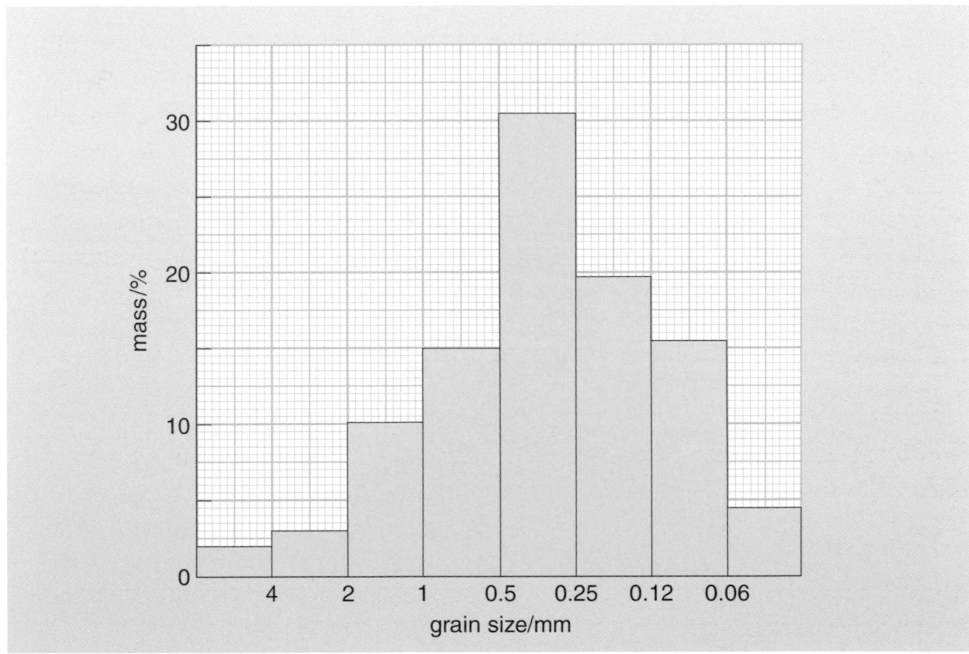

Figure 5.16 Sediment grain-size histogram based on data in Table 5.3.

Task 3

(a) In Figure 5.7a: (i) has a poorly sorted distribution and is likely to be river sand; (ii) is very well-sorted and likely to be desert sand; (iii) is fairly well-sorted and likely to be beach sand.

(b) Matching Figure 5.7a with Figure 5.7b: (a)(i) and (b)(iii) represent poorly sorted distributions (a river sand); (a)(ii) and (b)(i) are very well-sorted (a desert sand); and (a)(iii) and (b)(ii) are fairly well-sorted (a beach sand). Note that the narrow spread of well-sorted sand on the histogram (all the sand ends up in two or three sieves) results in a steep graph of cumulative frequency. Conversely, poorly sorted sand has a broader spread on the histogram, and the cumulative frequency graph is less steep.

Task 4

A steel nail removes grains from the sandstone more easily than from the igneous rocks, but most are too tightly held for a fingernail to work. The grains range from almost 2 mm in diameter to a size that is too small to be measured (<0.1 mm). (*Note*: some samples are coarser than others.) The sand grains are glassy and are mostly quartz. The finer material is soft and crumbly; probably clay. There is not a wide range of coarse grains, as very few have a diameter greater than 2 mm, but there is a considerable amount of very fine material. Overall, the sediment has a greater spread of grain sizes than a desert sand, or even a beach sand; it resembles a river sand.

Through a hand lens, most individual quartz grains are glassy and angular, much like those transported by water in the video sequence. They are not well-rounded and 'frosted' wind-blown grains. In places the grains are closely packed, but in others soft, pale powdery material (largely clay) surrounds them. You can also see lots of holes in the rock, especially on a cut surface. Water soaks rapidly into the rock, so there is a lot of open space between the grains.

Activity 6.1

Task 1

Table 6.2 shows the results of comparing the properties of slate, gneiss and schist. *Note*: your sample of schist may differ slightly in grain size, colour and degree of banding from the typical example described here.

Table 6.2 Completed version of Table 6.1.

Property	Slate	Gneiss	Schist
Grain size	Very fine; surfaces are smooth and most grains are too small to distinguish; only larger dark flecks (0.5 mm max.) are visible	Coarse; easy to see grains. Average size 3–5 mm. Some individual 1–2 mm grains of a dark mineral. Also tightly packed in layers	Medium; easy to see granular minerals (mostly 0.5–2 mm); difficult to distinguish platy minerals in tightly packed layers
Colour	Pale grey with dark flecks, fairly uniform	Pale (creamy/grey) bands and dark (black) layers	Silvery grey-brown, mottled cream, black and pinkish brown on cut surfaces. Rusty brown colour on broken surfaces. (Staining from iron compounds released on weathering.)
Texture	A scaly effect is apparent where lighting highlights edges to thin layers with flat surfaces. Not possible to see arrangement of fine grains. (Breakage is along parallel surfaces running through the rock, caused by aligned platy minerals.)	Irregular, sometimes lens-shaped bands of pale granular minerals, and dark sinuous and discontinuous bands of platy minerals	Uneven surfaces, sometimes crinkly, but fairly smooth, with a reflective sheen from planar alignment of medium- to coarse-grained platy minerals. In some samples, layers of dark and light minerals may be present (as in gneiss)
Minerals	Minerals unrecognisable. (Mainly fine-grained mica that you would see as a slightly reflective sheen in a hand specimen.)	Grey quartz, white feldspar, dark (biotite) mica	Mainly silvery and dark mica flakes, similarly sized glassy quartz grains and a few pinkish-brown garnet grains (*Minerals Gallery*)

Task 2

The grain sizes of the three rocks vary, and so does the nature of the layering. The order of increasing grain size is slate – schist – gneiss. In the same order, the layering becomes more uneven: flat in the slate (Figure 6.3a), uneven in the schist (Specimen 4), and undulating in the gneiss (Figure 6.3b). There is also greater separation between layers along which the rocks would tend to break. [In Section 6.1.2 you will see how these changes in character reflect an increase in grade of metamorphism.]

Activity 7.1

Task 1

The Devonian upper rocks are reddish to pink and layered on a scale of centimetres to tens of centimetres, suggesting a sedimentary origin. The layering is dominantly parallel, although small-scale cross-bedding can be seen in Figure 7.5b. They are moderately sorted sandstones (but note the conglomerate layer in Figure 7.5b). Like the Torridonian Sandstones, the Devonian upper sedimentary rocks are red-beds laid down in a strongly oxidising environment, i.e. on land, under moderate- to high-energy conditions. Being poorly sorted, they too were probably deposited by flowing streams.

Task 2

The grey Silurian lower rocks are also layered on a scale of tens of centimetres, but grains are not visible. They are fine-grained sedimentary rocks deposited under low-energy conditions. No cross-bedding is visible. Their grey colour suggests that the environment was non-oxidising. The presence of fossil trilobites (see the comments on Activity 2.2) indicates that they were deposited on the Silurian sea floor. These rocks are deep-water, marine mudstones.

Task 3

The bedding in the Silurian sedimentary rocks is almost vertical. This suggests extreme tilting, probably as a result of intense folding and crustal thickening through tectonic compression at some time between 420 and 380 Ma. The unconformity is almost planar, which implies that the mountains produced by crustal thickening had been eroded to an almost flat land surface by the time the Devonian red-beds were deposited. Both the unconformity and the Devonian beds dip gently northwards (Figure 7.5a), which suggests later, slight tilting of the crust.

Activity 7.2

Task 2

Figure 7.21 shows a sketch based on Figure 7.7a; it is useful to compare the two figures. Note that the student who produced this sketch has correctly concentrated on the main features, including the boundaries between the main beds of sandstones and the large-scale, high-angle cross-bedding within them that is typical of desert dunes. To save time, and to avoid unnecessary detail, only a few of the individual layer boundaries have been sketched in, as more-or-less continuous lines. The vertical feature near the centre is of little significance; the beds are not displaced across it (at least at this scale of view). So it is *not* a fault plane but merely a natural crack or joint.

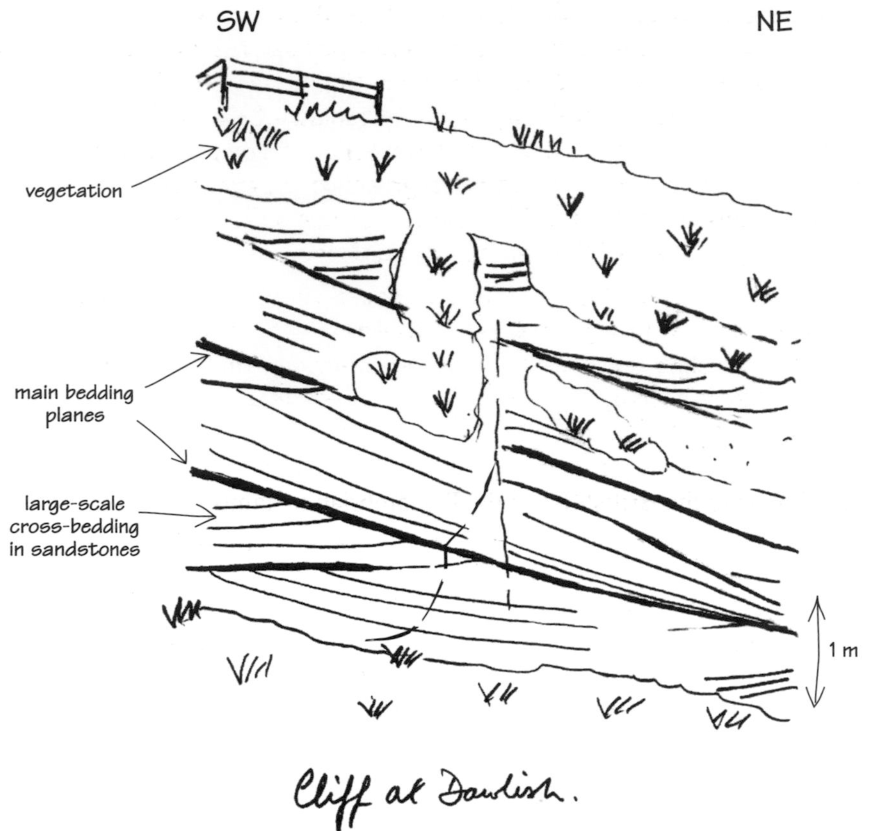

Figure 7.21 Sketch of the cliff section in Figure 7.7a.

Activity 7.3

Towards the end of the Precambrian (600 Ma), all continental crust was locked together in a supercontinent that extended from high northern latitudes to the South Pole, where glaciation was in progress. Northern Britain was close to the South Pole, and experienced this glaciation. Southern Britain was also at low southern latitudes, but several thousand miles away, to the east. At 560 Ma, glaciation had finished and sea-floor spreading had split three substantial continents from the supercontinent. The westernmost of these was to become modern North America, including the northern British Isles crust, at the northern side of the Iapetus Ocean. Spreading also resulted in oceanic volcanic arcs at subduction zones, where new continental material was evolving.

This break-up continued through the Cambrian, northern parts of the British Isles moving northwards, while their southern segment drifted over the South Pole, as a part of the remaining supercontinent. Between the Upper Cambrian (500 Ma) and the Middle Ordovician (470 Ma) one of the volcanic arcs collided with the westernmost of the isolated continents. This resulted in the first stage of the Caledonian Orogeny in the northern British Isles. At the same time, the southern segment broke away from the supercontinent to drift northwards.

By the Upper Ordovician (450 Ma), the Iapetus Ocean separating the northern and southern British Isles had begun to close. This happened by southward subduction beneath the southern segment, causing volcanism in Wales and the

English Lake District. By the Middle Silurian (430 Ma), the Iapetus Ocean had almost vanished, and two of the main drifting continents had begun to collide in what is now western Scandinavia. By the Lower Devonian (400 Ma), the two main continents had welded together, including both parts of the British Isles. From this time until the Triassic, the British Isles drifted steadily northwards. During the 450–400 Ma period, other small fragments of continental crust had split from the northern margin of the southern supercontinent. Sea-floor spreading to their south was driving them northwards too.

By the Upper Devonian (370 Ma), two main clusters of continental material had developed, separated by a closing linear ocean (called the Rheic Ocean). By Lower Carboniferous times this ocean was almost closed, a complex cluster of small continental blocks jostling in the east. From Upper Carboniferous to Lower Permian times (300–280 Ma), the final collision of the North America–Scandinavia and southern continents took place, which drove the Variscan Orogeny. This added the final parts to the British Isles: the Precambrian metamorphic rocks and Carboniferous oceanic crust on the two major, south-facing headlands of southwestern England (Figures 7.10 and 7.16). In the Carboniferous, the British Isles were at tropical latitudes, yet major glaciation was beginning at high southern latitudes, to linger until 260 Ma. By the Triassic (240 Ma), Pangaea was complete, running almost from pole to pole, the British Isles being trapped well within its northern part, at a northern latitude similar to that of the present-day Sahara desert. The last 'stitch' in the formation of Pangaea occurred when Asia collided with Europe along the line of the present Ural Mountains (260 Ma).

Activity 7.4

(a) The first sign – which is easily missed – that Pangaea's time was ending is a string of enclosed lakes running ENE–WSW through its central parts in the Upper Triassic (220 Ma). These are signs of a series of huge rift valleys that began to develop roughly along the join between what would become North and South America and Africa. Great thicknesses of evaporites formed in them. Through the Lower to Middle Jurassic (200–170 Ma) the rifts had joined to produce a seaway reminiscent of the modern Red Sea, but much bigger. Similar signs appear, at lower centre, of a split developing between Africa and the united India, Australia and Antarctica.

By the Upper Jurassic (150 Ma), both lines of rifting had formed narrow linear oceans, so that Pangaea had become three separate entities: North America–Europe–Asia, South America–Africa and India–Australia–Antarctica. It is interesting to note that the last two masses had been united continuously since the late Precambrian, a supercontinent with the memorable name Gondwana (named after the aboriginal Gonds of the Indian subcontinent). The Lower Cretaceous (120 Ma) marked the beginning of the separation of Africa and South America and India from Australia–Antarctica, which themselves separated at the end of the Cretaceous (65 Ma). India's course is dramatic, as seen in the animation frames up to 20 Ma. It drifted north and eventually met Asia at around 50 Ma, the collision creating the Himalaya and Tibetan Plateau, which continue to grow as Indian crust drives beneath that of Asia. Africa's slower northward drift, during roughly the same time, had a similar orogenic effect: the Alps and the Caucasus.

The other large tectonic feature of the Cenozoic is the final separation of North America from Eurasia from about 65 Ma. For much of the Mesozoic and to the present there were far more continents and surrounding shallow seas than at any previous time since 600 Ma ago – perhaps a major factor in encouraging the very rapid evolution and diversification of Mesozoic and Cenozoic faunas (Section 3.5).

(b) The proportion of shallow seas is the key to visualising global sea-level changes. In the Triassic to Lower Jurassic (240–200 Ma), they form a fringe around Pangaea. Once break-up was under way (170 Ma) there are signs of marine incursions in North America and Europe. These become progressively larger through the Jurassic and Cretaceous (to 90 Ma), and affect Africa and South America with huge inland seaways. During the Upper Cretaceous, into the Cenozoic and up to the present these gradually shrink. By 20 Ma, modern continental outlines are roughly as they are today.

The conclusion is that, accompanying the decisive break-up of Pangaea, some long-term process caused global sea level to rise (by as much as 300 m). The volume of the ocean basins must have decreased. That may have happened because of a combination of massive outpourings of flood basalts on the sea floor (this did happen in the West Pacific) and heating and therefore expansion of increasing zones of oceanic lithosphere along the growing length of mid-ocean ridges. From the Middle Cretaceous, the ocean-basin volume increased, so that sea level fell globally. The recent changes (since 2.5 Ma) in sea level are mainly due to the growth and melting of ice caps. Interestingly, during the previous ice age of the Carboniferous and Permian (frames from 340 to 260 Ma), although there is evidence that sea level did fluctuate in a similar manner, overall it must have been much higher than in the Cenozoic because vast areas of continent were flooded.

Appendix

The Geological Time Scale agreed by the International Commission on Stratigraphy (published in 2004) is repeated here for easy reference. It is available online at http://www.stratigraphy.org/ (last accessed September 2007).

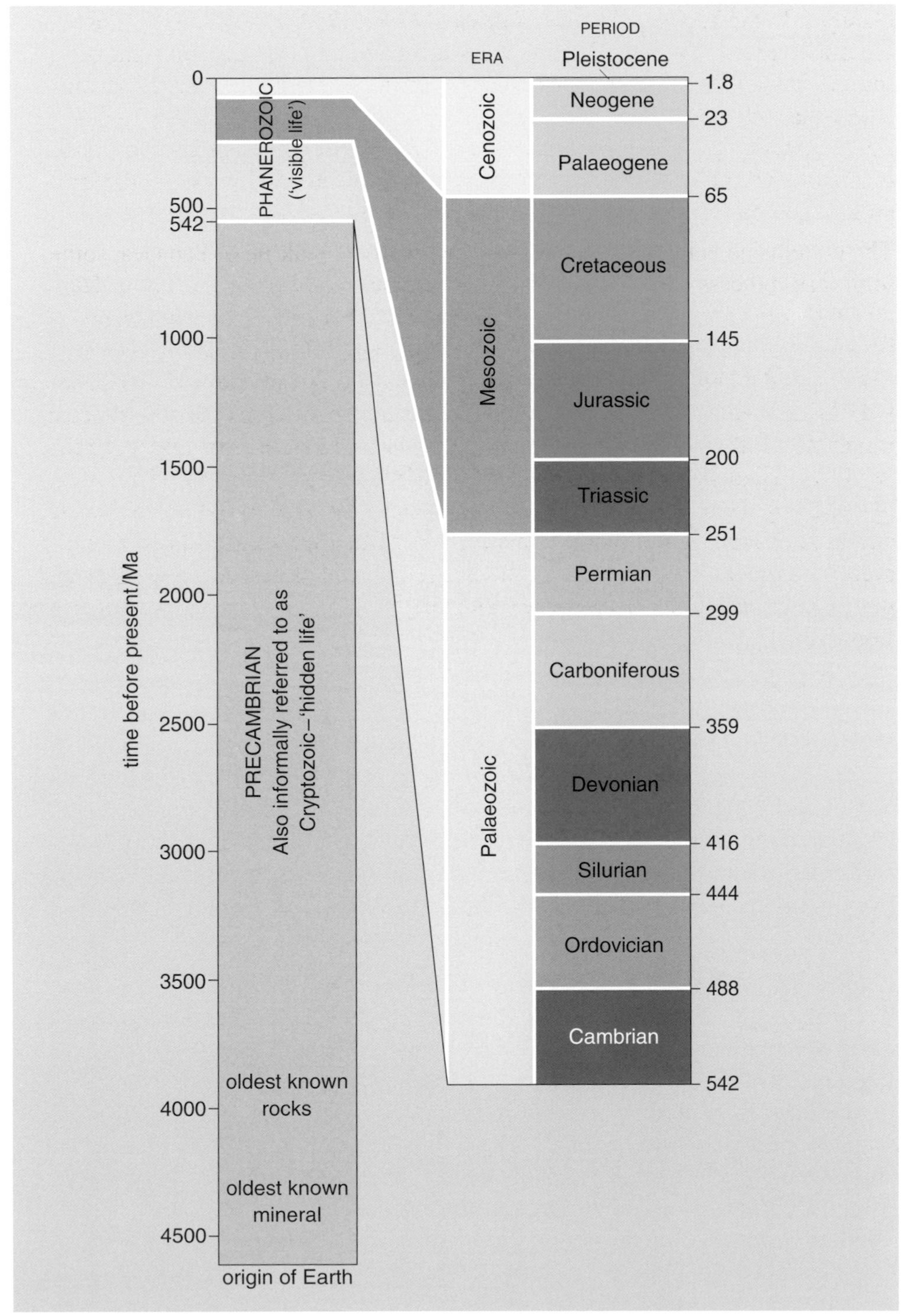

Figure A1 The main divisions of the International Geological Time Scale. (A repeat of Figure 2.15.)

Acknowledgements

The S104 course team gratefully acknowledges the contributions of the S103 *Discovering science* course team and of its predecessors. The author also wishes to thank colleagues especially Peter Webb, Steve Blake and Neil McBride for their many constructive comments that greatly improved the text.

Grateful acknowledgement is made to the following sources for permission to reproduce material in this book:

Figures

Cover: Eric Heller/Science Photo Library;

Figure 1.1: John Reader/Science Photo Library; Figure 1.2a: Javier Trueba/ MSF/Science Photo Library; Semsaw, S., Renne, P., Harris, J.W.K. et al. (1997) '2.5 million year old stone tools from Gona, Ethiopia', *Nature*, vol. 385, 23 January 1997. Nature Publishing Group. Reprinted by permission from Macmillan Publishers Ltd; Figures 1.2b and 1.2c: Pascal Goetgheluck/Science Photo Library; John Reader/Science Photo Library; Gravina, B., Mellars, P. et al. (2005) 'Radiocarbon dating of interstratified Neanderthal and early modern human occupations at the Chatelperronian type-site', *Nature*, vol. 438, Issue 7064, 3 November 2005. Nature Publishing Group. Reprinted by permission from Macmillan Publishers Ltd;

Figure 2.1: Moore, P.D, Challoner, B. and Stott, P. (1996) *Global Environmental Change*, Blackwell Science, Oxford; Figure 2.2a: © Anthony Gow, United States Army Corps of Engineers, Cold Regions Research and Engineering Laboratory, NOAA; Figure 2.2b: © Chris Gilbert, British Antarctic Survey; Figure 2.4: Jouzel, J., Johnsen, Lorius C. et al. (1994) 'Climate instabilities: Greenland and Antarctic records', Serie II, 1994. *Compte Rendu del Academie des Sciences*, Paris; Figure 2.6a: Misty Nikula (TREC 2006), Courtesy of ARCUS; Figure 2.6b: Anne Jennings, Institute of Arctic and Alpine Research, University of Colorado; Figure 2.9: W.B. Hamilton/US Geological Survey; Figure 2.11: Photographer Thomas McGuire/Earth Science World Image Bank, http://www.earthscienceworld.org/images; Figure 2.12a: © J.S. Watson; Figure 2.12b: Taken from www.geo.unimib.it/labs/photo1.htm, Universita Degli Studi di Milano Bicocca;

Figures 3.1, 3.5b and 3.11a: Courtesy of Dr Steve Drury; Figure 3.2a: Donald R. Lowe; Figure 3.2b: Courtesy of Professor Andrew Knoll; Figure 3.2c: Earth Science World Image Bank http://www.earthscienceworld.org/images; Figure 3.2d: © Society for Sedimentary Geology/www.earthscienceworld.org; Figure 3.4a: Reprinted by permission from Macmillan Publishers Ltd: *Nature*, vol. 391, 553–558, Xiao, S. et al. 'Three-dimensional preservation of algae and animal embryos in a Neoproterozoic phosphite', © 1998; Figures 3.4aiii and 3.4aiv: Reprinted from *Earth Science Review*, vol. 77, McCall, G.J.H., 'The Vendian (Ediacaran) in the geological record: Enigmas in geology's prelude to the Cambrian Explosion', pages 1–229, Copyright 2006, with permission from Elsevier; Figure 3.4av: From Glaessner, M.F. (1984) *The Dawn of Animal Life*, Cambridge University Press; Figure 3.4avi: Sprigg, R.C. (1947) 'Early Cambrian jellyfish from the Flinders Ranges, South Australia', *Transactions of the Royal Society of South Australia*, The Royal Society of South Australia; Figure 3.4avii: Brasier, M.D. et al.(1997) 'Ediacarian sponge-spicule clusters from southwestern Mongolia and the origins of the Cambrian faun', *Geology*, vol. 25, © Geological Society of America; Figure 3.4b: Chip Clark, National Museum of Natural History, Smithsonian Institution; Figure 3.5a: Plates 1–3 of Matthews, S. and Missarzhevsky, S. (1975) *Journal of the Geological Society of London*, 131, London; Figures 3.6a–3.6e: © Professor Simon Conway Morris and H.B. Whittington; Figure 3.6f: Courtesy of John Sibbick; Figure 3.7a: Blair, J.E. and Blair Hedges, S. (2005) 'Molecular phylogeny and Divergence Times of Deuterostome animals', *Molecular Biology & Evolution*, Oxford Journals; Figure 3.7b: Halanch, K.M. and Passamaneck, Y. (2001) *Integrative & Comparative Biology*, Oxford Journals; Figure 3.8: Estes, J. (ed.) (2007) *Whales, Whaling and Ocean Ecosystems*, University of California Press; Figure 3.9a: Based on data from Benton 1995, redrawn and embellished by John Sibbeck, Thames and Hudson Ltd; Figures 3.9b and 3.15: Sepkoski, Jr, J.J. (1990) 'Evolutionary faunas' in Briggs, D.E.G. and Crowther, P.R. (eds) *Palaeobiology: A Synthesis*, Blackwell Science Ltd; Figure 3.11a: Courtesy of Peter Sheldon; Figure 3.11b: Richard Grieve, Geological Survey of Canada; Figure 3.11c: Bruce F. Bohor, United States Geological Survey; Figure 3.12a: Benton, M.J. (1993) 'Dinosaur summer' *The Book of Life*, Ebury Hutchinson, Random Group (UK) Ltd; Figure 3.12b: Geological Society of Canada; Figure 3.12c: Courtesy of Dr Mike Widdowson; Figure 3.14: White, R.V. (2002) 'Earth's biggest 'whodunnit': unravelling the clues in the case of the end-Permian mass extinction', *Philosophical Transactions of the Royal Society of London Series A-Mathematical Physical and Engineering Sciences*, vol. 360, 2963–2985, © The Royal Society; Figure 3.16a: National Museums and Galleries of Wales; Figure 3.16b: Courtesy of Wendy Webb; Figure 3.17: © J.S.Watson; Figure 3.18: Daeschler, Edward B. et al. (2006) 'A Devonian tetrapod-like fish and the evolution of the tetrapod body plan', *Nature*, vol. 440, no 7085, p. 761; Shubin, Neil H., Daeschler, Edward B. and Jenkins, Farish A. (2006) 'The pectoral fin of Tiktaalik roseae and the origin of the tetrapod limb', *Nature*, vol. 440, issue 7085, April 2006. Nature Publishing Group. Reprinted by permission from Macmillan Publishers Limited; Figure 3.19: Benton, M.J. (1997) *Vertebrate Palaeontology*, 2nd edn, Chapman and Hall, by permission of the author; Figure 3.20: Stanley, S.M. (1993) *Exploring Earth and Life through Time*, W.H. Freeman & Co. Publishers;

Figure 4.2a: Courtesy of Marc Davies; Figure 4.2b: Courtesy of the Northern Ireland Tourist Board; Figure 4.3a: Press, F. and Siever, R. (1994) *Understanding Earth*, W.H. Freeman & Co. Publishers; Figures 4.3b and 4.4b: Courtesy of Andy Tindle; Figure 4.3c: Angus Miller, Geowalks; Figure 4.4a: Dunning, F.W., Mercer, I.F. et al. (1978) *Britain Before Man*, Crown copyright material is reproduced under Class Licence No C01W0000065 by permission of Controller of HMSO and the Queen's Printer for Scotland; Figures 4.14a and 4.14b: Courtesy of Dr Steve Drury;

Figure 5.1a: Courtesy of Chris Wilson; Figure 5.1b: Courtesy of J.G. Ogg; Figure 5.1c: Angela Coe; Figure 5.4: Courtesy of Evelyn Brown; Figure 5.5a: Courtesy of Andy Tindle; Figure 5.5b: Courtesy of Dr Steve Drury; Figure 5.12a: Dr Andy Sutton, www.andysuttonphotography.com; Figure 5.12b: DigitalGlobe Inc; Figure 5.13a: Courtesy of Professor Bill Church, University of Western Ontario; Figure 5.13b: Courtesy of NASA;

Figure 6.6a: From www.rocksforkids.com. Original source unknown; Figure 6.6b: From www.und.nodak.edu, University of North Dakota; Figure 6.7b: Courtesy of J.G. Ogg; Figure 6.7c: Courtesy of Professor Chris Hawkesworth; Figure 6.8a: Courtesy of M.S. Paterson; Figure 6.8b: Manuel Marques Lopez, www.nimbar.net; Figure 6.8c: From www.uwsp.edu, Kevin P. Hefferan; Figures 6.10a and 6.10c: Courtesy of Dr Steve Drury; Figure 6.10b: Courtesy of Rodney Gayer;

Figure 7.1: © British Geological Survey; Figure 7.2a: Courtesy of Dr Simon H. Lamb; Figures 7.2b, 7.3a, 7.3b, 7.4a and 7.4b: Courtesy of Department of Earth Sciences, Oxford University; Figures 7.5a, 7.5b, 7.5c, 7.6b, 7.7a and 7.14: Courtesy of Dr Steve Drury; Figure 7.6a: Courtesy of Martin Stokes; Figure 7.8: Miller Victor, C. (1961)' Identification and interpretation: approach and criteria', *Photogeology*, McGraw Hill; Figure 7.17: Mac Niocaill, C., van der Pluijm, B.A. and Van der Voo, R. (1997) 'Ordovivian paleography and the evolution of the Iapetus ocean geology', *Geology*, vol. 25(2), February 1997, Geological Society of America; Figure 7.18: © J.S. Watson; Figure 7.19: © Natural History Museum, London; Figure 7.20a: Angela Coe; Figure 7.20b: Taken from Teacher Resource Exchange. Original source unknown; Figure 7.20c: Courtesy of Peter Skelton;

Figure 8.2: From US National Intelligence Mapping Agency GTOPO30 digital elevation data, map designed by Steve Drury; Figure 8.3: Sepulchre, P. et al. (2006) 'Tectonic uplift and eastern Afira aridification', *Science*, vol. 313, Issue 5792, 8/09/2006, American Association for the Advancement of Science; Figure 8.6: Courtesy of NOAA; Figures 8.7 and 8.10: Courtesy of Dr Steve Drury from NASA SRTM data; Figure 8.8: From Roberts, N. (1998) *The Holocene*, Blackwell Publishing Ltd; Figure 8.9a: Courtesy of RWE; Figures 8.9b and 8.9c: DigitalGlobe Inc; Figure 8.9d: South Dakota School of Mines and Technology;

Index

Entries and page numbers in **bold type** refer to key words that are printed in **bold** in the text and that are defined in the glossary. Where the page number is given in *italics*, the index information is carried mainly or wholly in an illustration or table.

Q

R

S

T

U

V

W

Y

Z